Camtasia Studio® 5: The Definitive Guide

Daniel Park

Wordware Publishing, Inc.

Library of Congress Cataloging-in-Publication Data

Park, Daniel (Daniel Richard).
Camtasia studio 5 : the definitive guide / by Daniel Park.
   p. cm.
   Includes index.
   ISBN-13: 978-1-59822-057-5 (pbk., companion cd-rom)
   ISBN-10: 1-59822-057-8 (pbk., companion cd-rom)
   1. Camtasia studio. 2. Multimedia systems. 3. Digital video--Data processing.
   I. Title.
   QA76.575.P352 2007
   006.6'96--dc22   2007043591

Printed in the United States of America

ISBN-13: 978-1-59822-057-5
ISBN-10: 1-59822-057-8

10 9 8 7 6 5 4 3 2
0711

All inquiries for volume purchases of this book should be addressed to Wordware Publishing, Inc., at the above address. Telephone inquiries may be made by calling:

(972) 423-0090

Contents

Unit I: General Introduction

Unit II: Prep-work: What to Do before Making Your First Recording

Unit III: Recording with Camtasia Studio

Foreword

When Camtasia Studio was released as Camtasia in 1999, TechSmith anticipated that it would become the ideal tool for creating training and product demonstration videos, and its original feature set was designed specifically for that purpose. However, in the eight years since, we have watched and listened in amazement as people have developed their own novel uses for Camtasia Studio — most of which we never could have imagined. Today, Camtasia Studio's close integration with PowerPoint, Flash, and course management systems is a tribute to the innovative spirit of thousands of users. Their ideas have helped Camtasia Studio emerge to take its place among the leaders in multimedia and productivity software and to successfully bring the notion of screen recording to the masses.

As more and more people are realizing the advantages of recording presentations and delivering them online, this is the ideal time for Daniel Park to share his expertise. Daniel has been involved with TechSmith since Camtasia Studio was merely a concept. More than just a user of the product, his insights have contributed to the development of Camtasia Studio. But Daniel's depth of knowledge goes beyond simply understanding the "ins and outs" of Camtasia Studio. His experience as a multimedia consultant and stand-up trainer will help you master the art of "teaching by showing" any application, business process, job, web site, or workflow on a computer desktop.

In *Camtasia Studio 5: The Definitive Guide*, Daniel will help you understand how to make professional, effective content quickly and easily. He'll guide you through the simple-yet-powerful tools in Camtasia Studio that allow you to record the activity on a computer screen, add narration and video, and edit the recording like a professional videographer.

This book is a must-read for educators, marketers, salespeople, trainers, IT professionals, and anyone else who wants to create compelling video content. Using the techniques laid out in this book, you'll be able to demonstrate or teach *anything* that can be viewed on a computer screen.

Enjoy!

Bill Hamilton
President, TechSmith Corporation

Acknowledgments

There are a number of individuals who contributed their time and talent toward the production of this book, and they have my profound thanks.

First off, many thanks to the good people at TechSmith Corporation, the creator of Camtasia Studio. They've assembled an amazing piece of software (actually, several amazing pieces of software) that has, in one way or another, been my bread and butter for the past seven years. I'd like to send some extra love out to the following people:

■ **Betsy Weber,** chief evangelist and my main point of contact at TSC regarding the publication of this book. Betsy travels all over creation singing the praises of TechSmith products. She's the one who provides me with constructive criticism and, occasionally, free swag.

■ **Kari Bulkley,** project manager, who bears the brunt of all my bug reports and feature requests. And I make generous amounts of both.

■ **Troy Stein,** Camtasia Studio product manager, who has to endure all my platitudes about the future direction of the product.

■ **Brooks Andrus,** senior Flash developer, who shared his knowledge of cool ways to trick out your Flash productions. About half of the information covered in the customization chapter has been siphoned directly from him.

And extra super special thanks to…

■ **Dave O'Rourke,** lead programmer for Camtasia Studio, who has put up with my endless stream of technical questions with equally endless patience. Even my really dumb questions got a comprehensive (yet comprehensible) response. I almost feel guilty for not listing him as a co-author.

There are several other people I wish to thank, including:

- The folks at Wordware Publishing, especially **Tim McEvoy, Martha McCuller,** and **Beth Kohler.** You have been wonderful to work with in making this book a reality.

- **Scott Johnson,** creator of Extralife (www.myextralife.com), for graciously agreeing to do the cartoon strips for this book. I'm a huge fan of his work, and having the chance to share some of his strips (created just for this book, by the way) was a real treat.

- Microsoft PowerPoint MVP **Geetesh Bajaj,** who took the time to lend a critical expert's eye to the chapter on Camtasia Studio and PowerPoint.

- And finally, **María José** and **Rubén,** the two best things that ever happened to me.

Camtasia Studio® 5: The Definitive Guide

EXTRALIFE

by Scott Johnson

General Introduction

At the dawn of the year 2000, while working as a technical trainer and consultant for a local training firm in Michigan, I got an assignment to create some training content about a brand-new software product. The application was called Camtasia, and I was given the task of using Camtasia as the tool of choice to create some video tutorials *about* Camtasia. The program was fairly basic at that point: just a small screen recorder utility and a production tool that let you string together multiple clips. But it had two things going for it:

- It worked well, unlike similar products that had been offered up previously.

- It sported a brand-new compression algorithm that let you preserve the actions on your screen with *perfect* quality.

In the years that followed, Camtasia became more and more robust, eventually evolving into the comprehensive suite of applications now known as Camtasia Studio. And my, how things have changed! Users of Camtasia Studio now have no fewer than nine file types to choose from when producing video. They're also armed with new streams of content, such as picture-in-picture video and markers, and have a dizzying array of special effects from which to choose.

The two chapters in this unit will get you up to speed on what Camtasia Studio is all about and precisely how this book can help you become more familiar with it.

- **Chapter 1: Introduction to Camtasia Studio.** We'll talk about what Camtasia Studio does and what's new in the latest version. I'll also brief you on the system specs as well as tip you off about some handy third-party applications that can support your efforts with Camtasia Studio.

■ **Chapter 2: About This Book.** This brief chapter discusses the general style and formatting conventions used in this book and tells you about all the goodies you can find on the book's CD-ROM.

In one way or another, I've been working with Camtasia Studio (and its predecessor) for nearly its entire run. In that time, I've managed to win over a lot of converts. And I'm no salesman. A person's first experience with quickly shooting a tutorial video that would otherwise have necessitated pages and pages of instruction text is what usually leads to the "revelation." The benefit is just so clear and compelling that it leaves many wondering later how they ever got along without it.

Whether you're a novice or a power user, and whether you're merely dabbling in video creation or you want to learn every feature in detail, this book will have something to offer you. Welcome. Now let's get to work...

Chapter 1

Introduction to Camtasia Studio

This chapter will provide you with a quick introduction to the wondrous world of Camtasia Studio version 5. Since you've purchased this book, you probably already have at least a rough idea of what Camtasia Studio is and what it does. Even if you already know the application reasonably well, you may still want to skim this chapter, because there just might be some information contained herein that you didn't know before. To wit:

■ It discusses all the wonderful, brand-new features of Camtasia Studio 5. If you haven't upgraded yet, or if you've only upgraded recently and haven't yet explored all of its new offerings, I've got the skinny on it here.

■ It lists all the hardware and software you need to use the application effectively, including an updated set of minimum system requirements.

■ We also discuss third-party software applications that can augment the built-in abilities of Camtasia Studio 5.

What Is Camtasia Studio?

Camtasia Studio 5 is a comprehensive suite of applications that center around the recording, editing, and sharing of screen video content. Unlike other software demo applications that slap together a series of static screenshots and then animate the mouse to simulate movement, a video produced with Camtasia Studio is *true video*. Every animation, every move of the mouse, every *everything* is properly represented in your footage. If you see it on your screen, you can capture it.

But Camtasia Studio doesn't end with capture. It also sports a robust suite of editing tools. You can add callouts, quizzes, transitions, zoom and pan effects, and a host of other goodies. Combine your clips, trim them, add audio narration or camera video, and supply a title screen. When you're ready to share it with the world, you can produce your final video in any of nine file formats, optimized for different kinds of media (web, CD-ROM, e-mail, etc.).

The uses of Camtasia Studio run the entire gamut of business and personal applications, but its utility tends to fall into three main categories:

- **Training.** Bringing a new hire up to speed on your custom database program or providing your customer base with tutorials on your latest software package is a snap with Camtasia Studio. Video training content is infinitely scalable (send to one person or one million), replayable (train as often as you want, on your own time), and consistent (you know that *everyone* is getting the same high-quality material).

- **Marketing.** Post a video on your site that shows off all the fab new features of your software, and you'll suddenly have an automated sales force that's working for you all the time. When browsing your site for information about your products, isn't it amazing how some people don't really read? They get your number from the site, call you up, and then ask you all sorts of questions, the answers to which are plainly posted on the same web page. However, a great many of those who don't take the time to read *will* take the time to watch a video. A well-done marketing video prequalifies your customers; it teaches them all the benefits of your awesome new product so that you don't have to. Now, instead of calling you with a laundry list of questions, they're calling you with credit card in hand.

■ **Demo.** Rather than going hoarse at your next trade show by giving the same presentation over and over, you can automate it with a Camtasia Studio video. You can also use the video to demonstrate web applications in places with no Internet access. Demo videos (all kinds of video, actually) have the added advantage of traversing great distances; you don't have to be there in person. Yet even when demonstrating a software application in person, you can now ditch that boring PowerPoint presentation for something much more animated and interactive, and your audience will thank you for it.

Can Camtasia Studio be used for usability?

While this has traditionally been a use for Camtasia Studio, it has recently been supplanted by two newer TechSmith products, namely Morae and UserVue. These applications are far more robust in terms of collecting the kinds of information that usability professionals need. And yes, they too do screen recording.

Can Camtasia Studio be used to record games?

Yes, it can. You can get all the gory details about how to do this in Chapter 5, "Recording Your Screen."

Is Camtasia Studio only for Windows? What about other platforms like Mac and Linux?

Camtasia Studio is currently designed exclusively for the Windows platform. There are a few workarounds for using Camtasia Studio to record other platforms, and I'll discuss these options in Appendix B, "Recording Alternative Platforms."

Is Camtasia Studio spyware?

Not really. While the Camtasia Recorder *can* be set to run unobtrusively in the background and record everything the user sees on the screen, Camtasia Studio does not have the features offered by the major spyware applications, such as timed captures or the capture of keyboard activity. Spying on others is not Camtasia Studio's intended purpose.

What's New in Camtasia Studio 5?

As with any major release, the most recent version of Camtasia Studio sports a number of new features, which I'll tell you all about in this section.

This time around, the new feature set centers on four things:

- Usability enhancements, including a vastly improved Camtasia Recorder, project settings to let you set the dimensions at which you want to edit your project, and a more usable (and considerably less labor-intensive) zoom-n-pan experience.

- Visual enhancements, such as zoom-n-pan hints, three-dimensional callouts, new transitions, and the brand-new "Onyx" controller theme.

- Stability enhancements, including project file auto-save and a new 30 frames-per-second Timeline interface for a more predictable editing experience.

- Production enhancements, like FTP output, the ability to upload files to your Screencast.com (or FTP) *without producing first*, and the new ExpressShow template, which can deliver your Flash content as a single SWF file.

Let's quickly examine these groovy new features. They will all be discussed in greater detail as you work through the remainder of the book.

Usability Enhancements

With their usability products Morae and UserVue, TechSmith is becoming a guiding force in the usability industry. In version 5, they continue to "walk the walk" by providing additional enhancements to the user experience in Camtasia Studio.

New Welcome Window

In recent versions, Camtasia Studio has sported a "welcome" screen on startup as a launchpad to common tasks such as making a recording, importing capture files, or opening a project. In version 5, the welcome window also includes a recent projects list, access to a list of tutorial videos that address common concerns, and even options for capturing PowerPoint presentations or making voice narration files.

Camtasia Recorder Refinements

In Camtasia Studio 5, the Recorder application gets its biggest updates in recent memory. A new, radically simplified interface makes selecting your capture area a snap. Adding to the Recorder's ease of use is the built-in ability to automatically open any application dialogs or alert boxes *inside* the capture area. No more pausing to "fetch" errant dialogs! And speaking of pausing, the Recorder now offers the ability to record the location of your mouse cursor when paused, automatically resetting it when you resume. Finally, you can automatically resize the application you're recording to dimensions that you specify, so that you can now take advantage of every single pixel of screen real estate.

Project Settings

For larger, more complicated projects with footage from lots of different sources, editing all these segments together involved a certain amount of guesswork. If you had three clips of different sizes, and your desired output was yet another size, it would be nice to have an idea of what your final output is going to look like *before* you produce. Your Project Settings dialog can now help you do just that, providing a consistent editing interface that uses the dimensions at which you'll ultimately be sharing your video.

SmartFocus: Automated Zoom-n-Pan

When recording large application screens, it's often necessary to scale the content down to a manageable viewing size, which is of particular importance for mobile devices. However, screen content tends to look rather yucky when scaled, *unless* you make use of zoom-n-pan to show scaled footage at its normal size. The problem with this feature was that it was often rather time-consuming to set so many zoom points throughout the video. SmartFocus addresses this problem by automatically setting zoom-n-pan points based on the content. With Smart-Focus to do the work for you, there's no excuse to have a blocky, illegible video again. Add to that a sharp new zoom-n-pan interface, and you'll be able to produce content for *any* audience, regardless of the dimensions at which you recorded.

Visual Enhancements

Even after adding so many timesaving enhancements to your workflow, it's nice to know that TechSmith didn't hold out on delivering a little eye candy as well. You can utilize the following new techniques to further "wow" your audience.

New Special Effects

In Camtasia Studio 5, several of the standard special effects have received a facelift. Zoom-n-panners will love the Zoom Hints feature, which shows a border around the area into which you're about to zoom. Callouts have been augmented with a 3D effect for more eye-popping annotations. And at long last, those who love Camtasia Studio's transition effects now have six new, super-sexy transition effects such as Peel, Glow, and Cube Rotate.

Onyx Controller Theme

Adding to the Classic, Glass, and Matte themes, Camtasia Studio now gives you an additional choice with Onyx, a simple, attractive theme with a small footprint. Onyx is also the theme used for ExpressShow videos, which I'll talk about in a moment.

Stability Enhancements

As software products develop and are augmented with new features, application stability can often take a hit. Even I have found recent versions of Camtasia Studio to be a little crash-happy, which is why I was so thrilled to learn of the following two features.

Predictable Editing

As part of its Timeline editing in the past, Camtasia Studio has allowed users to zoom way in and select even 1/100ths of a second. Of course, with most screen videos averaging 15 frames per second, this level of granularity was an illusion, as you can't really select less than a single frame. With version 5, the application now bases its Timeline editing on frames rather than fractions of seconds, leading to both improved stability and improved ease of use.

Project Auto-Save

Nothing is more frustrating than performing hours of work on a project, only to have the application crash. With dawning horror, you realize you last saved your project over an hour ago. Ouch. Camtasia Studio now takes the sting out of the occasional crash by offering the ability to auto-save your project every so often. You can even choose the interval.

Production Enhancements

All your captures and edits don't mean a thing if you can't actually share the content. That's why Camtasia Studio is constantly refining the production process to ensure that new users as well as power users can easily get their videos "out there" for all to enjoy and learn from. In addition to a general aesthetic facelift, the Production Wizard sports the following new enhancements...

Upload Options: FTP and Screencast.com

Early versions of Camtasia Studio allowed you to produce your content, but then it was up to you to figure out how to get it online for others to view. With version 4, they introduced Screencast.com, a subscription-based video hosting service that lets you upload all videos and supplemental files, organize them, and control who has access to them. In this version, they acknowlege that many folks already have their own hosting solutions, and offer upload of produced content to any server via FTP. As if that weren't enough, version 5 will also let you upload files to your FTP site or Screencast.com *without* actually producing them first. Camtasia Studio can now be your conduit for getting all your previously created content files online.

ExpressShow

For those who have lamented the increasing number of supplemental files that accompany Flash videos, now there's a solution: ExpressShow. This new Flash template will let you pack it all into one SWF file, even content that has historically required multiple files, such as quizzes, captioning, and even a clickable table of contents. Complete with a YouTube-like front end and the new Onyx control bar, this is one stand-alone solution that can really stand on its own.

What Other Hardware and Software Do You Need?

System Requirements

While you're obviously going to enjoy smoother recordings with a faster processor, loads of memory, and a beefier video card, you may be surprised to know that Camtasia Studio can run, and run well, on a relatively modest machine. But before you take the time to actually install and run the program, it's probably a good idea to look over these minimum system requirements to make sure you don't need to upgrade your hardware. So, before you hop on this amusement park ride, please make sure your system is at least this tall:

- Microsoft Windows XP or Vista
- Microsoft DirectX 9.0 or greater
- A 1.0 GHz processor (though 2.5 GHz is strongly recommended)*
- 500 MB RAM (1.0 GB or more recommended)
- 60 MB hard drive space on which the application can reside

While these specs will cover the basics, there are additional minimum requirements to utilize some of Camtasia Studio's extended functionality. To wit:

- If you're going to add audio to your videos, at a minimum you're going to require a sound card, microphone, possibly a preamp, and some means of listening to the playback (speakers or headphones). A short buyer's guide for audio equipment can be found in Appendix C, "Equipment Buyer's Guide."
- Producing to Apple iPod format requires the use of Apple QuickTime 7.1 or later.

---

* I assume the developers were referring to a Pentium 4 processor when they wrote this requirement. Clock speed is only useful for assessing performance between two processors of the same type, so these numbers don't mean much by themselves. Example: a 1.8 GHz Core Duo is *much* faster than a 2.5 GHz Pentium.

- If you want to use the real-world video (picture-in-picture) capabilities of Camtasia Studio, you're going to need some sort of video device. While you may certainly use a high-end camcorder to create and import pristine video files, a simple webcam will also suffice. Camtasia Studio will detect the presence of a video input source automatically. For all the details, be sure to check out Chapter 5, "Recording Your Screen."

- If you want to record PowerPoint presentations, Camtasia Studio sports a special add-in for PowerPoint that allows you to access Camtasia Studio's functionality directly within PowerPoint. You'll need PowerPoint in Office 2000, Office XP, Office 2003, or Office 2007 in order to use the add-in. Chapter 8, "Recording Your PowerPoint Presentation," is entirely devoted to this topic.

Other Helpful Software

With the exception of Camtasia Studio itself, the only other software programs you truly need are (obviously) the applications you want to record. But there are a few kinds of third-party applications that can augment the built-in abilities of Camtasia Studio by streamlining your work processes or adding more functionality as needed.

- **Screen capture applications.** Screenshot apps like TechSmith's SnagIt allow you to quickly storyboard your video creations. Additionally, if your aim is to create a slide show of still images, a screen capture utility can help assemble your images easily and efficiently.

- **Animation programs.** Brief animated segments between screen recording clips can add refreshing and eye-catching variety to your videos. Since it records in real time, Camtasia Studio can capture animated content from programs like Adobe Flash or After Effects (or even Microsoft PowerPoint) to give your videos some added sizzle. In fact, Camtasia Studio offers an add-in for PowerPoint, allowing you to capture all your PowerPoint presentations without ever leaving the program. Please see Chapter 8, "Recording Your PowerPoint Presentation," for more information on how to use the add-in.

- **Titling applications.** While Camtasia Studio introduced title screen creation with version 3.0, there are times when more professional titling effects are called for. Titling programs will let you apply all sorts of fantastic Hollywood-style animated effects to your text, so that no one ever gets up and leaves during the credits.

- **Audio and video applications.** Even though Camtasia Studio is a total package solution with built-in audio and video editing, occasionally you might need to insert tracks or apply custom effects. One of Camtasia Studio's greatest strengths lies in its ability to produce industry-standard AVI files, which can be readily imported into applications like Adobe Audition, Serious Magic Visual Communicator, or Sony Vegas. So, if you need to apply a custom volume envelope to your audio narration or add a sepia filter to your video, you can rest assured knowing that your favorite third-party apps will play nicely with your content.

- **DVD burning software.** Your Camtasia Studio videos, when imported into a DVD burning suite such as Sonic MyDVD or PowerProducer, can produce high-quality DVDs for viewing on a television set. For specific tips on preparing your videos for DVD distribution, please see Chapter 12, "The Production Process."

While Camtasia Studio can stand on its own to produce amazing screen video, I do make various recommendations throughout the book for third-party software that I find helpful in accomplishing certain tasks. No one is paying me to mention these products. I bring them up because I like them and use them on a daily basis. These tools serve to augment Camtasia Studio; none of them are absolutely necessary to get the job done. But they do provide supplemental functionality not found in Camtasia Studio to produce eye-popping effects, give you more power and flexibility, and/or cut your time on task. I've managed to get permission from many of their various developers to put demo versions of these products on the companion CD. So feel free to check them out — you have absolutely nothing to lose.

Chapter 2

About This Book

Camtasia Studio 5: The Definitive Guide is designed to lead the user in an easy, stepwise manner throughout the entire video production process. I attempt to give you, the reader, a "best practices" set of procedures. I have sequenced the chapters in this book to follow the same general workflow of the application:

Record → Edit → Produce → Share

The individual chapters within these sections are presented in the order in which they appear in the program. For example, I discuss all editing functions available within Camtasia Studio in the order in which they appear on the application's Task List:

The Edit functions in Camtasia Studio's Task List.

In practice, these can be tackled in any order, so feel free to skip around the chapters and sections to read up on whatever function you wish to implement at the time.

What You Can Expect to Find in Each Chapter

Every chapter starts off with a one- or two-paragraph introduction that explains the points being covered in that chapter. Any procedural clarifications are clearly marked (they're surrounded by a gray bounding box), laid out step-by-step, and generally preceded by an explanation as to why this feature or procedure might be useful. The chapters also draw to a close with a summary of the material covered. Beginning with Chapter 5 (where we actually begin using the application), each chapter will conclude with a handful of exercises to test your knowledge and give you some hands-on practice toward mastery of the concepts covered. The data files for these exercises are included on the CD-ROM.

About the Companion CD-ROM

While flipping through this book for the first time, you probably noticed the CD inside the back cover. That CD-ROM actually has a veritable treasure trove of really useful stuff on it. For one thing, you've got a fully functional (as in *not* crippled in any way) trial version of Camtasia Studio 5. So if you haven't yet bought the application, you can still work all the way through this book, and already be an expert by the time you plunk down your money. In addition to Camtasia Studio, the CD-ROM also has free or trial versions of:

■ **TechSmith SnagIt 8.2.3.** This handy screenshot utility greatly enhances Camtasia Studio by giving you the ability to add still images of screen data for slide shows as well as the chance to effortlessly mock up your ideas prior to recording.

■ **AutoPlay Media Studio 7.0 from IndigoRose.** From a simple menu front end to a fully fledged custom application, this comprehensive package offers even non-programmers a means of creating content. I use it mostly in situations where I need a mind-blowing CD front end with capabilities that exceed those of Camtasia MenuMaker.

■ **BluffTitler DX9 7.14 by Outerspace Software.** This fun, versatile software is billed as a titling application, though I actually find it quite good for animation in general. It offers a variety of easy-to-implement effects, and it renders your content quickly and slickly. It's now one of my most often-used support utilities for Camtasia Studio work.

- **Color Cop 5.4.3 from Datastic.** A freeware multipurpose color picker utility. Good for getting a color's hexadecimal value (useful when editing a SWF XML document in Camtasia Studio or Theater) or RGB value (for setting Camtasia Player's background color through a command line parameter, for example).

- **IconWorkshop 6.1 from Axialis.** This comprehensive icon creation and editing solution can help you create custom icons for use with Camtasia MenuMaker, so that you're not stuck with only the MenuMaker icon for your otherwise polished CD-ROM front end. Please see Chapter 13, "CD-based Videos with Camtasia MenuMaker," for details.

- **Theater06 from TechSmith.** This is a special advanced (yet unfinished) version of Camtasia Theater that addresses many of the limitations of the current application. It is not officially supported by TechSmith, but it will allow you to string multiple SWF and FLV files together, including many of the themes and special effects currently missing in the official version.

- **Total Recorder 6.1 from High Criteria, Inc.** This application will allow you to record sound from your system (in other words, capture any sound made by the applications you're recording), even if your sound card doesn't support the recording of system sound. For more information, please see Chapter 10, "Working with Other Media: Audio, PIP, and Title Clips."

- **Visual Communicator 3 from Adobe.** This comprehensive video creation and editing application lets you produce eye-popping talking-head style videos, complete with hundreds of transitions, title screens, royalty-free music, and even chroma keying.

- **WildFX Pro 4.001 from Wildform.** One of the best titling programs out there, this handy animation application can do things with text that have to be seen to be believed. There are 400 available text effects for making your title screens jump up and dance, including dozens of customizable effects.

The other thing your shiny CD-ROM has to offer is loads and loads of project data. At the end of each chapter (beginning with Chapter 5), you'll find exercises that will give you hands-on experience with the program. If you proceed in a linear fashion through the book, you'll probably find that many of these data files aren't needed, and here's why: Several of these exercises build on earlier exercises from the chapters before it. If you completed the exercises from the previous chapter, chances are you'll already have a working version of the practice file in question. Note, however, that some files are not created in previous exercises, such as a sample graphic image for you to import as a custom callout. It would therefore be necessary to retrieve that file from the CD.

About the Screenshots in This Book

This book contains a multitude of screenshots (more than 350 of them, actually) to illustrate the various points brought up in this text. All screenshots were done using SnagIt by TechSmith Corporation (yes, the same company that makes Camtasia Studio). It's a marvelous tool for capturing, editing, and sharing still images of your screen, and a trial version of SnagIt 8.2.3 is available on the companion CD-ROM. This software is not crippled in any way, and can be used without restriction for a 30-day period, so please feel free to install and try it out.

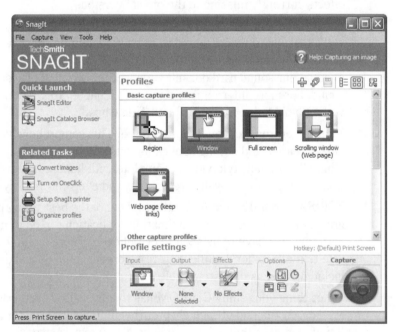

Most screenshots are taken of the application at its default settings. If you're opening Camtasia Studio for the very first time, the screenshots *should* mirror what you see on your screen. But if you've had Camtasia Studio for a while and have adjusted its many toolbars and settings, please note that your view of Camtasia Studio and its accompanying applications may look somewhat different.

About the Terminology in This Book

I have made every effort to keep the terminology used in this book as consistent as possible with the Camtasia Studio user interface as well as its pre-existing documentation. If alternate terms for the same thing exist as a general software convention, I try to point those out, so that those familiar with similar third-party applications have a frame of reference when discussing certain topics.

A side-note on political correctness: I liberally use the word "they" as a gender-neutral singular pronoun, as in, "When the user follows a link to this page, they will be presented with the navigation menu." While ungrammatical, I find it infinitely preferable to awkward constructions such as *he/she (his/her)* or alternating back and forth on a case-by-case basis to ensure that each gender gets fair play. So, until the grammatical prescriptivists devise a better system, that's the convention I'm sticking with.

And here's another blow to the prescriptivists: Whether doing stand-up technical training or writing documentation, I generally find it preferable to address the learner in an informal, conversational tone. In this book (and in other manuals I've constructed), I tend to write like I talk, which I believe makes the text a lot more approachable. But it also means that I freely start sentences with conjunctions, end them with prepositions, and occasionally make use of puns and other corny humor that some may find off-putting. If these sorts of things bother you, then you are more than welcome to go write your own book... ☺

Formatting Conventions

Hotkeys

Camtasia Studio employs a number of *hotkeys*, keyboard commands that the user can utilize to execute specific tasks. These are marked by first listing any needed modifier keys, such as Ctrl, Alt, or Shift (these can be combined), and then the appropriate alphanumeric or function key to execute the command. A plus sign (+) indicates that two or more modifier keys must be held down at once, while a hyphen (-) shows the key that must be pressed after said modifier(s) is held down.

Example:

Ctrl+Shift-M means that the user must first hold down the *Ctrl* and *Shift* keys together, then press *M*.

Special Sections

In an attempt to address the broad range of technical skill levels exhibited by those likely to read this book, this text contains both basic "how-to" procedures as well as special tips honed through my years of experience as a content developer. The former typically appeals to beginners, while the latter is more beneficial to those who are experienced with Camtasia Studio or similar products. As a result, certain passages are marked with visual cues so that you can tell at a glance what kind of topic you're dealing with. First, there will be a light gray box around all the procedural steps involved in accomplishing a certain task (for example, the steps you would need to execute in order to import media into Camtasia Studio's Clip Bin). Additionally, there are three other special sections I occasionally use throughout the course of this book:

These are the "secret documents" of the text, where I point out special tricks to help you accomplish certain goals or simply get more out of the program. It's just easier to relegate them to these sections as opposed to slipping them to you on microfilm...

These sections contain handy notes about the topic currently being discussed. They offer helpful reminders as well as background information.

 Here I talk about the complications you may potentially experience when working with a certain aspect of the software. If you're *really* lucky, then this section will also yield a *workaround* to the problem in question.

Emphasis

I place items in **bold** when introducing a concept for the first time in a chapter. When explaining a procedure, I will also set menus, hotkeys, and other commands in bold text. When you see something in bold text during a procedure, it's likely part of a command that you'll need to execute in order to successfully complete the procedure.

I use *italics* for words that are being introduced and defined. Additionally, italics indicate when a given word or phrase needs emphasis, as in, "You *must* complete the following items before moving on."

EXTRALIFE

by Scott Johnson

Prep-work: What to Do before Making Your First Recording

In this unit, we'll discuss how to best design your video content before ever even opening Camtasia Studio. I'll provide a brief introduction to curriculum design for each of the three major goals of Camtasia Studio video content: training, marketing, and demonstration. Then we'll work on scripting and storyboarding your creation. Feel free to skip this unit if you want to get right to the nitty-gritty of using Camtasia Studio, but I encourage you to come back to it at some point. These two chapters are useful, easy to read, and comparatively short. They contain a number of easy-to-implement yet powerful tips for refining your content and streamlining your work process.

In this unit, we discuss:

- **Chapter 3: Quick and Dirty Curriculum Design.** This chapter will help you focus your goals and select your audience, and will give all sorts of handy tips based on the kind of video you're creating.

- **Chapter 4: Scripting and Storyboarding.** Before diving in with your first recording, it helps (particularly for larger projects) to have some idea of where you're going. A script and storyboard can make the process flow a lot more smoothly.

Chapter 3

Quick and Dirty Curriculum Design

One of the wonderful things about a product like Camtasia Studio is its open-endedness. In other words, the software can readily adapt to the individual content needs of the person wielding it. Want a video tutorial to train new hires on filling out a supply acquisition form online? No problem. Need a demo of your software's new features to show to shareholders? You bet. Want a marketing spot to convince your target audience that they can't live without your program? Cake.

In this chapter, we'll discuss a number of items you'll want to keep in mind when creating each of these three kinds of videos. While it is well beyond the scope of this book to offer you a survey course on marketing or computer-based training, I have provided some general pointers to help your video content hit the mark. You'll also find a few good book tips at the end of the chapter should you desire to learn more (and I certainly hope you do). I decided not to inundate you with all kinds of extra background reading, opting instead to save you time by focusing on just a few really good resources, so I just picked out my top three faves for each genre. Remember, for each kind of video, there's no shortcut to great results, and a strong proficiency in Camtasia Studio alone is not sufficient to produce a truly world-class training (or marketing or demo) video. For each goal you want your video content to accomplish (you *have* established goals for your videos, haven't you?), I strongly encourage you to learn all you can.

Keep in mind that the following sections (indeed, this and the next chapter) have a fair amount of overlapping content. What I mention as a good technique to employ for a training video might also serve you well when creating a marketing spot, so I encourage you to read the chapter straight through rather than skipping around.

General Guidelines

Prior to delving into the various video types and what methods work best for each, I wanted to bring up a couple of items that are vitally important regardless of what kind of video you're making. The first section pertains to knowing what makes your target audience tick and how to reach them. The second is a checklist for dealing with the internal IT policies of your own organization.

Know Your Audience

You would think that this would be a no-brainer, but I can't tell you how many times I've seen videos where the creators clearly lost sight of the very people they were trying to reach. But *you* won't make that mistake, will you? Here are some thought-provoking questions that may help you figure out exactly who's watching. Later on, we'll examine our target audience even further through the lens of each video type.

Who's likely to see your video? Are you going to place the video content on your web site, with free access to anyone who wants to view it? In that case, try using a web analytics program to see who is accessing your site. If you have other (similar) videos, pay particular attention to who is viewing those. If you're a software company, and plan on restricting access to just your current customer base, it's time to start mining the customer database in order to assemble some basic information about where your customers are, who they work for, and what they've purchased. Why is this important? Well, friends, even the most basic vital statistics can tell you a lot about the direction of your videos.

- **Geographic location.** Especially if your customers come from all over the world, it's important to know where they are. If you have a lot of nonnative speakers of English in your customer base, you'll need to be careful to watch the pacing of your videos as well as the terminology you use. Your tone is important, too. What's engaging and cute in one culture could be offensive in another. If you have large concentrations of customers in a particular foreign country, consider a localized version of the video just for them (if you're making videos of your own software product, consider localizing the software itself, too).

- **Occupational data.** The professional lives of your audience should also be taken into consideration. Of course, this may already be inherent in the software you're trying to teach. For example, if the software in question is aimed at history teachers, then your job on this front is basically already done. Even if your target audience is a bit broader, at least knowing where the customer or prospect works can be of great advantage. Do they work for Fortune 500 companies? Are they mainly academics? IT professionals? Teenagers? If you're teaching to the average home user, slang phrases and cartoony title screens are more acceptable than they would be in a video aimed at corporate executives.

- **Purchasing habits.** What your customers are purchasing may not have much of an effect on the videos themselves, but their purchasing habits should have a profound impact on your priorities, and therefore the order in which you tackle the various video projects in your organization. When creating tutorials, concentrate first on the product that is selling the best. If a product is just being launched (or its sales are beginning to slip), a good marketing video may be just the ticket. In addition, your company can extrapolate other purchase information from its customer data that may have an effect on the videos you produce (or the format in which you produce them). For example, if you get a lot of volume license purchases, then consider creating a video series on CD- or DVD-ROM to include for free as a value-add.

Your web site can be a terrific tool for figuring out what your audience is looking for, especially if that's where your videos are destined to appear. Which pages are the most popular? How long do the users stay on a particular page? Analyzing these items could yield valuable insights as to which parts of your software are the most attractive to customers. Or which parts your users are really struggling with.

And for goodness' sake, don't forget to talk to the people in your organization who have the most frequent contact with your target audience. In the case of tutorials, this could be your support, QA, or training team. For demos and marketing spots, it's likely to be your advertising or marketing staff. These are the folks who are most likely to be in tune with the needs of your audience.

And here's a novel concept: In addition to collecting data about your customers (or clients or colleagues, etc.), why not simply ask them about the kinds of video content they'd like to see? This holds true for all video types, but especially for training videos. After all, who would know better than they what kinds of problems they're contending with? This can take the form of anything from an informal office poll to a fully detailed online survey (complete with door prizes, if you want a high response rate). But keep in mind that this should serve to augment your other data collection efforts, not supplant them. Customers and clients can tell you what they *think* they want, but they may not be able to articulate their *actual* need. Perhaps this is because they're unfamiliar with all the aspects of your software. Or maybe the solution that they really need just hasn't been invented yet, and is therefore outside the scope of their experience. In short, listen to your audience, but don't always do exactly what they say.

Determine All Technical Specs Ahead of Time

Although I strongly believe that learning (or selling or presenting) should never be a slave to the technology, the reality of our modern workplace is that the IT departments of many companies place stringent restrictions on what you're allowed to do from a technical perspective. You may be forced to use a particular operating system, media player, etc., while abandoning all others. Do make sure that you find out the policies of your particular situation so that you can safely work within the confines of those rules.

Keep in mind that some of these policies may not always be explicit, meaning that you're going to have to involve some other people. While some of you may be employed in an academic or small business situation where you're the sole decision maker (at least when it comes to producing video content), chances are that you're producing videos as part of a larger team effort. Be certain to include the decision makers from IT, management, and anyone else who has a stake in the content you're producing. Before recording a single frame of video on a new project, do make sure that you reach a consensus on the following points. Don't worry if you don't necessarily understand these concepts just yet; they're all covered in this book.

- **Method of deployment.** Will these videos be posted to your web site? The corporate intranet? Will CD-ROMs be created? What about a DVD for viewing on console televisions? These decisions will affect your video dimensions as well as the output format of your final production. And, whether online or on CD, it's never too early to start planning your menu navigation.

- **Maximum file size or bandwidth requirements.** It's especially important to clarify this if your organization will be hosting these videos on its servers. If you're deploying on CD-ROM, then you should try to compute how much space, on average, each of your planned videos is allowed.

- **Video dimensions.** Smaller video dimensions generally mean smaller file sizes. Larger video dimensions mean better visibility, but a corresponding high file size, plus the risk of those with smaller monitors not being able to view your creation without scrolling (bad) or scaling your content (even worse).

- **Will the videos be narrated?** Unnarrated video titles don't necessitate the hassle of setting up audio equipment, but you'll see a corresponding need for captions and text callouts. Narrated videos should ideally have a script in place prior to recording, so that you can appropriately time the recording of your segments. In fact, as you'll see in the next chapter, effective scripting and storyboarding is a good idea regardless of narration.

Tips for Making a Top-Notch Training Video

While Camtasia Studio is used for all kinds of purposes, training really seems to be the one that speaks to people. In the work that I do for my clients, more often than not they engage me to create an online tutorial, knowledge base video, or some other form of training. This can run the gamut from some quickie "Getting Started" videos (to give new downloaders a leg up) to a polished, menu-driven CD-ROM, complete with comprehensive tutorials on every aspect of the software, which can then be sold (or given) to those customers who have already made their purchase.

Why Train with a Video?

Training videos can serve to augment traditional stand-up training or, in certain instances, replace it entirely. While nothing's as good as being there, Camtasia Studio, with its inclusion of picture-in-picture camera video (so that you see the face of the trainer, hear the voice, and see the screen simultaneously), actually comes pretty darned close. Training videos also have the following advantages over traditional stand-up training:

- **Videos never tire of repetition.** If users don't understand something, they can always go back and view it again.

- **Videos are scalable.** Deploy your video content to 10 people or 10,000, without a lot of extra time, effort, or money.

- **Videos travel better than people do.** If you have 20 different people who require training in 20 different locations around the world, there's no need to summon them to one spot in order to deliver training.

- **Videos are always available.** Unlike trainers, who have a schedule to keep, videos are always at the ready, even at 3 a.m. If the trainees decide they've had enough for the day, they can come back to it the following day (or week) with no worries.

- **Videos are hassle-free.** Stand-up training involves scheduling, reserving a classroom, and communicating with both the trainer and trainees to make sure everyone shows up at the appointed time. Not to mention the coffee and donuts. The logistics of video deployment are quite a bit simpler.

- **Videos can act as a "front line of defense."** People in the IT support department love training videos because they know that those users who *never* read documentation might just take the time to watch a video. In fact, many companies build whole video reference libraries of solutions to common problems. When they receive an e-mail from a frantic customer or colleague, they can simply send a link to the appropriate video along with the tag, "Contact me again if you have any additional questions." Simple.

- **Videos can handle the training jobs no one else wants.** I've heard of several companies who now use training videos as part of their standard new employee orientation, helping them to teach the more mundane aspects of the job, such as requisitioning office supplies or filling out a timecard. Not placing this training burden on your staff means not having to remove them from their normal duties every time you bring on someone new.

But chances are I'm preaching to the choir here — after all, you probably wouldn't have purchased this book if you didn't already know that Camtasia Studio video content excels as a training device. So, let's move on to devising the best training program we possibly can. These tips are arranged in no particular order; they're mainly here to get you *thinking* about your audience and the information you want to convey to them *before* you sit down to forge your masterpiece.

Know Your Video's Purpose

You may be thinking, "But I *already* know the purpose. To teach people how to use the software. Duh!" But keep in mind that a tutorial can be designed to fulfill different needs. You should be considering the broader question of "Why is this video being created?" Is it to provide a basic introduction of the software to those who are trying it out? Is it an advanced tutorial for those who are already familiar with it? Is it a reference video designed to answer a frequently asked question, in order to expediently solve the user's issue and help take the load off of your support team? Knowing why this video (or series of videos) was commissioned in the first place is always a good start.

Learn the Basic Principles of Educational Multimedia

In the late 1990s, when *computer-based training* (CBT) started to gain some popularity as an alternative to traditional in-person software training, it was these same stand-up software trainers who were producing the first CBT modules. In their efforts to reach a broader audience, they created computerized training lessons, utilizing many of the same practices they had honed from years of experience in traditional training. Some of these techniques translated well to this new format; others did not. At that time, no major research in educational multimedia was available to the masses to help them adapt their training methods to a computer-based format. At least not until Richard E. Mayer's seminal *Multimedia Learning* appeared in 2001.

Throughout the '90s, Mayer and his colleagues conducted an endless stream of educational experiments on how we learn with the aid of various media (technological and otherwise). He found that people tend to learn much better from words and images than from words alone, thus lending empirical support to learning with multimedia. From the results of these studies, Mayer assembled a series of educational principles, the adherence to which greatly enhances multimedia learning. I strongly encourage you to go read one or more of his books on your own, but for now, please allow me to provide a condensed list of Mayer's principles. Hopefully, they will aid your training efforts as much as they've bolstered mine.

- **People understand a multimedia explanation better when words are presented as verbal narration alone, rather than both verbally and as on-screen text (redundancy principle).** This should already be familiar to those of you who have had to sit through a dull PowerPoint presentation where the host "presented" by reading all the bullet points off the screen. If we replace those bullet points with a chart, an animation, or a screen video, comprehension can be enhanced. Filling up the screen with narration text can waste a good opportunity for engaging the brain with visual media. There are a few exceptions to this principle, such as when introducing unfamiliar terms, or when the audience members are hearing impaired or nonnative speakers of your language. In those cases, you'd *want* to reinforce narration with text. Fortunately, Camtasia Studio offers text callouts as well as captioning to address these situations.

- **People learn better when information is presented in bite-sized chunks (segmentation principle).** For our purposes as video content providers, this principle has a profound impact on how we split up our content. For tutorial videos, I typically find that three to five minutes for each "chapter" works best. As you work your way through the book, I'll show you techniques for dividing your content automatically, and even creating a clickable table of contents, so that your users can seamlessly navigate your segments.

- **People learn better when information is presented using clear outlines and headings (signaling principle).** When utilizing Camtasia Studio, the signaling principle is instructive in a number of ways. First, it illustrates the importance of using title screens to announce your content. People seem to have an innate need to know what to expect. Title screens help to convey this information. The running time and duration displayed in the video's control bar aid in this as well, by informing the audience how long the video has been playing and, more importantly, how far they have to go. The users can then plan accordingly depending on how much free time they have in their day.

- **People learn better when information is presented in a conversational style rather than a formal one (personalization principle).** I think most people know this from experience on a conscious level, but I still see countless demonstration videos where the narrator is as stiff as a board. It's usually the result of committee review where any shred of the creator's personality is systematically removed for the sake of "professionalism." This is a mistake. When narrating your video segments, you need to stay warm and approachable, which includes both your terminology and your tone. And this doesn't mean I'm necessarily advocating the use of gutter slang. It is possible to be both informal *and* professional at the same time. It can be a balancing act, of course, but the rewards are great if successfully executed.

- **People learn better when on-screen text is presented near any corresponding images (spatial contiguity principle).** This principle comes into play when placing callouts in your video. As an example, take a look at the two screens below:

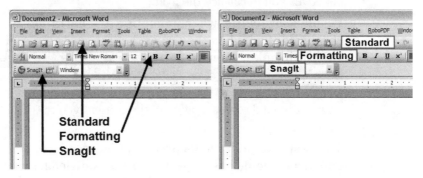

Which diagram do you find clearer?

So please don't glue the users' fingers to the monitor, forcing them to trace a maze of lines and arrows in an attempt to figure out what text goes to what graphic. It makes people confused, as well as making them smudge up their monitors with fingerprints...

- **People learn better when any extraneous information is removed (coherence principle).** This is definitely something you want to be cognizant of while recording. Remember to keep the focus on the material you want to convey, and eliminate everything else. If your Windows desktop is going to be recorded at any point, then for goodness' sake, change that funky desktop wallpaper to a solid color. Move any nonessential icons out of the recording area. Close any renegade windows. You want to make your recordings as clean as humanly possible. In addition to trimming out all the junk mentioned above, take care not to add irrelevant words, sounds, pictures, or music, as these can actually serve to hinder the audience from absorbing the material.

- **People learn better from animation and narration than animation with explanatory on-screen text (modality principle).** Of all the human senses, multimedia presentations typically engage two: sight and hearing. These are individual receptors, or pathways into the brain, and the reason that multimedia learning is successful has to do with the brain's efficiency at receiving information from both these pathways at once. But there can be bottlenecks, as the modality principle demonstrates. By presenting animation, and then adding written narration (as opposed to audio) on top of that, you're overloading one of the pathways, while the other one goes completely unused. When crafting your videos, it behooves you to balance the load.

- **People learn better when animation and narration are synchronized than when they're asynchronous (temporal contiguity principle).** When the video and audio are synchronized, the learner tends to more strongly build connections between the words and the picture, thereby improving their ability to form an accurate mental representation of the content you're trying to get across.

- **The design of multimedia presentations can have different effects on people based on their prior knowledge, visual literacy, and spacial aptitude (individual differences principle).** This is a fancy way of saying that everybody's different, particularly in terms of how they experience (and have experienced) the world.

There is no "one-size-fits-all" video experience that will appeal to everyone. But by following some of the principles above, your chances of truly getting the content across to your audience are actually quite good.

Recording Techniques for Training Videos

Here are a few handy tips for recording your training video once you've moved past preparation and into recording. While these techniques clearly do not fall under the category "prep-work," their use specifically for training merits a spot in this chapter.

Make Liberal Use of Attention-Getters

Tutorial content should ideally guide the user through the use of the software with as little effort required on their part as possible. Particularly if the procedure you're demonstrating has a lot of mouse movement and mouse click activity, using attention-getters such as mouse highlights, visual clicks, graphics and text callouts, and zoom and pan techniques can help to simplify what may otherwise be a long and confusing set of steps. Remember, what's obvious to you as a content expert may not be quite so clear to those who are just getting their feet wet with your software, which brings me to my next point...

Slow It Down

The pacing of a video can vary wildly depending on its purpose. A marketing spot needs fairly fast pacing to keep the viewer's attention while conveying the core benefits of the product in a 30-second to 2-minute long clip. Conversely, tutorial videos necessitate a much more relaxed pace. When running your audience through the procedural steps of executing a task on the computer, it's remarkably easy to lose them if you go too fast. Additionally, if you're likely to have non-native speakers of your language viewing your video content, you'll want to be especially careful with the pacing, and remember to slow down the pace of your narration as well.

The nice thing about having tutorials in video format is the ability to provide a control bar by which the users can navigate your video, even playing back segments they haven't thoroughly understood. While this is certainly an added benefit, not every user will take advantage of it (in fact, a few might not even know how the navigation works). Good controls, while helpful, cannot take the place of good pacing.

Don't Get Mired in the Details

Avoid the temptation to merrily skip from field to field in the program you're recording, explaining every little thing along the way.

Provided you've done a thorough assessment of your target audience, you probably have a decent sense of their general level of technical savvy as well as their pre-existing knowledge (if any) of the application(s) featured in your video. You can use this information to help you decide how granular you want to be in explaining the different aspects of the software. Rarely will you need to explain every field in every tab of every dialog box, or how to perform basic functions within Windows. For example, even novice computer users know how to close windows, open files, and select icons. If you make a point of telling them, "you'll need to double-click the program's icon in order to open it," then you're wasting valuable time, and you risk boring most of your users into exiting the video.

Set Specific Goals

It is my recommendation, regardless of video type, that you have certain predefined goals outlined before recording or even scripting begins. These goals need to be as specific as possible.

Bad example:

- Take users through the new features of the software.

Good examples:

- Show users how they can draw attention to certain words by utilizing the *italic*, **bold**, and underline commands.

- Help users to move projects from their desktop to their laptop computers by first exporting a project on one machine, and then importing it on another.

Do you see how these good examples delve into more detail? Also notice that in both examples, I've given the reason why this feature is beneficial. Writers do occasionally need to place extra emphasis on certain words. And road warriors must often transfer their work between their computers. This is a critical component. By remaining cognizant of exactly how the covered feature is going to improve the lives of your audience, your tutorial can stay focused on the most expedient way of attaining that benefit. And that's what we want: to get quickly yet comprehensively from Point A to Point B, giving users everything they need to know without adding a bunch of superfluous information. After all, this is a tutorial, not a knowledge dump. As tempting as it may be, you must do your best to avoid tacking on a series of "Oh, by the way…" remarks. While usually done with the good intention of being thorough, these additions typically only serve to confuse viewers and detract from that feature's main benefit.

Now, in the next section on marketing videos, we're going to talk a lot about benefits. The first thing taught in any book or course on copywriting is to always focus on benefits rather than features. Allow me to put forth the theory that training videos are no different in this regard. In order to create a top-quality tutorial, you must not only show them *how* to perform a given task, but also start out by telling them why they would *want* to. You're still focusing on the benefit, informing them as to how this feature is going to solve their problems. The difference with the tutorial video is that you then lay out the steps they'll need to perform in order to bring that benefit to fruition.

Tips for Making a Masterful Marketing Video

In this section, I'll be providing some general guidelines as to how you can make videos that will make you money. While tutorial videos have a decided focus on the *how* of using your software product, marketing videos instead focus on the *why*. Why should the audience care? Why do they need your product? How is it going to solve their problems, aid their efficiency, and generally improve their lives? It's up to your video to tell them. A smartly done marketing spot that truly addresses the users' needs will soon leave them smacking their foreheads and reaching for their wallets. Of course, in-person sales demos, brochures, and other media can do the same thing, so let's talk for a moment about the specific advantages offered by a video.

Why Sell with a Video?

There are a number of ways that a screen video can pull its weight as an essential part of an overall sales/marketing strategy. Consider the following:

- **Videos never take time off.** Consumers and even business-people don't always adhere to normal business hours when researching new software purchases. You may well have sales-people whose exclusive domain is to make cold calls, follow up on sales leads, and close the deal. But they can't be around 24x7. Videos don't sleep, don't take breaks, and, unlike your salespeople, can serve hundreds or thousands of potential customers at once.

- **People don't read.** When browsing your site, it's astounding how little people actually read. They will quickly scan a page's content, and decide within five seconds whether said content merits a second look. But it's amazing just how often those same people who shy away from a full page of the usual marketing blah-blah will take the time to watch a video. I once had a client who told me that after embedding a video I created for their home page, the average time that users lingered on that page more than tripled, and the number of both downloads and purchases increased substantially as a result.

- **Prequalify your leads.** A video can help take the heat off your sales team by addressing initial concerns and removing purchase objections before ever talking to a sales rep. Some people don't relish approaching a salesperson early on in their purchase process, out of fear that the rep will harass them with constant follow-ups. After watching the video and feeling a bit more comfortable with the product, the prospect can then target your sales staff with specific questions and, if all goes according to plan, their credit card number.

Know Your Video's Purpose

The ultimate purpose of any marketing video should obviously be "Sell more of our product." But the purchase process consists of numerous steps, and you'll need to determine exactly where you envision your marketing videos fitting into that process if you want them to be effective.

For example, does your product offer a free trial download? If so, then your video might serve as a springboard for increasing your download rate. In this case, you'll want to mention in the narration that you offer a demo, being sure to use words such as "new," "risk-free," "fully functional" (if applicable), and the mother of all magic marketing words, "free." If creating a Flash video, you might also want to add a clickable link to the end of your video that starts the download right away.

If you're selling higher-cost B2B software, and the goal is therefore to persuade the customer to call a salesperson, then placing all the appropriate contact information at the end of the video is essential. In fact, I had one client who had me add their toll-free number as a watermark for all their videos, so that a person could pick up the phone at any point while watching the video and immediately contact a sales rep.

Address the Customer's Need

As I mentioned earlier, the core component of the marketing video is to target the user's *need* rather than blathering on about features. The individuals you're trying to reach are busy people with problems to solve. It's the job of your marketing department to figure out what those problems are. It's your job as a video creator to convey the solutions to those problems in a quick and compelling way. At barest minimum, you have to know the difficulties that your potential customers are experiencing and how your solution helps alleviate that pain. This probably means having a good, long sit-down with the marketing team (that is, if you're not already part of the marketing team) to hammer these things out.

Unlike a demo video, where the target audience tends to be more specific, marketing videos are generally aimed at a very broad audience, possibly the entire potential customer base. But you should still try to find out as much about your target markets as possible, and address the needs that apply to the greatest percentage of them. If your target markets are really segmented, you may want to consider a special video for each group, rather than trying to kill multiple birds with one stone. As an example, let's take a product that I'm somewhat familiar with — Camtasia Studio. This is a product that appeals to a variety of groups, and for a variety of reasons. Let's look at a few possible markets, with a benefit for each one:

- **IT managers.** Construct a library of "how-to" videos so that users aren't bugging you all day long when they could be helping themselves.

- **Educators.** Put lessons online to help your students better prepare for their exams.

- **Law enforcement.** Collect computer-based evidence to help prosecute an online predator.

For each of these groups, we've identified the *unique selling proposition* (or USP), the main benefit that might convince one of these folks to dig out a credit card. The USP could actually contain several benefits. If you have three or four solutions that apply to each individual group of potential users, then it makes good sense to craft a video for each audience.

It might take some digging to find the USP. While it's beyond the scope of this humble book to give you a crash course in marketing, here are a few basic ideas as to where you might look:

- Go to conferences and trade shows that are specific to your business, and talk to your customers. If you have permission to contact them via other means such as phone or e-mail, do so. Ask them what prompted them to buy. You might also inquire about key benefits they've since discovered that would have made their purchase decision that much easier had they known about them at the time.

- Invest in a good web analytics package and take a good, hard look at what your visitors are doing. What pages are they visiting the most? Where are they spending most of their time?

- Mine the customer database. Take a look at what your customers do for a living (provided your software isn't exclusive to a particular industry). Who are your cash cows? What are the niche industries you might exploit?

Once you've found out what benefits make up your USP, you should try to rank them in order from most to least important. Why? One of the core tenets of selling is to always start with the most compelling benefit first and work your way downward. People may not stick around long enough to view the rest of the video if you leave all the good stuff for the clincher. Give them what they want to know up front.

Remember to Ask for the Sale

I have seen some truly amazing marketing spots created with Camtasia Studio, complete with a rock-solid USP, tight pacing, and terrific visuals. But then they trip right at the finish line by not telling the users what they need to do next! Remember, watching your video is but one step in the overall sales process. You need to do everything you can to guide viewers gently on to the next step. If that step is online purchase, you need to include a link to your purchase page. If it's to download your demo, you should provide a link to that. If it's to contact a sales rep, give the audience all the contact info they need, from phone numbers to e-mail addresses to your office hours (so that they're sure to actually reach someone).

And always, always, always specifically state in your narration what the next step is. When your video already has your prospects salivating over all the time and energy your software is going to save them, don't mess it all up by making them play detective in order to complete the purchase. Take them by the hand.

Tips for Making a Dynamite Demonstration Video

When Microsoft released the first version of PowerPoint back in 1990, no one was prepared for the way it came to change how ideas are presented in corporate, nonprofit, and academic environments alike. Unfortunately, the tool is really only as good as its wielder, and most PowerPoint presentations you'll see today are a listless sea of bullet points. Part of this is simply due to the way PowerPoint is constructed. After all, bullet points are astoundingly easy to do; they practically write themselves. One possible refuge from this tedium is a software product that can deliver with "bullet point ease" a series of visual elements that are much more compelling. So, let's talk about how Camtasia Studio can help you present like a pro.

Why Present with a Video?

Whether done as a critical part of an overall presentation or as a stand-alone kiosk-style demo, using screen video for demonstration offers a number of advantages, including the following:

- **Videos never tire of repetition.** In the past, I've gone to software trade shows where I had to deliver the same presentations 10 times or more in a single day. A video remains fresh from sunup to sundown, and it never gets laryngitis.

- **Videos don't require an Internet connection.** In demo situations where there's a risk of having no Internet connection, a video can show off your web application with no net access required. And on a related note...

- **Videos can show off intranet and enterprise-wide software.** You can record and demo content that would otherwise require being on-site at your company.

- **Videos can be there when you can't.** Emergencies can occasionally come up. Even if you can't make that conference due to a death in the family, you can still be there in spirit by creating a video demonstration. Sending off a video is also considerably cheaper and less time-consuming than sending human beings.

- **Videos can react quickly to time-sensitive opportunities.**
  Sometimes a situation will arise where you'll need to pitch your product to someone who needs to make a decision right away. Rather than flying all over the world to put out these fires, just fire off a customized demo video instead.

- **Videos can be an excellent primer for an in-person visit.**
  By sending your audience a demonstration video just ahead of your actual visit, you can make the time you spend with them much more focused, as opposed to expending a bunch of your allotted "face time" on covering the basics. Lingering questions can then be answered and any open issues clarified.

Of course, if you're utilizing a demo video to supplant an in-person demonstration, this has the obvious drawback of little or no interaction with the audience. Your audience can't easily get their questions answered; if it's not in the video, they're stuck. But a well-crafted, targeted demo video can greatly enhance or even replace an in-person demonstration. You just need to ask yourself the right questions about the video's purpose and audience.

Determining the Video's Purpose

Of the three video types, a demonstration video carries the broadest range of goals. Or so it would appear on the surface. The demo video is actually a cleverly disguised extension of the marketing and training genres, or perhaps some sort of hybrid thereof.

The difference that marks a video as a "demonstration" has to do with its target audience, which is generally narrower. Examples of demo audiences include your company's shareholders, the attendees of an industry-specific trade show or conference, or a potential client.

Despite all the different reasons people create a demonstration, when boiled down to their essence, there are really only two purposes: *training* and *selling*.

"Not my demo," you may be saying. "Mine is to show the new features of our product to management."

Nope. Sorry. Wrong. The real purpose goes deeper than that. Let me take an anecdotal moment to tell you why.

It may surprise you to know this, but my original vocational pursuit wasn't to become a video creation guru. This is pretty typical for multimedia designers. No one ever aspires to become one; we just sort of "fall into it" from other disciplines. I actually had a hankerin' to become an actor. I got bitten by the theatre bug (nasty little critter) at a young age, and declared my theatre major two weeks into my freshman year of college. I dove right into a variety of theatre-related classes, including acting courses based on the teachings of Konstantin Stanislavsky.

Stanislavsky put forth the notion that in order to create a truly realistic character, actors should study their character's *motivations*. You never tell someone a story just for the sake of telling it. The story is nothing without the *objective* behind it. Are you trying to impress? Flirt? Threaten?

Likewise, you never show features just for the sake of showing them. You've got to get at the reasoning behind it. So let's try this again:

"My demo is to keep management in the loop on all the new features of our product."

This is a little better. Keeping the folks informed is an admirable goal, but I'm afraid it's still not specific enough to really shape the construction of your demo. Aside from the fact that they probably determine your salary, why *exactly* are you keeping them in the loop?

"My demo is to keep management in the loop on all the new features of our product, so that they can get a look at the user interface screens of those features early on. That way, we can get feedback earlier in the process, and won't have to make major UI changes two weeks before the new version is supposed to ship. Unlike last time."

Okay, now that's a workable goal! By asking yourself some honest questions about *why* this video is being made in the first place, you can do a much more focused demo. In this case, getting management on board about your UI choices is the real objective behind the presentation. I would therefore contend that this is a "selling" video after all. Selling doesn't necessarily involve hawking a product or service. It's also possible to sell ideas, such as your design for the user interface of a new software feature. Of course, if you weren't the one who commissioned this video, then you need to have a chat with the person who did. An objective of "I'm making this demo video because my boss told me to" may be accurate, but it certainly won't help you refine the video's content. Find out why they want it made.

Finding Information about Your Audience

As I mentioned, it's the target audience that really designates your content as a demo video. While this may seem like a superficial distinction, it carries with it a variety of opportunities and obstacles that prompted me to designate the demonstration video as a separate type. Let's talk about some of these considerations.

Because the audience here is much more specific than that of a stock training/marketing video, this gives you the opportunity (or responsibility, if you're a pessimist) of really custom-tailoring your video presentation toward those individuals. For that, you're going to have to do a little homework. Possibly a lot. If this is a sales demonstration, and you're the fourth in a string of seven potential vendors being seen by this prospect, knowing their specific problems and offering a targeted solution to those problems can make all the difference.

If presenting to a larger audience (such as trade show or conference attendees), you'll want to gather as much information as possible about what makes these people tick. If you're not overly familiar with the target industry, then you need to give yourself a crash course. Try to gather some specific demographics on the people who will be in attendance at that event. The show's organizing body might be able to help you with that. Smaller audiences (such as a sales prospect) are a bit easier, because you'll probably have the ability to speak to a few of the major decision-makers ahead of time. If possible, pay them a visit. Sit down with them. Learn their story. Learn their needs.

When actually recording your video, do your best to incorporate examples from their world. If you have some sample fields to fill in, don't use generic data! This applies to both training and sales demos. Instead of talking about "widgets" and "ABC Companies," you should be speaking *their* language. You can use appropriate industry-specific terminology if you're certain everyone who's viewing your demo will understand it. Just keep in mind that your demo may end up being viewed by multiple departments, from the CEO to the IT manager to the order-takers on the sales floor. If every affected group will get different uses/benefits out of the software, consider doing a separate video for each one. Nobody wants to suffer through a long presentation of material that doesn't apply to them. The more you know about your viewers and their needs, the better your finished product will be. We'll talk more about this in the next chapter.

Additional Reading

Training Videos

Ruth Colvin Clark and Richard E. Mayer, *e-Learning and the Science of Instruction*, 2nd Ed. Jossey-Bass, 2008.

Richard E. Mayer, *Multimedia Learning*. Cambridge University Press, 2001.

Alan S. Pringle and Sarah S. O'Keefe, *Technical Writing 101: A Real-World Guide to Planning and Writing Technical Documentation*, 2nd Ed. Scriptorium Press, 2003.

Marketing Videos

Robert W. Bly, *The Copywriter's Handbook*, 3rd Ed. Henry Holt, 2005.

Robert B. Cialdini, *Influence: Science and Practice*, 4th Ed. Allyn & Bacon, 2000.

Bryan Eisenburg, Jeffrey Eisenburg, and Lisa T. Davis, *Persuasive Online Copywriting: How to Take Your Words to the Bank*. Wizard Academy Press, 2003.

Demonstration Videos

Cliff Atkinson, *Beyond Bullet Points*. Microsoft Press, 2007.

Peter E. Cohan, *Great Demo! How to Create and Execute Stunning Software Demonstrations*, iUniverse, Inc., 2005.

Robert Riefstahl, *Demonstrating to Win! The Indispensable Guide for Demonstrating Software*. Xlibris Corporation, 2000.

Summary

For each of the three common video types (training, marketing, and demonstration), there are techniques that will help you create compelling content. Regardless of the video type, you must consider two predominant factors:

- **Who is your audience?** In figuring out whom you're trying to reach as well as what that population's needs are, you can craft a video that addresses those needs.

- **What is your purpose?** While the purpose of your video may seem obvious, refining your objective(s) to be as specific as possible will aid you in planning a project that accomplishes its goals without a lot of superfluous fluff.

In the next chapter, we'll talk a bit more about how a video's audience and purpose can shape the visuals and especially the narration of your project.

Chapter 4

Scripting and Storyboarding

I once took an improvisation course as a college undergraduate. I, along with a roomful of fellow student improvisers, would ad-lib scenes based on a given premise. I can honestly say it was the most fun I'd ever had in an academic setting, almost like schoolyard recess for adults. Of course, I would have been dreadfully embarrassed had any of those scenes ever been recorded and put up on the Internet for all to see. While we occasionally mined a golden nugget or two from these scenes, most of the time they were a meandering muddle of mediocrity. Video creation works much the same way. Even though improvised recording is a terrific tool to get the creative juices flowing (and one which we'll discuss in detail a bit later on), this should be done only as a launchpad to a more structured approach. It is but one (early) step in the process, not the entire process in and of itself. Remember, if you fail to plan, you plan to fail.

So how do we remedy this? Well, now that you've gotten more acquainted with your audience, and hopefully have a better sense of purpose based on their needs (and on your goals for them), it's time to put it all down on paper. I typically do this in two steps:

- **Scripting**, where you clarify your basic message and draft the video's voice narration.

- **Storyboarding**, where you plan the visuals (be it in words, pictures, or video) and tighten up your script to match them. The storyboard is the plan from which your video will ultimately be created.

General Tips on Scripting

This section covers the basics of writing your narration script. Even if you're not planning on narrating your video, it's still a good exercise to put on paper the various points you'll want to convey. We'll be covering subjects such as information gathering, style and content, and using terminology. I'll conclude by mentioning a couple of scripting techniques developed by others that may help you in your own scriptwriting endeavors.

A lot of people have asked me whether it's a good idea to narrate your videos at all. After all, you'll need to invest in equipment as well as possibly hire voice-over talent, and the audio track can sometimes more than double the file size. In the end, it is really worth the hassle?

My answer is an unequivocal yes. As you read in the last chapter, Richard Mayer's studies tell us that engaging multiple pathways into the brain (e.g., sight and sound) greatly enhances learning. My own experience tells me that people typically respond more favorably to a technological medium when it's administered with a touch of humanity. After all, what are we really trying to do with these videos? I would argue that, more often than not, we're trying to convey the feeling of that human touch that accompanies an in-person training session (or sales demo or presentation, etc.), without all the cost and trouble of actually being there in person. It's that inherent "humanness" of a video to which the audience really seems to respond.

The trick lies in trying to figure out ways of pushing your personality, knowledge, and enthusiasm over the ether. Your voice is a big part of the equation. From infancy onward, we human beings are trained to respond to the human voice. By silencing your video, you're not only shutting off one of the learning pathways, you're robbing your work of the lion's share of its personality. The content takes on a more robotic feel, and the end result is listless and dull. After all, there's a good reason nobody makes silent movies any more.

Gathering All the Pieces

Before sitting down to write a single word of narration, you need to start out in information-gathering mode. In addition to the acts of finding out about your audience and discovering your purpose that we talked about in the previous chapter, it's a good idea to approach a few content experts so that you can collect their input. For example, you might approach the developers of the software for tips on the easiest way of executing a complicated process. Or you might want to speak with someone in your MarComm department about the survey they recently conducted, where users were given the chance to rate the usefulness of the software's various features. This could aid you in determining not only what topics to include in your video, but the order in which to place them and how long to linger on each point.

Once you've assembled both your own notes and the advice of others, it's time to compile it into a workable outline (assuming that one hasn't been dictated to you by management). While there are a multitude of software outliners and project management tools that can help you, I generally prefer 3x5 index cards or Post-it notes, with one talking point on each. It helps me to visualize the flow of my narration. Only after I've scribbled, laid out, shuffled, pondered, reshuffled, torn up a couple of cards, added a couple new ones, and shuffled the order once again do I know that I'm ready to put my outline into Word or some other tool. But everyone has their own process; do what makes you comfortable.

Avoiding the "Blank Page" Syndrome

Once you have a good sense of what you want to cover and how, it's finally time to hunker down and get typing. Unfortunately, this is where a lot of people become paralyzed. You fire up a new word processing document, and there's just something about the vastness of that blank screen, with its I-beam cursor blinking tauntingly at you, that seems to freeze the creative juices right in their tracks.

The best tip I can recommend here is to go back to the good work you did during your preparation. Return to your assessments of the audience and purpose, and determine how those things interact with the outline you've established. Once you've got that blueprint in place, trust me, the text will practically write itself. Focus on your objective, and start typing content that speaks to that objective.

If you're still stuck, there is one technique I use that helps me overcome writer's block without fail. I simply make a rough recording. Remember at the beginning of the chapter, when I said that improvisation can be an effective tool if used appropriately? This is where ad-libbing is the most helpful. Jot down your video's main objective, and tape it to the top of your monitor. Then record a tutorial/marketing/demo video without the help of any notes or scripts. Just pretend that a representative person of your target audience is in the room, and start talking to that fictitious person, recording all the content with the video's overriding purpose in mind. Remember to record your audio narration at the same time. Then, preview and analyze your recorded content. Even when wading through all the "umms" and the uneven pacing, provided you've remained focused on the objective, I guarantee you'll find *something* salvageable to include in your script. Additionally, it can really help you target potential problems in your thought process as well as any lingering technical issues. You'll learn all about recording your first video in the next chapter.

What to Write: Form and Content

Included in this section are a few content and style tips to keep in mind when hammering out a script for a video audience. First, let's talk a bit about the wording we use in a video script.

Make the Wording Audience-Appropriate

When doing videos about software, you're bound to be producing for both technical and decidedly nontechnical audiences. Remember, in each and every video project you undertake, part of your discovery process with the target audience is figuring out which applies (if not both). The technical savvy of your group will have a profound effect on the terminology you employ. For example, if you're doing a marketing spot designed for general public consumption, don't use a lot of technical jargon that would mystify anyone not in possession of a computer science degree. If you must introduce an unfamiliar term, take a moment to explain it.

And this isn't just limited to techie words. The same concept applies to marketing buzzwords, industry jargon, and any other kind of gobbledygook that might not be immediately apparent to certain members of your audience. If this is a special demo video aimed at your sales and marketing staff, you can probably get away with using industry-specific terms and acronyms such as ROI, B2C, CPC, M-O-U-S-E, etc. However, any techies or administrative staff viewing your video would probably be lost. Try to play to the lowest common denominator, even though you're often walking a fine line between insulting their intelligence on the one hand and leaving them completely confused on the other. If you have distinct audiences with vastly differing areas of expertise, consider a separate video for each group.

That said, you'll want to "speak their language" as much as possible where it doesn't obscure your point. When citing examples, make them appropriate to the industry of your target audience rather than using generic filler content. For example, when demonstrating a particular feature of your new home design software, fill in the software's various fields with terms that an actual contractor (or architect, or whoever your target audience happens to be) would really use when using your product in a real-world situation. So, if you're showing off the Door & Window Inventory List feature, ask yourself which field entry would be more compelling: "Widget" or "Loose pin back flap hinge." Using the former is tantamount to saying, "I understand nothing about you or the things you care about," which doesn't do much to make a sale or establish yourself as a content expert.

Be Consistent in Your Terminology

Okay, I have one final point to make before I shut up about terminology. For some odd reason, presumably in the interest of adding variety to the narration, many writers of narration scripts will invariably use two or three different terms for the same concept. This is severely detrimental to helping your audience comprehend the content. It's the kiss of death for a tutorial video.

In this book, for example, I always call a video a *video*. I don't say movie, or film, or motion picture. And all of these are terms with which the general populace is pretty familiar. Imagine my throwing around a few highly technical, polysyllabic words, all of which meant the same thing. The only instance in which I find such usage appropriate is when you actually introduce the words at the same time. Here's an example from Chapter 7 of this very book:

> A *key frame* is a frame that has a complete picture in it. Also called an I-frame (short for "intra-frame"), a key frame anchors your video by providing a fully assembled image every so many frames.

Even when presenting both terms at once, I'd still typically use one of them pretty much exclusively, only mentioning the other once as background information.

Possible Scripting Techniques

While there are any number of methods for approaching the actual crafting of a video script, I've found two that are particularly helpful with certain video projects, and I'd like to share them with you here.

- **The "Sesame Street" technique.** This organizational scripting technique is sometimes credited to the Children's Television Workshop and its educational research in developing its *Sesame Street* TV series. It actually predates Big Bird and Cookie Monster in its use by trainers, marketers, salespeople, and professional speakers, yet is still often lovingly referred to as the "Sesame Street" technique.

    The premise is simple. First, tell them what you intend to show them today. Show them. And then tell them what you've shown them. This *tell-show-tell* technique tips off the audience as to what to expect, reinforces that expectation with the actual material, and then closes by summarizing all the important points. In fact, as you read through this book, you'll quickly realize that each chapter is laid out much the same way, with a topic introduction, the actual content, and then a handy summary.

A brief introduction not only prepares the audience for the content, it selects the audience as well. Viewers can therefore tell in the first 30 seconds whether this video contains information that will be useful to them. Due to the shorter length of most screen videos, I tend to gloss over the summary portion, even skipping it entirely if the video is less than seven minutes in duration.

I use this technique all the time. Its inherent sense of structure really seems to speak to people. Additionally, it helps you organize your own thoughts as well as get you thinking about the overall flow of the piece.

- **Storytelling.** In his book *Beyond Bullet Points*, management consultant Cliff Atkinson concocted a method of conducting a PowerPoint presentation that avoids the "bullet point syndrome" with which most of us are all too familiar. He suggests using your presentation to tell a story, casting your audience in the role of protagonist. Much like a stage play, this story consists of multiple acts where your characters (audience) must overcome obstacles in order to reach their overriding objective (à la Stanislavsky).

While intended for the PowerPoint set, this book offers a remarkable, alternate way of constructing your video scripts. By offering an appropriate metaphor for the current difficulties and future opportunities of your audience, you can construct a compelling story that guides them from problem to solution.

Of course, a brief synopsis doesn't really do the technique justice, so make sure you check out Atkinson's book for more details (a full reference to which can be found at the end of the previous chapter).

I've been on the business end of this technique several times, and I can tell you that when it works, it works remarkably well. There have also been a couple of instances when I've seen this technique fail miserably, mainly because its creator chose the wrong metaphor or didn't fully commit to the story. When done half-heartedly, it comes across as artificial, contrived, and, well…, cheesy. But when done well, it can accomplish the objective you've established as well as connect with the audience on a more basic human level than might otherwise have been possible.

General Tips on Storyboarding

Once you have a script in hand, the next step in the process is to craft your storyboard. The storyboard is the blueprint of your video. At a glance, you'll be able to view the visual details of each segment and the accompanying narration simultaneously.

Choose a Presentation Layout You're Comfortable With

The key to making a useful storyboard is to lay out each scene in a separate box, with the visual cues on one side and the audio narration on the other. The storyboard is doing its job if you can glance down and instantly know what you're doing in the next clip.

The layout will obviously vary according to personal taste, but if it will help you, I'm only too happy to share how I lay out my storyboards. Here goes:

The narration script provides a base. The first step is splitting up the individual pages and paragraphs into distinct *shots*, those points at which there is some major change to the visual elements on-screen. I'm not a big fan of letting the audience view a single application window throughout the entire course of the video. I think it's much better to mix things up a bit. Plan a wide variety of shots that will elicit the most clarity for the topic at hand. As your skills progress, you can do more advanced zooming and panning shots, both for the sake of homing in on a particular interface element and for artistic effect. To aid me in this endeavor when first starting out, I devoured a few introductory books on film directing, and I can't tell you how much this exercise helped the preparation of my various shots. I encourage you to do the same.

Once you've separated your narration into corresponding shots, try placing them into individual boxes so that there is a distinct visual separation of elements. The Table feature of Microsoft Word works admirably in this regard. In my table, I include two columns. On the left is where I place my visual elements. I paste my narration on the right. I'll also typically change the page's orientation from portrait to landscape in order to get a bit more elbow room on the horizontal axis. To do this in Word, simply choose **File > Page Setup…**, and then click the **Landscape** button on the Paper Size tab.

Next, it's time to fill out the column for our visual cues. It's fairly quick and easy to simply type in a textual description of how you envision the scene playing out, making sure to include any planned on-screen text. This is what I do most of the time. For the visual thinkers out there, you may be more comfortable including a mocked-up screenshot, or even a link to a rough draft video clip. While the inclusion of actual visual images is certainly more work than typing out a quick description, for complicated scenes, it can save you time in the long run by allowing you to examine the picture for potential trouble spots, something most of us are unable to do in our mind's eye. Additionally, an image can give you all the information you need at a glance when actually getting down to the business of starting a capture.

Now, keep in mind that you can also insert a *hybrid* visual, which is an image accompanied by explanatory text, usually detailing the action that a still image cannot capture. Observe:

Visual	Narration
After clicking the cell, zoom over with the mouse to the AutoSum button, and then zoom back to show the result.	You can quickly tally a series of numbers in your Excel worksheet by selecting the next cell in the series and then clicking **AutoSum**. This will give you the total of all numbers in the series, without having to enter any formulas or cell references.

As you can see here, we've got a screenshot and some descriptive text that explains the animations. You can also see that I've intentionally blown up the size of the narration text. Since this is the script from which I'll probably end up reading, I tend to ignore standard formatting conventions, and instead go with formatting that lends itself to script reading, such as enlarging the text. I also make sure to use a *serif* font (a font with little "feet" at the bottom of most letters), as research demonstrates these fonts to be the most readable for large blocks of text (which is why the body text of most books and magazines is comprised of serif fonts).

Storyboard Flow

As soon as you've got all your visuals in place, the next thing you need to work on is making sure the storyboard has a nice rhythm and flow.

Each point should segue naturally into the next, both visually and in its narration. This is trickier than it sounds. You may have to do some last-minute juggling of the order of your items in order to establish transitions that feel natural and not forced. Remember, regardless of video type, everything in your video is about progression. In a training video, for instance, you're guiding the users procedurally through your content, with advanced topics building on top of the basics. Marketing videos also have a progression. Your task is to take the audience by the hand and guide them ever so gently toward the sale. This is done by conveying benefits (in descending order of importance), using the power of those benefits to sweep away any lingering objections, and finally, giving them all the information they need in order to take the next step.

The rhythm of your storyboard also plays a large role in terms of how well it flows. Have you spent an appropriate amount of time on each point? Double-check to ensure that everything has been appropriately clarified, and that most users won't be left with a series of burning questions when the video is done. Unlike an in-person demonstration, you won't be there to answer questions. It therefore falls on the individual users to contact you for answers, and most won't bother.

Conversely, you should also ask yourself if you aren't taking up too much time on topics of lesser importance. In a marketing spot, for example, if you spend 10 seconds on your primary benefit and 70 seconds on the last benefit in the list, then you know you have a problem. It may be time to do some creative editing of your narration (and possibly your video) to correct the distribution of content.

Picture-in-Picture (PIP)

I wanted to make one final point before we move on to actually using the program. Camtasia Studio offers the ability to include a *second* video stream in your video project, either in a side-by-side format or a true picture-in-picture (with one video image superimposed over the other).

This opens up a new world of possibilities in terms of "staging" your work. While generally intended as a way for you to capture your face when delivering a presentation or walking someone through a software procedure, there are a number of other uses you should definitely consider when putting together your storyboard:

- **Live-action sequence.** Camtasia Studio can import AVI, MPEG, and WMV files, so why not take things up a notch with the introduction of some real-world video segments? In our home design software example from earlier in the chapter, you could give your video a new dimension by showing how a particular blueprint plan evolved into a finished house.

- **Diagram or animation.** If a table, diagram, or animated figure would help illuminate the current topic, you can show it without having to leave the procedure you're working on.

- **Close-up shots.** Sometimes you need to focus in on a particular part of the user interface, and Camtasia Studio's zoom and pan effects are quite useful to this end. But if you'd like to show a close-up while allowing the user a bird's-eye view of the entire window at the same time, a PIP video fits the bill nicely.

- **Déjà vu: Recalling an earlier segment.** Training videos tend to proceed in a stepwise manner, with advanced topics building upon the basic ones. With PIP, you can quickly remind your audience of something you've covered previously while simultaneously forging ahead into new material.

As you can see, this picture-in-picture technology offers all sorts of neat ways to lay out your content visually. We'll be talking more about this handy feature in Chapters 5, 10, and 11, but in the meantime, don't forget about it when designing your storyboards. Rather than being forced into a strictly linear progression of images, PIP can let you produce content that has the potential to be even more engaging.

Summary

In this chapter, we discussed several techniques for scripting the narration of your video, and then building a storyboard around it that placed the narration within the context of the envisioned screen visuals.

- **Scripting the narration.** As it conveys the feel of an in-person demonstration, audio narration is a critical component of your video. In order to best leverage that power, it is far better to script your narration ahead of time as opposed to winging it. After speaking with content experts and reviewing your audience and purpose, you're ready to begin crafting a script. Remember to use consistent terminology that is appropriate to your audience. Making use of the special "Sesame Street" technique or the storytelling methods can also be quite helpful if used appropriately.

- **Storyboarding your visual content.** After writing out your narration, you can use it as the basis for a storyboard by adding visual cues (in the form of text descriptions or graphics) to individual sections of narration. Be sure to select a layout for your storyboard that matches your own personal workflow. Pay close attention to how your storyboard flows from one point to the next. And finally, don't forget about the possibilities offered by Camtasia Studio's picture-in-picture technology, which can afford you the opportunity to storyboard more visually complex, engaging scenes.

In the next chapter, we're going to get really crazy and actually start working with the program. We'll begin with the first step of recording your initial footage, using the Camtasia Recorder.

EXTRALIFE

by Scott Johnson

Recording with Camtasia Studio

The Camtasia Recorder is the part of Camtasia Studio that captures all your screen activity and saves it as a video file. It is these files that make up the components of your final video presentation. As such, the Camtasia Recorder is generally considered the backbone of the application. Unfortunately, this can lead many users to believe that the Recorder is pretty much all there is to Camtasia Studio, when in fact the application offers so much more. This unit is devoted to recording your screen content. While it is only the first step to taking your storyboard and giving it life, it's a critical step. No matter how refined your editing skills, a world-class product comes from world-class footage, and with the Camtasia Recorder, that's exactly what you can provide.

This unit is divided into four chapters:

- **Chapter 5: Recording Your Screen.** This is the nuts-and-bolts introduction to using the Recorder. It also provides a step-by-step guide for recording different kinds of content, and concludes with a series of "best practices" tips I have honed through years of working with the program.

- **Chapter 6: Special Effects of the Camtasia Recorder.** This chapter expands upon the basics by teaching you how to add great special effects to your recordings. From autohighlight to zooming, you'll learn all about techniques that give your videos some added zing.

■ **Chapter 7: Recorder Tools Options.** This chapter is devoted to setting the Recorder's various options according to your needs and preferences. Adjusting audio and video settings, hotkeys, program preferences, and the addition of camera video are all discussed here.

■ **Chapter 8: Recording Your PowerPoint Presentation.** This chapter focuses on the Camtasia Studio add-in for Microsoft PowerPoint. While not about the Camtasia Recorder per se, the add-in is based on the same Recorder technology, and gives the user an alternate (and *improved*) means of recording PowerPoint presentations.

Chapter 5

Recording Your Screen

In this chapter, you'll have your very first introduction to the Camtasia Recorder. This handy application acts like a video camcorder shooting a desired scene, like your nephew's graduation. Only this time, the desired scene is happening on your computer screen, and the camcorder isn't made of plastic and microchips but rather of code. Now that you've selected your audience (well, sometimes they select *you*), storyboarded the different elements you want included, and (hopefully) crafted a script, we're ready to actually start recording content.

The cool thing about Camtasia Recorder is that once you've set up the scene, you can record it over and over until you're happy with the result. In the case of your nephew's graduation, if you miss out on your brother pouring a beer over the lad's head in a specially concocted rite-of-passage ceremony, that's a moment that's gone forever. Even if you can convince your nephew to sit patiently as he's doused with another brewski, it just won't be the same. Fortunately, computer software gives a much more consistent performance, and it never tires of repetition. Therefore, I encourage you to really take your time with this step, and make sure that your base clips represent the cleanest footage you can get. After all, bad editing of good footage can still create a passable product, but good editing cannot salvage bad footage under any circumstances.

In short, your clips created with the Camtasia Recorder are where the success of your overall project begins. Ready to dive in? Good.

Making Your First Recording

If the first thing you did after installing Camtasia Studio 5 was to launch the main application (this is logical, after all), you were probably presented with a dialog that looked something like this:

Choosing the option **New Screen Recording** brings up the Camtasia Recorder. In version 5, this application has been drastically revamped, both in aesthetics and functionality. Gone is the wizard from previous versions that guides you through the basic steps associated with making your first recording. Instead, there's a new, simpler interface that's a snap to use.

But before we dive into making our first capture, I want to take a brief moment to introduce you to the new Camtasia Recorder window. Out of the box, it looks like this:

To make a capture, we need to first tell Camtasia Recorder exactly what portion of the screen we want to record. This can be done by clicking one of two buttons: **Select area to record** or **Last area**. The latter option is obviously out, since this is our very first capture and there *is* no last area. So go ahead and choose *Select area to record*.

You're presented with a special selection tool that can function in a few different ways depending on what you want to capture. With it, you can select a region of the screen, a window, or the entire screen.

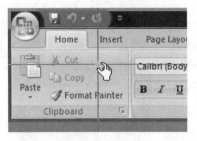

Just pass your mouse cursor over any window and click when the frame is around the desired area. Note that this also works for many individual components of a window; in this case we were able to single out a toolbar.

Let's explore how this works. As you move your mouse cursor around the screen, a red border will highlight any windows or portions thereof that it can detect underneath the cursor. If your desire is to capture one of these areas, just click when its edges are enclosed in the red border. The entire screen can be captured in much the same way — just move your mouse cursor to the top of the screen, and the entire screen will highlight.

 If you're on a machine running Windows Vista running the default Aero theme, keep in mind that the window detection mechanism doesn't tend to include the drop shadows around the edges of the window. If you want to include these, you'll need to manually adjust your capture area, which we'll talk about in a moment.

Of course, you aren't confined to these automatic selections. If you take another look at the capture selection tool, you'll see that your hand-shaped mouse cursor is centered over a set of thin red crosshairs. Clicking and dragging will allow you to select your capture area by hand. For example, you can have your capture area encompass three different application windows. As you're dragging, notice that you see a set of dimensions inside a small window:

These numbers represent, in pixels, the width and height of the respective capture area. If you're targeting a particular size for your output, you'll want to pay attention to these numbers. Unless you have a very steady mouse hand, it's hard to exactly nail down your desired set of dimensions, but that doesn't really matter, as these numbers are readily adjustable.

Regardless of what area of the screen you select, you'll next be presented with the capture area, along with a rather curious new dialog, titled **Camtasia Recorder Selection Area**. You've also probably noticed that everything outside the capture area is grayed out. Let us quickly dissect both the capture area itself and its corresponding dialog.

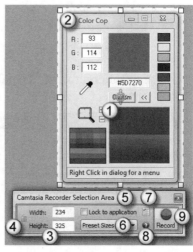

① **Move handle.** This small anchor sits in the middle of your capture area, allowing you to click and drag it to move the entire capture area around.

② **Resize handles.** Eight of these tiny white boxes surround the capture area, letting you make size adjustments on the fly.

③ **Width and Height boxes.** Once you've dragged (or clicked a window) to select your capture area, you can refine it by typing values into the Width and Height fields. It's nice for perfecting a hastily dragged "good enough" region selection to exactly match your desired size.

④ **Lock aspect ratio.** If you'd like your adjustment in the Width field to be proportionally reflected in the Height field (and vice versa), click this padlock icon to lock the aspect ratio.

⑤ **Lock to application.** This doesn't seem like an important option at first glance, but it's an astounding new development in making your recording a snap. First off, locking the capture area to the application means that no matter how you move or resize the application window, the capture area will follow. But the coolest part is that the reverse is also true. Say you needed the video to be 800 x 600 pixels. Just select the window for capture, choose *Lock to application*, and then type 800 x 600 into the Width and Height fields. Now you have a window that fits perfectly inside your desired recording area — not a pixel is lost.

Not only that, but once you lock the capture area to an application, any pop-up alerts or other dialogs that come up as part of the application are *automatically* centered within your capture area. No longer do you have to interrupt a recording to fetch errant dialogs! This is a huge advantage, and we'll talk about it more fully in Chapter 7.

⑥ **Preset Sizes.** Rather than typing values into the Width/Height fields, you can choose from a list of presets. This drop-down list shows both common capture sizes as well as the five most recent areas you captured. This can be extraordinarily handy when making multiple captures for the same project. Using the same size and location for each capture lends consistency to your video by making sure that all the windows are in their proper place. We'll talk more about this when we discuss *Last area* capture.

⑦ **Options.** This merely brings back the main Camtasia Recorder interface, so that you can set additional options as appropriate.

⑧ **Help.** A context-sensitive help window will appear.

⑨ **Record.** This starts the recording process in motion.

If you made a mistake and want to cancel, you may freely do so by closing the Camtasia Recorder Selection Area window. If you're ready to go, you can go ahead and click the **Record** button, or press **F9**, which is the default hotkey for toggling Record/Pause.

When you do so, you see the four corners of your defined capture area flash green and black. That means that you're now recording everything that happens in this space. Another visual indicator that you're currently recording is the Camtasia Recorder icon in the system tray, which flashes red and green while recording, and stays red when paused or stopped. Beneath your capture area (provided you're not recording full-screen) is a special Recording toolbar for controlling the recording. It looks like this:

By default, you can utilize it to pause/resume the recording, stop it entirely, or delete it and start over. You can click to hide the the toolbar if it annoys you. And on the right-hand side of the toolbar is a section for monitoring the running time and the volume of your narration if you opted to record it (more on this in a bit). You can also adjust the recording volume using the accompanying slider. I personally don't care for the toolbar, opting instead to make use of keyboard hotkeys for controlling my recording. If you *do* opt for the toolbar, we'll discuss how it can be toggled and even customized with additional tools when we get to Chapter 7. We'll cover hotkeys there as well.

At any rate, we are now recording. Press **F9** again to pause the action. You can toggle between play and pause by pressing F9 repeatedly. One insanely cool new addition is Camtasia Recorder's ability to mark the position of your mouse cursor upon pausing. When you resume recording, the mouse is automatically placed right back where you left off. This wonderful feature avoids the dreaded *apparating cursor syndrome*, where it looks to your audience as if the USS *Enterprise* suddenly "beamed" your mouse cursor from one end of the screen to the other. We'll talk about how to toggle this feature in Chapter 7.

When finished with your recording, press **F10**. At this stage, you're presented with a Preview window containing the clip you just recorded, including your camera video if you opted to record that stream. If everything looks okay, click **Save**. If everything looks less than okay, click **Delete**, and you're booted back to the Recorder's main interface, where you can begin another recording from scratch using the settings you already specified.

Now, assuming you liked what you did and clicked the Save button accordingly, you're presented with a standard Save Recording dialog, where you can specify a name and file path for your new video file. By default, this file is in CAMREC format. Camtasia Recorder also supports the ability to record to an industry-standard AVI. We'll discuss how to change the output format (and under what circumstances you'd *want* to) in Chapter 7, "Recorder Tools Options."

At any rate, after clicking the **Save** button on this dialog, you'll get a small box with your Post-Save Options, which asks the burning question, "What would you like to do next?" If only all computer applications were so simple and direct. You've got three options here:

- **Edit my recording.** Choosing this option will automatically import your recording into Camtasia Studio for further editing, opening the application if necessary. If you're already working on a project, your file will be added to the Camtasia Studio Clip Bin and Timeline automatically. You can edit your recording right away, or go back to the Recorder and create a new clip, bringing it into Camtasia Studio to join the first one. We'll discuss editing your work in Chapter 9, "Working with Camtasia Studio."

- **Produce my video in a shareable format.** The CAMREC files produced by Camtasia Recorder contain your video footage, camera video (if recorded), and any markers you may have added during recording (more on this later). It is not a format that can be read by any standard media player. If you do not wish to edit your creation, instead opting to share it immediately with others, then select this option. The Production Wizard will appear, letting you select the file output best suited for the situation. To find out more about the Production Wizard and all the various output types at your disposal, please go straight to Chapter 12, "The Production Process."

■ **Create another recording.** This saves your video using the specified file path and file name, and then takes you back to the Camtasia Recorder so that you can record your next segment. If you're like me and want to do all your recording at once before having to worry about mucking around with the editing process, then this option is for you.

So that's it. You've just made your very first video. Now, that wasn't too hard, was it? Of course, we have yet to fully acquaint ourselves with the Recorder interface and learn about all it can do for us. Along the way, I'll also show you the additional streams you can record: audio, camera video, and markers.

Setting Up Your Recording

So, you've gotten your feet wet with a quick introduction to recording. Of course, there are many more options that we haven't yet covered for setting up a world-class capture. In this section…

■ We'll start off with a discussion of the additional content streams beyond screen video that are available for you to capture and use in your projects.

■ Then, we'll talk further about the Last area capture selection tool and its importance in attaining consistency in your captures.

■ Later, we'll explore all the nooks of Recorder's user interface and how it can be customized to suit your needs.

■ We'll then round things off with advice for recording in special circumstances, such as media players, games, and animation tools.

Choosing Which Streams to Include

In addition to the screen video that Camtasia Studio is famous for, the Recorder also offers to record a few additional streams of data to go along with it. Two of these streams, audio and camera video, are adjustable directly from the Recorder's main interface:

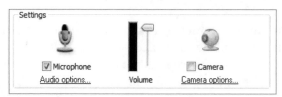

Audio

When recording your segments, you always have the option of narrating them as you go. Clicking the **Microphone** check box will record your audio narration during recording (it's checked by default). Clearly, you must also have the appropriate equipment (a microphone and, if necessary, a preamp) hooked up to your machine before this option becomes viable. While recording your narration this way is certainly an option, juggling the screen recording and remembering your lines at the same time can often prove too much to handle. As a matter of personal taste, I prefer to record my audio during the editing process. You can read all about your options for recording and editing your narration in Chapter 10, "Working with Other Media: Audio, PIP, and Title Clips."

Of course, there are times when recording a voice-over as you go is perfectly appropriate, such as when you're giving a quick "how to" to a friend or colleague, and they probably won't mind the "umms" and awkward timing as long as the information is good, so go right ahead if the video isn't for public comsumption. With this option enabled, you can lay in an audio track with your voice narration that will be perfectly synchronized with the screen video, and there's a certain convenience with getting all your content created at once.

In addition to the Microphone check box, you can also enable audio recording by choosing **Capture > Record Audio.**  Additionally, you can toggle the audio using the first button on the Audio toolbar, which you can bring up by choosing **View > Audio Toolbar.** Let's explore this toolbar a bit further.

The next two buttons will insert mouse click and keyboard sound effects whenever you click the mouse or press a key. Done in small doses, they can help convey to the user exactly when you clicked or typed, and depending on the application and circumstances, this could be critical information. Don't overdo it, though; torturing your audience with the constant clickety-clack of keypresses and mouse clicks is unlikely to win you any fans. Finally, there's a button on this toolbar I like to call the "panic" button. It instantly mutes all audio recording as well as audio effects. When enabled, all other audio options are disabled. You can also set a hotkey for the mute function, so that you can access it even when the Recorder user interface isn't visible (see Chapter 7 for more information on setting hotkeys).

All four buttons on this toolbar are *toggle* buttons, meaning that they can be turned on and off by clicking multiple times. Additional settings for these tools can be found in the Effects Options and Tools Options dialogs, which are discussed in Chapters 6 and 7.

Once you've decided what audio streams you want included (narration, mouse clicks, keystrokes, etc.), it's time to set up the device, source, and volume for your recording. If the volume meter on the main Camtasia Recorder window is showing activity when you speak into your microphone, then you're probably more or less set. If the meter is flatlining, then you'll need to make adjustments. This is done by clicking the **Audio options...** link from the main Recorder window, which will spit you out onto the Audio tab of the Options dialog. You can set these options manually, and indeed, we'll discuss the technical details of these settings in "The Audio Tab" section of Chapter 7. But this time, let's set up our audio by clicking the **Audio Setup Wizard...** button, located toward the bottom of the tab.

When choosing your settings, the first thing you'll want to do is select an **Audio device**. This is most likely your sound card, though audio interface boxes also count as audio devices. This device can support one or more **Recording sources**. You can have Camtasia Studio auto-select your **Microphone** input (for recording from the mic) or **Speaker audio** input (for recording your system sound). If desired, you can even choose to have Camtasia Recorder record from your microphone and from your computer system at the same time. To custom-manage your source, you can also select an input manually. Finally, be sure to check your **Input level** to ensure that Camtasia Studio is receiving audio. You can adjust the recording volume level with the accompanying slider bar.

Camtasia Studio essentially leaves your system audio settings alone. For example, when you launch the Camtasia Recorder, the application does indeed switch your audio settings to your last known settings within the application, but when you exit, it cleans up after itself by setting everything back to your standard system settings.

In Windows Vista, the audio drivers for most sound cards are still very young and unrefined at this point, and it's likely that recording your speaker audio won't be an option for you, at least not without some major tweaking. Check back with your manufacturer often, as new drivers are released all the time. For tips on circumventing this limitation, see "Recording System Sound" in Chapter 10.

Of course, if you'd rather have Camtasia Studio determine the best recording volume, the following screen in the wizard, **Tune Volume Input Levels,** can do exactly that. Just click **Auto-Adjust Volume**, and then speak into the mic normally (or run the system sound on your computer). Camtasia Studio will automatically set the optimal recording volume based on this input. Keep in mind that Chapter 10 contains a wealth of information on adding audio to Camtasia Studio, so that's the first place to turn if you have questions.

Camera Video

Right next to your audio settings on the main Camtasia Recorder interface is a check box for another content stream. Checking **Camera** will record a second video stream from your webcam (or video camcorder) in addition to your screen video, so not only will your audience be able to view your screen, they'll also be able to see *you*. Like your audio narration, the camera video will be perfectly synchronized with your screen video, and during the editing process, you can superimpose one over the other in a process called picture-in-picture (or PIP). Those who will ultimately produce their projects to Flash have the additional option of laying out their screen video and camera video in a side-by-side format. If you want to see what the camera sees, choosing **Camera Preview** from the **View** menu will show your camera video in a preview window while you're recording.

If you chose to engage the Camera Preview, you'll also see a preview window of your pretty face (or your ugly mug, depending on your level of self-esteem) plastered on the screen. I'm ready for my close-up!

If what you see in the preview is blank or simply not what you're expecting, click the **Camera options...** link, located right under the Camera check box. Here you can select from the different available video camera devices and see a preview of what each looks like. You may also adjust each device's **Camera Properties** as well as the **Video Format** of the camera output by clicking the corresponding button. You should probably leave these on their default settings for now; we'll discuss them in a bit more detail in Chapter 7, "Recorder Tools Options." Should you end up making a complete mess of your video format settings, a click of the **Default** button will reset them to their factory defaults, restore your default webcam device, and reinitialize the video stream. It's a handy safety net if you really screw things up good, which I tend to do as a matter of course.

For your convenience, both the Record Camera and Camera Preview commands can be toggled by way of the Camera toolbar, as shown here:

Don't worry if you don't currently see the toolbar; it's hidden by default. We'll discuss this as well as the other toolbars at your disposal a bit later in this chapter.

One last note about recording camera video: If you've altered your file settings such that you're recording to an industry-standard AVI rather than Camtasia Recorder's proprietary CAMREC format, you cannot record camera video. You simply can't store a second video stream inside an AVI. If you need camera video, use CAMREC instead. So, if you receive an error message when trying to enable camera video, do the following:

1. From the **Tools** menu, choose **Options...**.
2. On the **Capture** tab, select **Save as CAMREC**.
3. Click **OK**. Try enabling Record Camera again.

Markers

While not technically a stream, the welcome addition of markers packages another useful set of information in with your video recording, and as such bears mentioning here. Like the camera video and audio narration streams, it too is perfectly synchronized with your screen video. A *marker* is just what it sounds like: a placeholder in the video that marks something of note. While markers can also be added within Camtasia Studio after recording has already taken place, they're often handy at record time when you want to mark a new section or witness other events you want to make note of.

Most people use markers to denote a new topic or some other change. For our own practical purposes, the markers in Camtasia Studio are used for three essential reasons:

■ **Basic editing.** While recording the latest video clip in your project, say you screw something up. Hey, it happens (in fact, for me, it happens often). Rather than stopping and then restarting the process over from scratch, you just insert a marker. This marker serves to remind you, "Hey, I just messed up and now I'm starting over." When you conclude your recording and move into Camtasia Studio for editing, you can see your marker at a glance and instinctively know to delete everything that came before it. With the aid of markers, you no longer have to go blindly searching for different "takes" inside a long video. You already marked them.

■ **Setting up a table of contents.** Markers can also be utilized to take advantage of a great feature in Camtasia Studio. When recording a lengthy video, say you decide to add a marker for every new topic. When you start editing in Camtasia Studio, all your added markers can be given meaningful names, from which you can automatically set up a table of contents for your footage. When watching your video, as soon as the user clicks the link with the corresponding marker name, the video's playback head moves immediately to that spot.

- **Chopping up a lengthy video file.** If you're recording a really long video, consider adding a few markers at pivotal points. When producing your file, you can tell the Production Wizard to split your video into separate files based on your markers. That way, when circumstances force you to record a marathon session, you can easily break it into palatable chunks. They're easier to sit through, and the file size is infinitely more manageable.

So, how do we add a marker? You can put this wonderful technology to work for you just by hitting a specified hotkey while recording your video. By default, this hotkey is **Ctrl+Shift-M**. You can add a marker at any point during recording. So as not to detract from the recording, you won't hear a tone or see any kind of visual indicator that a marker was added, but as soon as you conclude your recording and bring it into Camtasia Studio, sure enough, there it will be. We'll talk more about working with markers in Camtasia Studio when we get to Chapter 9, "Working with Camtasia Studio."

> As with Camera video, recording markers won't work if you have the Camtasia Recorder set to record to AVI format. Only CAMREC files can make use of markers at record time, so if you need to use this feature, make sure you've got Save as CAMREC enabled. It's located on the General tab in the Tools Options dialog.

Capture Area Selection Revisited: Last Area

Now that you're armed with some additional content streams, perhaps you have a mind to capture your next clip. Remember our two capture selection buttons?

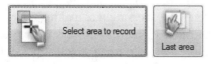

We did *Select area to record* last time. This time, let's choose *Last area*. Rather than having to take time selecting a new recording area, you can get right down to business, which can be a real time-saver. But that's not all. It has the added benefit of providing *consistency* between your clips.

So what do I mean by this? Say you're recording a video of your favorite application. The work day ends, and you shut down your computer. You come back the next day and fire up your application. Provided the program adheres to standard Windows conventions, the application window should reappear in the same location, at the same dimensions, that you left it. Now you start up Camtasia Recorder. If you choose Last area, the recording area will also appear at the same size and dimensions as before. If you fail to do so, and try to reselect a recording area by hand, you're unlikely to get a pixel-perfect match of your capture area settings from last time. This results in a jarring visual shift when stringing together the video clips from yesterday and today. Using Last area will help you avoid that subtle "pixel jump" that would otherwise mar your project and expose you as an amateur.

And don't forget: The last five captures are saved in the drop-down list of your Camtasia Recorder Selection Area window. So even if you made a quick capture or two since last working on your big project, you can easily recover the capture area settings you need to keep working.

Now that we've established what area we're recording, it's time to figure out what other kinds of information we want to include in our video.

The Camtasia Recorder User Interface

By design, the user interface of the Camtasia Recorder window is highly customizable. If you don't like the Statistics and Properties area of your window, just collapse it. Never use the Zoom & Pan toolbar? Turn it off, and it won't distract you ever again. In this section, we'll talk about adjusting the views and toolbars of the Recorder as well as examine the other elements of your main user interface.

Adjusting Your View

The Camtasia Recorder window is designed to have a small footprint so that it stays out of the way of whatever application you're recording. Depending on your needs, you have the option of making the window even smaller by only keeping those elements you're actually going to use. Let's begin by cutting the view down to its smallest possible size. From the **View** menu, choose **Compact**. Notice how the main inter- face disappears, and you're left with only the title bar, menu bar, and status bar. Of course, you can still access all needed commands through the menu bar, and to an extent through keyboard hotkeys as well. And if you miss the main interface, it's easy to get it back by choosing **View > Standard**.

When looking over the View options, you probably noticed that you had six toolbars at your disposal: Main, Annotation, Audio, Cursor, Zoom & Pan, and Camera. By selecting toolbars from this list (using either the View menu or its corresponding button on the Main toolbar), they can be toggled on and off. In the View menu, a check mark appears next to the enabled ones.

The Main toolbar sports three buttons: Toggle View, Options, and Help, all of which I'll discuss in a moment. The Audio and Camera toolbars involve the inclusion of additional streams with your video. The other three toolbars are devoted to special effects, and we will cover them in detail in the next chapter.

By default, the toolbars appear in a particular order, but if you don't like the way the Recorder organizes your toolbars within the palette, you can click and drag on the toolbar's handle to move it around the palette to a location you like better:

With the exception of the Main toolbar, all toolbars in Camtasia Recorder have a handle with which you can move them around.

Finally, note that your View options sport two other settings, from which you can bring up windows that aid in recording:

- **Camera Preview.** If you're recording to a CAMREC file (which is the default), you can bring up a preview window that monitors what your video device (webcam, camcorder, video capture card, etc.) is currently capturing. Obviously, you have to have some sort of video device attached to your computer. You can initiate the preview before the capture begins, but to continue viewing it while recording, you'll have to have Record Camera enabled.

- **ScreenPad.** This window will allow you to place graphics on your screen, which you can then record. A pre-established library of graphics is at the ready, and you can also add your own graphic files. While this feature has been largely supplanted by callouts in Camtasia Studio, the ScreenPad still has its uses. You'll find a full tutorial on the ScreenPad in Chapter 6, "Special Effects of the Camtasia Recorder."

Other Menu Options

At this point, we have covered the tools available from the Capture and View menus. Obviously, there's more ground to cover. There are entire chapters devoted to the remainder of the menus, but since we're talking about the user interface (of which these elements are a part), I'd be remiss in not mentioning them here as well as telling you where to find out more.

III: Recording

- **Effects.** This is a handy menu for selecting the options of the various toolbars without actually needing to bring those toolbars up. It also includes access to the comprehensive Effects Options dialog. These will all be addressed in Chapter 6, "Special Effects of the Camtasia Recorder."

- **Tools.** From this menu, you can instantly launch any of the other programs in the Camtasia Studio suite of applications, as well as Screencast.com, TechSmith's video hosting service. To get the skinny on all the fantastic preferences in the Tools Options dialog, be sure to check out Chapter 7, "Recorder Tools Options."

For direct access to any tab in either the Effects Options or Tools Options dialogs, just enable the Main toolbar, and click the drop-down arrow next to the Options button.

- **Help.** In addition to accessing Camtasia Studio's detailed help files, you have a number of other options such as instructions for getting support, version/upgrade information, and other tools. The help tool on the Main toolbar will take you directly to the help file.

  For details about the various options on the Help menu as well as other resources you have at your disposal, turn to Appendix D, "Getting Additional Help."

The Statistics and Properties Area

If you haven't yet adjusted any of the Recorder's internal settings, then the Recorder window should minimize automatically when recording begins. However, if you pause the action, the Camtasia Recorder window reappears, and we get the chance to view the Statistics and Properties area of the main Camtasia Recorder user interface:

Statistics:	
Frames:	51
Rate:	14.50 frames/sec
Length:	00:03
Zoom:	652 x 864 (100%)
Audio:	
Properties:	
Size:	652 x 864
Colors:	16777216
Rate:	15 frames/sec
Codec:	TSCC

Resume Stop Delete

With the Recorder's Statistics and Properties info, you can tell a lot about the current recorder settings as well as how the capture is going.

Under Statistics, you have the following pieces of information:

- **Frames.** This is the total number of frames you've recorded at this point. If the Report dropped frames check box on the Capture tab in the Tools Options dialog is checked, then the total number of frames dropped due to system load will also be reported on this line.

- **Rate.** This is the actual number of frames per second at which you are currently recording. If the system cannot handle recording at your specified frame rate (which can sometimes occur if you're recording animations or other kinds of content where the screen image radically changes), you'll see this number begin to drop.

- **Length.** The current running time of your video. It's an easy way to check how long the current clip is getting. Keep in mind that this displays the actual running time of the video, not necessarily how long you've been recording. (It's important to make this distinction for when we discuss time-lapse recording in Chapter 7, "Recorder Tools Options.")

- **Zoom.** This shows the current zoom level (in terms of both pixel dimensions and percent of original video dimensions) at which you are recording. We'll discuss zooming and panning in greater detail in Chapter 6, "Special Effects of the Camtasia Recorder."

- **Audio.** If you opted to record audio narration, you should see a bar that indicates the presence of sound. To check your audio levels, simply speak into your mic. If nothing happens on the bar, then it's a sure sign that your hardware isn't set up correctly, your recording volume is too low, or you have the wrong recording device selected. For tips on troubleshooting your audio, please refer to Chapter 10, "Working with Other Media: Audio, PIP, and Title Clips."

We also have four additional pieces of information in the Properties area:

- **Size.** These are the specified dimensions of your video, regardless of any zoom functions.

- **Colors.** This is the color depth of your video, and usually ranges from 256 to 16,777,216. This value is taken from the color depth of your monitor, not from any setting within the Camtasia Recorder. To change this setting:

  1. Choose **Start > Control Panel**.

2. Double-click the **Display** icon (in Windows Vista, it's **Person-alization > Display Settings**). The Display Properties (Display Settings) dialog opens.

3. If using Windows XP, click the **Settings** tab.

4. Choose a color depth from the Color Quality (or Colors) drop-down list.

5. To save your settings, click **OK**, then **Yes**.

6. If recording from PowerPoint, close and then reopen the application. PowerPoint optimizes its templates based on the current color depth. If you lower the color depth without executing this step, some banding may occur in template backgrounds with color gradients.

I generally choose Medium (16 bit) as my color depth when recording. It tends to save a bit on file size compared with 32 bit (depending on your method of compression), and the visual difference is nearly imperceptible.

- **Rate.** This is your specified frame rate. It is set on the Video tab of your Tools Options dialog (to which I've devoted an entire chapter later in this unit). Remember that this value only mirrors your desired setting; it is not necessarily reflective of the *actual* frame rate (which you can see in the Statistics area).

- **Codec.** This is the compression algorithm used to compress your video into a manageable size. It will almost always be the TechSmith Screen Capture Codec (TSCC). You'll have the opportunity to learn much more about video and audio codecs in later chapters.

The Camtasia Recorder System Tray Icon

There's one final part of the Camtasia Recorder interface you should be aware of. When running Camtasia Recorder, there is a small icon in your system tray that you can use to access much of Recorder's functionality without ever needing to see the main user interface of the Recorder application. When the Camtasia Recorder window is *minimized* (whether automatically at record time or executed manually by you), then the system tray icon is the only part of the Camtasia Recorder you'll actually see. If you decide that you miss the Recorder window, you can always bring it back by double-clicking the system tray icon, regardless of whether the application is currently recording, paused, or stopped.

Whether the Recorder window is visible or not, you can access a whole heap of Recorder functions by right-clicking the system tray icon to display its context menu.

The commands you can execute are as follows:

- **Control the actual recording.** Record/Pause/Resume, Stop, or Delete.

- **Select or toggle any toolbar item.** Choose **Effects**, and then drill down to your desired option. Check marks (for those items that can be toggled) or bullets will display next to any effects options that are already enabled.

- **Options.** Pick a tab, any tab, and it will launch either the Effects Options or Tools Options dialog, with the desired tab already open.

- **Exit.** Quit the Camtasia Recorder without even having to bring up its window.

So there's your whirlwind tour of the Camtasia Recorder user interface. Now that you've familiarized yourself with the basics of recording and gotten to know how the interface works, it's time to discuss some "special case" kinds of recording situations where you'll need to adjust some settings in order for the capture to function correctly.

Special Circumstances

When crafting your videos, there are certain situations that will require you to adjust settings, either within the Camtasia Recorder itself or within the application you're recording, so that you can execute the capture successfully. Examples of this include games (and other applications that utilize DirectX), media player content (such as videos), and Flash animations. Another special circumstance is that of recording PowerPoint presentations. Because there's so much to know about capturing PowerPoint, I have split this particular topic off into its own chapter, which you'll find at the end of this unit.

Recording Games

The capture of computer games is something users have enjoyed doing with Camtasia Studio since its inception, and for a myriad of reasons:

- Game companies use it to create video trailers of their upcoming games.

- Action gamers record their games to document their high score or create tutorials on how to find "Easter eggs" and other secret areas.

- Players of MMORPGs (massively multiplayer online role playing games), such as EverQuest and World of Warcraft, utilize Recorder to make "home movies" of their virtual characters and friends.

Unfortunately, you have a few roadblocks standing in your path. Nothing insurmountable, mind you, but you should at least be cognizant of them:

- Today's games are pretty processor-intensive, as is the recording of video content. To record the latest games, you will require a higher end system, which means a fast processor and a heavy-duty graphics card.

- In Windows XP, keep in mind that Camtasia Studio works best when display acceleration is *disabled* (Vista doesn't allow you to disable it). Well, folks, most current games (at least the really graphic-intensive ones like first-person shooters) require your display acceleration to be *on*. So there's obviously a conflict here. Again, a good video card may help you record at a decent frame rate even when your display acceleration is on.

- The TechSmith Screen Capture Codec (TSCC) excels at encoding most kinds of screen video content. It likes backgrounds that don't change much, and solid blocks of color with no color gradients or photographic content. Doesn't sound like your average game, does it? Remember when I said that TSCC should be used almost all the time? Well, this is one of the exceptions. To record our games, we'll require a different codec, one that plays nicely with cinematic screen content.

These roadblocks aside, don't let the seemingly stiff hardware requirements put you off. While there are obviously limitations as to what you can do with a less-than-top-of-the-line system, there are some tricks you can employ to get the smoothest captures possible from even the most demanding games.

Here's a step-by-step guide to **capturing games with Camtasia Recorder**.

1. If using Windows XP, check to see whether the game in question really does require *display acceleration* to be enabled. I'll discuss display acceleration at length in Chapter 7, but for now, let's just go ahead and turn it off globally, like so:

    a. Choose **Start**, and then select **Control Panel**. Double-click the **Display** icon.

    b. On the Settings tab, click the **Advanced** button.

    c. Click the **Troubleshoot** tab. Under Hardware Accelera-tion, drag the slider all the way to the left from Full to **None**. Click **OK**.

    If your game runs fine without it, so much the better.

2. If the game refuses to run at this point, then it does in fact require dis-play acceleration. Turn it back on (repeat step 1, this time dragging the slider to the right). Also, in the Camtasia Recorder, we need to make sure that Recorder doesn't disable the acceleration for us. Choose **Options...** from the **Tools** menu.

    On the Capture tab, make sure that the **Disable display acceleration during capture** check box is *unchecked*. Oth-erwise, display acceleration will be disabled when you try to record, resulting in either a completely black game screen or a spectacular crash. Either way, the capture won't be suc-cessful. Again, you need WinXP for this option to even be visible.

3. While on the Capture tab, there are a few more settings that will make your life easier. Three of them, actually. While these aren't "have-to" settings, I find them helpful.

    ■ **Pause before starting capture.** This setting is handy for making sure that the recording doesn't actually start until you're ready for it to start.

- **Report dropped frames.** When checked, data will show up in your Statistics and Properties area during recording that displays the number of frames dropped. It's useful for determining whether your system can handle the load you're giving it.

```
Statistics:
Frames:    114 (16 dropped)  ◄━━━
Rate:      11.00 frames/sec
Length:    00:07
Zoom:      652 x 864 (100%)
Audio:     ▇▇▇▇▇▇
           ────────────◖

Properties:
Size:      652 x 864
Colors:    16777216
Rate:      15 frames/sec
Codec:     TSCC
```

Not sure if your system is capturing the game adequately at your current settings? Check to see if you're dropping any frames.

[● Resume] [▢ Stop] [✗ Delete]

- **Round frame size to a 4 pixel boundary.** Certain codecs can only tolerate capture dimensions where the x and y coordinates are in multiples of four. The TechSmith Screen Capture Codec does not have this limitation, but since you'll be working with other codecs when recording games, it's best to keep this setting checked.

4. Now we need to set a *frame rate*, the number of frames per second captured by Camtasia Recorder. This is usually set to **Automatic**, meaning that Camtasia Studio will capture as many frames per second as the processor will allow. When recording a game, however, you're going to want a little breathing room so that the game itself doesn't lag.

   Let's go back into our Tools Options Video tab. Then go ahead and click the **Manual** button, and enter a frame rate into the Screen capture frame rate field. Usually 10 to 15 frames per second will do the trick, although you may need to experiment to find that happy medium between smooth game play and a smooth capture.

5. As long as we're here on the Video tab, let's go ahead and change our codec to one that's better equipped to handle game content. Codecs may be a completely foreign concept to you now, but not for long. They'll be covered in full in Chapters 7 and 12. Don't worry for now; just follow these handy instructions and you'll be fine.

Click the **Video Compression...** button. In the dialog that appears, click the **Compressor** drop-down menu to choose a new codec. I'd recommend some flavor of MPEG-4 codec, such as DivX, Xvid, or 3ivx. Xvid is open-source and therefore free; the others may cost a bit of money depending on the exact iteration of the codec you choose. Keep in mind that if kept in this format, your audience will also need to have the same codec installed on their machines, so you might want to think about converting it to a more distribution-friendly format later. We'll talk about this in Chapter 12, "The Production Process."

6. By clicking the **Configure...** button, you can specify a bit rate, and can sometimes choose between better compression and faster compression. If the capture makes the game lag, you can try reducing the bit rate and/or opting for faster compression. Different codecs have different configuration settings; feel free to experiment to see what works best for you.

7. If you also want to include the game's audio, you'll need to set up the operating system to record your system sound. Just click the **Audio** button on the main Recorder interface to open the Audio Setup Wizard, and then choose **Speaker Audio (what you hear)**, if available. Full instructions on how to do this can be found in Chapter 10, "Working with Other Media: Audio, PIP, and Title Clips." Do keep in mind that when you start recording an additional stream, you place extra load on an already taxed processor. Don't record the audio unless you think it's really necessary.

8. In an effort to keep the system from choking during capture, it's important to give Camtasia Recorder as small a recording area as possible. Smaller dimensions mean less load on the processor. Most games support different screen resolutions to accommodate both high- and low-end systems. A game may look positively glorious in 1024 x 768, but it will certainly capture better at 800 x 600, since it takes fewer resources to record this smaller area. Now, most games offer a Video Options screen, where you can set the resolution directly within the game. If that's not the case with your game, then we'll need to **reset our screen resolution:**

Just go to **Start > Control Panel**. If using Windows XP, double-click the **Display** icon*, and then choose the **Settings** tab. If using Windows Vista, go to **Personalization > Display Settings**. Then drag the Screen resolution slider down to **800 x 600**, as shown here:

If you try to capture your game and the recording is still quite choppy, you can try taking the resolution down even further to 640 x 480. Note that Windows doesn't particularly like this resolution, and takes extra steps to hide it from you. Here's how to flush it out:

From the the Display Properties dialog where you changed the resolution the first time (it's called Display Settings in Vista), click the **Advanced** (**Advanced Settings**) button. On the Adapter tab, click the **List All Modes...** button. Choose one of the 640 x 480 modes, and click **OK**.

If you're capturing a game that supports being opened in a window, then reducing the screen resolution may not be necessary. But it's important to know, just in case.

9. Making sure that Camtasia Recorder is still running, launch your game. At the game's title menu, try pressing **Alt-Enter** to see if the game supports running in a window. If it does, you can try resizing the window down even further to get a better capture. If not, you can still capture the screen, but you have a bit less control over the video dimensions and the portion of the screen you want to capture, as you're pretty much stuck with a full-screen recording.

10. Press the **Record** hotkey (F9 by default). If the game supports running in a window, go ahead and select the game's window or a region thereof. Otherwise, choose the full screen. Keep in mind that the act of selecting the capture area and starting the capture may minimize the game — press Alt-Tab to get back to it. Play the game as you normally would. Stop the recording whenever you wish by pressing the **Stop** hotkey (F10 by default). Preview and save the file as you would any other.

* If you have Windows XP and do not see the Display icon, then the Control Panel is probably in Category View. Click Appearance and Themes, and then choose Change the screen resolution.

Recording Media Player Content

People utilize Camtasia Studio for all kinds of reasons. One unconventional (and perhaps unintended) use for Camtasia Studio has been the conversion of media player content from a proprietary format into an industry-standard AVI (as well as several other file formats). Many people attempt to record videos directly from a media player window, but not all succeed. Why? That darned display acceleration is getting in the way again. Depending on the media player, its version, and the content, it doesn't always interfere; but when it does, it must be disabled or you'll end up recording nothing but a black screen. You can turn off the display acceleration globally, as demonstrated in the previous section on game capture. However, there's usually a way to turn off display acceleration within the individual media player instead of having to do so globally. You can keep display acceleration active for general purposes (playing games, using CAD programs, etc.), but shut it down for a particular media player. I'll show you how to do this for the "big three" players: Windows Media Player, QuickTime, and RealPlayer.

To disable display acceleration in **Windows Media Player**, do the following:

1. From the **Tools** menu in Windows Media Player, choose **Options...**, and then click on the **Performance** tab. If you have Windows Media Player version 6.4 or earlier, choose instead **View > Options > Playback**.

2. In the section labeled Video Acceleration (which, depending on the version, can also be called Hardware Acceleration), drag the slider all the way from Full to **None**.

3. Click **OK**, and then restart your video, recording the window per usual.

To disable display acceleration in **QuickTime**, do the following:

1. From the **Edit** menu, choose **Preferences**, and then **QuickTime Preferences** (may also be called Streaming Transport in earlier versions).

2. In the dialog that appears, click the **Advanced** tab. For earlier (tabless) versions of QuickTime, choose **Video Settings** from the drop-down list.

3. Click the **Safe mode (GDI only)** radio button. Click **OK** to save your settings, then click the X in the upper right-hand corner to exit the dialog.

 It is unnecessary to disable display acceleration in QuickTime for recording video content from the QuickTime plug-ins for Internet Explorer and Firefox. If your QuickTime movie plays inside your browser, it can be captured, even if display acceleration is enabled.

To disable display acceleration in **RealPlayer**, do the following:

1. From the **Tools** menu, choose **Preferences...**
2. Click the **Hardware** category.
3. In the section marked Video Card Compatibility, move the slider all the way to the left, from Best Performance to **Most Reliable**. Click **OK**.

The actual process of capturing media player windows is fairly similar to that of capturing games. Therefore, please at least skim the previous section. Pay particular attention to the proper selection of a codec, as the same codecs work for both games and real-world video. The default TechSmith Screen Capture Codec doesn't work well for either. One exception: Unlike game content, media player windows are small and don't commandeer the entire screen, so there's no need to adjust your screen resolution. You may freely skip that step.

 Prior to starting a cavalcade of captures from the various media players, do keep one thing in mind. If you find a particular video in only one proprietary format, there may be a good reason for this. Doing things like format conversions and editing the intellectual property of others is of questionable ethics and legality, and may carry penalties ranging from bad karma all the way up to fines and jail time. Do your best to respect the rights of the copyright holders.

Recording Flash Animations

Adobe Flash, for those who aren't familiar with it, is a wonderful tool for creating animated content. The small size of its SWF and FLV files, coupled with the fact that every major web browser can play them, make it ideal for distribution on the web. The SWF file format has in fact become so ubiquitous that Adobe Flash is far from the only software program that can create SWF files. Many applications now offer export to SWF, including Camtasia Studio.

But the Flash authoring tool can do things that Camtasia Studio cannot, such as animated cartoons, dynamic title screens, and other whiz-bang motion effects. For this reason, I see Macromedia Flash as being complementary to Camtasia Studio. I occasionally turn to the Flash authoring environment whenever I want to add a little sizzle to my video with dancing text, diagrams that fly around the screen, and other really cool special effects.

While a tutorial on using this handy application goes far beyond the scope of this book, if you happen to be familiar with Flash, and you happen to create something in Flash you want as part of your Camtasia Studio video, and you happen to wonder how this can be accomplished, never fear. I can get you the rest of the way there. Here's what you need to do:

■ First, unlike the previous two cases (games and media players), display acceleration may be fully *disabled*, and it won't impact your ability to successfully record a Flash movie.

■ You also don't need to actually produce your project to a SWF file in order to record the content with Camtasia Recorder. Recording your video from inside the authoring environment will work just fine. In fact, utilizing the authoring environment is actually preferable in this case because you can adjust the movie's frame rate (more on this in a moment).

■ Unfortunately, the Recorder's Window capture doesn't automatically detect the edges of the Stage. You need to select Region, and when it comes time to record, draw your region around the edges of the Stage, like so:

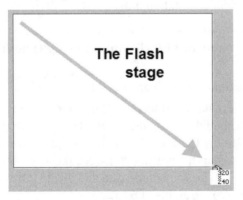

Be sure to make good use of the pixel dimension indicator shown here. You can obviously resize and reposition the capture area frame if the placement isn't quite right.

Making judicious use of Last area capture comes in very handy here — barring some boneheaded maneuver on your part like resizing your project window or scrolling the Stage, you should only have to set the capture area once.

■ Go ahead and start the recording process. Making sure that your playback head is at the beginning of the desired sequence in Flash, press **Enter** to play back your content. Once finished, stop the recording and save it as you normally would. Poof, done.

Or are you? Recording animated content is still pretty processor-intensive, and even if the Recorder doesn't report any dropped frames, you may notice in the video's preview that your content came out rather choppy. And there's nothing worse than a jerky animation. I've seen this phenomenon even with high-end systems. Fortunately, I invented a workaround that takes care of this little problem, and it involves the use of Camtasia Recorder's **Time-lapse** feature.

It works like this: In order to make sure that the Camtasia Recorder captures every single frame of your desired content, we're going to slow down the playback so that the Recorder has a better opportunity to do its thing. (I usually make it 1/3 speed.) Then, using time-lapse recording, I'll record the slowed-down content at a certain number of frames per second (I usually go with 15 fps, but whatever you're comfortable with is fine), and then set the playback speed to 3x that frame rate (45 fps in my case). So, you're recording an excruciatingly slow movie, but when recorded and played back, your video will play the content at normal speed, and completely jerk-free. Clear as mud? Perhaps going step-by-step will alleviate any remaining confusion. Note that these instructions presume the use of Macromedia Flash MX 2004 (basic or professional), Flash 8, or Flash CS3. You may need to check your documentation if using other versions.

So, here's how you **record Flash content using time-lapse recording**:

1. Launch Macromedia Flash and open the desired .fla file.

2. Click anywhere on the Stage, and then look in the Properties palette. You should see an editable field labeled Frame rate. I usually create my Flash movies at 15 frames per second (I believe the default fps is 12; fortunately, these are both divisible by three). Take your frame rate and divide it by three. This would give me an fps of **5**.

3. Open Camtasia Recorder if you haven't already done so. Bring up your Tools Options Video tab. At the bottom of this tab is the **Time-lapse capture** check box. Check it. Now click the **Time-Lapse Setup...** button.

4. A dialog appears that allows you to set the capture frame rate as well as the rate at which the video is played back. In the AVI capture rate section, enter **15** frames per second (or whatever frame rate you generally use). In the AVI Playback Rate section, enter a frame rate equal to three times that of your capture rate. For me, this would be **45** frames per second. This produces a dialog that looks like the following:

5. Click **OK** twice. Now we're ready to record. Start the Recorder if needed, and then select your Stage for recording as previously instructed. Pause the recording if necessary.

6. If you have enough screen real estate, try to position the Recorder window so that it appears next to the Stage, outside the recording area. It's useful for keeping an eye out for any dropped frames as well as monitoring the developing length of your video in the Length field of your Statistics and Properties area. Remember, this is the length of the final video, which will be three times faster than the rate at which you're currently recording. As such, one second will tick by in the Length field for every three seconds you've spent recording.

7. Begin recording. Making sure that your Flash Stage is the active window, press **Enter** to start the playback head in motion. Stop the recording and save when finished.

When you play back your video, you'll notice that the animated effects now flow like water. This is a great technique because it's easy to do and it doesn't add appreciably to the file size. In fact, when adding this clip to your overall presentation, it won't hurt the smoothness of your animation to produce the entire video back at 15 fps (or whatever setting you typically use). However, there are a couple of caveats you need to be aware of:

■ When recording in Time-lapse mode, both the audio and camera video streams are disabled, so if you need to add either of these elements, you will need to do so after the recording process, while editing in Camtasia Studio. If you're working from a script, you'll want to play back your Flash file several times to make sure the timing is right (using your original frame rate, of course). Make any needed adjustments *before* doing your recording.

■ There's no visual indicator on the main interface that Time-lapse capture is on. If you use Time-lapse mode fairly often, always double-check to make sure it's only enabled when it needs to be. So, before moving on to other kinds of content, make sure you go back into the Video tab and shut it off, or your next recording is guaranteed to be ruined.

Recorder Workflow Tips

Now that you have familiarized yourself with the basic functions of the Camtasia Recorder as well as experimented with customizing the program's interface, it's time to give you some additional tips to make your recordings flow as smoothly as possible. Following these basic guidelines will save you many hours of retakes, thus sparing your sanity and reducing your total production time. And who could say no to that?

Work from a Script

I've said it before, but it bears repeating: If you're not recording using a roadmap such as a storyboard or narration script, then your video is likely to be a meandering, disorganized mess. If you really care about delivering the content in a professional way, follow a script. After all, you can't arrive at your desired destination when you don't know where you're going half the time.

The same goes for audio narration. Even if you know your content backward and forward, something *happens* when that little Recorder icon starts a-blinkin'. You stammer, groping for the right words (yet seldom actually finding them), and the final result just isn't good enough for prime time. I know you have a deadline to meet, but trust me when I tell you that an hour of preparation will save you three on the production end.

Take the Time to Set Up Your Shot

Just as a videographer scouts a location to determine its fitness for filming, so should you plan ahead to get the best possible footage. Preferably, all your shot information should already be detailed in your storyboard, so that when we get to the recording phase, all you have to do is follow along.

Open your needed application windows for the clip and get them set up, making sure that all essential elements actually fall within the recording area. Don't be afraid to make bold choices in terms of laying out your application windows. Overlap them or place them side-by-side. Try to make as much use of the space provided by your recording area as possible.

If you're only recording a single application, you might want to resize it so that it fills up as much of the recording area as possible. Fortunately, the Lock to application feature is there to ensure a consistently perfect fit.

Also, make sure that your captures are *clean*. By this, I mean setting your preferences and visuals to mimic what users are likely to see on their own systems. Take care to leave out any unnecessary actions, windows, or other distractions that will detract from your message. If part of the desktop will be visible in your recording, use a solid-color background (I use white) and get rid of any superfluous icons. Also, while the Camtasia Recorder's special effects are great in certain situations, they too can become a distraction if overdone, so try to make your special effects implementation meaningful (in other words, thematically related to the actual content) rather than using them just because you can.

Don't Mess with Your Windows

Provided your application has been programmed to adhere to standard Windows conventions, its window has the convenient ability to reappear in the exact same place you left it, at the exact same size, even if it's been months since you last opened it. Likewise, Camtasia Recorder has the ability, utilizing its Last area capture feature, to record a given capture area over and over. Same size, same location. This can afford you a great level of consistency when recording multiple clips and then combining them into a single video project. Using Last area capture, you can splice together 10 different clips recorded on 10 different days, and it'll still look like you managed to do everything perfectly in a single take.

So don't go screwing it up by moving or resizing your windows! If you record a new clip where the window size or placement is off, even by a few pixels, you'll notice a rather disconcerting shift when splicing your clips together. It looks amateurish and crude. Should you ever happen to find yourself victim of this phenomenon, you've only got a few options:

- ■ Live with it.

- ■ Meticulously move and/or resize your windows to match the old settings as best you can. Then record a test clip, import it into Camtasia Studio next to one of your other clips, and observe the transition from one clip to the next to see what, if anything, needs adjusting. Repeat as necessary (and since this is a precision art, it's likely you'll need to repeat *often* to get it perfect).

- ■ Cover up the discrepancy during editing by placing a transition or title screen between the clips, which sometimes works, but is often just as conspicuous as leaving it be.

As the old saying goes, nothing is as expensive as regret. All of the above options either compromise the video's quality or waste your valuable time. Better to avoid this situation altogether.

Timing Is Everything

If you're like the vast majority of us who write a script before recording your video, yet record the actual narration after your video capture is complete, you want to make sure that you give each action appropriate breathing room. An *action* is defined as one step in whatever multi-step process you're attempting to document in your video. Since you're going to be narrating the action as it unfolds, it's important to keep one eye on the script so that the timing of your piece remains consistent. If you proceed too quickly from action to action, you won't have enough time to squeeze in the commentary without sounding like the announcer from the old MicroMachines commercials.

It's far better to err on the side of too much lag time between actions, as you can always easily trim out part of that pause during editing if you find it too lengthy. While it *is* possible to extend a frame at production time to accommodate longer narration, it's a hassle to have to fix something in post that you should have gotten right at record time. Also, frame extensions tend to clutter your editing work, taking what should have been one clip and turning it into three. So take your time, keep your script in plain view, and the pacing of your video will drastically improve as a result.

If there is a complicated set of actions that need to be explained in great detail, consider using time-lapse capture to slow things down. Likewise, if you want to gloss over a long set of features in your program, you can also utilize time-lapse to speed through it, showing off everything in just a few seconds. You can read more about how to perform a time-lapse capture in Chapter 7, "Recorder Tools Options."

Avoid the Scroll Wheel

Very often, you don't even think about it because that little wheel has become so ingrained in our collective work processes. But bear in mind that your audience can't see your mouse or what you're doing with it. All they see is the content inexplicably shifting around on your screen. Try to be cognizant of this while recording. Use the scroll bar instead of the wheel in order to give the good folks at home a visual cue as to what's happening. Of course, if the audience can't see the scroll bar, then they *still* won't have a visual cue, so remember to actually include the window's scroll bar as part of your recording area.

Pause when Needed

When recording a clip that features multiple processes, all of which have multiple steps, it's insanely easy to get lost or mixed up, and suddenly you have no idea what's coming next. Be sure to make liberal use of that F9 key. It's such a simple thing, I know, but it's easy to forget it's there amid the chaos of recording. Pausing the action will allow you to quickly consult your script or storyboard to see the next action or procedure you wanted to cover. Once you've gotten your bearings, simply hit the hotkey again to keep going.

Finally, you may want to pause often if you're ever creating a tutorial of an application with a lot of text fields to fill in. Nobody wants to sit and watch you painstakingly type each letter. It's usually better to pause, type in the field, and resume. To the user, it will look like the fields are just filling in automatically, which isn't entirely "natural," but I find it preferable for the sake of saving time. Some people accomplish the same thing by pasting their text, but I prefer the former solution simply because it's more relaxed — just pause, and fill in fields at your leisure.

Split Things Up

If you have the task of creating a two- to three-minute tutorial video, you might be tempted to do it all in a single take in order to keep things simple. Try to resist this temptation, because the final result is usually anything but simple. For one thing, by splitting things up into more palatable chunks, you'll more easily be able to work through the content. Nothing is more frustrating than meticulously creating a five-minute clip, only to screw it up right at the finish line. For another, recording multiple clips means more opportunities to set up interesting shots. After all, there's a reason why film directors shoot their movies from multiple angles. It gives you choices. Having your screen set up in a particular way may work wonderfully for one topic, but could actually obscure your point when moving on to the next.

Summary

The Camtasia Recorder is used to record the basic footage used in your videos. After recording, your video clips can be imported into Camtasia Studio for editing and further processing.

Here's the basic procedure for **recording a video clip** with the Camtasia Recorder:

1. Open the application(s) you wish to capture, and arrange these windows on your screen.

2. Open the Camtasia Recorder. Choose whether you want to include camera video and/or audio, selecting these elements from the Capture menu.

3. Select your capture area by clicking either **Select area to record** (for a new region or window) or **Last area** (to replicate the most recent capture area).

4. Click the **Record** button (or press the corresponding hotkey, **F9** by default). Execute the actions you want to capture. You may pause at any point by pressing F9 again.

5. When finished, click the **Stop** button (or press the corresponding hotkey, **F10** by default).

6. View the recording in the Camtasia Recorder Preview. Click **Delete** to trash the capture and start over, or choose **Save** if you're satisfied and wish to continue.

7. If you chose Save, you're prompted to provide a file name and location. Navigate to a folder, type a file name, and press **Enter.**

8. After saving, you're presented with the options of editing your recording within Camtasia Studio, producing your recording right away into a shareable file format, or returning to the Recorder to make another recording. Make your choice and click **OK.**

III: Recording

Other Tips

■ Pressing the **Marker** hotkey (**Ctrl+Shift-M** by default) during recording will add a marker to your project that can be used to facilitate editing, put together a table of contents, or more easily split up a lengthy recording.

■ The Camtasia Recorder's user interface is fully adjustable. In addition to having two different views, you have several supplementary toolbars that can be enabled/moved/disabled at will.

- Recording certain applications, such as games, media player content, and Macromedia Flash, requires that specific steps be taken in order to achieve a quality capture.

Now that we understand the basics of recording, we'll spend the rest of this unit covering other Recorder-related topics such as implementing special effects, adjusting your preferences, and making use of the Camtasia Studio Add-in for PowerPoint. Stay tuned.

Exercises

1. When setting up your recording, try experimenting with the different capture area selection methods. Which method would you choose if you were recording...

    a. a tutorial about the various toolbars in Microsoft Word?

    b. a usability session where *all* the users' actions on the computer needed to be captured?

    c. a series of videos about a web application?

    d. a Palm OS utility?

2. What commands must be executed in order to include audio and PIP streams with your screen video? Try making a sample video with these streams enabled, and then check out your Preview window. Did everything show up as expected?

3. Toggle the view of your Camtasia Recorder application a few times. Which view do you like best? To save on screen real estate, remember to turn off any toolbars you don't think you'll regularly use.

4. Take a look at the Statistics and Properties area of the Recorder window while recording (if the window's not visible, try double-clicking its blinking task bar icon). When might the knowledge of the frame rate come in handy? What about the length?

5. After recording a 60-second sample video, try analyzing it according to the Recorder workflow tips laid out in this chapter. How did your video come out? Did you run into any unexpected problems? Take a look at the sample video located in the Chapter 5 media folder on the companion CD. What problems can you identify?

Chapter 6

Special Effects of the Camtasia Recorder

Now that you've mastered the basics of recording screen video footage, we can learn how to make even greater use of the Camtasia Recorder by adding some record-time special effects to the mix. Used sparingly, these effects can do much to add some needed pizzazz and professionalism to your video.

In addition to merely looking or sounding cool, several of these effects are helpful in conveying additional useful information. For example, when using the Recorder to do systems monitoring, annotations like the computer name or a date/time stamp can help you to accurately label your videos as well as isolate any problems that occur. Visual and audio mouse click effects can let the audience know exactly when and where you clicked on a particular object.

While a number of these special effects have been largely supplanted by the effects in Camtasia Studio, at least for larger projects, I still find the Recorder effects useful for mockups, smaller videos, and informal work where I'm not necessarily going to be editing and producing a final cut within Camtasia Studio. As we go through this chapter, I will alert you to instances where the effects possibilities are identical or similar between the Camtasia Recorder and Camtasia Studio. In almost every case, you'll want to perform those effects in Camtasia Studio instead, due mainly to the fact that Camtasia Studio effects are infinitely *editable*. They can be altered or removed at will, as opposed to the effects in the Camtasia Recorder, which are essentially "baked into" your base video footage. With Recorder-based effects, if you want to make any changes later, you're basically stuck with rerecording the entire clip. There are exceptions to this rule, of course, and I'll try to point these out as well.

In the previous chapter, we explored the View menu in Camtasia Recorder. Opening this menu reveals six toolbars: Main, Annotation, Audio, Cursor, Zoom & Pan, and Camera. The Audio and Camera toolbars were discussed in the previous chapter, as they pertain more to the inclusion of additional content streams in the video than to special effects.

Any of these toolbars can be toggled on and off by either of the following methods:

- From the **Effects** menu, click the name of the toolbar you want to toggle. A check mark next to the toolbar name indicates that it is currently visible on the toolbar palette.

  or

- From the **Toggle View** drop-down arrow on the Main toolbar, choose the name of the toolbar you wish to toggle.

To turn on one of your special effects, simply click its corresponding button. The buttons of all currently enabled effects will have a "pressed-in" effect:

In this Annotation toolbar, the System Stamp, Watermark, and Autohighlight effects are enabled.

Note that you needn't necessarily have a particular toolbar up and visible in order to make use of its options. There are a few ways of enabling or disabling the options without clicking the corresponding buttons on the various toolbars.

You can toggle the settings of the different toolbar options as follows:

- From the **Effects** menu, mouse over the appropriate submenu, and then click on the effect you wish to enable/disable. A check mark will appear next to those enabled items that can be toggled off. A bullet will appear next to selected items that cannot be toggled (one item in the list must always be enabled).

or

- Right-click on the Camtasia Recorder system tray icon, and from the **Effects** submenu, mouse over the submenu of the desired toolbar, and then select the effect you wish to enable/disable.

or

- A couple of the more often-used commands (e.g., turning on audio recording) can be accessed directly from the main Camtasia Recorder interface.

The Annotation Toolbar

The **Annotation** toolbar provides a means of adding text annotations, frames, and drawings to your recordings. It gives you several different ways of meaningfully "marking up" your video content to make it more accessible to your audience.

System Stamps

The Annotation toolbar consists of six tools, the first of which is called **Add System Stamp**. This setting stamps one or more pieces of information onto your video. These are not visible at record time; they can be seen only when the video is played back. The details of what actually gets displayed are buried inside the Effects Options dialog.

Here are a few common ways of **opening your Effects Options dialog**:

- From the **Effects** menu, choose **Options….**

  or

- Click the **Options** drop-down arrow in the Main toolbar. This option has the added benefit of allowing you to choose the exact tab you want.

  or

- Right-click the Camtasia Recorder system tray icon. From here you can either choose **Effects > Options…**, or choose **Options** and then click on the exact tab you want to bring up.

In this particular case, we want the **Annotation** tab of the Effects Options dialog.

| Annotation | Sound | Cursor | Watermark | Zoom |

System stamp

☑ Time/Date   [Time/Date Format…]

☐ Elapsed time

☐ Computer name   [Arrange Stamp…]

☐ User name

☐ Show Stamp for   [3]   seconds   [Options…]

Preview:

11:38:01 AM 9/17/2007

Caption

[▼]   [Options…]

☐ Prompt before capture

Highlight

Width: [8]   pixels   ■   [Color…]

ScreenDraw

☑ Disable keyboard and cursor effects during ScreenDraw

As you can see, we have four different system stamps from which to choose:

- **Time/Date.** The current time and/or date. Useful for systems monitoring and usability testing, when you need to know exactly when something occurred.

- **Elapsed time.** Shows how much time has passed since the capture began. Any time in which the Recorder was paused does not count. How long does it take to perform a specific action? Now you can document it, and compare it to how long it takes the competitor's product to do the same thing.

- **Computer name.** The name given to the computer as specified in the Windows System Properties. Good for monitoring systems and other kinds of testing where you're likely to be working with a large number of computers.

- **User name.** Shows exactly who is logged onto the machine at the time of recording.

For the Time/Date stamp, you have the ability to adjust the formatting for the stamp. Just click the **Time/Date Format...** button. The following dialog appears:

Use the options in this dialog to format your Time/Date stamps.

In the Display section, you have the option of choosing whether you want to display just the time, just the date, or both. If you opt for both, you can also stipulate the order. Time and Date also have their own sections from which to choose a particular format for their display. You can pick a format from the scrolling list, or choose **Custom Format** and create your own. Here's a quick guide to the time and date formatting codes:

Code	Definition	Example
Time Codes		
h	Hour — single digit	6:35:49 PM
hh	Hour — double digit	06:35:49 PM
H	Hour — single digit (military time)	9:03:14
HH	Hour — double digit (military time)	18:35:49
m	Minute — single digit (seldom used)	6:9:49 PM
mm	Minute — double digit	6:09:49 PM
s	Second — single digit (seldom used)	6:09:7 PM
t	AM or PM (single character)	6:35:49 P
tt	AM or PM (two characters)	6:35:49 PM
Date Codes		
M	Month — single digit	3/05/2007
MM	Month — double digit	03/05/2007
MMM	Month — three characters	Mar-05-2007
MMMM	Month — full name	March 5, 2007
d	Day — single digit	3/5/2007
dd	Day — double digit	3/05/2007
ddd	Day of the week — three characters	Jun-10-07 (Sun)
dddd	Day of the week — full name	Sunday, June 10, 2007
y	Year — single digit (seldom used)	3/5/7
yy	Year — double digit	3/5/07
yyyy	Year — four digits	3/5/2007

As long as you don't inadvertently enter any of these codes, you can add all sorts of text (e.g., Date:) and symbols (slashes, commas, colons, hyphens, etc.) to punctuate your formatting. You can check your work by keeping an eye on the live preview at the bottom of the dialog. Click **OK** when you're happy with the formatting.

If you've selected more than one system stamp to appear on the screen at once, note that you can easily change how the items are ordered. Just click the **Arrange Stamp...** button in the Annotation tab. Then select the desired system stamp, and click the **Up** or **Down** buttons to move this item upward or downward in the list order. The stamp will take the top to bottom order of these items and arrange them on screen from left to right. Click **OK** to continue.

Beneath all the system stamps, you have one more check box labeled "Show Stamp for ___ seconds." Rather than risk annoying the user by showing an obtrusive system stamp for the whole duration of the video, you can check this box and enter a value into the seconds field, which will get rid of your stamp(s) after the specified number of seconds have elapsed from the beginning of recording.

But you may be wondering, "Can I control what the stamp looks like? Font, size, color, all that jazz?" Actually, you can. Clicking on the **Options...** button in the System stamp section will bring up the following dialog:

Change the options in this dialog to make your system stamps all pretty.

The System Stamp Options dialog offers numerous options for changing the look of your text:

- **Style.** You can choose Normal text (no shadow), Drop shadow (a small shadow appears beneath the text), or Outlined shadow (shadow appears all around your text, providing a 3D effect).

- **Transparent background.** By default, the Recorder places a colored background behind your text to ease legibility (particularly for graphically detailed videos). Rendering the background transparent, however, gives the text more of a cinematic quality. In addition, selecting a transparent background allows lengthy text to wrap, which is useful if you've selected multiple system stamps.

- **Position.** While Recorder doesn't give you pixel-perfect control over a system stamp's position, it does allow you to set it in one of nine sections of your video window. Just click the button of the desired screen section.

- **Font...** Allows you to choose a font, style, and size for your system stamp text.
- **Text Color...** Alters the color of your text.
- **Background Color...** Provided you don't have Transparent background enabled, this will change the text's solid background color.
- **Shadow Color...** If you've chosen Drop shadow or Outlined shadow as your style, this is the color of your shadow.
- **Outline Color...** If you've selected Outlined shadow as your style, this will change the color of the outline.

You have a live preview of your options in the lower right-hand corner of the dialog. When satisfied with your choices, click **OK**.

As you can see, enabling Add System Stamp on the Annotation toolbar is just the beginning. It's in the Effects Options dialog that things really get interesting. When you're finished tweaking your settings, it behooves you to do a test recording so that you can see what the system stamp(s) will look like in the final capture before you actually do it. After all, there's nothing more frustrating than spending 20 minutes recording a clip, only to discover that the system stamp looks terrible at its current settings.

Captions

The next tool in your Annotation toolbar is **Add Caption**. Captions function very similarly to system stamps, except that a caption can be anything you want. Let's head back into the Annotation tab of your Effects Options dialog to see how this effect can be set.

In the Caption box, simply type in what you want the caption to say. When you enable captions by clicking the Add Caption button on your toolbar, this caption is emblazoned on your recording (during playback, not during recording):

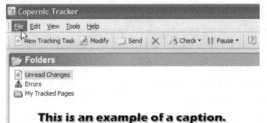

Captions can be anything your heart desires, from copyright information to special instructions to "Bob rulez!"

This is an example of a caption.

The Caption field also comes with a drop-down list from which you can select the most recently used captions, so if you have just a few that you use often, you're not constantly having to retype them. Of course, you can also adjust the formatting of your caption, using the same kind of dialog as with your system stamps. Just click the **Options...** button inside the Caption section of the Annotation tab and adjust any settings as necessary.

There's one additional option here that you might find handy. Clicking the **Prompt before capture** box will present you with a dialog when starting recording that lets you type in a new caption each and every time, using the currently entered caption as the default:

Enter Caption

Whatever you do, don't click this button!
Whatever you do, don't click this button!
Spinach and lima beans are good for you.
Buy Camtasia Studio 5: The Definitive Guide.
This is an example of a caption.

Options...

As you can see, this dialog has the same drop-down list for selecting recently used captions as well as an Options... button for adjusting the caption's formatting.

 Unlike system stamps, a feature that is not replicated at all on the editing side, captions have been more or less supplanted by callouts in Camtasia Studio. I would use captions only if you want a particular message "welded" to the content, as captions are very difficult to remove later. I personally prefer to always have the option of editing or striking content at a later time, and the Callouts feature in Camtasia Studio supports this as well as offers a fuller array of capabilities in general (for more information about callouts, please see Chapter 11, "Editing Effects"). But if the difficulty in removing a caption is tolerable or even desirable for you (e.g., security reasons), then by all means, use captions. They, along with system stamps, are a quick and easy way of labeling individual video clips.

Watermarks

The next button on the Annotation toolbar is the **Add Watermark** tool. If you've ever seen network television, then you've probably seen a great many watermarks already (in fact, most cable channels use them now, too). The CBS eye and NBC peacock are examples of watermarks*. They sit in the lower right-hand corner of the screen, branding the content, and you therefore have the constant reminder that the show you're currently enjoying is broadcast into your home courtesy of them.

---

* In the television "biz," a watermark is called a "bug." The software industry, however, avoids this term for obvious reasons.

Now you can brand your videos in very much the same way. This is usually a corporate logo of some sort, but it can be just about any image you want. To give you a sense of the possibilities, Camtasia Studio comes with a sample watermark image to play with:

Now imagine your logo in place of the Camtasia Studio "C"...

While the watermark can be turned on and off through the Annotation toolbar, the real action once again is happening in the Effects Options dialog, this time on the Watermark tab:

Obviously, the first thing we need to do is specify what file you want to use. If you're looking at this dialog for the first time, you're likely to see a path to the Camtasia Studio logo. You can change this by typing in a new path or by clicking the **Browse** button (with the folder icon) in order to navigate to your watermark. This can be any image file you like, as long as it's in an accepted file format (BMP, GIF, JPG, or PNG). While any of these formats will work, I would strongly recommend using a 32-bit PNG image, as the watermark feature allows per-pixel transparency information in this format. Unlike other image formats that only offer whole-image transparency (if any at all), 32-bit PNG images have a special alpha channel that can assign a different transparency level to each and every pixel in the image. Confused yet? Basically, this means that whatever's behind it, the watermark's edges will never look jagged or have a weird color outline. This is particularly nice if your video has a lot of visual detail. You can create 32-bit PNG images in recent versions of higher-end imaging applications like Adobe Photoshop.

At the top of the tab, you have a check box called **Include watermark in video**. This merely enables or disables the watermark in your recordings; it's the same as clicking Add Watermark on your Annotation toolbar. There's also a small preview window that will let you see more or less what your watermark will look like. It comes up whenever you enter the dialog. If you closed it inadvertently, you may reopen it by clicking the **Preview...** button.

Now, let's move on to some of the watermark effects. When you select an image to use as your watermark, you can alter its appearance, size, and location inside your video window. Let's first look at the Effects section. For starters, you have the ability to display your image with an Emboss effect. Embossing the watermark makes it look like you made a stamp out of the image and then stamped it in foil. This can be combined with the built-in Depth (how strong you want the emboss to be) and Opacity (the watermark's level of transparency) slider controls to produce a subtle, ghostlike effect. From the Direction drop-down list, you can choose one of eight directions for the light source. Depending on the levels of depth and opacity, the differences between these directions can be subtle or striking. View them all and then settle on the one you like best.

Of course, if you uncheck Emboss, the image actually looks a lot more like the image you remember. While the Depth control is strictly in the domain of embossed watermarks, you can still control the Opacity. If your image has a background you wish to be rid of (so that it appears to "float" on the screen rather than being confined to a box), click the **Use transparent color** check box, and then click **Color...** to select the color used for the transparency. For example, you'll pick white if the background of your watermark is white (which it probably is). Poof! The background disappears.

The next section controls the scaling of the image, where we can alter its size relative to our capture area. Clicking the **Preserve image size** check box will maintain the size of the watermark image at 100% of its original dimensions no matter what, and consequently, all other scaling options will be disabled. If unchecked, you can use the **Image scale** slider to increase or decrease the size of the watermark. Note that the percentages listed here indicate the percentage of total available space within the recording area, not the percentage of original image size. Setting the slider to 100% means that the watermark will consume 100% of the recording area on either the horizontal or vertical axis. Unchecking **Keep aspect ratio** will stretch the image to conform with both axes, but will probably end up making your watermark look like its reflection in a funhouse mirror. Best to leave this option enabled. Lastly, when scaling your content, the watermark can be blown up to several times its original size, and this can make the resulting image look pixelated and jagged. To combat this, make sure **Use smooth scaling** is enabled. This will apply a special smoothing algorithm to reduce the jaggedness. I recommend keeping this option enabled unless it interferes with the transparency of your watermark image.

Now that we've changed the appearance and size of the watermark, let's complete the package by changing its position. Just as with system stamps and captions, you have nine buttons that will let you place your watermark in a general section of the screen. With watermarks, you can go a bit further, using the **Horizontal offset** and **Vertical offset** sliders to place your image more exactly. When centered on the vertical axis, the vertical offset will be disabled. The same goes for your horizontal offset when centering horizontally. If you place the watermark dead center on your recording area, both offset controls will be disabled.

Just like your system stamp and caption effects, you won't see the actual watermark at record time. Also, do keep in mind that you have the same watermark options when producing in Camtasia Studio, which, once again, has the advantage of making your watermark editable. So, unless you're branding your content for security purposes and don't want anyone messing with the watermark under any circumstances, I'd highly recommend adding the watermark there. Then you can move or resize the watermark, change it, or get rid of it entirely, based on your future whim.

Autohighlight and Highlight

When creating your videos, you may want to draw attention to a window, toolbar, or some other specific area of the screen. Imagine if you could place a colored box around that particular object so that your audience can focus just on that one item, like so:

A colored box is great for cutting through the clutter and letting your audience know exactly which toolbar to look at.

With the next two tools on the Annotation toolbar, **Autohighlight** and **Highlight**, you can do just that.

①The Autohighlight tool. ②The Highlight tool.

While similar, these two tools work a bit differently. The colored box from the Autohighlight tool is designed to follow your mouse cursor as it moves about the screen. Say you were creating a tutorial on the various toolbars of Microsoft Word, for example. The autohighlight box would appear around the toolbar upon which your mouse cursor was currently resting, and when you moved the mouse cursor to the next toolbar, the box would follow you, and the audience's attention would focus on that toolbar instead.

Just enable Autohighlight and then start the recording as you normally would. Unlike the Annotation tools we've discussed thus far, you can actually see the autohighlight during record time. Once recording is in progress, the colored box appears and follows your mouse cursor from object to object. The autohighlight box will not display when recording is paused or stopped.

The Highlight option is slightly different, in that the colored box does not follow your mouse cursor. Rather, you choose the object you want to have the focus, thereby "setting" the highlight.

Here's how to **highlight an object**:

1. With the Recorder open, click the **Highlight** button. A thin red rectangle will appear around the nearest object, and you can move it by mousing over the various objects on your screen. When over your desired object, left-click to drop the highlight in place, and the box will become its usual thickness and color (which you can change — more on this in a moment).

2. Record your presentation as usual.

3. The highlight box will remain in one spot during your recording and, unlike Autohighlight, can be initiated or canceled at any time, regardless of the Recorder's current mode (recording, paused, or stopped). You can use this to your advantage if you wish to move the highlight box. Simply **Pause** the recording, and then uncheck the Highlight box. Then check it again, and select a new object. Resume recording. All the audience will see when playing back the video is the highlight suddenly moving from one object to another. This gives you the freedom of moving the box around without necessarily having it "joined at the hip" to your mouse cursor.

You may be wondering whether you'll always be stuck with a red box at the default thickness. Good news: You won't be. So let's change some things around. Again, choose **Options...** from the **Effects** menu, this time returning to the Annotation tab. In the Highlight section, you can adjust two factors, which apply to both the Highlight and Auto-highlight tools. First, you can change the width, which is the line width of your highlight box in pixels. Just enter a value into the Width field. Then, click the **Color...** button to adjust the box's color.

When I really want to focus *exclusively* on a particular toolbar or some other element, I can use the Highlight feature to blacken out everything else on the screen for a few moments, so that only the toolbar (or whatever object you wish) is visible, like this:

Here's the same window from the previous example, except that this time, the SnagIt toolbar is the only thing visible.

Here's how it works:

1. In the Highlight section of your Annotation tab (Effects Options dialog), set Width to **500*** pixels, and Color to **black** (or some other color of your choosing).

2. Begin recording normally (with Highlight *off*). Then, just before you're ready to discuss the object in question, **pause** the recording.

3. Enable **Highlight** and then click on the desired object. Now only your object is visible; the rest of the screen is black. **Pause** again when finished discussing the object.

4. Remove the highlight. If it happens that your Recorder window is also completely obscured by your highlight, you can disable the highlight by right-clicking the Camtasia Recorder system tray icon, then choosing **Effects > Annotation > Highlight**. If even your task bar is obscured by your highlight, a press of the **Alt-Tab** hotkey should reveal it.

5. Resume the recording when ready.

---

* It doesn't have to be exactly 500 pixels; it depends on your recording area. The trick is to have the box obscure your entire recording area (other than the desired object, obviously), but still leave the task bar and/or Recorder application window visible, as you'll need one of those later to turn the highlight back off.

Here are a few more tips and caveats regarding the use of Highlight and Autohighlight:

- Keep in mind that you can enable Highlight or Autohighlight, but not both at once.

- If you click the Highlight button but change your mind before laying it down, a right-click will cancel the operation.

- With both Highlight and Autohighlight, you're relying on the Camtasia Recorder's object detection capabilities, which are pretty acute at detecting windows and portions thereof. But if you can't seem to highlight just the object you want, you can use the Callouts feature in Camtasia Studio to mimic a highlight during editing. While it cannot offer the convenience of Autohighlight in following your mouse cursor around, callouts are handy for drawing a quick bounding box and, unlike the highlighting features, can do so with pixel-perfect accuracy (plus you can edit or remove the box later if desired). So, if you're trying to highlight a nontraditional object or group of objects, callouts are probably the way to go. If you insist on using the Recorder for this effect, then you can draw a box using the Frame tool of the ScreenDraw function, which, as luck would have it, is the final tool on your Annotation toolbar.

ScreenDraw

When explaining a detailed procedure in your video, it may come in handy to start drawing all over the screen in order to make your point. Just like John Madden dissecting a complicated play, you can scribble notes, draw arrows, and highlight "players" (in our case, windows and toolbars are standing in for linebackers and tight ends). It's incredibly easy to do, and fun to boot!

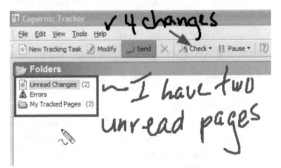

I used ScreenDraw to paint this graffiti all over my capture.

ScreenDraw is the final button on our Annotation toolbar. When glancing at it over in the Recorder, you may notice that it's grayed out. The ScreenDraw function can only be enabled when the Recorder is in record or paused modes; you can't do anything with it when Recorder's at a full stop.

Let's play with ScreenDraw a bit by trying the following:

1. Start a new recording. If desired, you can start out in paused mode in order to avoid having to make a long recording while you experiment. One cool thing about ScreenDraw is its ability to let you create drawings either during the actual recording or when paused, and each has its own effect. You can keep recording when drawing to show the actual process, à la John Madden. Or you can pause, draw, and then resume. To the viewer, it then looks as if the drawings just appeared like magic.

2. Click the **ScreenDraw** button on the Annotation toolbar.

3. Now, when inside the recording area (ScreenDraw only works inside the recording area), notice that your mouse cursor looks different. Click and drag the mouse. Congratulations; you just used the pen to draw a line.

4. But why stop there? Notice that your capture rectangle toolbar now has a special ScreenDraw toolbar underneath it:

You have an arsenal of six tool buttons plus an Undo button. Click the **Arrow** tool on the far left. When mousing back over the capture area, notice that your mouse cursor has changed once again. Each tool has its own cursor to indicate which one you're currently using.

5. These tools all have certain defaults, but these can be readily customized by clicking each tool's corresponding drop-down arrow. Click one of the tools' drop-down arrows and choose a new tool, color, and/or width. This becomes that tool's new default. These tools are incredibly useful in that you can now store up to six of your most often-used ScreenDraw settings without having to constantly reset.

6. Of course, you might have all your defaults set just the way you like, but then also have the occasional one-off ScreenDraw annotation for which you don't want to set a default. **Right-click** within the capture area and, in the context menu that appears, notice that all your standard tools are available. Change them here in the context menu and notice that these changes do not affect anything on the toolbar.

7. When inside the drop-down and context menus, you may have observed that each tool had a letter next it. Press **E**, and then click and drag. You now have an ellipse.

8. These hotkeys don't just select different tools; you've got hotkeys for all the attributes of those tools as well. Press **G**, then **7**, then **T**. Draw another ellipse. This one looks a lot different from the first, as it's now green, has a line width (thickness) of 7 pixels, and is translucent (meaning that the lines in the ellipse shape are now see-through).

9. You also have a couple of hotkeys for tidying up. Press **U** for undo, and the last shape you created disappears. When finished, press **Esc** to remove all your lovely artwork and exit ScreenDraw.

As you can see, ScreenDraw relies very heavily on hotkeys in order to make your choices. Especially if you're not working within the confines of a default toolset, hotkeys are by far the easiest way of working with ScreenDraw. You'll find that it can be profoundly helpful to memorize these commands. While the context menu and drop-down tools are always there to help if you get stuck, accessing either of these can be impractical if you're drawing while recording. Always looking to help out my fellow artists, I've put together a table of all the Screen-Draw commands and their corresponding hotkeys, so feel free to keep your book open to this page when drawing all over your screen:

Command	Hotkey	Notes
Tools		
Frame	F	Hold down Shift to draw a square.
Highlight	H	Width function is disabled, since highlights have no frame.
Ellipse	E	Hold down Shift to draw a circle.

Command	Hotkey	Notes
Pen	P	
Line	L	
Arrow	A	
Width		
Line width	1-8	Press any number from 1 to 8 to alter the border thickness.
Color		
Blue	B	
Black	K	
Cyan	C	
Green	G	
Yellow	Y	
White	W	
Magenta	M	
Red	R	
Translucent	T	Lets the user see through the shape's ink to whatever lies beneath it. Highlights are automatically translucent.
Clean-up		
Undo	U	Removes last object. Repeat for multiple undos.
Stop drawing	Esc	Removes all shapes and exits ScreenDraw.

In the Annotation tab of the Effects Options dialog, you'll find one setting that pertains to ScreenDraw:

ScreenDraw
☑ Disable keyboard and cursor effects during ScreenDraw

If you have turned on the keyboard and mouse cursor audio effects, you probably won't want your audience to endure all the clicking and clacking associated with drawing objects and using the keyboard hotkeys. After all, the sound effects are supposed to be instructive about the application you're currently capturing. These effects are therefore unnecessary and distracting when caused by your recording activities. That's why it's generally best to keep this setting enabled.

Here are a few additional things you'll want to keep in mind when using ScreenDraw:

- If you're adding ScreenDraw elements at record time, you may not wish to have the various tools' custom mouse cursors displayed to your audience. Hiding the mouse cursor (I'll explain how later in this chapter) will also work on these custom cursors.

- While there is a certain amount of overlap between ScreenDraw and the Callout tools in Camtasia Studio, they're really used for different purposes. While I lean toward the effects offered by Camtasia Studio due to their nondestructive editing capabilities, ScreenDraw is one of the Recorder-based effects I still frequently use. Unlike callouts, ScreenDraw objects can actually be animated if drawn at record time. It's a terrific effect.

- In order to quickly start and stop ScreenDraw, I strongly recommend enabling the ScreenDraw hotkey. Choose **Options...** from the **Tools** menu, and then click the **Hotkeys** tab. In the ScreenDraw hotkey section, specify your chosen hotkey, along with any modifier keys. For full details on specifying hotkeys, please see Chapter 7, "Recorder Tools Options."

The Audio Toolbar

The next toolbar is the **Audio** toolbar, which can include one or more of the following: voice narration, mouse click sound effects, and keyboard sound effects. While these options were covered in Chapter 5, "Recording Your Screen," there is one additional aspect of the Recorder's audio effects I'll mention here: choosing audio files for your keyboard and mouse click sound effects.

Out of the box, the Camtasia Recorder includes audio files that simulate a mouse-down sound, a mouse-up sound, and a keypress sound. Should you wish to change these, you can do so in the Effects Options dialog. Simply choose **Options...** from the **Effects** menu, and then click the **Sound** tab.

Once you have the desired sound files on your system, you can use this tab to link to them. This can be done either by typing in the file path or by clicking the **Select Sound File** button (![select sound file icon]). Once you have a sound linked, you can test it by clicking the **Test** button (![test icon]). Finally, both the mouse and keyboard effects have master volume sliders where you can adjust the overall loudness of the effect. Click **OK** to lock in your changes.

The Cursor Toolbar

When previewing your first recordings, you probably saw your mouse cursor whizzing around the video screen, just as if you had been watching it live. This is the default setting for capturing your mouse cursor, though it may surprise you to know that this is only one of five settings on your **Cursor** toolbar, which looks like this:

Unlike most of the tools on the other toolbars, these tools are not toggle buttons — only one can be selected at any given time. The cursor tools are (from the left):

- **Hide cursor.** The mouse cursor does not appear at all in your video recording.
- **Show cursor.** The cursor appears normally. Unless you've enabled a custom cursor (more on that in a minute), the appearance of your mouse cursor will be exactly what it was at record time, including any application-specific changes (changing into a

hand pointer cursor when mousing over a web link) or changes in system state (an hourglass cursor during a wait, etc.).

- **Highlight clicks.** Every time the mouse is clicked, a colored pool of rings (or a solid circle, depending on the settings) emanates from the mouse cursor. It is a visual indication that the mouse was just clicked. You may assign separate colors to left and right mouse clicks. It's a really useful tool for demonstrating a complicated procedure with lots of clicks involved, especially if you're not doing any audio narration.

- **Highlight cursor.** If the application you're recording necessitates a lot of mouse movement, consider turning on Highlight cursor. This draws more attention to your mouse cursor by placing a perpetual highlight over the cursor that follows it around. It's an effective way of making sure that your cursor never gets lost in the background. The color and shape of this highlight are editable, and we'll learn how coming up next.

- **Highlight cursor and clicks.** The previous two tools combined. It can be useful in certain situations, but for general purposes, I find it overkill.

As promised, let's now talk about how we can edit all our cursors, clicks, and highlights for a custom effect. As you might have guessed, this involves going back to the Effects Options dialog once again. Choose **Options...** from the **Effects** menu, and this time give the **Cursor** tab a click.

The Cursor tab of the Effects Options dialog, where you choose a custom cursor, change the shape and color of the cursor highlight, or alter the size and appearance of your visual mouse clicks.

The first section, called **Cursor,** is where we can specify a custom cursor for use with the recording. Custom cursors lend a certain amount of realism to particular recording applications. For example, when given the task of creating a series of videos on Palm software using the Palm OS Emulator, I utilized a custom cursor in the shape of a pen stylus. This was a nice, professional touch that did much to "Palm-ize" the video. Click the **Cursor Setup...** button to get started.

You have three options in the Cursor Setup dialog:

- ■ **Use actual cursor.** The default. Your cursor appears normally and automatically adapts to both applications and state changes (such as changing to a pointed finger when hovering over a hyperlink).

- ■ **Use custom cursor.** Here you may choose one of Camtasia Recorder's custom cursors from the drop-down list.

- ■ **Use cursor from file.** This option will let you specify a cursor file on your system to use as a custom cursor, either by typing in a file path or clicking the **Open** button ( ) and browsing to it. By default, Camtasia Recorder uses the C:\Windows\Cursors directory, which should already have a number of icons with which you can experiment. Camtasia Recorder can make use of either cursor (.cur) or icon (.ico) files for its custom cursors. Unfortunately, it does not support animated cursor (.ani) files*.

You can also create custom cursors with any cursor or icon creation utility. IconWorkshop from Axialis (www.axialis.com), a demo of which is included on the companion CD, can create .ico files to use as custom cursors. If you do decide to use a custom cursor, please note that you'll only see your standard cursor during the recording process. This will be replaced with the custom cursor at playback.

---

* Well, it does and it doesn't — you can't browse to an .ani file, but you can type in a file path to an .ani file. The cursor will then appear in your recording, but it won't be animated.

Keep in mind that custom cursors lose their ability to change based on certain situations. The cursor will always remain the same, and will therefore no longer change into an I-beam cursor when mousing over editable text, for example.

Let's move on to the **Highlight cursor** section of the Cursor tab. You have a preview that shows what your highlight will look like at its current settings. There are four basic properties that we can change about this highlight: shape, size, color, and opacity. Let's look at these in order.

While the default highlight is a circle, a simple pool of color like a spotlight, this is only one of 19 options available in the Shape drop-down menu. The shape's size can be adjusted by moving the Size slider back and forth, and you can choose a different color from a wide palette of choices by clicking the Color... button. For the opacity of the highlight, we have three choices:

- **Translucent**, where everything under the highlight appears unobscured.

- **Semi-translucent**, where a dither effect is applied to the highlight, making it partially translucent and partially solid, in a checkerboard pattern.

- **Opaque**, where the highlight color is solid, and nothing in the video window can be seen underneath it.

Simply play with the settings until the preview reflects your wishes, click **OK**, and then record normally. The highlight won't show up until you play back your recording.

Moving to the **Highlight mouse clicks** section, we also have a preview (although this time the preview doesn't really do the effect justice, since it doesn't capture the animation). Here you see a set of three controls for each mouse button (left and right): shape, size, and color. The Shape drop-down menu will let you choose between Rings (a circle that expands outward, like a ripple on a pond) and Circle (similar, except that the circle is filled rather than empty). The Size and Color... controls work similarly to the cursor highlight controls. When finished, simply click **OK** and then record your video per usual. As always, you won't actually see the mouse click highlights until playback.

The Zoom & Pan Toolbar

While working on your projects, you'll invariably run into situations where your video will need to cover a broader portion of the screen than will fit into recording dimensions. It's also likely you'll encounter the opposite problem of having too broad a view, and will need to zoom in on a particular area of the screen. Either way, the **Zoom & Pan** toolbar has you covered.

The toolbar has six buttons, only the first two of which are clickable when the Recorder is in stopped mode: AutoPan and AutoZoom. We'll discuss the panning features first.

AutoPan

Say you're recording a particular region of the screen, and suddenly you realize that a function you need to discuss lies outside your recording area. Camtasia Recorder supports panning capabilities that will let you move the recording area to include the new item. You can do so manually by clicking and dragging the frame of the recording window to the new location, either during recording or when paused, depending on whether you actually want to show the movement. For a more refined panning solution, though, just click the **AutoPan** button.

When enabled, the recording area will attempt to keep the mouse cursor centered by following the cursor's movement around the screen rather than remaining stationary. Since the recording area can pan to every corner of even a very large screen area, this can be useful for recording particularly large applications that consume most of the screen.

AutoPan can be toggled on and off by clicking the AutoPan button, but you'll get the most mileage out of this function by selecting and using an AutoPan hotkey. Choose **Options...** from the **Tools** menu, and from the **Hotkeys** tab, click **Advanced....** Then choose a hotkey (plus any desired modifier keys) and click **OK**. During recording, a simple press of your hotkey will toggle between having the recording area follow you like a lapdog and bringing it to a dead stop. The latter is useful for "re-anchoring" the recording window so that you can more easily mouse around the current recording area without making your audience seasick with superfluous motion.

III: Recording

While the speed at which the recording window follows you is partially dependent on the power of your processor and video card, there is also a setting that lets you adjust the relative tightness of AutoPan's "mouse magnet." From the **Effects** menu, choose **Options…**, and then move to the **Zoom** tab. While most of these options are specifically related to the Recorder's zooming capabilities, there is also a slider called **AutoPan speed**, with which you specify how fast you want the recording area to "snap" to your mouse movements. While I generally prefer to have my AutoPan speed on the faster side, it depends on your mousing habits and, of course, your personal taste.

> Keep in mind that the AutoPan function (and AutoZoom, for that matter) changes large portions of image background with every frame, and as such, can bloat the file size a lot. It's back to the classic trade-off between special effects sexiness and a svelte file size. It's less of an issue with the newer codecs that are very forgiving of this kind of content, but just bear in mind that your core footage is going be rather large.

AutoZoom and the Other Zoom Functions

Setting the size of your video dimensions is always a dance between keeping the file size low while making sure it fits on the viewer's monitor on the one hand, and making sure you cover all aspects of an application and its interface on the other. I just showed you panning techniques that let you move that recording area around the screen to capture different segments of the screen, even if they're all over the place. The counterpart to these techniques, zoom, also allows you to capture more of the screen than your capture area would normally allow, or even to move in closer in order to concentrate on just one small section of your otherwise spacious recording area. These two sets of techniques can also be used in concert to create different effects.

The rest of the buttons on the Zoom & Pan toolbar apply to zooming, the first of which (and the only one that is immediately selectable) is AutoZoom. When this feature is disabled, you can use the different zoom tools (which we'll discuss in a minute) to instantly move closer to or farther away from the action. During recording, this has the effect of the recording area growing or shrinking in size. During playback, the size of the video window remains constant — it's the content itself that does the growing and shrinking. Enabling AutoZoom adds a special effect to this function by animating the zoom, thereby looking a lot more like the zoom on a video camera. Rather than putting your audience through the jarring effect of instantly being placed closer to the action, you can glide them in with an exhilarating *whoooosh* (well, it's exhilarating to *me*, but then, I don't get out much…). Just click the **AutoZoom** button to include this effect.

> When recording with AutoZoom enabled, there will be a slight pause during the zoom to encode the AutoZoom effect. This is normal.

You may notice that the other zoom buttons on the Zoom & Pan toolbar are grayed out. This is because you can't zoom in either direction if you're not recording (or paused). Just enter record mode, and suddenly the following tools become available to you:

- **Zoom Out** and **Zoom In.** This will increase or decrease the size of your recording area while keeping the playback size constant, producing the effect of zooming out or in. If desired, you can set hotkeys for both of these functions by choosing **Tools > Options… > Hotkeys tab > Advanced….**

- **Zoom To.** This tool allows you to set the level of the zoom by clicking on the button's drop-down arrow. You can select a percentage of the zoom in specific increments, or choose **Full Screen, Window,** or **Region***. Clicking on the button itself will always take you back to 100%, regardless of the percentage at which you started (more on this later).

- **Zoom Undo.** Actually, this should be called Zoom Undo/Redo, as it's a toggle button that can quickly alternate between your last two zoom settings. If you find that you're using two levels of zoom pretty much exclusively, then this is a handy button to keep at the ready.

As you saw during our discussion of the AutoPan function, the zoom tools can be customized in a number of ways. Let's go back to **Effects > Options…,** and then return to the **Zoom** tab.

---

* When choosing one of these latter options, you may end up with more recording area than specified, due to the fact that the recording area *must* maintain the aspect ratio of its original dimensions. In fact, if the dimensions of the recording area don't correspond to those of your screen, then choosing a Full Screen zoom simply won't work.

As you can see, most of these options are devoted to zoom functions:

- Just like with AutoPan, there is a special slider to adjust the **AutoZoom speed**. The whooshing zoom effect will speed up or slow down accordingly.

- **Zoom level at start of capture** lets you set whether you want to begin the recording zoomed in or out. The default is 100%, meaning no zoom. Simply type your percentage into the corresponding field. Just remember that this option is set; otherwise, what you record and what your audience sees will be two very different things.

- When you choose **Center zoom effect**, the new zoomed recording area will always be centered over the old one. In practice, the recording area will zoom in/out, and then automatically pan over until it's appropriately centered. This option is *off* by default, though I actually find it to be a rather nice effect.

- When you select **Use smooth scaling**, you're instructing Camtasia Recorder to use a special smooth interpolated scaling algorithm to remove the pixelation that occurs when zoomed out. In English, now: This option helps maintain the smoothness of graphics and the legibility of text when you're zoomed out, since these elements would otherwise look all blocky and gross. While your frame rate can take a hit due to the processing power involved in computing this algorithm, if you've got gigahertz to burn, I'd recommend keeping it *on*.

- Similar to the previous option is **Use smooth scaling during AutoZoom**, which applies the same smooth scaling algorithm to the actual AutoZoom effect. It suffers the same limitation as the Use smooth scaling option. Given that the AutoZoom effect only lasts a second or two, it is obviously less critical here to make sure everything's nice and legible, and a result, this option is *off* by default.

- **Show zoom rectangle during AutoZoom** allows you to track the progress of the zoom by showing a zoom rectangle during both recording and playback. This zoom rectangle consists of a black border that highlights the area you'll be zooming to. While seeming like a good idea in theory, in practice I think it adds unnecessary clutter. It is *off* by default.

Two quick warnings regarding AutoZoom and AutoPan:

- Both of these effects, due to the fact that they precipitate a lot of background movement, can really bloat your file size. If bandwidth is an issue for you, consider making use of instant zoom and pan effects rather than the animated versions.
- All the effects offered by the Zoom & Pan toolbar can be accomplished with the Zoom-n-Pan tools within Camtasia Studio. If you need to perform complicated zoom and pan effects, or you simply want any effects to be editable or removable, I strongly recommend that you implement those effects inside of Camtasia Studio instead.

The Camera Toolbar

Your **Camera** toolbar sports two buttons that control whether you wish to add a camera video stream to your recording, and whether you wish to preview that stream in its own window when making said recording.

These two options were discussed in the section on additional data streams in Chapter 5, "Recording Your Screen." You have some additional options that let you change the video source as well as alter settings specific to your video device. As these options are located in the Tools Options dialog, they will be addressed in detail in Chapter 7, "Recorder Tools Options."

The ScreenPad

One additional item that bears mentioning in this chapter is the Camtasia Recorder ScreenPad. The **ScreenPad** is a mini-application within Recorder, a separate window that lets you drag graphical elements such as callouts, arrows, and boxes onto your screen for recording (or just looking cool). The elements float above the other content on your screen, and can be used for adding stylistic notes, captions, and other graphical objects to your captures.

Because there's a lot of content to this section, I'll do you a favor and say it up front: A good 95% of the ScreenPad's functionality has been replaced by Camtasia Studio's Callouts feature. Don't get me wrong: The ScreenPad is still a great tool, but its utility is fading against the more advanced backdrop of the clickable hotspots, drop shadows, and fade effects offered by Camtasia Studio. I strongly encourage you to use callouts instead, and am really only including this section on the ScreenPad for the sake of completeness.

To open up the ScreenPad, simply choose **View > ScreenPad**. The ScreenPad appears in a small window, and its content is based on a "library" metaphor. There are three types of libraries available:

- **Layout library.** These libraries consist of groups of other ScreenPad elements that you have opted to save in a particular configuration for easy reuse. Unlike the other two library types, only one layout library may be open at a time.

- **Shape library.** A shape library contains graphical objects of all sorts. These can be either created by hand in the internal editor (discussed in a bit) or imported from a graphic file. In the included My Shapes library, you have all manner of callouts, arrows, and boxes that you can customize for your needs.

- **Text note library.** This library contains text boxes. There are a number of default notes in the My Text Notes library. You can create your own notes of various sizes, fonts, colors, and borders. They can contain default text (that you specify) or simply be blank. You can always tell a text note from a shape, as a text note will show a different icon when mousing over it:

This is a text note.

To set a ScreenPad object on your screen, drag it out to its desired location or simply double-click the shape within the ScreenPad. Multiple objects can be added to the screen — these objects can be layered by dragging them over the top of one another. The order is determined by the order in which these objects were clicked, with the most recently clicked object on top.

In addition to what you're given in the default My Shapes library, you can also import just about any image you want as a new shape. Just choose **New Shape…** from the **Edit** menu. In the New Shape dialog (under Background Image), choose **Image file**, and then browse to your image. You can use BMP, GIF, or JPG files.

So what if you want to get rid of one or more objects? Just right-click on the object, and then choose **Close** from the context menu* that appears. To get rid of *all* your objects, choose **Close All Objects**. And if your various computing activities ever corrupt the display of one or more objects, simply refresh them by clicking **Refresh Objects**. As you've probably noticed, there are a great number of functions in this context menu in addition to the ones I've already mentioned.

Edit Text...
Edit Image...
Edit Opacity...
Resize...
Clone
Save
Save Layout
Close
Close All Objects
Refresh Objects

The context menu of a shape object. The menu for text notes looks slightly different.

Let's discuss a few of these options in greater detail.

Editing Text

Both shapes and text notes allow you to add or edit text, but they have different ways of going about it. With text notes, you can edit the text simply by double-clicking the object or choosing **Edit Text...** from the object's context menu. The text will highlight and you can enter whatever you wish. Should you desire to alter the font or any of the text's other characteristics, then right-click the text note and choose **Edit Settings....**

Editing a shape's text is a bit trickier. You start the process the same way, either by double-clicking the shape or by choosing **Edit Text...** from the context menu. The Text Tool and Edit Text dialogs appear, as shown in the following figure.

---

* While I find the use of the context menus to be incredibly helpful (and hence use them in my instructions), note that most of the commands available in an object's context menu can also be found in the menus of the main ScreenPad user interface.

The two dialogs you need to edit the text of a shape object.

The Text Tool dialog allows you to type in your text as well as specify formatting information, such as font, size, color, alignment, and style. The Edit Text dialog lets you move or resize the text box in order to change the text's placement on top of the shape. To move the text box, place your mouse inside the box, then click and drag to a new location. To resize, click and drag on one of the box's eight frame handles. You can also use the scale sliders at the bottom of the dialog to adjust the size of the shape itself. You can elongate the object to better fit the text by leaving **Keep scale factors equal** unchecked and by adjusting only one of the sliders, but to maintain the highest quality and avoid an undesirable "stretch" effect, keep the scale factors equal.

Editing the Object Itself

But the text isn't the only thing you can change about these objects. As you first saw when editing the characteristics of one of your text notes, most of the object's properties can be adjusted by choosing **Edit Settings…** from the context menu. In addition to editing the text itself, you have the following capabilities:

Name	Icon(s)	Notes
Font...	Font...	Lets you adjust the font, font style, and size of your text.
Horizontal alignment		Choose from left-justified, centered, or right-justified text.
Vertical alignment		Place text at the top, middle, or bottom of the text box.
Font style	**B** *I* <u>U</u>	**Bold**, *italic*, and <u>underline</u> toggle buttons.
Word wrap	☑ Word wrap	Choose whether you wish to have longer text wrap to the next line.
Text color	Text color:	Click to choose the color of your text.
Bkgd. color	Bkgd. color:	Click to choose the color of the box.
Width (pixels) Height (pixels)	Width (pixels): 219 Height (pixels): 137	This is the size of your box in pixels. You can adjust these numbers to exactly specify the object's size.
Style	Style: 3D Border	Choose the kind of frame border you want from a drop-down list.
Width (pixels)	Width (pixels): 10	Choose how wide you wish the frame to be. The upper limit of this value is dictated by the size of the object.
Color	Color:	Click to pick the frame's color. This option is not available for all frame styles.

This is a rather comprehensive list, and adjusting these settings can produce just about any kind of text box you can imagine. But Screen-Pad's shape objects take things even further. Unlike your text notes where only certain properties can be adjusted, you have pixel-perfect control over all your shapes. To get started, just right-click on any shape object, and then choose **Edit Image...** from the context menu. The Edit Image dialog appears, and you'll see the image in a window to the left.

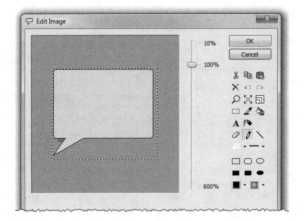

This is your workspace, where you can edit the image using the tools on the right. Between them is a slider that allows you to adjust the level of zoom on the object. This has no bearing on the size of the image itself, only on the view of the image in your workspace, so that you can more easily edit the object. As you can see, you have a metric ton of editing tools at your disposal, which are detailed in the table below.

Tool	Description
✂	Cuts your selected area from the image for pasting into another part of the image. If the entire image is selected, everything will be cut.
📋	Copies your selected area from the image for pasting into another part of the image.
📋	Pastes anything cut or copied from the image. You are unable to paste in objects or text from other sources. If your selection area is too small to accommodate the clipboard contents, you'll be asked if you want the contents cropped to fit the selection area.
✗	Clear removes the image or any selected part of it.
↰	Undo gets rid of your most recent change. Click Undo multiple times to purge an entire chain of oopsies if desired. The Ctrl-Z hotkey will do the same job.
↱	Redo redoes the doings you just undid. Pressing Ctrl-Y will work wonders as well.
🔍	Magnify will zoom in on your image to let you more easily work with it. Moving the zoom slider downward will accomplish the same thing.
⤢	Size to fit window zooms the image to the exact point where the entire contents of the image will just barely fit within the editing window.

Tool	Description
🔲	Clicking Resize will bring up a dialog that lets you adjust the size (in pixels) of the selection rectangle. The default values are the full dimensions of the current image. Reducing these values will automatically crop the image. If you have already reduced the size of your selection rectangle in the editing window by clicking and dragging on one of its frame handles, then checking the Crop to selection rectangle box will crop the image to the current size of the rectangle. Additionally, you can set the color depth of the image here.
▭	Select Area will let you click and drag a subset area of the image so that you can work with that portion exclusively. This area is represented by a dashed frame in the editing window. It can be resized by clicking and dragging on one of the frame handles. You can move a selection (and the content it encompasses!) from its original spot by clicking and dragging it.
🖊	The Select Color eyedropper tool will let you click any color in the editing window, and this color will then be represented in the Foreground Color box, allowing you to draw, airbrush, flood fill, and add text in this color.
🪣	Flood Fill will fill any enclosed area of the image (using automatic border detection) with the color in the Foreground Color box.
A	To insert text into your image, just click Add Text. A dialog will appear that will let you enter your text as well as adjust its format. You can change the placement of the text by moving or resizing the selection frame for the text in the editing window, which completely encompasses the image by default. Note: Unlike the text options for shape objects discussed earlier in this chapter, this text is not editable once you've laid it down. I therefore do not recommend using this tool unless you really, really want the text there forever.
🖌	Airbrush is like a spray paint canister that you can use to touch up your shapes for an artistic effect. Either that, or use it to "tag" your shapes with all sorts of juvenile graffiti.
⌀	While you can remove a large section of the image by selecting it and choosing Clear, Freehand Erase lets you control an eraser manually. Just click and drag over the area you want to erase.
✏	Freehand Draw acts like a pencil or a paintbrush, letting you draw all over the image by clicking and dragging.
╲	The Line tool allows you to draw straight lines. Just click, drag, and release. It's a swell complement to the wavy lines of the Freehand Draw tool.
▦ ▾	Clicking the drop-down arrow of the Eraser Width tool lets you choose the width of your Freehand Erase command.

Tool	Description
▬ ▾	Pen Width is similar to Eraser Width, except that it applies to the width of your lines (for the Freehand Draw, Shape, and Line tools).
▢▢▢ ▬▬●	These tools allow you to draw a Rectangle, Rounded Rectangle, and Ellipse, respectively. Choose the upper row if you want a transparent (frame only) shape, or the lower row if you would like the shape filled in with the foreground color, thus creating a solid (borderless) shape.
■ ▾	For Foreground Color, click the drop-down arrow to select a new color, and any subsequent lines, drawings, shapes, and paint effects will show up in that color.
◉ ▾	The Transparency Color tool is used to select a color in the image that will show up as transparent. Just click the drop-down arrow to select a color, or alternately (and more easily), click the Select Color tool, position the dropper over the color you wish to make transparent, and then right-click.

Editing Opacity

Now that you have some ScreenPad shapes and text notes on the screen and have edited them to your liking, let's try adjusting their opacity. After all, totally opaque images are so passé. Transparency's where it's at, and you can set the opacity of both shapes and text notes anywhere from 100% opaque (totally solid) to 1% opaque (almost totally invisible). By adjusting this setting, you can create cool ghost-like semi-transparent effects. To do so (with either shape type), simply right-click the shape and then choose **Edit Opacity....** The following dialog appears:

Either drag the slider or simply enter a number from 1 to 100 into the % field. The ScreenPad image in question will automatically update to reflect the change, so you can preview it before clicking **OK**.

Resizing ScreenPad Objects

Both text notes and shape objects can be readily resized. Since text notes are vector objects, however, they resize much better than do shapes, which may experience some pixelation when scaled way up or down. The technique for resizing an object depends on its type:

- **Text notes.** You can do an "eyeball" adjustment by simply clicking and dragging on the object's border. For a pixel-perfect adjustment, however, you should right-click the note, choose **Edit Settings...**, and then alter the **Width** and **Height** fields in the Notes section.

- **Shapes.** Right-click the shape and then choose **Resize...** from the context menu. You can adjust the shape by percentage of the original size, anywhere from 10 to 600. The scale (the ratio of horizontal to vertical) will be kept even by default, but you can uncheck **Keep scale factors equal** if you want to stretch your shape. Note that even when executing this command more than once, the value entered will always reflect the percentage of the *original* shape (the one currently sitting in your ScreenPad library) as opposed to the percentage of the shape's most recent size. For example, say you resized the shape to 200%, making it a lot bigger. If you resized again, this time entering 115%, the shape would be 115% of the size at which it started out, thus making it significantly *smaller* than it is currently. Click **OK** when you're happy.

Cloning and Saving Objects

Every instance of an object on your screen is based on some sort of "pattern," which is the corresponding shape in your library. At this point, it's important to clarify the difference between *screen objects* and *library objects*, and how these two interact. A library object is the original shape or text note that sits in your library. You can clone objects within libraries by copying and pasting them in one of the following ways:

- Use the context menu. Just right-click the object and then choose **Copy** or **Paste** as appropriate.

- Select the desired object and then use **Copy** or **Paste** from ScreenPad's **Edit** menu.

- Select the desired object and then use the **Ctrl-C** and **Ctrl-V** hotkeys.

You can paste copied items into either the same or a different library (provided that library is for the same object type), and it's a good practice to do so if you plan on editing an object extensively. That way, you still have the original until you decide you like your new creation better. Library objects can be edited the same way as screen objects, either by right-clicking the object and then choosing the appropriate command from the context menu, or by selecting the desired object and then clicking a command in the Edit menu. You can get rid of any object in any library by selecting it and pressing **Delete**.

Now, once you drag that object onto the screen, a separate instance of it is created, which I call a screen object. This object can be edited to your heart's content, and it will have zippo effect on the library object that spawned it. If you do edit the screen object and, in the end, prefer the changed version and want to save the changes back to the original library object, you may do so by right-clicking the screen object and then choosing **Save** from the context menu. You will see its corresponding library object automatically update. The changes are then saved.

The cool thing about ScreenPad objects is that you can spawn a gazillion of them from either the same or different library objects, literally populating the entire screen if desired. If you want another instance of your object on the screen, just drag it out again. However, there may be times when you edit a screen object and want to spawn a new copy of that edited object *without* saving it back to the library object. No problem. Just right-click the desired screen object and choose **Clone**. A brand-new instance of the edited object appears on your screen.

Working with Layouts

As you continue to work with your ScreenPad objects, eventually you'll come to a point where you'll need to save groups of them so that you can maintain more detailed layers of objects. This is where layouts come in. A *layout* is a saved configuration of objects where the properties of every object on your screen are preserved, including their exact locations. Say you've got a bunch of screen objects laid out and are just finishing with your recording session for the day. All you need to do is save these objects as a layout, and you can start fresh the next day, with all the ScreenPad objects displayed just as they are right now.

Here's how you **save a ScreenPad layout**:

1. Assemble the various ScreenPad objects on your screen as desired. Make sure that their placement and layering is exactly as you'd like them. Remember that you alter the order of layering by clicking on each object in ascending order (the most recently clicked object will be on top).

2. Right-click on any screen object and choose **Save Layout**, or choose **Save Layout** from ScreenPad's **Edit** menu.

3. The ScreenPad will pop up with a new layout. A generic name (*Layout-xx*) is given to it, but this name is already high-lighted and ripe for renaming. Type in a name and hit **Enter**.

4. Later, when you want this layout to show up, simply double-click the object in the ScreenPad or drag it out onto the screen. No matter where you drag it, the layout's objects will assume the position in which they were saved. Be careful not to call the layout multiple times, or you'll have objects on top of objects.

If your needs change and you want to move these elements around, simply do so and then create a new layout from them. If you work with ScreenPad layouts frequently, there are hotkey functions available to help you be more efficient. From ScreenPad's **Options** menu, choose **Hotkeys…**. There you will find three layout hotkeys available for your use:

- **Next Layout hotkey.** If you have multiple layouts in your current layout library, this will cycle forward in order by one layout.

- **Previous Layout hotkey.** If you have multiple layouts in your current layout library, this will cycle backward in order by one layout.

- **Show/Hide Layout hotkey.** This will toggle the current layout on and off.

These hotkeys are particularly useful for when you've developed a "stock" library of layouts you use fairly frequently. Now you can save time by quickly cycling among them.

 The actual execution of these hotkeys can be a little buggy. I've found that it helps tremendously to have your current layout library open before using these hotkeys.

Customizing the ScreenPad

In addition to creating custom categories by adding libraries, you can alter the view in your ScreenPad in several key ways. First, you can view the objects in each library by **Icons and Names,** by **Icons Only,** or by **Names Only.** Make your choice from ScreenPad's **View** menu.

Note that this is a global setting, meaning that all libraries will be affected, not just the one currently open. If you do decide to view the object names, you can change them by clicking twice (*not* double-clicking) on the object's name text.

Within the ScreenPad, a library object's icon is generally just a shrunken view of the object itself (except for layout objects, which always use a stock icon). You can change icons for any library object (including layouts), if desired. Choose **Edit > Icon,** and then choose either **Change Icon…,** which lets you select a new icon from any .ico, .exe, .dll, or .bmp file, or **Edit Icon….** This option gives you an editing window similar to that of the Shape editing functions. A current version of the icon will appear in the editing window, and you may change it to your liking.

Summary

In addition to basic recording capabilities, a number of functions are built into the Camtasia Recorder that can produce an array of eye-catching special effects. While some of these effects have been largely supplanted by the tools within the Camtasia Studio editing application, most have retained their usefulness for specific situations:

- The **Annotation toolbar** gives you various methods of marking up your content. You can choose to add system stamps (for stamping your videos with specific information), captions (for making a statement with text), watermarks (for branding your videos), Autohighlight and Highlight (for placing colored frames around content), and finally, ScreenDraw (for marking up your video with shapes and drawings).

- The **Audio toolbar** lets you opt to add voiced narration or system sounds to your recordings. Additionally, you can record keyboard and mouse click sound effects for your video.

- The **Cursor toolbar** allows you to hide or show the mouse cursor when recording your video. If shown, you can opt to show graphically when the user has clicked the mouse. A highlight can also be placed around the mouse cursor to let the audience more easily follow the cursor visually. The size, shape, and color of these elements can be easily adjusted. If desired, you may also pick a custom cursor for your recording.

- The **Zoom & Pan toolbar** lets you focus in on specific segments of the screen, even those that fall outside your current capture area. In addition to an array of tools to help you zoom in for a detailed view of an area (or zoom out to gain perspective), the AutoPan and AutoZoom tools can smoothly animate your zooming and panning for a more professional effect.

- With the **Camera toolbar**, you can choose whether to include video (and possibly audio) from a web camera or video device in addition to your screen video. You may also turn on a preview window of this video stream so that you can see exactly what is being captured.

- The **ScreenPad** provides a means of decorating the capture area with callouts, arrows, text boxes, and other graphic objects. Multiple ScreenPad objects can be saved as a single layout.

But special effects aren't the only way you can customize the recording experience with the Camtasia Recorder. In the next chapter, we'll look at adjusting your preferences in the Tools Options dialog.

Exercises

1. Add one or more system stamps/captions to the next video you create. If including multiple stamps, place them in different locations so that they don't overlap. Use different formatting options for each one. After recording, preview your video. Does it look as expected?

2. Record a brief video that showcases one or more application toolbars (any Microsoft Office product should work). Use the highlight feature to make only *one* of the toolbars visible, using the information in the "Autohighlight and Highlight" section of this chapter as a guide.

3. In a new recording, enter ScreenDraw mode. Draw a green squiggly line that's 5 pixels wide. Make the next shape a translucent blue rectangle (frame) with 8-pixel wide borders. If you're feeling adventurous, try changing these shape settings using only the keyboard shortcuts.

4. Experiment with the various ScreenDraw effects in both record and paused modes. Preview your work. Which mode do you prefer?

5. Edit your cursor effects (Effects > Options... > Cursor) to create a highlight cursor effect in the shape of an orange star. Similarly, change the color, shape, and size of one of your mouse click effects. Then, record a test video with the Highlight Cursor and Clicks tool enabled. Preview the results.

6. Drag a few of the shapes from the default ScreenPad library onto your desktop. Now, import one or more of the sample images from this chapter's folder into a new library, and place a few instances of those on your desktop. Try saving a group of shapes as a layout. Check your layout by closing all objects and then adding the layout to your desktop.

Chapter 7

Recorder Tools Options

In the last two chapters, we explored the basics of making a recording as well as some record-time special effects you can implement. This chapter further explores the capabilities of the Recorder by teaching you how to set its various preferences, such as file settings, codecs, and hotkeys. And that's just skimming the surface. In Camtasia Recorder, you've got a vast number of behind-the-scenes options that affect the Recorder's functionality to some degree. Be warned: There's a lot of tweaking you can do to alter and extend the core capabilities of the Recorder, and the Tools Options dialog is where it all happens.

To **get to the Tools Options** dialog, do one of the following:

- Click the **Tools** menu, and then choose **Options**....

    or

- Click the **Options** tool on the Main toolbar.

 The Options tool.

 If both the Options menu item and the Options tool are grayed out, this means that you can't enter the dialog because you're recording (or in paused mode) right now. Just stop the recording, and you'll find that you can access the Tools Options dialog once again.

Is your Tools Options dialog open? Good. As you can see, the dialog contains six tabs: Capture, Video, Audio, Camera, Hotkeys, and Program. Note that the Capture tab comes up first by default. As a shortcut, if you know which tab you want to work in prior to opening the Tools Options dialog, you can click the arrow next to the Options tool, and then actually select a particular tab from either the Tools Options or the Effects Options dialogs, as seen here:

Every Options tab is available in one handy list.

Let's discuss these tabs.

The Capture Tab

The **Capture** tab actually has a dual function, controlling both how files are saved (File Options) and how the recording is actually executed (Capture and Performance Options).

File Options

Let's begin with the File Options. Starting with version 3, the Camtasia Recorder introduced a new file system to incorporate streams of additional content without making you contend with a gazillion files. Now you have a choice between industry-standard AVI files and proprietary CAMREC files. The latter encapsulates both the screen video and, if desired, its corresponding camera video as well as video markers into one handy file. In the future, it's likely that CAMREC files will be expanded to include additional streams of data. For now, which format you choose depends on your specific needs. If you don't need to include your face as part of your video or add markers at record time, and you would like the ability to import your video into third-party editing applications (Adobe Premiere, Sony Vegas, etc.), then AVI is for you. If, however, you want to keep everything within Camtasia Studio, or if you need to include camera video or markers, then choose CAMREC.

Starting with version 5, one compelling reason to choose CAMREC is that the Recorder can use this format to store special metadata about the action happening inside your capture area. When editing in Camtasia Studio, you can use this information to apply SmartFocus, a special command that can automaticlly set zoom-n-pan keyframes based on what's happening in the recording. Especially if you plan on scaling the video content for mobile audiences, this is a wonderfully time-saving feature that helps you avoid the drudgery of setting zoom points manually. But it doesn't work with AVI.

To choose between AVI and CAMREC, just click the corresponding radio button. If you try to access any of Recorder's marker or camera video features, you will receive an error message if AVI is selected here. No worries — just come right back and change it to CAMREC.

Notice here that you also have a button labeled **File name options...** available to you. The options contained in the dialog that follows can really help you streamline your work, and here's how. By default, the Camtasia Recorder has a specific way of handling your file data. It prompts you for a file name upon saving, and opens to the most recent folder you last saved to. This is adequate for most users. In fact, most regular users aren't even privy to the fact that these settings are adjustable. Little do they know the files can be automatically saved without having to bother with this dialog at all.

Normally, when you finish your recording, you are prompted to save the file. You must give it a name and specify the desired folder (if it differs from the folder to which you saved last). **Ask for file name** is the program's default. You can, however, set your **Output file name** to be automated. Choosing **Fixed file name** will *always* save your file under a particular name, automatically overwriting the previous iteration. When you clicked on Fixed file name, did you happen to notice that the **Output folder** field became active? Whenever using Fixed file name, you *must* specify an output folder. You can do so by clicking the folder icon next to the Output folder field to browse for the folder, or simply click the field's drop-down arrow to choose from a list of usual suspects. Keep in mind you will get no warning that you're overwriting your old file; Camtasia Recorder will just do it. This method is particularly handy if you're the sort of person who does a million retakes until the video sequence you're working on is perfect (just remember to change the file name here when it finally *is* perfect, so that you don't go overwriting your perfect clip). So, if you've selected this option, the Recorder already knows both the name of your file and the location when recording, and as such you will not be prompted upon saving. At all. So, if you ever start a new video session, finish the recording, and don't get the expected Save As... prompt, this tab is the first place to troubleshoot.

The final file output option is **Automatic File Name**. With this method, you specify a prefix (some project-related word or acronym), and the Camtasia Recorder will save the file with your chosen prefix plus a three-digit number, starting with 001. With each successive file save, the Recorder automatically increments this number so that no existing files get saved over by your new file. Even if you start a new recording session several days later, the Recorder will not "start over" and inadvertently overwrite your old files. It quickly scans your output directory, finds all files with your established prefix, and then increments one digit upward from the highest number it finds. So even if you've moved or deleted some files, all files in your directory will be listed sequentially from first to last.

Capture Options

Let us move on to your **Capture Options**, which will help give you a finer level of control over exactly how the capture is executed. Here we have a number of check boxes:

- **Minimize to system tray during recording.** Checking this option gets the Camtasia Recorder window out of your way when recording is engaged and brings the window back when the recording is paused or stopped. This will ensure that you don't inadvertently capture the Recorder window instead of the desired application. This setting is *on* by default.

- **Pause before starting capture.** This setting starts your recording in paused mode, so that you can do one final sanity check to make sure everything's in place before the capture actually starts. This setting is *off* by default. I used to swear by it, but the setting is now less critical now since the advent of the Camtasia Recorder Selection Area window, since it already lets you see what you'll be capturing prior to recording.

- **Solid capture rectangle.** This check box will change the capture rectangle into a solid rectangle rather than one with angles at each corner. That way, you can have a pixel-exact view of those elements that are included in the capture. If both Hide capture rectangle and Solid capture rectangle are checked, the capture rectangle will be invisible during recording and solid when paused. This option is *off* by default.

- **Hide capture rectangle.** Normally, the capture rectangle is visible during record and paused modes (solid green when paused;

blinking green and black while recording). When this option is enabled, the capture rectangle is invisible. In fact, the only visible indication that you're recording is the Camtasia Recorder icon in your system tray, which blinks red and green during capture. Only when paused is the capture rectangle visible (in solid green). Why would you want to turn off such a helpful visual indicator like the capture rectangle? Well, you may find that even the corner handles of the capture rectangle get in the way of desktop elements, and it's nice to make them invisible for an unobstructed view. You may also find the incessant blinking an annoyance, especially on longer captures. And finally, some screenshot applications and other graphic applications can auto-select individual objects on the desktop, and the capture rectangle can confuse the program, as it sees the capture rectangle and everything inside it as one large object. Hiding the capture rectangle will let you perform the capture while preserving this auto-select functionality. This option is *off* by default.

■ **Report dropped frames.** This is a handy option that will help you monitor how well your system is coping with the capture, telling you in the Recorder's Statistics and Properties area just how many frames the system couldn't capture due to performance issues.

According to these statistics, we haven't dropped a single frame. Yea!

For weaker systems, this is a good way to quickly tell if you're getting in over your head in terms of your Recorder settings or the content you're trying to capture. Obviously, if you choose to enable this option, don't also check Minimize to system tray during recording, as the Recorder window needs to actually be *visible* during recording for it to be of any use. This option is *off* by default.

■ **Round frame size to a 4 pixel boundary.** When compressing your videos, several video codecs (Microsoft Video 1, among others) require that all videos have horizontal and vertical pixel dimensions that are in multiples of four. The TechSmith Screen Capture Codec (TSCC) does not have this limitation. But even if you're only ever planning on using TSCC for your captures (and good for you if you are; that's exactly what you *should* be doing!), you may want to switch to a different codec when producing your final project, and it's nice to have all your bases covered. Unless you absolutely need to have pixel-exact captures, this limitation shouldn't trip you up very often — the heights and widths of every commonly used screen resolution just happen to all be divisible by four, anyway. This option is *on* by default.

- **Capture layered windows.** There are some translucent or irregularly shaped windows, such as the Office Assistant in Microsoft Office, that appear to "float" above the other windows, completely untethered to a standard rectangular window. It's actually not far from the truth — these are called *layered windows*, as the content is actually rendered on a separate layer *above* the desktop action.

Layered windows such as Mr. Clippit here can be readily captured when this option is checked.

Checking this option will allow Camtasia Recorder to record both the desktop screen activity and this additional layer. With it, you can literally capture *everything* you see on your screen. So why not leave it on all the time? Well, capturing these additional layers can really take a toll on your system performance, and your maximum frame rate will definitely take a hit. If you're not recording a video that features any layered windows, it's best to keep this option off until you really need it. It is *off* by default.

 For those of you who capture camera video in addition to screen video, keep in mind that the Camera Preview is itself a layered window, which is how you can see the window on-screen yet not record it with the rest of your content. If you want to capture layered windows *and* watch your Camera Preview, make sure it's well out of the way of your capture area.

- **Disable screen saver during capture.** On longer unmanned captures (such as a lengthy web conferencing session), you might run into problems with the screen saver suddenly kicking on and obscuring everything you're capturing. This option temporarily disables the screen saver. It is *off* by default.

- **Restore cursor location after pause.** Say you're in the middle of making a capture, and you need to pause in order to copy some information from another application. With this option enabled, Camtasia Recorder remembers exactly where your mouse cursor was when you paused. The moment you resume, the cursor is placed right back where you left it. Now playback will be flawless, and it won't look to your audience as if the cursor was magically teleported from one side of the screen to the other. Restore cursor is one of those "don't know how I ever lived without it" sort of options. It's *on* by default, and I strongly recommend keeping it that way.

- **Force popup dialogs into the recording area.** When recording various applications, you're likely to run into the issue of warnings, alerts, and other dialog boxes popping up as you're working with a particular application. This option helps to ensure that all the application dialogs show up in the center of your capture area. Dialogs that are larger than the capture area will appear with the top-left corner in the top-left corner of your capture area. It is *on* by default.

> Keep in mind that in order for this feature to work, you'll need to have Lock to application enabled in the Camtasia Recorder Selection Area window so that the Recorder knows which dialogs to target. Also, due to the fact that different applications often use different technologies for popping up those dialogs, the feature won't work with every dialog in existence. But it will work with most.

- **Show toolbar underneath capture rectangle during recording.** By default, whenever you're performing a screen recording that doesn't consume the full screen, Camtasia Recorder places a small toolbar just below your capture rectangle that lets you quickly pause, resume, stop, etc. It you never use this toolbar, you can turn it off permanently by clearing this check box.

- The **Customize Toolbar…** button will let you add, remove, and reorder some of the tools on the toolbar:

In this dialog, it's easy to add buttons for ScreenDraw, markers, and a command for hiding the toolbar. The arrow buttons on the right-hand side of the dialog will let you reorder them.

Performance Options

Finally, we come to **Performance Options**. As you can see (at least you can if you're running Windows XP; more on this below), there's really only one option: **Disable display acceleration during capture**. This option keeps your system from choking during recording. If you look in your Statistics and Properties area and see that your captured frame rate is only 3 or 4 fps when it should be 15, chances are you're recording with display acceleration enabled. Disabling should bring your actual fps in line with the frame rate you specified.

Why does this make such a difference? When working with your computer, your system normally relies on your video card to assume the load in displaying images on your screen. Especially for processor-intensive programs like games, video, or CAD applications, your video hardware uses display acceleration, which optimizes all those little bits to efficiently travel from your system memory to your video memory. For just about every application *except* screen capture, this tends to speed things up considerably. However, for screen capture and screen recording applications like Camtasia Studio, the data needs to flow in the *opposite* direction, from video memory to system memory. Like a fish trying to swim upstream, the data flow of hardware acceleration actually works against the Camtasia Recorder doing its job. Following our "river" analogy, disabling your hardware acceleration calms these waters, giving the Recorder a much easier time of recording your screen data. In fact, disabling hardware acceleration is probably the single most important thing you can do to improve your maximum frame rate.

Please note that the option to disable display acceleration is only present if you're running Windows XP. Because Windows Vista is so heavily dependent on the graphics card to ensure normal functioning, it does not allow the user to disable graphics acceleration. Users of Vista will therefore need a much more powerful system in order to reliably capture video from their screens. If you're having trouble on Vista, you'll want to try abandoning the sexier Aero theme in favor of Classic. To do this, go to **Start > Control Panel > Personalization**, and click the **Theme** link. In the drop-down list, change the theme to **Windows Classic**. If that doesn't work, try recording a smaller capture area. If that doesn't work, you may need to upgrade your machine.

Note that checking this option disables the display acceleration only during the recording process (i.e., the program is either in record or paused mode). You will see the screen quickly and temporarily go black when first entering record mode, and again when stopping the recording. This is from the Camtasia Recorder turning the display acceleration off and then back on again when finished. If you're doing multiple takes, this constant screen flashing can get old rather quickly. This is why I generally tend to turn off the display acceleration globally, which is a setting in Windows XP. Keep in mind that this affects all applications.

Here's how to **globally disable your display acceleration**:

1. Choose **Start**, and then select **Control Panel**. Open the Display Properties dialog by double-clicking the **Display** icon.

2. Click the **Settings** tab. This is the tab that controls the screen resolution and color depth of your monitor. In the lower right-hand corner of the dialog, you will see the **Advanced** button. Give it a click.

3. Click the **Troubleshoot** tab. Under Hardware Acceleration, drag the slider from Full to **None**. Click **OK**.

4. At the end of your session, repeat steps 1 through 3, this time dragging the slider from None back to **Full**.

One final note about hardware acceleration: Some applications, such as games, media players, and CAD programs, need hardware acceleration in order to function. If the application you want to record refuses to run, you'll need to keep the display acceleration enabled. You can still record it, but you may need to make some concessions. Please see the sections called "Recording Games" and "Recording Media Player Content" in Chapter 5, "Recording Your Screen."

III: Recording

The Video Tab

The **Video** tab is where you can tweak all aspects related to the capture of your video stream, which include the selection of your video codec, your frame rate, and the possibility of doing time-lapse or single-frame recording.

The Video tab of the Tools Options dialog.

The topmost section of the tab, Video configuration, is the most important. **Automatic** is selected by default. This essentially puts the Camtasia Recorder on autopilot, using the settings that generally work best for most users. Note that the settings in the Manual configuration options section are all grayed out. When Automatic is enabled, the Camtasia Recorder records your videos with the following settings:

- The frame rate is automatically determined by the individual constraints of your system.

- The codec used to encode your video will be the TechSmith Screen Capture Codec (TSCC). Don't worry if you have no idea what a codec is; we'll be discussing it later in this chapter.

- Time-lapse capture is disabled. That is, the recording rate and the playback rate are the same.

Now, go ahead and click the **Manual** option; all the settings that were formerly gray and unusable suddenly spring to life! We're going to learn how to adjust each of these to suit our individual needs.

Frame Rate

Let us now dive into these manual settings, the first of which is **Screen capture frame rate.** It breaks down like this: A video file is really nothing more than a series of still pictures arranged in a specific order and played back sequentially, using a media player. These pictures, when played back in rapid succession, simulate movement. A single one of these pictures is called a *frame*. By adjusting the frame rate, you tell the Camtasia Recorder how many pictures it should take of your desired content in a single second. It takes many frames per second (or *fps*) to fluidly depict motion. Your average video camcorder captures motion at 30 fps. Motion pictures (film) are somewhat slower at 24 fps.

So how many frames per second do you need to fluidly capture a screen video? Generally, about 12 to 15 fps is ideal, and this is what I would recommend at the record phase. Later, should you need to pare down the file size a bit, you can then reduce the frames per second at production time. Though somewhat less fluid, you may find that 5 fps is perfectly acceptable for some applications. Go less than that, and things start to get really jerky. But for the recording of slide show applications (such as an animation-free PowerPoint presentation), you'll probably discover that a mere 1 or 2 fps works just fine.

Yes, the frame rate does have an effect on your file size. Just how much of an effect it has depends on the kind of content you're recording, specifically how much motion you've got. For relatively static movies, the difference will be much less pronounced. If a particular frame didn't change at all since the frame before it, it's likely that that frame will have a size of *0 bytes*. Whether you have 5 of these frames in a second or 15, it obviously won't have an appreciable effect on the file size. But if you have motion all over the place, then it behooves you to set your frame rate as low as you can while still maintaining fluidity.

Video Compression

Next, we're going to adjust exactly how the Video track is encoded in our video file. First, let's click on the button labeled **Video Compression....** This will bring us to a dialog designed to let us alter the following codec-related options:

- Choose a video codec
- Enter the number of key frames or the data rate
- Configure the individual codec's options
- Find out more information about the codec

So, What's a Codec, Anyway?

The word "codec" stands for COmpressor/DECompressor. When you record video with Camtasia Studio (or any other video application), that image is digitally converted into binary code, those many many many zeroes and ones that represent all the qualities of the moving picture you just recorded (note that there are also audio codecs; more on those in a bit). A *codec* is a special mathematical algorithm that compresses that code into a smaller file size by implementing a sort of "shorthand" for the code, saving on storage space and speeding up transmission over a network. Different codecs utilize different methods to accomplish this. The codec also decodes all that material so it can be displayed at playback time. The goal of any codec is to maintain as much of the video's quality as possible, while at the same time ensuring that the file in question doesn't take up half your hard drive space. Quality high, file size low. At least in theory.

In practice, there are a number of compromises to be made. First off, keep in mind that some codecs are designed for a specific purpose. For example, there are certain audio codecs that excel at compressing the human voice, but any music in the file will either bloat the file size or merely sound terrible. As another example, the TechSmith Screen Capture Codec (TSCC), as the name implies, can create astoundingly small files of screen video content. The algorithm in this particular codec is designed to efficiently compress large blocks of similar colors that change fairly seldom, as is usually the case in the video of a standard Windows software program. However, as demonstrated in our audio codec example, every codec has a flip side, a set of weaknesses you'll need to keep in mind when using it. In the case of TSCC, it fares poorly when it comes to compressing photographic data, real-world video, color gradients (one color changing gradually into another), and dithered backgrounds (a solid color "polka-dotted" with a different color to make it appear lighter or darker, often used in 8-bit color image formats like GIF to simulate a larger palette of colors). For example, to compress a movie featuring a NASCAR race (a veritable sea of diverse color and motion!), TSCC wouldn't be an appropriate choice at all.

As a rule, codecs (both audio and video) fall into two basic categories: lossy and lossless. A *lossy* codec reduces those file sizes by sacrificing quality. In fact, for most lossy codecs, you can adjust the quality level according to the needs of your project. If you need to transmit long videos over the web, you can crank the quality way down in order to squeeze your work into teeny-tiny files. But be prepared to put up with blurry, artifact-laden video as a result. Or, you can go the opposite way, opting for a superior-looking product. While your file size will certainly be smaller than its uncompressed counterpart, it will be significantly larger than the aforementioned web-ready files. Both extremes can be found in a single codec.

The TechSmith Screen Capture Codec (TSCC), by contrast, is a *lossless* codec. It reduces file size by representing its video content in a more efficient way. But absolutely no quality is lost. So what happens when you try to compress the kind of data that TSCC doesn't handle particularly well (photos, gradients, and the like)? Simple. The codec compresses the content really inefficiently, and the file size bloats exponentially. In fact, depending on the amount of inappropriate content, the resulting file *could* be even larger than if you had left the file completely uncompressed (though this is unlikely).

Its weaknesses aside, TSCC is by far the best codec out there in terms of making screen videos. This is the codec that Camtasia Studio defaults to, and if Automatic on the Tools Options dialog's Video tab is selected, this is in fact the only codec the Camtasia Recorder will *ever* use. Except in very rare circumstances, it's probably the only codec you should use, too.

Now, when checking out the resulting files of your recordings, you may occasionally notice an unusually large file. In this event, you should probably go back and examine the video for the kind of content TSCC typically chokes on. There are, of course, many reasons discussed in this book why your file size might be larger than expected, everything from the video dimensions to the color depth to the compression of your audio (see Appendix A, "Tips for Reducing Your File Size" for a comprehensive list). When it comes to video compression, however, the offending content falls into two basic categories:

- **Lots of colors.** TSCC compresses large blocks of a single color really well. The more colors change from pixel to pixel, the less efficiently it will compress. This applies to photos, detailed line art, and color gradients.

- **Lots of motion.** The compression algorithm in TSCC assumes that not much is going to change visually from frame to frame. That's why it excels at screen data, since it's very often the case that the background will remain static, with only the mouse cursor moving around and pointing at different things. Numerous scene changes, complex animations, or even (egads!) real-world video tend to mean lots of color and motion, and therefore lots of speed bumps in TSCC's compression.

Does this mean you shouldn't have *any* of these elements in your video if recording using TSCC? Nope. You just need to exercise a little common sense in keeping these items to a minimum. However, please note (this is important): Even if you have tons of photographic and real-world video content, if it's at all possible to use TSCC for *recording*, I strongly encourage you to do so. If you record using a lossy codec, and then produce a final cut later on with a lossy codec (regardless of whether it's the same codec or a different one), image quality will continually decrease. Ever try making a photocopy of a photocopy? The same principle applies here. Your video will always look a little bit worse than the video from which it's produced. It's therefore far better to record with TSCC, and then, if the content demands it, produce your final cut in Camtasia Studio using a more forgiving lossy codec like MPEG-4.

Personally, I would only choose a different codec on the recording side under the following two circumstances:

- You have a lot of content that TSCC handles poorly and are not planning on editing the clip later in Camtasia Studio (in other words, recording is your final step), in which case you may want to consider a variant of the MPEG-4 codec.

- You're dealing almost exclusively with lengthy, real-world video content, to the point that the system chokes or the file space needs become prohibitive. In this event, you might simply be better off recording your video clips uncompressed, and then selecting an appropriate codec upon production of your final video.

If your recording needs are such that you absolutely *must* select a different codec, simply click on the drop-down menu under the heading **Compressor**, and you'll see a list of the video codecs installed on your system. I've provided a description of some of the likely contenders in the AVI section of Chapter 12, "The Production Process."

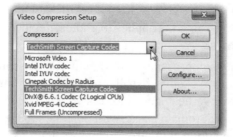

A list of the compressors installed on my system. Depending on the software you have installed, your list may look different.

Please note that Microsoft Windows and its accompanying Windows Media Player come with certain codecs automatically. More are likely to be added as you install different video software applications (for example, TSCC was included when you installed Camtasia Studio). So don't fret if your list doesn't look exactly like mine.

Remember back when I said that the word "codec" stood for COmpressor/DECompressor? This means that when playing back an AVI file you created with Camtasia Studio (or any application, for that matter), it is necessary to have the same codec installed on the playback machine. So, whoever wants to actually view your video will need the same codec you used to *compress* the video so that they can *decompress* and view it on their end. What does that mean for you? Well, keep in mind that the TechSmith Screen Capture Codec is not one of the standard codecs that accompanies Windows. That means that if we're not careful, we could have a distribution problem when trying to share our work with others. Anyone who has ever installed Camtasia Studio gets the codec installed automatically. For anyone else who needs to view TSCC-encoded AVI files, there are a few options:

- Download and install TSCC from TechSmith's web site. The codec is free and freely distributable, so anyone who needs to view TSCC-encoded content can simply download it and they're good to go.

- Download and run Camtasia Player from TechSmith's web site. The Camtasia Player is a simple AVI player that has the TechSmith Screen Capture Codec baked right in. And unlike Windows Media Player, it won't scale your content to fit inside a window, and thus risk making the text in your video completely fuzzy and illegible. It's a great little AVI player that I use to view all my AVI files, and it too is completely free of charge. There's an entire section devoted to the Camtasia Player in Chapter 15, "Other Output Options."

- If you don't want your users to have to download anything prior to viewing your videos, you could use the Pack and Show functionality within Camtasia Studio to turn your AVI video into an executable (EXE) file that can be played on any machine. We'll discuss this a bit more in Chapter 15, "Other Output Options."

As the Camtasia Recorder only spits out AVI files (remember, CAMREC files also use AVI for the actual screen video footage), I have therefore only discussed our AVI options here. However, do keep in mind that we'll have a great many more possibilities for distributing our content when we get to the Production Wizard within Camtasia Studio and its dizzying array of output methods. But for the time being, let's continue our discussion of codecs and the other options here on the Video tab. Now that we know a bit more about video codecs, it's time to choose one and set its options.

When you clicked the **Video Compression...** button, you were presented with a list of codecs. Each one has its own unique set of options. Depending on the codec you select, it's possible that certain options will be disabled. For example, in the following figure we see that with TSCC (our default codec), you can alter the number of key frames but not the quality or data rate.

The compression options for the TechSmith Screen Capture Codec (TSCC).

The Compression Quality Slider

The Compression Quality control is a manual slider that lets you set the general quality of the video picture. It's only available with (certain) lossy codecs. Set the slider low, and you'll get a comparatively small file, but the quality will suffer. Move the slider up, and you'll take full advantage of the quality capabilities of the codec, but you'll need a bit more drive space to accommodate the resulting file. Exactly *how much* difference in quality or file size you'll experience depends on the individual codec as well as on your content. Simply experiment, and you'll find a nice compromise between size and quality.

What's a Key Frame?

As I mentioned in our section on frame rates, a *frame* is one single picture that makes up your video. Perhaps you've seen those old flipbooks that had a drawing on each page, and flipping the pages made it look like the image was moving. One of those pages would constitute a frame. A *key frame* is a frame that has a complete picture in it. Also called an I-frame (short for "intra-frame"), a key frame anchors your video by providing a fully assembled image every so many frames. The compressor looks at this frame independently of any content that preceded it. However, there is a second type of frame, called a *delta frame* (or D-frame)*. These frames follow the key frame, and are all based on

---

* In addition, there's actually a third type of frame, called a bi-directional frame (or B-frame), but since TSCC doesn't use B-frames, I'll leave them out of the discussion for now.

the key frame before it. They comprise most of your frames. Basically, only the parts of the image in the delta frame that have changed since the previous frame get encoded, going backward to the most recent key frame.

For lossy codecs, the more key frames you have, the better the video's quality, but keep in mind that key frames do take up more file space than do D-frames. Videos created with lossless codecs always maintain their perfect quality, but adjusting the key frame rate does have an effect. Set the rate lower, and you're likely to decrease file size, as key frames take up more space than other kinds of frames. However, set it too low, and your audience could run into seeking issues when scrolling through your video. Say, for example, that you have a key frame every 200 frames, starting with frame 1. Moving the playback head to frame 199 might cause the playback to hang for a second or two, because frame 199 builds on frame 198, which in turn builds on frame 197, and so on, all the way back to the most recent key frame (in this case, frame 1). The TSCC codec defaults to one key frame every 80 frames, and there's really no reason to change this. TSCC is comparatively efficient at compiling a full image from the last key frame and any delta frames that follow it.

Specifying the Data Rate

Utilized in some of the lossy codecs, this option gives you the ability to specify the *data rate*, that is, the amount of file space (in this case measured in kilobytes, or KB, per second). Ever see advertisements for the Priceline.com travel service that allows you to "set your own price"? It sort of works like that. You give the codec a certain number of KB per second to work with, and the codec does its best to work within those parameters, giving you the best quality it possibly can at the desired file size. The higher the number, the better the quality.

Other Compression Options

You may have noticed that this little dialog sports two additional buttons, **Configure...** and **About....** Both of these buttons are context sensitive. Clicking them will pull up dialogs created by whatever third party produced the codec in question. The Configure... button will allow you to play around with any additional options allowed by the codec. This can include anything from setting the number of passes (i.e., whether the video is compressed on the fly or it's analyzed first to achieve better compression) to specifying the pixel aspect ratio. This dialog will look completely different from codec to codec, and it is well beyond the scope of this book to address the configuration options of each codec, with the noted exception of the TechSmith Screen Capture Codec.

In the TSCC Configuration dialog, you have one simple control — a slider that lets you adjust the quality of compression. You can choose somewhere on the spectrum between **faster compression**, where the video doesn't take as long to compress (save), but you may have a slightly larger file, and **better compression**, where the codec takes its own sweet time compressing your file, but once it's done, you'll have a smaller file for your efforts. Note that you can always opt for a spot somewhere in the middle. Whichever place on the spectrum you choose is a matter of personal taste, depending on how patient you are (the length of your average video clip is obviously a consideration here) and the extent to which file size is a consideration for you. My personal choice (and, probably not coincidentally, the application's default) is to have the codec set to *faster* compression during the recording stage when capturing the files with Recorder, and have it set to *better* compression in the main Camtasia Studio application to produce your final video, since that's likely to be the file you're actually sharing.

Now, on to the About... dialog. This is simply general info about whatever codec you've selected. It's useful for finding out version information as well as the organization's web site should you want more information about the codec (or the latest download). And that's all there is to the Video Compression Setup dialog. Go ahead and close it for now.

Screen Capture Mode

At the bottom of the Video tab, you've got a few options pertaining to the screen capture mode. At least 90% of the time, you'll be working with **Normal screen capture**. This is your standard capture mode that records your video at a set number of frames per second and then outputs them to a file. All recordings we've done up to this point have been normal screen captures. But there are a few specialty capture modes that can be extraordinarily useful in certain circumstances. Let's discuss these now, starting with Live output capture.

Live Output Capture

In addition to outputting an AVI/CAMREC file using the Camtasia Recorder, you also have the option of having the Recorder act as a "live camera." The Recorder films all the action as it normally would, only rather than saving that content as a file, it passes that video material to third-party programs that can make use of live camera content, such as webcam and video conferencing applications. The **Live Output** feature lets these applications use the Camtasia Recorder as a video source, and the Recorder can therefore provide these applications with a video feed that can be broadcast over a network or the Internet. Rather than using a real hardware camera, which would transmit a video image of you, Camtasia Recorder is providing the video image, this time of your screen.

To turn on Live Output, choose **Live output capture** as the screen capture mode. Now, when you hit the Record button (or its corresponding hotkey), the Camtasia Recorder isn't actually saving any data, but rather feeding that data to the other application. Before we start streaming our screen, however, let's set a few additional options. This is done by clicking the **Live Output Setup...** button.

Live capture rate allows you to specify just how often the video frames are updated during capture, and is measured in frames per second (fps). This can be used to more tightly manage your system resources, as capturing video of your screen and encoding this information for streaming concurrently can take quite a toll on your system.

Now that we've turned on Live Output and specified the Live capture rate setting, it's time to choose the **Default Video Format...** button. Here you can choose the **Image Format**, selecting from an 8-bit (256-color) palette, 16-bit (65,536-color) RGB output, 24-bit (16,777,215-color) RGB output, and 32-bit (4,294,967,296-color) RGB output. Next, we need to select our **Image Dimensions**. You can either select from a list of common dimension standards by clicking the drop-down menu or specify a **Custom Size**. Simply check the corresponding check box and then enter the width and height of your recording area in pixels. Note that the size settings of the live output server will override any default you set here, so if the size of your recording differs from what you expected, examine the settings of the third-party application and set the output dimensions there.

To summarize, if you have a web conferencing system or some other live encoding software and wish to broadcast your screen using the Camtasia Recorder, here's how to **set up and execute a Live Output capture:**

1. Select **Live output capture** from the list of screen capture modes on the Video tab within Tools Options. Click **Live Output Setup....**

2. Specify the **Live capture rate.** Five frames per second is adequate for most uses.

3. Click on the **Default Video Format...** button to stipulate the default image format and image dimensions of your capture. Click **OK.**

4. Choose **OK** twice more to exit the Tools Options dialog.

5. Start the encoding application to which you want to send the Live Output stream.

6. Once you've tweaked the desired settings in this application, click **Record** in the Camtasia Recorder to begin the output.

Note that all the Recorder-based special effects (such as cursor highlights, annotation effects, and zoom and pan) still function with Live Output and will be viewable on the other end. Also, keep in mind that Live Output automatically makes a recording based on the dimensions stipulated by the live output server (or, if none are specified, by the dimension settings in your Camtasia Studio Video Capture Format dialog, available by clicking **Default Video Format...** on the Live Output Setup dialog). The standard input options such as Screen, Window, Region, and Fixed Region are not available.

 A few older live encoding applications will only let you have one default video capture device. You open your encoding app and try to select the Camtasia Studio Video Capture driver, only to discover that you can't select it — you're stuck with the driver for a webcam or video capture card. If this is the case, you'll need to temporarily disable the offending device(s) if you wish to use Live Output. Please consult your Camtasia Studio documentation for instructions on how to do this.

Unfortunately, there's not a lot of call nowadays for Live Output. Most web conferencing applications have screen broadcast capabilities built in. Also, the Camtasia Recorder will *not* record camera video when Live Output is enabled, so if you had hoped to broadcast both your screen video and a webcam stream of your face, then you are, sadly, out of luck. With its real-world uses dwindling as current web conferencing software becomes more sophisticated, Camtasia Studio no longer even installs Live Output by default. The option to install this functionality must be checked during initial installation. If you try to use Live Output and find an alert message that the Camtasia Video Capture driver isn't installed, you'll need to go back and reinstall the application, this time checking the box labeled **Install Live Output Support.**

Single-Frame Capture

Under normal circumstances, engaging Record will begin the capture at the frame rate you established on the Video tab of the Tools Options dialog, and the capture will continue until you stop it (or until you run out of drive space). But there is another capture mode that pays no attention to the specified frame rate. Single frame capture lets you manually take a single-frame shot with every click of the Record button (or press of its corresponding hotkey). This allows you to do stop-frame animations, slide shows, and custom time-lapse effects that speed up or slow down as needed. Like the shutter button of a camera, this option will let you snap individual shots of the capture area as desired. In fact, if you have the Record function mapped to a hotkey (such as F9), it's possible to do a "burst" capture by holding down this key.

Directing the action is easy. You can incrementally move or resize elements within the capture area in order to achieve different motion effects. When finished with your capture, choosing Stop will save the chain of individually captured frames as an AVI or CAMREC file.

Please note that single-frame capture also plays nicely with time-lapse capture when assembling a slide show presentation. For example, in the Time-lapse Capture Setup dialog, setting the capture's playback rate to one frame every five seconds will produce an AVI where every frame displays for five seconds, which is ideal for a slide show. Keep in mind that the capture rate settings in this dialog will be ignored, as the capture rate in this instance still just depends on how often you press the Record button.

Time-Lapse Capture

Have you ever watched nature shows on the Discovery Channel? Nature videographers are big fans of time-lapse photography. They may speed up the action to show the complete life cycle of a daffodil in 20 seconds. They may also slow time down to reveal the grace and beauty of a cheetah chasing down a gazelle (though it becomes markedly less graceful and beautiful when the cheetah actually catches it).

Camtasia Studio allows you that same kind of precision. Want a quickie marketing spot to show off all the neat features of your new art palette in just a few seconds? Or perhaps you'd like a tutorial that dissects a complicated step-by-step procedure? You can easily speed up or slow things down accordingly.

Notice here on the Video tab that the **Time-lapse capture** check box is unchecked by default. If you check it, you now have a button available that will lead you to a dialog where you can adjust the capture and playback rates. This supplants the usual frame rate control, which is now grayed out. Go ahead and give the **Time-Lapse Setup...** button a click. Here's what the dialog looks like:

The Time-lapse Capture Setup dialog. With the settings shown here, the video would play back at three times the speed at which it was captured.

Note that this dialog is split into two parts: capture rate and playback rate. Also note that we're not necessarily talking about frames per second here. You could set Camtasia Recorder to record a certain number of frames per *minute*, even per *hour*. For example, you could set Recorder to periodically take a frame of a program's status window (say, every five minutes), and be able to browse the whole night's activity in less than a minute when you come in the next morning.

Another handy use for time-lapse capture is the ability to more fluidly capture animated sequences from applications like Microsoft PowerPoint or Adobe Flash. This is particularly handy if your system specs are less than cutting edge. I explain in detail how to do this in Chapters 5 and 8.

So how does it work? Just enter the desired number of frames per second/minute/hour in the **AVI capture rate** field, and Camtasia Studio will record your video at that frame rate. When you enter a different value into the **AVI Playback Rate** field, special information is embedded into your video file, instructing the media player to play back your file at this rate. So, if you set the video to record at 5 frames per second but play back at 25 frames per second, the resulting video will display five times faster. Neat, huh?

There are a couple of caveats of which you need to be aware, however. First, rather than mucking around with speeding up or slowing down your corresponding audio recordings, Camtasia Recorder *entirely disables* the simultaneous recording of audio during capture. Of course, if you want to narrate the time-lapse segment, nothing prevents you from doing so later when editing the clip in Camtasia Studio. But you can't record audio at capture time. After all, what good is audio narration if you end up sounding like Darth Vader or Alvin from the Chipmunks?

Second, keep in mind that your Statistics area inside the Camtasia Recorder interface will show the actual length of your video when played back, not the elapsed time you've been recording. If you take our example above where you recorded at 5 fps and played back at 25 fps, this means that five seconds would elapse during capture before you would see one second tick by on the video's length.

Statistics:		See the length of
Frames:	204 (0 dropped)	this video so far?
Rate:	5.00 frames/sec	Eight seconds.
Length:	00:08	We've actually
Zoom:	640 x 480 (100%)	been recording for
Audio:		40 seconds.
Properties:		
Size:	640 x 480	
Colors:	16777216	
Rate:	5 frames/sec	
Codec:	TSCC	

Pause　　Stop　　Delete

Also, while the Video section of your main Recorder interface tells you when time-lapse capture mode is engaged, it's rather easy to miss. Make sure you go back into your options and disable it when you no longer need it. I've had to rerecord many a clip from inadvertently leaving my Time-lapse capture check box enabled.

The Audio Tab

Now that we've tackled our video settings, it's time to work on audio. Unless you're doing a time-lapse capture, the Camtasia Recorder allows you to record audio narration (or audio from your system) during your video capture. Here on the **Audio** tab of our Tools Options dialog, we can influence several aspects of recording this audio, from choosing a codec to selecting a capture device. We'll discuss all of these options in turn.

Selecting an Input: Audio Devices and Sources

In the last few chapters, we've discussed audio narration and sound effects, and how to implement them in your recordings. Here on the Audio tab, we'll be able to tweak the audio, both for input and output. On the input side, you've got three basic qualities to adjust:

- The capture device
- The input source
- The recording volume

Adjusting the audio capture device, source, or volume here changes these settings *globally*, not just in Camtasia Studio. By clicking the **Device** drop-down list, you can set which audio driver you wish to use when recording your sound. This driver is typically tied to a sound card or audio interface device. The options in this list will vary depending on the hardware and software on your system. Except in rare circumstances, you're going to choose the driver that corresponds to your sound card or audio interface.

Of course, every device will offer one or more sources. If you've ever looked at the back of your computer and located your sound card, you know that you've probably got four or five jacks all lined up in a row. A few of these are for output, like your speakers, but at least a couple of them are likely to be input jacks, like a microphone, MIDI device, or line in jack. Most sound cards also support the ability to record from the system itself; that is, record what you hear on your computer. To record a particular source, just select it from the **Source** drop-down list. Now, it's very likely that you'll be completely mystified as to the functions of some of the sources you'll find. A full discussion of audio equipment and source selection can be found in Chapter 10, "Working with Other Media: Audio, PIP, and Title Clips."

Next on the Audio tab, you'll find a volume meter as well as a slider tool for adjusting the sensitivity of your recording. To test the volume, get some sound cranking through the selected device and source (i.e., speak into the mic, or play some sound on your computer if recording from the system). You can then get a sense of where to set the volume slider (try to keep the input in the orange part of the meter without going into the red).

Of course, if you're not sure which device or source you need, help is just a click away. If you click the **Audio Setup Wizard...** button, you'll find the same simple Audio Setup Wizard that we first saw in Chapter 5.

Selecting an Output: Audio Format

Let's move on to our Audio Format settings. Microsoft designed AVI files to be ready for sound. The audio track contained in an AVI file is Microsoft Waveform Audio (WAV), which can either be part of an AVI or exist as a stand-alone file. In fact, you can use Camtasia Studio to actually split an AVI, saving the WAV data as a separate file. More on this in Chapter 9. For now, go ahead and click the **Audio format...** button. Now, just as there are video codecs for compressing video, the AVI file system also has a number of audio codecs for getting the size of the audio track down. Since uncompressed audio (called PCM, or pulse code modulation) can take upward of 172 KB *per second* for CD-quality audio, it is imperative to have good audio compression to keep those file sizes manageable. Virtually all audio codecs are *lossy*; to keep the audio lossless, you have to keep it uncompressed.

The default recording format for the Camtasia Recorder is the TechSmith LAME MPEG Layer-3 codec, a very high-quality MP3 encoder. This yields a highly compressed file with very little loss in quality. While seeming like an ideal solution, I tend to ignore the good but lossy default in this case, and I encourage you to do the same. Here's why:

I am of the opinion that, as with video compression, you should refrain from doing *any* lossy compression here at the recording stage unless recording the AVI is your final step (no editing). If this is the case, please see the AVI section of Chapter 12, "The Production Process" for a breakdown of the more common audio codecs. Otherwise, you should be recording an uncompressed sound file using PCM, working with PCM all through the editing process, and *then* choosing a codec for compressing the final distributed product.

Now, when selecting a compression method, in fact even with uncompressed (PCM) audio, you'll have a few choices to make in terms of the codec's attributes. You have three basic attributes that need to be set: the sample rate of your recording, the bit depth, and whether you wish to record in mono or stereo. The **sample rate** is, simply put, the number of samples (digital snapshots of an audio waveform) per second. The higher the sample rate, the greater the number of sound frequencies that can be reproduced (and, of course, the larger the file). In order to accurately reproduce a particular frequency, the sample rate has to be set to *double* that frequency. This is called the Nyquist frequency, and is the reason why audio CDs use a sample rate of 44,100 Hz (44.1 kHz). Its corresponding Nyquist frequency is 22,050 Hz, just outside the range of human hearing (20,000 Hz). When you record your audio with the Camtasia Recorder, it's always best to start with a high sample rate in order to achieve the highest quality possible, and then sample down if needed.

Next comes **bit depth,** also called *bit resolution*. Bit depth refers to the number of unique amplitude levels in your recording, and generally, you have two choices: 8 bit and 16 bit. Just as 8-bit color depth gives you a maximum of 256 colors to play with, 8-bit resolution provides you a maximum of 256 levels of amplitude. This produces a 48 dB dynamic range. A resolution of 16 bit gives you 65,536 amplitude levels, doubling the dynamic range to 96 dB. Some audio applications can now provide up to 32-bit resolution, though these are still the exception (Camtasia Studio does not), and many of today's sound cards cannot yet support 32 bit. For recording your initial clips, I'd recommend setting the bit depth to 16-bit resolution.

And lastly, we have the choice between **mono** and **stereo**. This one is usually a no-brainer. Ninety-nine percent of the time, you're going to choose *mono*. Why? Because you're probably recording your own voice from a single microphone. One mic, one source. And when you only have one source for recording, it makes no sense to create a stereo WAV file from it, as the exact same thing would be playing from both speakers anyway. A monophonic signal will take up half the file space, and give you the same result. Of course, stereo signals do have their uses in screen recording, albeit rare. For those readers who have been spending their entire lives in a cave in Siberia and have never owned a hi-fi, a stereo signal is one with two channels, a left channel and a right channel. This allows for spatial positioning of sound content on a spectrum from left to right. There are only two reasons you would ever want to set the Recorder's signal output to stereo:

- You and a colleague are both narrating the video using separate microphones, and wish to separate the voices into distinctive channels. Even then, I'd probably record mono to save on file space, unless your voices are so similar that you fear your audience wouldn't be able to tell you apart otherwise.

- You are recording system sound from an application with stereo sound. Once again, practicality would probably win out over precision, and I would actually still select mono to cut the file size in half.

For those keeping score at home, my recommendation for recording audio is 44.1 kHz, 16 Bit, Mono. Here in the Audio Format dialog, I can click the **Attributes** drop-down menu, and make my choice. Note that the data rate appears next to every possible attribute combination, a handy reference for finding an acceptable set of attributes. From this, I can see that my chosen attributes will give me a data rate of 86 KB/sec. So, if I have two minutes of video, the audio portion will take up about 5 MB. Large, but not unwieldy. Obviously, don't forget to factor in the Video track when guesstimating the file size.

PCM uncompressed audio and its endless combinations of attributes.

Also, notice here that we have a handy way of saving off presets of codecs and attributes we use a lot. We can call these up by utilizing the drop-down box labeled **Name**. As you can see, you have four presets already done for you. You can clear any or all of these if desired by selecting the preset you want to disappear and clicking **Remove**. To add a new preset, simply choose the desired codec and attributes, and then click **Save As....**

A list of audio presets. As you can see, it's easy to add presets as your needs grow more complex.

Especially if you're working with a lot of different output formats, setting up your audio properties this way can be a real time-saver. Also, keep in mind that you have access to the same library of presets regardless of whether you're in the Camtasia Recorder or the main Camtasia Studio application, which is rather practical.

The Camera Tab

With the addition of camera video to your repertoire of recordable streams, you now have the **Camera** tab to select the appropriate video device and adjust the camera's settings. If you're going to record camera video, then the first thing you need to do is to choose from the drop-down list of **Available video devices**. If you only have a single webcam attached to your computer, then that's probably the only video device you'll see. However, there are other devices that can also be attached and used as a video device besides webcams, such as:

- A digital video camcorder, attached to your computer via IEEE 1394 (FireWire) or USB
- Certain digital cameras
- A video capture card that records video from an analog source (such as a VCR)
- A television capture card

The **Camera Properties…** button allows you to adjust a variety of settings for your webcam or other video device. While I can't tell you exactly what you'll see when clicking this button (as all these settings come directly from the driver software of the individual device), you're likely to see some or all of the following:

- Screen image settings (contrast, hue, saturation, gamma, etc.)
- Gain control (adjusting the level of exposure, for example)
- Image mirror (flipping the captured image on the vertical and/or horizontal axis)
- Other enhancements such as low light boost and anti-flicker compensation

Like Camera Properties, the **Video Format…** button also offers settings from the capture device's display drivers, this time focusing on the file output settings. While obviously varying from device to device, you can generally alter settings like:

- The video frame rate
- The number of colors
- The dimensions of your video output (window size)
- Key frame control
- Overall image quality/compression

If you start monkeying with these various settings and get in too far over your head, note that you also have the **Default** button at your disposal. A click of this handy "do-over" button will reset the Video Format options, restore the default video capture device, and reinitialize everything.

Note that this dialog also sports a useful **Preview** window. This window will not only let you ensure that you have the correct video device selected but will also update in real time, so if you altered any of the camera properties, you'll see those changes right away in the preview. It's a practical way of helping you figure out which tweaks enhance the video quality and which detract from it.

When capturing the stream from your webcam or video input device, this data is saved in WMV format inside the CAMREC file, using the WMV7 codec. This codec features fast encoding so that your captures with camera video don't experience too much of a slowdown.

When you're finished adjusting your settings, click **OK** to exit the dialog.

The Hotkeys Tab

While the Camtasia Recorder interface allows for complete mouse-driven control of the program, some users are simply more comfortable and efficient using their keyboards. The **Hotkeys** tab of the Tools Options dialog will allow you to stipulate *hotkeys*, which are keys or combinations of keys that will execute a given command. You have a few hotkeys set up for you by default. Pressing the **F9** key will start or pause the recording. It's the same as clicking the Record button on the Main toolbar or choosing Record from the Capture menu, except that multiple presses of the hotkey will toggle between record and pause. Pressing **F10** will stop the recording, the equivalent of clicking the Stop button or selecting Stop from the Capture menu. Pressing **Ctrl+Shift-M** will add a marker to your video that can later be manipulated in Camtasia Studio (if grayed out, then Recorder is currently set for recording to AVI; use CAMREC instead). **Ctrl+Shift-D** will activate ScreenDraw. These hotkeys can be fully configured on this tab, so if you already have these keys assigned to something else or you simply want a hotkey that's easier for you to remember, just change it.

To assign a hotkey to a function, you must first select a key, which can be pretty much any of the alphanumeric keys, function ("F-") keys, or the Print Screen key (PrtScr). In addition to this key, you can add a custom combination of extension keys, if desired. The Control (Ctrl), Shift (Shift), and Alt (Alt) keys are available, either singly or in combination. Just check the appropriate boxes. The command is then executed by holding down any applicable extension key(s), and then pressing the main key. For example, if you have the Record/Pause command mapped to Ctrl+Alt-R, you would hold down the former two keys, and then press the latter.

Just as Record/Pause is a toggled command, the **ScreenDraw** hotkey will also toggle your last chosen ScreenDraw tool on and off. You can find out all about the ScreenDraw tool in Chapter 6, "Special Effects of the Camtasia Recorder." Note that you also have the option of configuring hotkeys for five lesser-used commands. To reach these options, simply click the **Advanced...** button. You can assign hotkeys for the following commands:

- **AutoPan.** When pressed, Camtasia Recorder's AutoPan mode will engage, and the capture area (if less than full screen) will begin to follow the mouse cursor as it moves about the screen. Pressing the hotkey again will disengage AutoPan, and the capture area will remain in the current location.

- **Hide Tray Icon.** This hotkey will toggle the visibility of the Recorder's icon in your Windows system tray.

- **Zoom In** and **Zoom Out.** Each successive press of one of these hotkeys will zoom farther. You can zoom as far out as full screen and as far in as 1,000% or more of the original recording window.

- **Mute.** This hotkey essentially silences all sound in the recording, be it microphone audio, mouse cursor sounds, or keyboard sounds. You can still hear sound coming from the system, but nothing will be recorded. Pressing the hotkey again will re-enable whatever sound functions were active prior to the mute.

The Program Tab

The final tab in the Tools Options dialog, **Program**, allows you to adjust some general Recorder-related settings. Here we see two sections: Program options and Temporary file folder. Let's talk about the **Program options** first. Notice that you have four check boxes:

- **Always on top.** This option keeps the Camtasia Recorder window on top and visible at all times. Any opened windows will still appear below the Recorder window.

- **Enable tips.** This option keeps a handy array of tips at your disposal. When experimenting with certain options for the first time (e.g., Time-lapse capture), a special tip dialog appears, explaining the feature in question. Note that you have the option of disabling *individual* tips by unchecking the Show tip again box within that dialog. This check box is merely a handy tool for enabling/disabling these tips globally.

- **Display recording preview after recording is stopped.** Remember the window that pops up after each recording and plays back your video? The recording preview allows you to quickly go over your work, and either discard it if you think it's utter crap or give the file your stamp of approval so that you can save it. I personally find it an invaluable tool. However, for some applications (systems monitoring, for example), previewing the file before saving is unnecessary. Also, some may prefer to disable it as a matter of personal taste, wanting to save themselves a little time by skipping the preview. This isn't really a time-saver in my opinion, but it's nice that Recorder gives you the option. You can turn the preview off by clearing this check box.

- **Display options dialog after recording is saved.** When this option is checked, you're presented with an additional dialog after saving your file. It provides you with a few choices regarding what you want to do next. Three of them, actually:

    - **Edit my recording**, which brings your freshly recorded video into Camtasia Studio for further editing.

    - **Produce my video in a shareable format**, which skips the editing process and produces your clip as a stand-alone video in any of nine different file formats.

    - **Create another recording**, which takes you right back to the Camtasia Recorder, so you can get busy recording your next clip.

Unchecking Display options dialog after recording is saved is basically the same as always checking the third option. After saving, this dialog won't appear, and you will always return to the Recorder to capture additional clips. Whether you'll want to check this box depends on your own personal workflow.

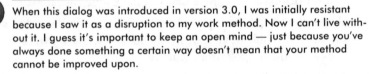

When this dialog was introduced in version 3.0, I was initially resistant because I saw it as a disruption to my work method. Now I can't live without it. I guess it's important to keep an open mind — just because you've always done something a certain way doesn't mean that your method cannot be improved upon.

Returning to the Program tab, you probably noticed here that you also have a field for specifying the application's **Temporary file folder.** This is the directory where Camtasia Recorder will store data as it's being captured, right up until the moment you finish the recording and save it as an AVI or CAMREC file. It will default to the Temp folder on your C: drive, but feel free to change it if you have another fast drive with more space. For instance, I have a large scratch drive where I save all my video work — my temp file is on this drive as well.

Summary

In this chapter, we explored the Tools Options dialog. We learned how to alter the Recorder's various preferences by tweaking options on the dialog's six tabs:

- **Capture.** Set various capture and performance options as well as choose how and in which format the recorded file is saved.

- **Video.** Select a video codec, change the frame rate, and select a screen capture mode.

- **Audio.** Choose an input device and source, set volume sensitivity, and choose an output format and accompanying attributes.

- **Camera.** Choose an appropriate video device for the capture of camera video content, and access the camera properties and video format options as well.

- **Hotkeys.** Specify keyboard hotkeys for up to nine commonly used commands.

- **Program.** Set general program preferences as well as stipulate a temporary file folder for storing recordings in progress.

So now you've mastered all the options of Camtasia Recorder, both for special effects and for the application's various preferences. In the next and final chapter of this unit, we'll be talking about recording your PowerPoint presentations using the Camtasia Studio Add-in for PowerPoint.

Exercises

1. Set up and execute a time-lapse capture, using the settings to make a video that plays three times *slower* than usual. Preview the results. Remember to turn off time-lapse recording when finished.

2. Save an audio preset called "Master Quality" in **PCM** format with attributes of **44.1 kHz, 16 Bit, Mono**.

3. On the Hotkeys tab of the Tools Options dialog, a number of commands do not yet have hotkeys assigned. Assign a hotkey to each command, and test out your established hotkeys while recording.

4. If working on Windows XP, access the Capture tab of the Tools Options dialog, and uncheck **Disable display acceleration during capture**. Try making a test recording. Does it play back as smoothly as before? Try disabling display acceleration globally using the instructions in this chapter. Unless you regularly play games or use CAD applications, you may want to leave it off all the time.

Chapter 8

Recording Your PowerPoint Presentation

When it comes to sharing information with customers, clients, and colleagues, Microsoft PowerPoint has been the number one application for over a decade. While terrific for in-person demonstrations, PowerPoint does leave something to be desired when trying to package your presentation for viewing when you may not be there. That's why Camtasia Studio has been so popular with PowerPoint gurus all over the world. A couple of years ago, Camtasia Studio developed a special add-in module for Microsoft PowerPoint* that allowed users to record their presentations without ever starting up the Recorder. The add-in sits right in your PowerPoint toolbar, always at the ready, and offers much (but not all) of the functionality of the Camtasia Recorder.

The Camtasia Studio Add-in for PowerPoint.

In addition to recording the presentation window, this add-in can also import the recorded presentation directly into Camtasia Studio, complete with markers for each slide. These markers are automatically labeled using titles from the presentation, and are ideal for quickly setting up a table of contents for use in exporting to the web. Additionally, your PowerPoint notes can be imported for those wishing to add captions to their videos.

---

* The instructions in this chapter are specific to PowerPoint 2007, but other versions should work similarly. The Camtasia Studio Add-in supports PowerPoint 2000, XP, 2003, and 2007.

Why Record Your PowerPoint Presentations?

You may be thinking, "My PowerPoint presentations can *already* be viewed by other people, online or off. Why in the world would I want to convert them to a Camtasia Studio recording? That sounds like a lot of effort." Good question. To answer it, let's discuss some of the things a video can offer that a standard PowerPoint presentation cannot.

Almost as Good as Being There

For every person who attends your live presentation, 30 or more people may end up viewing it in archived form. Will those people receive the same benefit when paging through your PowerPoint file after the fact? Will this presentation contain your narration, your ink comments, even your face? I know that when looking over a PowerPoint file from a presentation I wasn't able to attend, I simply couldn't shake the feeling that I was viewing a "ghost" of a presentation. Yes, I had the raw slide data, possibly even some notes if the presenter was diligent. But without the presenter to guide me through the content, I got lost very quickly. Imagine if you could take the "live-ness" of your PowerPoint file and preserve it as part of your presentation. With Camtasia Studio, you can do just that.

Audio and Video

While PowerPoint does allow you to add audio narration to your slides, it does not let you use audio codecs to compress your narration, so a lengthy presentation can get quite unwieldy. Also, PowerPoint does not allow you to include a video of yourself. With the camera video options in Camtasia Studio, you can actually film yourself giving the presentation. This video is placed in a small video window, either inside the video window itself (picture-in-picture) or in a special side-by-side format. This second video stream is perfectly synced to your screen video. In addition to being a great supplement to your archived presentation, the camera video can also serve as a rehearsal tool. Just hit Record, practice your presentation, and then you can analyze your presentation style, timing, and appearance.

Ink Annotations

One of the great features of PowerPoint is ink annotations, the ability to take your mouse and scribble all over your presentation to draw attention to certain points. This is now made even easier with the use of a tablet PC. The problem is that once your presentation is over, you either have to discard them or (provided you have a more recent version of Microsoft Office) save them as static drawings within your presentation, thus making your slides look cluttered and ugly. But when you record the presentation with the Camtasia Recorder, the actual animation of drawing those images is preserved. Just as if you were there.

Portability

To view a PowerPoint presentation, you must have either Microsoft Office or Microsoft's free PowerPoint player. Camtasia Studio allows you to avoid the issue of viewer software by outputting your presentation in a number of formats, such as AVI, MOV, SWF, and WMV, among others. So, no matter what the audience, you'll have a way to reach them.

Better Playback Control

When I open a PowerPoint file, it opens in Edit mode. I have to click to start the actual presentation and, depending on how it's set up, it will either automatically take me through slide by slide based on timed events, or I have to manually click. I also have no idea how long it will take to view the presentation in its entirety. With most of the output formats offered by Camtasia Studio, however, you have VCR-like controls as well as a view of the elapsed time and total running time. I can tell exactly where I am in the presentation, and how long I have to go. Plus, navigating through a very long presentation is a lot simpler.

Interactive Features

With the addition of Flash hotspots and quizzing, you can add some interactivity to a formerly flat and linear presentation. If you want to poll your users or test their knowledge about your video content, it's pretty straightforward to do so with Camtasia Studio's quizzing and survey features. If you want to add a button that, when clicked, automatically takes you to a web site, you can do that too.

Security

You may have presentations that you want to distribute, but you'd rather not have users editing your content. While PowerPoint 2002 and later give you the ability to issue a password so that users can't edit your file, this also means that people with versions prior to 2002 won't be able to view your presentation *at all*. Besides, there are utility programs out there that can easily crack any Office password. Fortunately, Camtasia Studio allows you to distribute your PowerPoint slide content in a number of formats, none of which will allow even the most determined would-be plagiarist to mess with it.

Capture of Third-Party Applications

During your PowerPoint presentation, you might have cause to reference Word docs, Excel spreadsheets, or any number of other third-party applications and documents to help you get your point across. Camtasia Studio effortlessly captures *all* that appears on your monitor, so that you can distribute these segments along with your PowerPoint content in one cohesive package.

Camtasia Studio Add-In Toolbar

Now that we've talked about the *why* of making a video out of your PowerPoint presentation, let's move on to the *how*. For this, it's time to explore the actual toolbar:

The Camtasia Studio Add-in for PowerPoint toolbar.

Simply launch PowerPoint, and the add-in appears in your toolbar palette automatically. The toolbar sports six buttons:

- **Launch Presentation and Start Recording.** This will put PowerPoint into Slide Show view and begin the recording process.
- **Record Audio.** If pressed, this button will record all sound from the microphone while the capture is in progress. As I'll discuss in a minute, it can also be set to record any sound from the system, such as sound effects within PowerPoint or any prerecorded narration embedded in the PowerPoint file. It is *on* by default.

- **Record Camera.** When clicked, this will enable the capture of camera video. This video data is saved as a separate stream inside the resulting CAMREC file. During editing, you can superimpose this video over your screen video, setting its size and position as desired, or place it next to your presentation in a side-by-side layout. Your webcam, camcorder, or other video device *must* be connected and the appropriate driver software installed in order to use this option.

- **Show Camera Preview.** Clicking this button will bring up a preview window of your camera video, so that you can make sure the camera is properly aimed, and that you stay in-frame and in-focus during the entire recording session. This window will appear on top of your presentation, but not to worry — it won't be recorded. The opacity of this window is somewhat reduced so that you can see what's underneath it while recording. As with the Record Camera option, it only works if you actually have a camera plugged in. Also, keep in mind that you can still view the camera preview even if you elect not to record the camera output during capture.

- **Camtasia Studio recording options.** This will let you adjust the add-in's recording preferences. The details of this button and its corresponding dialog are discussed in the following section.

- **Open help topic.** Brings up the help topic on the PowerPoint add-in.

Add-In Options Dialog

The second button from the right on the toolbar is Camtasia Studio recording options. Clicking this button brings up the Camtasia Studio Add-In Options dialog. This is essentially a one-screen amalgamation of all the effects and tools options from the Camtasia Recorder that are most pertinent to recording a PowerPoint presentation.

The dialog is divided into four sections: Program (which includes the Watermark options), Video and Audio, Picture In Picture, and Record Hotkey. Let's look at each of these in turn.

Program Options

There are six preferences in the Program section, all of which can be toggled on and off. They are:

- **Start recording paused.** Leaving this box checked will start the recording in paused mode, so that you can do a final sanity check prior to beginning the recording. It's also handy for getting everything set up while people are filing into your presentation, and then postponing the actual recording until you begin to speak. This avoids having to edit out the 15 minutes of "audience murmur" you unintentionally recorded before your presentation got underway.

- **Record mouse cursor.** This option, which is checked by default, will include the mouse cursor when recording your presentation. This is a matter of personal taste. If you plan on using Power-Point's Pointer Options settings to do any drawing on the screen, I would recommend that you keep it enabled. If you feel that the mouse cursor will distract the viewer, then turn it off.

- **Highlight cursor.** If Record mouse cursor is enabled, then you also have the option of having a highlight appear around the mouse. It takes the form of a translucent circle that moves with the mouse cursor in order to help the user keep better track of the cursor. Like the cursor highlight of the Camtasia Recorder, it is only seen at playback time, *not* at record time. Unlike the

Recorder's cursor highlight tool, you cannot configure the cursor highlight to use other shapes, colors, and opacities — I'm afraid you're stuck with a small, mustard-yellow, translucent circle. But it does get the job done.

- **Edit in Camtasia Studio when finished.** When checked, Camtasia Studio will automatically launch upon the conclusion of recording, and your saved project will be immediately imported, ready for editing. If unchecked, your work is saved, but Camtasia Studio will not open.

- **At end of presentation.** While you can always stop the recording using the Ctrl+Shift-F10 hotkey (or some other hotkey that you specify), you can choose what will happen when you get to the end of the presentation. You can have the recording end automatically, continue recording, or prompt you about what to do.

- **Include watermark.** This option lets you add a watermark to your recordings. We'll discuss this option in detail a bit later in its own section.

Video and Audio Options

This section of the dialog allows you to choose the settings that affect how your video and audio streams are recorded, such as frame rate, codecs, audio source, and record volume.

- **Video Frame rate.** The frame rate is the number of frames per second at which the add-in records your presentation. You may either choose a frame rate from the drop-down list or simply type a number into the field. The frame rate you select will depend on your content. If your presentation has a gazillion animations like bouncing text and wacky slide transitions, you'll want to go with a higher frame rate so that you can capture all these elements fluidly. On the other hand, if your presentation is pretty static, and the only movement that happens on the screen is the appearance of the next slide, then you can easily get away with four (or even fewer) frames per second.

- **Record audio.** Checking the Record audio box will include audio with your presentation, either from a microphone, the computer's own system sound, or both at once. Just make the appropriate choice in the **Audio source** drop-down list. Note that the system sound option is good for recording presentations where the audio narration has already been recorded within PowerPoint. However, keep in mind that this option might not be available to you if your sound card doesn't support recording audio from the system (fortunately, most modern cards do, though this is more of a crapshoot for users of Windows Vista, as most audio drivers for Vista are pretty unrefined at this point). It may be time for an equipment upgrade if your sound card can't manage this.

■ **Volume slider.** No matter which option you choose, you have a Volume slider that will let you quickly adjust the recording volume for your selected audio source. You can test the volume by speaking into the microphone and monitoring the activity on the colored volume bar. Ideally, your volume should be within the range of yellow/orange, without going into the red area (where some clipping may occur). For the full lowdown on recording audio narration, please see Chapter 10, "Working with Other Media: Audio, PIP, and Title Clips."

■ **Advanced... button.** This button brings up a dialog allowing you to change the default codecs and choose an audio recording device.

You're presented with options for both video and audio. Let us first tackle the former. A click on the **Video Setup...** button will let you choose the video codec from a drop-down list. The default is the TechSmith Screen Capture Codec, and I strongly recommend you leave it alone. Even if you have a ton of animations, TSCC can most likely capture it all without dropping any frames. Then, if you find the resulting file size too large, you can encode using another codec after you've edited your project. The only possible exception I can think of is if you have many real-world videos embedded into your slides — this may necessitate a codec like MPEG-4. But

I would still give it a shot with TSCC, just so that you can have a lossless original.

You may notice here that the default key frame rate for TSCC is lower than it is in the Camtasia Recorder, at one key frame per 300 frames. Since PowerPoint slides tend to remain static for longer periods of time, you can get away with fewer key frames. Please see the previous chapter for a full discussion of key frames and delta frames.

Let's move on to the **Audio Options**. First, you'll need to choose an **Audio Device** from the drop-down list, indicating which device you wish to record from (usually the sound card). It can be set to make use of the Windows default, or you can choose something different. You will also see details of the chosen audio codec as well as that codec's attributes on this screen. To change them, just click the **Audio Setup Wizard...** button.

The wizard dialog is exactly the same as in Camtasia Recorder, allowing you to choose a manual input if one of the preselected sources doesn't cut it for you. To change the output format, just click the **Audio Format...** button. Again, notice that the default is MPEG Layer-3 (TechSmith LAME). Remember that I warned you about using lossy audio codecs for recording in the previous chapter, but since live presentations aren't done in a pristine studio environment, using a lossy codec here probably isn't as big a deal. However, when making archival copies of presentations, if you have a nice audio setup and a system that can handle the load, I would recommend setting the codec back to uncompressed (PCM), at 44.1 kHz, 16 Bit, Mono. Since you may want to distribute this file on the web at some point, you'll obviously want to use a different audio codec later in the production process. But if you have the drive space and enough processing power to make a fluid capture, I'm generally for creating the highest-quality original possible, and then compressing and downsampling as needed.

Click **Next**, and you'll be able to have the wizard automatically set the recording volume, if desired. Click **Finish** when satisfied.

Keep in mind that if you ever lose your bearings when experimenting with the video and audio codecs, you can always go back to the factory defaults by clicking the **Defaults** button in the Advanced Video and Audio Setup dialog.

Now, getting back to the Advanced Video and Audio Setup dialog, notice that there's one more set of options we haven't yet touched, specifically **Output File Type**. This will let you choose how the video is saved. You can either save it as a CAMREC file, with the camera, marker, and caption streams encapsulated into the file, or you can save it to AVI with a project file. The project file will house your marker information and captions, but camera video will not be recorded. The latter option also doesn't give you the option of whether or not to include captions from your PowerPoint notes — it does so automatically.

With CAMREC, the import of captions is fully adjustable. It defaults to asking you at the end of every recording whether or not you want your notes imported as captions. But you can also set it either to *always* import your notes, or *never* to do so, without bothering to prompt you. These options are hidden within the main Camtasia Studio application. Go to **Tools > Options...**, and click the **PowerPoint** tab to adjust this setting.

Both CAMREC and AVI are perfectly viable options, though I personally prefer the convenience of having everything tucked into a single CAMREC file. When finished with the Advanced options, click **OK** to return to the Add-In Options dialog.

Picture In Picture Options

This section controls the implementation of camera video in your PowerPoint recordings. Camtasia Studio offers you the ability to include a camera view of yourself. You can present this extra video stream either superimposed over your screen video or in a side-by-side formation, so that you never need to worry about the camera video covering up something important on your slide. This has exciting implications for PowerPoint. You can essentially hand someone a presentation you gave some months ago, and rather than having to decipher your cryptic titles and brief notes from the PowerPoint slides, they're practically transported into the front row of the lecture hall where you delivered that presentation. They can view the slides, hear your voice, and see your face.

■ **Record from camera.** If you're the kind of presenter that stands stock-still at the podium, you can probably get away with using a simple webcam. However, if you're like me and you like to move around a bit, it probably behooves you to recruit a volunteer to shoot you with a camcorder that is attached to your computer via IEEE 1394 (FireWire) or USB. You'll end up with better, more professional footage.

To enable the camera video, click the **Record from camera** check box. Make sure that there's actually some sort of video capture device attached to your computer; otherwise, this entire section will be grayed out.

- **Camera Setup... button.** To choose a capture device and adjust settings, click **Camera Setup...**. Just as with the Camera tab of the Tools Options dialog in Camtasia Recorder, this dialog will let you pick a capture device from the drop-down list. As a courtesy, it also offers **Camera Properties...** and **Video Format...** buttons that link to the various settings of your video device's camera driver. These settings are different for every video device, so please consult your device's documentation to learn about all the different settings.

Record Hotkey Options

This is just a quick preference setting that allows you to adjust the hotkey that toggles the Record/Pause and Stop commands. The Record toggle hotkey is **Ctrl+Shift-F9** by default, and Stop is **Ctrl+Shift-F10**. You can use any combination of the Ctrl, Shift, and Alt modifier keys plus alphanumerical characters, F-keys, or the Print Screen key (PrtScr). The Escape key (**Esc**) will stop the presentation and possibly the recording as well, depending on what you've chosen in the **At end of presentation** drop-down list.

Watermark Options

Do you have a corporate logo or other image you want to use to "brand" your video? Consider using it as a watermark. Just click the **Include watermark** check box (located up in the Program section of the dialog) to get things started. But we're obviously not done yet, as we must at least choose the image file that will serve as our watermark. This is done by clicking the **Watermark...** button. You'll need to specify a file path of the image to use in the **Image Path** field. You can type the path into the field

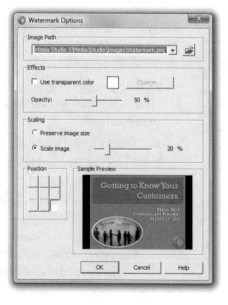

directly, click the drop-down arrow to select from the most recently used watermarks, or click the **Browse** button to maneuver through your directories to find the file.

There are also some preferences that can be set on the Watermark Options dialog. These options are a somewhat watered-down version of the Watermark tab in the Camtasia Recorder Effects Options dialog, but the basics are all represented.

You can do any of the following within this dialog:

- Select a color within the image that will be transparent
- Change the opacity of the watermark, from fully transparent to fully opaque
- Scale the image to an appropriate size
- Choose from any of nine screen positions

> In Chapter 6, "Special Effects of the Camtasia Recorder," I cautioned you against using watermarks within the Recorder except in very rare circumstances. This caveat applies here too. Using watermarks at record time means that you will not be able to change or remove them later. If you're going to use a watermark, it's far better to do so in Camtasia Studio, where you can always change your mind if you later decide you want to change it or remove it entirely.

Recording Your Presentation

Okay, let's get down to business. I know I've been building it up for about 10 pages, but the actual execution of a PowerPoint recording is surprisingly simple.

Here's how you get started with **recording a PowerPoint presentation**:

1. Open PowerPoint. Open the presentation you want to record.
2. Click the **Record** button. The presentation will launch into Slide Show view.
3. A small box appears in the lower right-hand corner of your screen, reminding you of the hotkeys at your disposal as well as allowing a last-minute tweak of your recording volume (if you're recording audio narration, that is). Click the **Click to begin recording** button.

4. The presentation (and recording) will begin in earnest. Just give the presentation as you would normally, maintaining the same pacing you've practiced.

If you need to pause for any reason, you may do so by pressing the established hotkey (**Ctrl+Shift-F9** by default). When paused, that small graphic box in the lower right-hand corner of your screen will reappear. It looks like this:

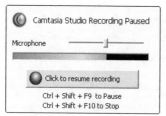

My recording is officially paused. As you can see, my volume levels for this recording look just about right.

To unpause the recording, either click the button marked **Click to resume recording** or simply hit your Record/Pause hotkey again. If you are recording audio, be sure to speak loudly and clearly. You may wish to use a wireless lavaliere microphone so that you aren't tethered to the podium. Also, do note that you might have to do some "creative cabling" to get your audio going to both your computer (for recording) and the PA system (so that your live audience can actually hear you). Fortunately, most conferences and business events have on-site technical staff who are usually happy to help. When you've finished your presentation, hit your Stop hotkey (or **Esc** if you have auto-stop set up) to stop the recording and return your presentation to Normal view.

Once you've stopped the capture, a dialog appears, asking you for a file name and location. If you chose in the Advanced dialog of the Camtasia Studio Add-In Options dialog to save your project as AVI/CAMPROJ, then two files will be created. Both will have the name you specified (e.g., *myname.camproj* and *myname.avi*).

Moving Your Project to Camtasia Studio

After saving your file, Camtasia Studio launches (provided you didn't turn this off in the Add-In Options dialog) and opens your project file. You're also presented with a dialog that gives you two or three additional options:

So, what *would* you like to do?

- **Produce your recording.** By choosing this option, you're essentially telling the program that you don't wish to do any editing. It's just perfect as is, and you want to move straight to producing your creation in a shareable format.

- **Edit your recording.** Since you already have your project open within Camtasia Studio, choosing this option doesn't do much beyond clearing this dialog.

- **View in Camtasia Player.** (Only available when saving as AVI/CAMPROJ.) This will open your video file in Camtasia Player so that you can preview it first. Note that after viewing and closing the video in Camtasia Player, your project file will still be open in Camtasia Studio so you can then move straight to editing and/or production.

While we're not going to tackle editing in earnest until the next unit of the book, there are a couple of items specific to the add-in I'm going to point out in a moment.

Keep in mind that if you'd rather circumvent this dialog in the future, you can always turn it off by clearing the check box marked **Show this dialog again**. It can also be toggled within Camtasia Studio, on the **PowerPoint** tab of the **Tools > Options...** dialog.

When looking over your video project in Camtasia Studio, you probably noticed the presence of markers, those little green diamonds that appear above the video segments in their own track. The Camtasia Studio Add-in for PowerPoint automatically takes the titles of these slides and uses them to name your markers. Why is this important? Because when actually producing your video, you can use these markers to automatically create a table of contents for your material. The finished product will have an accompanying HTML file with a dynamic menu containing your marker names. When the user clicks on a menu item, the playback head goes straight to that point in the video.

Of course, as with any automated process, the system isn't perfect. The add-in relies only on the slide's title text for the marker name. People who aren't PowerPoint power users can end up doing some pretty wacky things to get their presentation to look the way they want. It's possible that the slides contain *only* title text (in other words, they used a smaller version of the title text for their body text). In this case, *all* of the slide text would end up in your marker name. Or, you could have the opposite problem, where the author used only body text or even no text at all (for example, when the whole slide is one large graphic). In this case, there will be no marker name whatsoever. You may also experience cases where the title is simply too long to make an effective menu link. If you're the one creating the PowerPoint presentation, you should be cognizant of these issues if you know you'll want to record it at some point. If you're recording someone else's work (hopefully with their permission), keep in mind that you might need to edit some or all of the marker names, depending on how the author actually created all those pretty slides. Please see Chapter 9, "Working with Camtasia Studio," for instructions on renaming markers.

Additionally, if you have any notes in your PowerPoint presentation, you'll be presented with a small dialog asking whether you want to import them as captions in your presentation*. Captions allow hearing-impaired and nonnative speaking individuals to enjoy your video. We'll discuss captions in detail in Chapter 11.

---

* If you're recording to AVI/CAMPROJ, you won't be consulted — your note text will be imported as captions whether you like it or not.

Reducing the Dimensions of Your Presentation

If you've followed the chapter thus far, you have probably already successfully made your first recording of a PowerPoint presentation. If you've actually produced it in a shareable format (or previewed it in Camtasia Player), you may have noticed one disconcerting thing: the *SIZE*. You were probably recording a full-screen presentation at your monitor's standard resolution. This leads to a rather large video window that is unwieldy both in terms of file size and interface (the navigational controls could be obstructed, you may need scroll bars to view all the content, etc.). Clearly, this needs to be addressed. We have two options for doing so:

- **Reduce your monitor's resolution.** By reducing the resolution of your monitor to 800 x 600, or even 640 x 480, you can still do a full-screen capture, but the resulting file will consume less file space and be more likely to fit on the user's monitor when viewed. This can be done either globally (within Windows) or from within PowerPoint (and will return to your standard resolution when the presentation concludes).

- **Record your presentation in a window*.** This has the advantage of allowing you to resize your presentation to pretty much any dimensions you want (and PowerPoint scales the slides' text and images remarkably well, even at smaller dimensions). The one disadvantage is that you cannot use any of the pointer options (such as pens and highlights) during your slide show.

Reducing Your Screen Resolution

You can reduce your monitor's resolution globally by following the instructions in Appendix A, under the section called "Keep Your Dimensions Small."

---

* This option is only available for PowerPoint XP and later. If you have PowerPoint 2000, then you must reduce your monitor resolution in order to capture your video at smaller dimensions.

To **reduce the resolution within PowerPoint**, follow these instructions:

1. In PowerPoint, choose **Set Up Show...** from the **Slide Show** menu (in PowerPoint 2007, choose **Set Up Slide Show** from the Slide Show tab).

2. In the **Performance** section, choose a new resolution from the **Slide show resolution** drop-down list, preferably **640 x 480** if the presentation still looks good.

3. Click **OK**. Click **Record** to capture your presentation as usual. The screen will probably go blank at the beginning of the presentation as the system changes the screen resolution. Once finished, the screen will go blank again while Windows changes the resolution back to what it was previously.

 Since changing the resolution on the fly like this usually takes a few seconds, you may end up inadvertently recording a couple seconds of your presentation's Normal view at the beginning and/or end of your capture. You can easily edit out these portions later in Camtasia Studio.

Recording Your Presentation in a Window

To set up PowerPoint to **play your slide show in a window**, please do the following:

1. In PowerPoint, choose **Set Up Show...** from the **Slide Show** menu (in PowerPoint 2007, choose **Set Up Slide Show** from the Slide Show tab).

2. In the **Show Type** section, click the **Browsed by an individual (window)** radio button. Make sure that the **Show scrollbar** button is *unchecked*. Click **OK**.

3. Before you start recording, let's look at our presentation in Slide Show view so that we can adjust the size of the window to our liking. Go ahead and start the slide show.

4. Your presentation appears in a window. You may need to take it out of maximized mode. Click the **Restore** button ( ) in the upper right-hand corner of the screen in order to resize the window.

5. Resize by clicking and dragging on the lower right-hand corner of the window. Try to resize your window with the same aspect ratio as full screen, or your recording will have black bars appearing either at the top and bottom or at the sides of your video window.

> If you're trying to attain a particular set of screen dimensions, it may prove challenging to get that slide show window to just the right size. Recorder's Lock to application feature isn't going to help us in this case, since we just want the presentation pane, not the entire window. But here's a handy tip that'll make things much easier. First, select your desired capture dimensions within the Camtasia Recorder. I find it easiest to manually input a width and height in the Camtasia Recorder Selection Area window. Then move the capture area to be somewhere in the middle of the screen. Finally, resize the PowerPoint slide show window so that the presentation just barely overlaps the edges of the capture area.

6. Click the **Record** button. A blinking recording frame will appear around your window.

    Note that clicking on the screen to advance the slide does not work when showing your slide show in a window. Use the PageUp/PageDn or the Left/Right arrow keys instead.

7. You can pause and stop the recording per usual.

Final Recording Tips

While the above two methods can help ensure that your presentation videos are of reasonable file size and dimensions, I do have a few other miscellaneous tips to share for really getting the most out of your PowerPoint recordings.

Capturing Video Content within PowerPoint

If the PowerPoint presentation you're trying to record has any videos placed inside one or more of its slides, you may notice that you're getting a solid black rectangle where the video should be when previewing your recording. As with media player content, this is due to display acceleration being enabled.

You can try turning off display acceleration within PowerPoint itself by choosing **Set Up Show...** from the Slide Show menu, and then making sure that **Use hardware graphics acceleration** is unchecked. However, even with this option disabled, it has been my experience that if PowerPoint detects a system with video acceleration capabilities, it will attempt to make use of them anyway. If you're still running into problems, I'd advise you to turn off display acceleration globally, which affects all Windows programs. Remember that this is only for Windows XP, as Vista doesn't allow you to disable hardware acceleration.

Here are some instructions for **globally disabling your hardware acceleration**:

1. Choose **Start**, and then select **Control Panel**. Double-click the **Display** icon.

2. On the **Settings** tab, click the **Advanced** button.

3. Click the **Troubleshoot** tab. Under **Hardware Acceleration**, drag the slider all the way to the left from Full to **None**. Click **OK**, then **Yes**.

Capturing Smoother Animations

As I mentioned in the section on recording Macromedia Flash files in Chapter 5, "Recording Your Screen," sometimes your animated content just doesn't seem to capture very well. Although you may have a relatively new system with a decent video card, you might notice some choppiness in your animations, even if the Recorder window is reporting zero dropped frames. As with Flash, you can remedy this by slowing down the content and then doing a time-lapse capture to give the recorder more time to process the information.

But PowerPoint presents us with a few unexpected snags. Unlike Flash, there's no way to set the frame rate *globally* for you to record the whole presentation at one-third speed, for example. No sir, that would be way too easy! Instead, you need to slow down *each and every* animation on an individual basis. It's slow, meticulous, mind-numbing work, and if you happen to have 1,000 animations in your presentation, it probably won't be worth it to you in the end. Also, the add-in does not support time-lapse capture, meaning that we have to use the Camtasia Recorder, thereby sacrificing all the cool automatic splitting and marker features that the add-in brings to the table. And lastly, recording a presentation at one-third speed is obviously not an option if you're doing it before a live audience — this option is therefore only for those who want to make a high-quality video of a presentation they're not doing live. But for those who have the determination to get the best possible capture quality for their PowerPoint animations, the payoff can be big.

Here's how to **slow down those animations** and **set up time-lapse capture** in the Camtasia Recorder to speed them back up later:

1. Make a copy of your animation-laden PowerPoint presentation in Windows. Open the copy for editing.

2. If using PowerPoint 2000, XP, or 2003: Bring up your Task Pane (if not already present) by pressing **Ctrl-F1**. Click on the Task Pane name at the top of the pane to bring up a menu list of other task panes.

3. Choose **Custom Animation**, near the bottom of the list.

   or

   If using PowerPoint 2007: On the Animations tab, click the **Custom Animation** button.

4. The Custom Animation task pane appears, with a complete list of every animation in the current slide, in order of appearance. In order to effectively do our time-lapse capture, we're going to have to slow all of these down.

5. Click on an animation effect to select it, and then click the drop-down arrow on its right-hand side to bring up a context menu for that effect. Choose **Timing...** from the list.

6. A dialog appears, allowing you to adjust several aspects of the effect's timing. Only two of the settings are important for our needs: **Delay** (the number of seconds after the previous animation that the current one begins to play) and **Speed** (how quickly the animation itself is displayed). For both of these, take the field's current value, and **multiply it by three**. Don't alter any of the other fields.

In this particular case, I would type "3" into the Delay field, and "1.5" into the Speed field in order to slow this effect down.

Some objects may have "On click" listed in the Start field, meaning that this particular effect is waiting on input from the user (a mouse click) in order to start playing. While it sometimes works to record such prompted animations if you can time it out okay, it's tricky because you have to remember to give each animation *three times* the delay before moving on to the next. In short, timing it manually is a chore. I therefore recommend putting all animations and slide transitions on a timer prior to recording. Make a copy of your original file, and try to get the timing of the animations to adhere to your narration script. Utilizing the Advance slide automatically after ___ field within the Slide Transition task pane (in PowerPoint 2007, it's on the right-hand side of the Animations tab), you can also have the presentation move automatically from slide to slide, eliminating your need to baby-sit the computer at all during recording.

The slowed-down version of the presentation would then be a copy of this copy. If you do add the automatic slide transitions I just mentioned, remember to slow these down by a factor of three as well; otherwise, the slide show will proceed to the next slide before all your animations on the current slide have had a chance to run.

7. Click **OK** to save your changes. Repeat the process with every animation in the current slide. Then move on to all your other slides. Depending on how animation-intensive your presentation is, this could obviously take a while.

8. **Save** the file. This is the one from which you'll be recording, so keep it open.

9. Since the Camtasia Studio Add-in for PowerPoint does not yet support time-lapse recording capability, we'll have to do this the old-fashioned way, with the Camtasia Recorder. Open the Recorder now.

10. Choose **Options...** from the **Tools** menu. On the Video tab, check the **Time-lapse capture** check box. Then click the **Time-Lapse Setup...** button.

11. In the dialog below, you can set the frame rate for capture and playback. In the AVI capture rate section, enter your usual frame rate (I use **15** fps). In the AVI Playback Rate section, enter a frame rate equal to three times that of your capture rate. I would therefore enter **45** frames per second:

12. Click **OK** twice. Now choose your recording area: the entire screen if you're doing a full-screen recording, or you can select smaller dimensions if you have the slide show set to display in a window.

13. If there's audio narration in your presentation (linked to an external file) that you also want to record, it will have to be added later in Camtasia Studio, since audio recording is disabled when making a time-lapse capture. To learn how to do this, please see Chapter 10, "Working with Other Media: Audio, PIP, and Title Clips."

14. Begin recording. Start the presentation in Slide Show mode, and then select your capture area. Press your **Record** hotkey to begin the recording. If you've set up your presentation to proceed from animation to animation and slide to slide on a timer, you should be able to simply walk away from the computer, returning only to stop the recording once the slide show concludes.

15. Use your **Stop** hotkey to end the recording, saving the file per usual.

16. *Optional*: A file that plays back at 45 fps is going to be somewhat large. It has been my experience that you can use Camtasia Studio to reproduce your video at 15 fps without any major impact on the smoothness of your animations. Feel free to give it a try and see if it works for you.

Playing Camtasia Studio Video Content within PowerPoint

Up to now, we've talked exclusively about getting information *from* PowerPoint *into* Camtasia Studio. But what if you wanted to do the reverse? Say you have a wonderfully set up PowerPoint presentation and, during your presentation, you want to access some screen video content to show to your audience. What's the best way of going about it?

If you've worked with PowerPoint for any length of time, you probably already know that PowerPoint supports the ability to place video content inside a slide within your presentation. I do *not* recommend this. Screen videos placed directly in the slide tend to look just awful as a result of PowerPoint automatically scaling the content in order to fit the slide frame. Inserting a video in this manner works fine for real-world content, but not so much for screen videos. Any text in the video is rendered practically illegible.

Linking to Camtasia Player

But there is a way to access videos directly within PowerPoint, and it has none of the aforementioned problems. In essence, it involves linking your presentation to your external AVI video file, which will then open in Camtasia Player. No scaling, no yucky quality.

Here's how to set up PowerPoint to **play videos using Camtasia Player**:

1. Open PowerPoint, and navigate to the slide where you want the video to be displayed.

2. In order to call the video, we're going to need some kind of button that, when clicked, will call up Camtasia Player and your video. One way to do this is to add an action button. From the Drawing toolbar (usually located at the bottom of your application window), click **AutoShapes**, and then choose a button from the Action Buttons submenu:

In PowerPoint 2007, go to the **Insert** tab and click the **Shapes** button. The action buttons are located at the bottom of the pop-up dialog.

or

Choose an object on your slide to act as your button. It can be a text box, a graphic, in fact *any* object as long as it's not grouped. Right-click on your object, and then choose **Action Settings...** from the context menu that appears. In PowerPoint 2007, click the object and then click the **Action** button on the **Insert** tab.

3. On the Action Settings dialog box, click the **Run program** radio button. It's time to link to our video file.

4. Enter **CamPlay.exe** into the Run program field. Now Power-Point needs to know where to look for this file. You can browse for it, but to avoid accessibility issues later on in case the presentation file gets moved, it's best to place a copy of both CamPlay.exe and your video file directly in your project folder, so that they're much more likely to stay with your project (and it simplifies the file path). The CamPlay executable is only 474 KB. Just copy it over from your program directory. By default, it's located here: C:\Program Files\ TechSmith\Camtasia Studio 5\CamPlay.exe.

5. Now we have to specify both the video file and how you want Camtasia Player to open it. On the same line in the Run pro-

gram field, enter a space, any command line parameter options (completely optional), and then the file name (also technically optional, but who needs the player without the actual video?). For those who are wondering, command line parameters can help you stipulate exactly *how* you want the file opened and displayed. For example, if you want it to open in full-screen mode or loop the video until the user closes it, you can use

The commands and arguments in the Run program field are instructing the program to launch Camtasia Player, open myvideo.avi without a title bar, and automatically exit when finished.

command line parameters to accomplish this. For a comprehensive list of command line parameters, and for more information about the Camtasia Player in general, please see Chapter 15, "Other Output Options."

6. So, by now we should have a dialog that looks roughly like the figure on the previous page.

   Click **OK** to exit the dialog.

7. When running your slide show, simply click the chosen action button when you're ready for the video to begin. Camtasia Player will launch your video using the parameters (if any) you specified. When finished, simply continue the presentation.

Opening Camtasia Player through PowerPoint in this way can sometimes make the security features of Microsoft Office a little grumpy. If you end up getting a security warning message that is disruptive to your presentation, you can temporarily lower PowerPoint's security settings by clicking on the **Tools** menu, and from the **Macro** submenu, choosing **Security...**. Set the security level to low until your presentation is over, and then reset it to its original level.

Embedding Animated GIF Files

If you really want to embed a video into the actual presentation, there is one other option, provided the video's dimensions are small and its length is short (under 20 seconds). You can convert your video into an animated GIF (done within Camtasia Studio), and then import this image into your presentation. As a truly embedded part of the file, you needn't worry about broken links when moving your presentation file around, and GIF files actually add precious little to the overall file size. The only hitch is that you're confined to 256 colors.

Here's how to **embed an animated GIF** in your PowerPoint presentation:

1. In Camtasia Studio, produce your video as an animated GIF. We'll go into detail about this process in Chapter 12, but in terms of PowerPoint, there's only one additional thing you need to know. Since you're probably only going to want the video to play once, during production you would therefore set this option in the Production Wizard by entering a **1** into the Play ___ time(s) field, like so:

   Animated GIF Encoding Options
   Select the settings for saving your video. The Aut
   quality for your produced video.

   Options
   Colors: Automatic ▾
   Frame rate: Automatic ▾
   ○ Loop indefinitely
   ● Play   1   time(s)

   However, due to a glitch in PowerPoint 2003 and 2007, this number must be set to the number of times you want the video to play *plus one*, so you would most likely enter a **2** here. The rest of the default options should work fine.

2. Open PowerPoint, and navigate to the slide where you want to embed your new GIF image.

3. From the **Insert** menu, go to **Picture**, and then choose **From file...** (in PowerPoint 2007, choose **Picture** from the **Insert** tab).

4. Navigate to your animated GIF file and choose **Open**. The image will appear on your PowerPoint slide. It will not be animated until you view it in Slide Show mode.

5. You can move or resize this image at will, with no major scaling issues. You may wish to experiment with scaling your GIF in order to get the best possible image quality for the screen resolution at which you'll be presenting.

Troubleshooting the Add-In

What If the Add-In Doesn't Open?

When opening PowerPoint, the Camtasia Studio Add-in should appear in your toolbar palette automatically. Emphasis on *should*. If it doesn't, it could be for one of the reasons listed below. Fortunately, they can all be remedied, and I'll explain how as we go. As these are listed in order from least to greatest effort required, you might want to try them in order.

■ You or someone else inadvertently turned off its toolbar in PowerPoint. From the **View** menu inside PowerPoint, go to **Toolbars**, and then make sure there's a check mark next to **Camtasia Studio** in the submenu that appears. If not, click this option.

■ If you see that there's a check next to Camtasia Studio in the Toolbars submenu, look around. The add-in could simply be docked in a weird place (check the sides and bottom of your application window), or it could be floating (not docked at all). Look at your second monitor if you have one; it could also be there. In PowerPoint 2007, it's going to be located on the **Add-Ins** tab.

■ If Camtasia Studio isn't listed in PowerPoint's Toolbars submenu (or on the Add-Ins tab) *at all*, you may have inadvertently disabled it in Camtasia Studio. From the **Tools** menu in Camtasia Studio, choose **Options...** and select the **PowerPoint** tab. Make sure that **Enable PowerPoint Add-in** is checked, and then click **OK**. Likewise, should you ever wish to disable the add-in, this is the place to do it.

■ You elected not to enable the add-in during Camtasia Studio's installation process. Fortunately, even if you disable the add-in, Camtasia Studio still installs this capability, so no reinstallation is necessary. Again, simply go into **Tools > Options...** (**PowerPoint** tab) and enable it.

- On very rare occasions, a third-party add-in designed for a Microsoft Office product can, through some unexpected turn of events, cause the application to crash. The next time the application is started, it will disable the add-in until you manually re-enable it. To see if this is the case, do the following:

  - In earlier versions of PowerPoint, return to PowerPoint and choose **About Microsoft Office PowerPoint** from the **Help** menu. In the dialog that appears, click the **Disabled Items...** button. If the Camtasia Studio Add-in shows up in the list that appears, select it and then choose **Enable**. Click **Close**, and then **OK**.

  - In PowerPoint 2007, click the **Office** button (circular button in the upper left-hand corner of the screen), and choose **PowerPoint Options** from the bottom of the menu. Click the **Add-Ins** category. At the bottom of the dialog, under **Manage**, choose **COM Add-Ins**, and click **Go....** Check the box next to **Camtasia Add-in**, and click **OK**.

My Recording Looks Weird. Why Are All Those Lines of Color There?

Microsoft PowerPoint offers a great many templates to aid even novice users in creating an attractive presentation. Many of these templates contain *color gradients*, subtle shifts in color that can be rather pretty, provided your system supports the number of colors for which the template was designed. Some templates can support multiple color depths. However, certain templates are only designed for a high number of colors, and if your system isn't correctly set, you force the template to use fewer colors than it was designed for, and instead of subtle shifts, you get solid blocks of color (called "banding").

Fortunately, **changing the color depth of your monitor** is a quick and easy way to eliminate this problem:

1. Choose **Start > Control Panel**.

2. *In Windows XP:* Double-click the **Display** icon. The Display Properties dialog opens. Click the **Settings** tab.

   or

   In Windows Vista: Double-click the **Personalization** icon. Click the **Display Settings** link.

3. Choose a color depth from the **Color Quality** (or **Colors**) drop-down list, at least 16-bit, and probably 32-bit if you want to play it safe.

4. To save your settings, click **OK**, then **Yes**.

5. Close and then reopen your PowerPoint presentation.

Summary

Recording PowerPoint presentations is a common use of the Camtasia Recorder. Its ability to better capture the "live" aspects of the presentation, such as audio narration, camera video, animated drawings, etc., can really give an extended afterlife to a presentation you've already done before an audience. With Camtasia Studio's Flash output, you can then offer additional interactive features such as custom navigation, clickable hotspots, and quizzing.

Here is a summarized version of turning your PowerPoint presentation into a first-rate video experience:

1. Launch PowerPoint, and then open your presentation.

2. On the add-in's toolbar, select the **Camtasia Studio Recording Options** button, and set your preferences in the dialog that appears.

3. Choose whether you wish to record the presentation in full-screen mode (with either the current resolution or a different one) or inside a window. Make the appropriate adjustments in the **Set Up Show...** dialog, available from the **Slide Show** menu (or tab).

4. Click **Record**. You may toggle between record and paused modes by pressing **Ctrl+Shift-F9** (or whatever hotkey you selected in the Recording Options dialog). Press **Esc** to finish recording and exit Slide Show view.

5. Save your files. The project file will open automatically in Camtasia Studio, where you can then edit out segments, adjust marker names, time your captions, and otherwise prepare the file for output to a shareable format.

And speaking of Camtasia Studio, the next chapter begins our unit on the main Camtasia Studio application, where we take all the wonderful footage we produced in this unit, and then put it through the rigors of editing and production. Congratulations! You're ready for the next step.

Exercises

1. Without looking back at the text, try to think of at leave five advantages video presentations have over PowerPoint files.

2. Take a look at the sample PowerPoint presentation in this chapter's media folder on the companion CD. There are several animations. Using the techniques described in this chapter, make a smooth, correctly paced capture of these animations with Camtasia Recorder's time-lapse capture.

3. Capture part of a PowerPoint presentation (either the sample file or one of your own), utilizing one of the two techniques mentioned in this chapter for reducing the dimensions of your video presentation. Now try the other technique. Which do you prefer?

4. In the sample PowerPoint presentation on the companion CD, there's a "Play" symbol graphic on the final slide. Copy both the presentation and an included sample video from the same folder to your hard drive. Following the instructions in this chapter, set up your presentation to link to that video using Camtasia Player.

5. In your professional career, chances are you've had to give a PowerPoint presentation at some point. Would it be useful to preserve it as a video? If you've given a presentation recently, try archiving it as a video using the Camtasia Studio Add-in for PowerPoint.

EXTRALIFE

Editing within Camtasia Studio

Now that we've recorded all our raw footage, it's time to bring it all into Camtasia Studio for editing. This includes everything from splicing together clips and cutting out unusable content, to inserting additional media streams like audio and PIP, to adding special effects like callouts, transitions, and zoom and pan. There are even some interactive elements that can be added, such as clickable hotspots and quizzes. In this unit, we'll cover all of the above, and then some.

This unit contains three chapters:

■ **Chapter 9: Working with Camtasia Studio.** Here, I'll guide you through the program's user interface as well as teach you how to import all that wonderful footage you just created. Then you'll get a crash course in editing your clips: how to shorten them, split them, and combine them with other clips to create a fluid and robust presentation. Finally, we'll discover the utility of working with markers in Camtasia Studio.

■ **Chapter 10: Working with Other Media: Audio, PIP, and Title Clips.** After cleaning up your screen video footage, check out this chapter for aid in adding new streams of content to augment your base footage. The addition of custom title clips, recording of audio narration, and the post-production recording of camera video for picture-in-picture are all addressed.

- **Chapter 11: Editing Effects.** In this chapter, we'll learn how to add a little moxie to our videos in the form of picture-in-picture editing, screen transitions, callouts, interactive Flash hotspots, zoom and pan effects, and quizzing features. With Camtasia Studio 5, you also have the ability to enhance your audio narration, survey your audience, and add captioning to aid in achieving Section 508 compliance.

Chapter 9

Working with Camtasia Studio

By working through the previous unit, you've probably managed to create some quality footage of your favorite applications. If you've been smart, you've been doing your recording in a lot of smaller pieces in order to set up the best possible shot for the segment in question. It's now time to put all those little pieces together. Camtasia Studio offers what is called a *nonlinear* editing system, meaning that the different clips in your presentation don't have to be laid out in a particular order on the fly. They can be cut, moved, and reordered an infinite number of times, at your leisure. This gives you the incredible flexibility to experiment until you get it just right.

If you've worked with Windows Movie Maker or other mid-level timeline-based editing systems, you'll probably find Camtasia Studio's layout pretty similar to what you're used to. If you've never used a video editing application of any sort, not to worry: The learning curve is comparatively light. But before we get down to the business of editing and importing your clips, let's take a quick gander at the user interface of Camtasia Studio.

The Camtasia Studio User Interface

When first opening the application, you're presented with a Welcome dialog that gives you several choices for getting started:

- **New Screen Recording.** We've already been here. If needed, check out Chapter 5 for a refresher.

- **New PowerPoint Recording.** This is also fairly well-covered territory. The principal difference here is that selecting this option will automatically launch PowerPoint as well as prompt you to open the desired file. From there, just do what you practiced in the previous chapter.

- **New Voice Recording.** This option opens up the Voice Narration tool for recording an audio segment. If you would prefer to record your narration prior to editing segments, or if this is going to be an audio-only presentation, then this is where you need to be. We'll discuss the Voice Narration tool in detail in the next chapter.

- **Import Media.** Assuming you've already done your recording, this option will let you bring all these gorgeous files into Camtasia Studio for editing. This handy command will bring in all associated media files at once: video files (.camrec, .avi, .mpeg, .mpg, .wmv), audio files (.wav, .mp3, .wma), and images (.bmp, .gif, .jpg, .png).

- **Recent Projects.** If you've already created a project or two in Camtasia Studio, then they'll be listed here, so you can skip the File menu and get right to business. The **more...** link brings up the standard Open dialog for opening not-so-recent projects.

- **Tutorial Videos.** A series of starter videos that TechSmith created for the newbs. By the end of this book, you'll be light-years beyond them.

Go ahead and click **Close** for now. Here's a quick breakdown of the Camtasia Studio interface:

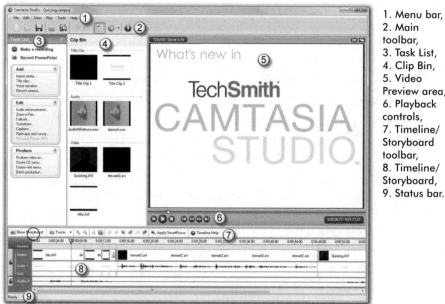

1. Menu bar,
2. Main toolbar,
3. Task List,
4. Clip Bin,
5. Video Preview area,
6. Playback controls,
7. Timeline/ Storyboard toolbar,
8. Timeline/ Storyboard,
9. Status bar.

Here's a brief description of each of these interface parts:

① **Menu bar.** As with most applications, Camtasia Studio's menu bar contains almost all the available commands of the application, split up into six handy menus.

② **Main toolbar.** The most often-used menu commands are present here so that you can more easily access them. If you don't use the toolbar and wish to turn it off to conserve space, you may toggle it by choosing Toolbar from the View menu.

③ **Task List.** This special pane allows access to groups of commands for special purposes. It is divided into five sections:

▪ **Make a recording.** This button brings up the Camtasia Recorder, and is aimed at those who first opened the main Camtasia Studio application before making their first recording.

If you're ever working in Camtasia Studio and discover that you need to make another recording, pressing Ctrl-R will minimize Camtasia Studio and open the Recorder.

▪ **Record PowerPoint.** This is a similar option for people who want to start recording a PowerPoint presentation. It launches PowerPoint and prompts you to open the file you want to record.

IV: Editing

- **Add.** Lets you import the various kinds of media supported by Camtasia Studio. Also used to create title screens, record voice narration, and capture camera video.
- **Edit.** All of the spiffy special effects we'll be covering in Chapter 11 are present and accounted for here.
- **Produce.** This section is all about sharing your content. You can produce a video here, as well as access menu creation tools for both CD-ROM and the web. Camtasia Studio's batch production tool is also available here.

If you have no use for a particular set of functions, note that each of these individual sections can be closed by clicking its corresponding arrow button (⊗). The Task List can be closed entirely by clicking the X in the Task List title bar, or it can be toggled on and off by choosing Task List from the View menu.

④ **Clip Bin.** This is a sort of holding area for any imported media, including Camtasia Recorder (CAMREC) files, title clips, images, audio, and video. Each of these media types appear in the Clip Bin, split into their own categories. There are also different views available to you should you wish to use them. I'll show you how in a moment.

⑤ **Video Preview area.** Depending on your actions, the preview area will show either the contents of the Timeline/Storyboard or a particular Clip Bin item. It's useful for viewing your editing changes and examining the flow of your developing video in general, so that you have a sense of what it's going to look/sound like *before* you produce it.

⑥ **Playback controls.** These DVD-like controls allow you to navigate the current contents of the Video Preview area. You can also view both the elapsed time and total running time of said contents.

⑦ **Timeline/Storyboard toolbar.** This toolbar offers basic controls for editing the contents of the Timeline or Storyboard. The toolbar will look slightly different based on which view you're currently using.

⑧ **Timeline/Storyboard.** This area offers two different views for working with your video content: Timeline view and Storyboard view. Both views have their uses, and in a moment you'll learn how to leverage the power of each.

⑨ **Status bar.** Displays the definition of the currently selected item from the menu bar or Main toolbar. Simply mouse over an item you wish to learn more about. If you don't use the Status bar, you can turn it off to free up a little extra space by choosing Status Bar from the View menu.

Don't worry that we've only glossed over some of these items. Most of them will be covered in much greater detail a bit later on. For now, though, I think we've learned enough to start importing our work.

Importing and Using Your Media Clips in Camtasia Studio

Okay, we've got some clips we want to work with, but in order to do anything with them in Camtasia Studio, we have to import them first. Even if you're not sure you're going to use a particular clip, it's best to import and have it at your fingertips should you end up needing it.

To **import one or more clips into Camtasia Studio**, do the following:

1. From the Welcome dialog (that little box that appeared when you first opened the program), click **Import Media.**

   or

   From the Add section of the Task List, click **Import media....**

   or

   Choose **File > Import Media....**

   or

   Click the **Import Media Files** button on your toolbar.

   or

   Right-click within the Clip Bin, and then choose **Import Media...** from the context menu that appears.

   or

   Press **Ctrl-I.**

2. In the dialog that appears, select the media file you wish to import. You can select multiple files by clicking and dragging, or by **Ctrl-clicking** on individual items. You may also either narrow your search to a particular media type or include all media types by making an appropriate choice from the **Files of type** drop-down list.

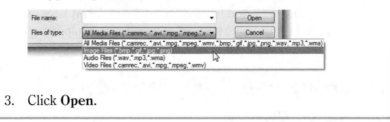

3. Click **Open**.

With no fewer than *six* different ways of doing the same thing, do you get the sense that perhaps this is a really important command? Notice that all the clips you imported now show up in the Clip Bin. Don't worry if you missed a clip or you have need for various clips located in different directories. You may continue to import at will without losing anything currently located in the Clip Bin.

Utilizing the Clip Bin

The Clip Bin holds five categories of media:

- **Camtasia Recording File.** These are the CAMREC files you recorded. They're in a different category than your standard videos due to the different media streams they contain (or perhaps I should say *can* contain — you need to have actually recorded those streams in order for them to be present).

- **Title Clip.** No more having to assemble a title screen using a huge, cumbersome image editing package and then importing it as an image. Camtasia Studio offers a one-stop workshop for constructing title and ending screens, and I'll show you how to add these in Chapter 10.

- **Image.** If, for example, you wish to use Camtasia Studio to create a slide show out of a series of still image files, you can easily do so. Still images also work well for displaying charts, diagrams, and contact information.

- **Audio.** If you have background music, sound effects, or narration that you recorded outside of the Camtasia Recorder, you can add it to your video project.

- **Video.** These files can be real-world camera video or animations, including your picture-in-picture (PIP) video. Additionally, if you recorded to AVI while working in the Camtasia Recorder, then these clips will mostly consist of all the wonderful screen video footage that you captured. If you captured narration or mouse/keyboard sound effects at the same time, the audio track will be imported as well.

Each type of media has its own category in the Clip Bin, and all media of a particular type are neatly arranged within that category in alphabetical order (by default, anyway). Depending on the number of clips you have imported, you may want to make a little additional elbow room for them — the width of the Clip Bin can be adjusted by clicking and dragging the left edge of the preview area.

> Keep in mind that you can **view the contents of your Clip Bin** in different ways. These view options can be accessed in one of two places:
>
> - Choose **View**, and then the **Clip Bin** submenu.
>
>   or
>
> - Right-click within the Clip Bin area.

You have three basic sets of choices for altering your Clip Bin view:

- **Thumbnails vs. Details.** By default, the Clip Bin displays your clips in Thumbnail view, meaning that each clip is represented by a miniature image of the content (except for audio, which gets a generic icon), with the clip's file name appearing underneath. But you can also set your Clip Bin to display in Details view, which has the advantages of (a) fitting more clip information into a smaller area, thus reducing or eliminating the need to scroll, and (b) providing additional useful information about the clips, such as size, dimensions (for images and videos), and duration (for audio and video).

- **Sort order.** As I mentioned earlier, the icons appear alphabetically by default. But you have several additional sort orders at your disposal, including size, type, dimensions, and duration. Choosing the same item twice will sort your content according to that sort option, but in *descending* order. In addition to the options listed above, you may also specify the sort order within the Details view by clicking on any heading.

IV: Editing

- **Show in Groups.** Whatever sort order you choose, your Clip Bin items are sorted by media type. If you'd prefer that the Clip Bin ignore this distinction and simply lump all your media together, you may do so by unchecking Show in Groups.

If you've inadvertently added a clip that you know you won't be using, you can get rid of it by right-clicking the clip and then choosing **Remove from Clip Bin** or by simply selecting the clip and pressing **Delete.**

CAMREC files, while extremely useful in Camtasia Studio because they neatly package several streams into one file, don't play nicely with other third-party software applications. If you want to be able to use your CAMREC video with other programs, you'll need to pull out the AVI video (and possibly the WMV file of your PIP track) contained in the file. Fortunately, Camtasia Studio includes a built-in extractor tool. Just right-click any of your CAMREC files, and choose **Extract Camrec Contents…**. You'll be prompted to choose a folder where the AVI file will be saved. It's possible to extract several files at once by selecting several CAMREC files before executing the command. You can also extract one or more streams from a CAMREC file in the Windows Explorer by right-clicking it and choosing the appropriate option from the **Extract** submenu.

Previewing Your Clips

So what good are these handy little clips sitting in the Clip Bin? From here, you've got two choices regarding what to do with a clip: You can view it directly or you can add it to your Timeline/Storyboard for inclusion in your final video. If you wish to preview any clip in the Clip Bin, simply give it a double-click. Alternatively, you can also right-click the clip, and then choose **Preview Clip**. The selected clip will display right within the preview area. For video and audio files, you'll be able to use the playback controls to play, pause, stop, and otherwise move the playback head around. You'll also be able to see the elapsed time of the clip as well as its overall duration.

Want even more information about a particular clip than what is visible in the preview area? You can also view a particular clip's properties. Just right-click the clip, and then choose **Properties…** from the context menu that appears.

Camtasia Studio

C:\myvideo.camrec

Screen Video Properties:

screen_stream.avi

Length:	0:02:11;28
Size:	2.37 MB (2,495,488 bytes)
Modified:	9/18/2007 1:34:24 PM

Audio Format:
No Audio

Video Format:

Width:	640
Height:	480
Colors:	16M
Frames:	1979
Rate:	15.00 Frames/Second
Format:	TechSmith Screen Capture Codec

Camera Video Properties:

camera_stream.wmv

Length:	0:02:12;00
Size:	3.91 MB (4,102,000 bytes)
Modified:	9/18/2007 1:34:24 PM

Audio Format:

Rate:	44.100 kHz
Sample:	16 Bit
Channels: Stereo	
Format:	Unknown

Video Format:

Width:	320
Height:	240
Colors:	16M
Frames:	1980
Rate:	15.00 Frames/Second
Format:	Unknown

OK

Here are the properties of one of my CAMREC clips. For audio, images, and title clips, you'll see a different set of properties.

You'll find different kinds of information based on the type of clip selected, but the Properties dialog can include things like file size, duration, dimensions, when the file was last modified, etc.

Adding a Clip to the Timeline or Storyboard

It's important to note that the presence of certain media in the Clip Bin does *not* automatically mean they'll be part of your video — it only means that they're *available* to you if and when you wish to use them. To actually include these elements in your final video, you will need to add them to the Timeline or Storyboard. The Timeline and Storyboard offer two different ways of viewing your content. The **Timeline view** is the default view of Camtasia Studio. This view shows the different elements in your video as part of its total duration:

IV: Editing

The **Storyboard view**, in contrast, shows the individual video and image clips in chronological succession, as if they were index cards:

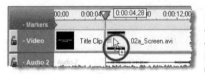

In the next section, we'll talk a lot more about these two views, the purpose of each, how to work within them, their limits, etc. What's important for this section is that you know how to effectively add clips to both views.

Without further ado, this is how you **move your clips out of the Clip Bin** and into the spotlight:

- Right-click the desired clip in your Clip Bin, and choose **Add to Timeline** (or **Add to Storyboard**, depending on which view you have enabled). The clip will automatically be placed after all the other clips currently in your project.

    or

- Click and hold on your desired clip, dragging it down onto the Storyboard or Timeline. In both views, you can specify the chronological order.

    Here I am dragging a clip to my Timeline. If I drop the clip here, it will appear between my title clip and 02a_Screen.avi.

    If you have other clips already in your video, you can drop the current clip at the beginning or end of the sequence, or any point in between, depending on where your mouse cursor is when you release the button.

Audio clips do not show up on the Storyboard. If you're in Storyboard view and you attempt to add an audio clip to your video, it will automatically switch to Timeline view.

Keep in mind that you can add multiple clips to either the Timeline or Storyboard at once. Just select all the clips you want to add from the Clip Bin. Any standard method of multiple file selection will work here:

- To select a sequence of clips, click and drag an area over your clips to select them.

or

- Click the first clip in the sequence, then Shift-click on the last clip.

or

- To select/deselect individual clips, Ctrl-click on them.

Then simply follow either of the methods for adding clips to the Timeline or Storyboard discussed above. The order in which the clips will be added is taken directly from whatever sort order is currently in effect in your Clip Bin, so it behooves you to sort your Clip Bin content in the order that most closely approximates your desired video order *before* adding them to your video.

Adjusting Your Project Settings

When you add your first clip to the Timeline, notice that a special dialog appears:

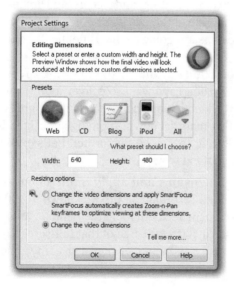

The **Project Settings** dialog lets you select the editing dimensions of your project as well as the means by which those dimensions are achieved. Why is this important? Well, keep in mind that the dimensions at which you recorded your clips may not necessarily be ideal when it comes time to share that content with the world. You might have recorded an application at 1280 x 1024, the full dimensions of your monitor, but you want people to be able to comfortably view it in a web page without having to scroll around. Or perhaps you recorded at a comparatively reasonable 640 x 480, but then need to share that video on a mobile device that has a maximum resolution of 320 x 240. The fact that the various clips and images on your Timeline might also be of different sizes implies a level of complication that your Project Settings can help resolve.

This dialog will help you determine the best dimensions for the content based on your desired output. Once you decide on a set of dimensions, then those are the dimensions at which you'll be editing your overall project. Say, for example, that you choose standard Blog output at 400 x 300 pixels. All images and clips on your Timeline will then be displayed at a resolution of 400 x 300, meaning that you now have a consistent editing environment that will be exactly the same as your final output. No surprises.

In the **Presets** section of this dialog, you can set the dimensions in a number of ways. You can simply choose the defaults for going to Web, CD, Blog, or iPod. The All drop-down list includes some additional options, including QuickTime and Windows Media. The two options at the end of the All drop-down are also quite useful: Custom, which reflects your most recent setting, and Recording Dimensions, which is the actual original size of the clip you're dragging down onto the Timeline. If multiple clips are going to the Timeline, then the Recording Dimensions will reflect the largest of these.

Next, we come to **Resizing options**. If you're taking larger content (say, a full-screen recording) and want to deliver it for a smaller format (for example, embedded in your blog), then you've got two basic options for sizing that material down: zooming or scaling. In almost every case, you'll want to choose the former. Let's examine these two options to understand why.

■ **Change the video dimensions and apply SmartFocus.** Instead of scaling that full-screen recording all the way down to 400 x 300, it's easy to use SmartFocus to zoom in on the content. Your audience will therefore see a 400 x 300 area of that full-screen recording at any one time, but at 100% of its original size, meaning that the quality will remain perfect.

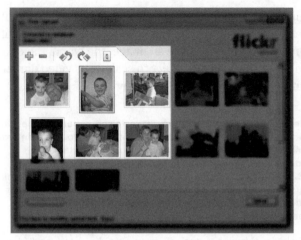

When zoomed into an area, only part of the original capture area will be visible. However, this portion will be shown full-size with perfect quality. And if the action shifts to another part of the capture area, SmartFocus can shift the focus right along with it.

So what is SmartFocus? Here's a little background: Camtasia Studio has supported the creation of zoom and pan points for a long time now. The problem was that the process of manually setting all those points was pretty laborious, which led a lot of folks to simply not bother with it. Scaling the content, while producing less-than-desirable quality, was much faster, easier, and hence deadline-friendly.

Now that SmartFocus has arrived on the scene, you have no excuses. This technology uses a complex algorithm to determine where the action is on your screen. It then automatically creates the zoom and pan points *for* you, following the action around your capture area. As with any automated process, it may require some manual tweaking, but it does offer an amazing, high-quality viewing experience for surprisingly little effort. We'll talk more about SmartFocus when we get to the Zoom-n-Pan Effects section of Chapter 11.

- **Change the video dimensions**. By contrast, this option simply scales your original content down to fit the desired dimensions. This tends to result in incredibly poor quality. Why? As you probably know, your screen is made up of pixels. Say that part of your video contains a cluster of these four pixels:

blue	black
white	red

When material needs to be scaled down, it needs to take these four pixels and make just one. But what color to make it? Obviously,

IV: Editing

quality takes a major hit. Real-world video can scale quite well, but screen video, with its hard lines and small text, does not. And of course, the more you scale an image, the worse the effect. My recommendation is therefore *not* to scale your video dimensions, as seemingly easy an answer as it may be.

Often, the best way to avoid the zoom vs. scale conundrum is simply to capture your video at the same dimensions with which you plan on producing. Mind you, it takes a little planning. Plus, the content and distribution method often make it impossible. For instance, you can't make a 320 x 240 iPod tutorial about Adobe Photoshop without zooming or scaling; it's a logistical impossibility. But if you can finagle it so that your capture area and final output dimensions are the same, it helps avoid a bit of labor.

So, now that you've selected your editing dimensions and set resize options (if applicable), just click **OK**. You can always return to the Project Settings dialog by clicking the Scale button in the upper left-hand corner of the video preview:

In addition to toggling the Video Preview between Shrink to fit and 100% Scale modes, this button also lets you access the Project Settings dialog at any point.

Basic Editing in the Timeline View

Now that you have some clips on the Timeline, it's time to learn how we can wield its power to make those clips dance and sing. The Timeline view opens by default, and for good reason: All your editing happens here. Before we delve into the details, I'm going to give you a bird's-eye view of the Timeline and its functions. First off, your Timeline view looks a bit like this, and contains the following components:

1. Editing toolbar, 2. Time reference area, 3. Video seek bar, 4. Playback head, 5. Tracks, 6. Track locks, 7. Scroll bar.

① **Editing toolbar.** This is where you can execute editing commands such as zooming in and out on the Timeline, cutting selected segments, splitting clips, alternating between the Timeline and Storyboard views, adjusting your audio on the fly, and selecting which tracks you wish to view.

② **Time reference area.** This bar shows the running time of your video being incremented across the Timeline. It gives you a good idea of the length of each segment and how it contributes to the overall running time. The time reference area will be incremented differently depending on your current level of zoom.

③ **Video seek bar.** This little green triangle represents the spot on your Timeline from whence you'll begin playback. The seek bar is also used for the selection of clip sections so that they can be edited or removed. Selected portions are highlighted in blue.

④ **Playback head.** This vertical line shows where you currently are in the playback of your Timeline. If you click Stop, the playback head will return to the seek bar.

⑤ **Tracks.** In addition to the Video and Audio tracks, virtually all special effects have their own track so that you can easily see exactly where they appear on the Timeline.

⑥ **Track locks.** These can lock specific tracks (or groups of tracks) so that they are unaffected by any editing you do to a specific part of the Timeline.

⑦ **Scroll bar.** If you zoom in on your Timeline to the point that your clips can no longer be displayed within your Camtasia Studio application window, the scroll bar appears so that you still have access to your entire Timeline. You can also scroll your content with your mouse wheel if you have one.

The Timeline view offers the most complete picture of your video and all its elements. After all, the Timeline is not only where you can arrange the videos, images, and audio clips from your Clip Bin, it's also where you manage special effects like Callouts, Picture-in-Picture, and Quizzes. Each of these elements displays in the Timeline in its own track. More on tracks in a bit. For now, we'll be focusing mainly on the Video track and Audio 1 track, as these are the tracks that are open by default.

All the imported video and image clips are placed in your Video track. If the video clip in question contains any narration or mouse/keyboard sound effects in its audio track, you'll find this information in the Audio 1 track. And yes, there is an Audio 2 track (hence the need for a numerical designation). Audio 2 is where the imported audio clips go when you add them to your Timeline. Both audio tracks appear as waveform images on your Timeline. We'll talk more about Camtasia Studio's audio capabilities in Chapter 10, "Working with Other Media: Audio, PIP, and Title Clips."

Viewing Your Work on the Timeline

Concentrating on our Video track, if you add a series of videos and still images, you'll see a multitude of boxes representing these clips on the Timeline. Within each box, there is a thumbnail image that signifies the clip's contents. You've probably noticed that all of these boxes are of varying sizes. This is because the width of the clip's box on the Timeline is demonstrative of the clip's actual length. Check out the row of numbers between your Editing toolbar and your Video track:

| 00;00 | 0:00:00;12 | 0:00:00;24 ▼ | 0:00:01;06 | 0:00:01;18 | 0:00:02;00 |

This is the time reference area. It is your guide to gauging just how long your video is getting as you add and edit your content. It also offers the most convenient way by far of instantly moving to any point in your video. Place your mouse cursor over any point on the time reference area and click. What just happened? Your seek bar (that little green upside-down triangle) immediately jumped to where you clicked, and the content of the Video Preview area changed. You are now at the exact point in your video that you selected. If you click the **Play** button within the Video Preview area, the video will play from that point forward. Click **Stop**, and the playback head will return to the seek bar.

> The time reference area is now based on frames rather than on fractions of a second. For example, the time designation 1:38:20;16 means one hour, 38 minutes, 20 seconds, and 16 frames (out of 30). This ensures that the smallest selectable unit is one frame.

The one problem with moving the seek bar around using the time reference area is that you can't really see where you're going in the preview area until you click. You can remedy this with an alternate way of moving through your video: the preview area's **scrubber bar**. The scrubber bar is that little round button on a slider, which looks like this:

Just click and drag the playback head around, and you can see in the preview area exactly where you are and where you're going. Notice that the seek bar in the Timeline follows you as you do so.

Previewing Your Content

The ability to control your Timeline's playback doesn't stop with the basics. You have a range of choices for moving around in your video preview as well as adjusting its view. Here's a quick reference table that may help:

Name	Button	Menu Command	Hotkey	Notes
Play	▶	Play > Play/Pause	Ctrl-Space	Toggles between Play and Pause.
Pause	⏸	Play > Play/Pause	Ctrl-Space	
Play from beginning	▶			Plays the video from the beginning, regardless of where the seek bar is on the Timeline.
Stop	⏹	Play > Stop	Ctrl+Alt-Space	
Beginning	---	Play > Beginning	Ctrl-Home	Returns to the beginning of the Timeline.
End	---	Play > End	Ctrl-End	Moves to the end of the Timeline.
Previous Clip	⏮	Play > Previous Clip	Ctrl+Alt-←	This command and the next will quickly move you from one clip to another on your Timeline.
Next Clip	⏭	Play > Next Clip	Ctrl+Alt-→	
Step Backward	◀	Play > Step Backward	Ctrl-←	Holding down this and the next hotkeys will rewind/fast forward through your content.
Step Forward	▶▶	Play > Step Forward	Ctrl-→	

Name	Button	Menu Command	Hotkey	Notes
Previous Marker	---	Play > Previous Marker	Ctrl-[	This command and the next let you quickly move from marker to marker on the Timeline. We'll discuss markers in detail later in this chapter.
Next Marker	---	Play > Next Marker	Ctrl-]	
Toggle Shrink-to-Fit mode	800x600, Shrink to fit	View > Shrink to Fit		If the dimensions of your clip are larger than the preview area, this command toggles between scaling your content down and displaying it full-size with scroll bars. Can also bring up your Project Settings dialog.
Full Screen	▣	View > Full Screen	Alt-Enter (can also press Esc to exit)	Displays your content in full-screen mode, meaning that you will not have access to the Timeline or any other part of the Camtasia Studio interface, so you'd better be comfortable with the playback hotkeys before doing it.
Detach video preview	▣			Undocks the preview area to its own window, where it can be dragged to another part of the screen, or even to a second monitor.

I'm a big fan of using hotkeys to get around. Once you've got them down, navigating even a complicated series of clips becomes child's play. Plus, hotkeys are the *only* way to rewind or fast forward in your Video Preview. And finally, once you've learned these hotkeys, learning to select content for editing with the keyboard is just a matter of adding the Shift key to the mix (more on this coming up).

In brief: Learn them. Use them. They'll make your work that much easier.

Moving, Selecting, and Trimming Your Timeline Content

Moving Clips Around on the Timeline

In moving clips from the Clip Bin onto the Timeline, you learned that you can manipulate the order of clips on the Timeline. By dropping a new video clip over a particular pre-existing clip on your Timeline, we note that it and all the clips to the right of it move over to the right in order to make room for this new addition (as opposed to New Edition, the '80s pop group with Bobby Brown). Keep in mind that you can pick up clips on the Timeline whenever you want, and then drag them around to adjust the order. When dragging, the Timeline will adjust automatically, so you know that when you release the mouse button, the clip will remain exactly where you want it.

Audio and PIP clips behave a little differently than video clips on the Timeline. Video clips always appear next to one another in direct succession. They may be reordered at any time, but there can be no pauses between them. Audio clips in the Audio 2 track as well as video in your PIP track have some "give" to them. They're a lot more flexible in terms of where they can be placed.

Selecting Content for Editing on the Timeline

Now that we know how to move around in the video and play back our content in the preview area, we're one step closer to doing some editing. But we have to first *select* the content in our Timeline that we want to apply those editing changes *to*. Selected content on the Timeline is highlighted in blue, like this:

0:00:54;00	0:56;00	0:00:58;00	01:00;00	0:01:02;00
	Quizzing.AVI	Quizzing.AVI		Quizzing.AVI

Once a segment is highlighted, it can be edited.

The easiest way to select the segment is by clicking and dragging on the **time reference area.** Just place your mouse cursor where you'd like the selection to begin, click and hold, drag the cursor to the end point of the desired selection, and then release. The reverse also works (selection from the end to the beginning). When mousing over either end of the selection, its triangle will glow red. This can be handy when doing a very fine selection where the two ends are close together, as the red highlight indicates which side of the selection will move when you click and drag. Zooming in on the Timeline can help with this problem as well — more on that in a moment.

You may notice when dragging around to make your selections that your selection occasionally "snaps" to objects, such as the beginning or end of video and audio clips, as if they were magnetized. This is done intentionally to facilitate the editing of your clips without accidentally overlapping and clipping out content you don't want to lose. I personally find it helpful, but if it annoys you, you can turn off this snapping effect for the various objects that support snapping. Simply choose View > Snap-to, and then choose the object type you want to disable from the submenu.

In addition to selecting with the mouse, there are more precise selections that we can make using the keyboard hotkeys. Now, assuming you've been a good student and have learned all the basic playback hotkeys, adding the power of selection is a breeze. Just hold down the **Shift** key in addition to the desired key combination.

For example, we learned you can step forward in the Timeline by pressing **Ctrl-→** (as well as hold this hotkey down to fast forward). By pressing or holding **Ctrl+Shift-→**, you do pretty much the same thing, except that you're selecting as you go. You can also select from a certain point to the beginning or end of its clip by making use of the Previous Clip/Next Clip commands (**Ctrl+Shift+Alt-→** and **Ctrl+Shift+Alt-←**), or even select from a point all the way to the beginning or end of the *entire Timeline* with the Beginning and End commands (**Ctrl+Shift-Home, Ctrl+Shift-End**).

Of course, nothing prevents you from using a *combination* of your mouse and keyboard selection techniques. I do it all the time. Just do a general selection with your mouse cursor, and then use your keyboard hotkeys to refine it by stepping the selection forward or backward a little at a time. Note that you only have control over one end of the selection, namely the last end (where your finger left the mouse button). So if it's the *beginning* part of the selection that you need to finely adjust, perform your mouse selection starting at the end of the desired selection and then going back to the beginning.

Zooming In and Out on the Timeline

If you want to do any detailed selections inside a lengthy video, you'll be subjecting yourself to a lot of frustration if you don't learn how to zoom. Zooming in and out on your Timeline is a wonderful way to either magnify a small portion of a single clip so that you can perform extremely fine editing, or pull back to get a broad overview of the entire Timeline. And of course, there are numerous small increments between these two extremes. When zooming in, the width of each of your clips appears longer. Additionally, you'll notice that the time reference area has shifted, and that the increments between time designations have changed to reflect the current zoom level.

Zooming in or out doesn't just affect the view of your clips — the Timeline *functions* differently, too. Specifically, stepping forward or backward (either with selection or without) is *finer* when zoomed in. That is, each step consists of fewer frames. The opposite is true when zoomed out. So, when using the keyboard hotkeys to step the selection gradually forward or backward, you might find that the granularity of your selection is just too coarse. If so, the problem may simply be that you aren't zoomed in far enough.

On your Editing toolbar, you can easily zoom by clicking the **Zoom In** and **Zoom Out** buttons.

These buttons zoom in increments, so clicking them multiple times will have a cumulative effect. Note that there are also five keyboard hotkeys for zooming, all of which can be found in the View menu of Camtasia Studio. They are:

Zoom Type	Hotkey	Note
Zoom In	Ctrl-+ (plus)	Zooms in incrementally.
Zoom Out	Ctrl-— (minus)	Zooms out incrementally.
Zoom to Fit	Ctrl-F9	Sets the zoom so that the whole Timeline fits precisely within your application window.
Zoom to Selection	Ctrl-F10	Zooms in on your current selection, fitting it to the exact width of the Camtasia Studio application window. You must have a segment selected in order to use it (which should go without saying, but I thought I'd state it for the record).
Zoom to Maximum	Ctrl-F11	Zooms as far in as you can possibly go, allowing you to select individual frames if desired.

Trimming Content from the Timeline: Method 1

So, we've learned how to make selections, and even to zoom in for a closer look. What's the real-world use for all this? Well, friends, selecting content designates it out of all your other content to be on the business end of your editing commands. For audio segments, this may mean fading in the sound or cranking up the volume, but for video segments, it pretty much means only one thing: deletion.

After importing your raw footage, it's entirely likely that you'll find segments within your clips you'll want to get rid of. Whether it's a bad take, an errant window opening in the middle of your recording area, or a pause big enough to drive a Mack truck through, we all have content we'd rather leave on the cutting room floor, so to speak. To cut a particular segment, the first step is to simply select it.

After selecting the doomed material, it's a simple matter of **executing the cut** by doing one of the following:

- Click the **Cut Selection** button on the Editing toolbar (✂).

  or

- Choose **Cut Selection** from the **Edit** menu.

  or

- Press **Ctrl-X**. Note that this differs from most other applications in that the cut material is *not* placed in the clipboard for later pasting. It's just plain gone.

Boom. Done. Note that no gaping holes are left — everything to the right of the cut segment now butts right up against everything to the left. For the visually inclined, here's a quick before-and-after shot to illustrate:

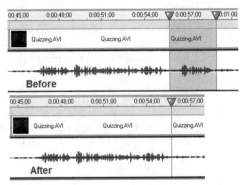

Also, keep in mind that your cut can be within a single clip or can span many clips. If you can select it, you can trash it. But there's something important you need to make note of: Camtasia Studio utilizes what is known as *nondestructive editing*. This means that your original clips (those little guys sitting in the Clip Bin) are *untouched*.

How does Camtasia Studio do this? Well, your project file references all the clips you dragged down to the Timeline, and in its internal data structure, all your little edits are noted. The preview compiles this information on the fly while you're playing back the content of your Timeline, but those referenced files are not actually changed in any way. This gives you tremendous flexibility. In addition to not having to make a bunch of file backups, you have the freedom to reuse your clips for different purposes. You could theoretically drag the same clip from the Clip Bin to three different locations on your Timeline, making different edits to each one. Camtasia Studio would track all this, and the original file wouldn't be harmed.

If so desired, you can bring back your deleted material by choosing **Undo**. If you don't dig your undo, it's easy to **Redo** what you did (or is it *un*did?). These commands can be executed thusly:

Name	Menu Command	Hotkey	Main Toolbar Button
Undo	Edit > Undo	Ctrl-Z	
Redo	Edit > Redo	Ctrl-Y	

Keep in mind that, depending on the size and complexity of your cut, it may take Camtasia Studio a few seconds to get everything reassembled. If you really mess things up, you always have the option of trashing the clip, and then dragging the original clip down from the Clip Bin to re-edit as needed. If you want to get rid of an *entire* clip, no selecting is necessary. Simply click on the clip and press **Delete** (or right-click the clip and choose **Remove from Timeline**).

Trimming Content from the Timeline: Method 2

Sometimes you might just need to trim a few seconds off the beginning or end of the original clip. You know, those moments when you were busy fumbling around the Recorder, trying to get it to start or stop? Obviously, you don't want to keep those parts.

Now, while Method 1 would also work just fine for getting rid of those portions, there is an alternate way. Go ahead and click on one of your clips in the Timeline. It should look like this:

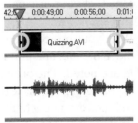 The beginning and end of each clip can be dragged to make it shorter.

You see those little triangles on each end? By placing your mouse cursor over one of these (until your cursor turns into a dual-headed arrow (↔), you can **click and drag** to shorten the clip on either end. Now, you do have to be ever-watchful of your mouse cursor placement. Since the end of one clip and the beginning of the next are so close together, you can end up manipulating the wrong clip if you're not careful. The advantage that this has over Method 1 is that you can always elongate the clip back to its original size (but not longer, since by definition a video only has a finite amount of material to work with), effectively undoing your cut, even if you originally did it 100 commands ago. Audio clips can be shortened the same way. Images, however, are a different story….

If you dragged any images from your Clip Bin onto the Timeline, you may have noticed your image had a duration of five seconds on the Timeline. Why five seconds, you ask? Well, since static media elements like images (and title clips, which we'll talk about in the next chapter) have *no* pre-established duration, Camtasia Studio assigns it one for display in your video.

I bring this up because the duration of an image on the Timeline can also be changed with Method 2. Simply by clicking and dragging on the clip's border, it can easily be shortened or, since an image has no inherent duration, *lengthened*. You can take that five-second image clip and make it .1 seconds or 1,000, whatever suits your needs.

The recently added clip doesn't have to be five seconds, of course. That's just the default set by the program — a default that can be altered at will.

If you want to **change the default length for images** on the Timeline, do the following:

1. In Camtasia Studio, choose **Options...** from the **Tools** menu. It should automatically open to the **Program** tab.

2. In the section marked Default duration (seconds), alter the **Images** field by clicking the spinner arrows or simply entering a number directly into the field. The field supports a range from 1 to 60 seconds. Click **OK**.

3. Drag an image clip from the Clip Bin onto the Timeline. The duration of the clip will reflect the new setting.

Please keep in mind that, just as with Method 1, your video's audio track will be gobbled up at the same rate as the Video track when reducing the length in this manner. Any special effects caught in the crossfire will also be gone. However, unlike Method 1, this method will not touch your Audio 2 track or your PIP tracks. We'll learn more about singling out individual tracks for editing when we talk about locking our tracks, coming up in a minute or two.

Advanced Editing Techniques

Splitting a Clip

Say that you have a wonderful video clip, every second of which is solid gold. You don't want to trim out any of it. But you would like to add a segment right into the *middle* of the clip that nicely illustrates one of your points. You already know by now that you can freely move clips around to reorder them. But to stick one clip in the middle of another? Well, friends and neighbors, you can accomplish this worthy goal by *splitting* the clip into two pieces. Once split, the two pieces act like separate clips, and can be individually moved and edited. And yes, you can insert other clips in between them.

IV: Editing

To **split a clip** into two parts, do the following:

1. Place the seek bar where you'd like the split to occur by clicking the appropriate spot on the time reference area.

2. Execute the split by clicking the **Split** button on the Editing toolbar (⬚⬚).

   or

   Choose **Split** from the **Edit** menu.

   or

   Right-click the video clip in the Timeline, and then choose **Split**.

   or

   Press **Ctrl-D**.

3. The clip is split into two pieces. Both parts will have the same name (the original clip's file name), so be careful when moving them around that you're not editing the wrong portion inadvertently.

Extending a Video Clip

It happens to the best of us. You record a clip with the utmost care, believing that you have the timing of the piece exactly lined up with your planned narration. You read your script aloud while playing back the contents of your Timeline, with one eye on the preview area and the other on the piece of paper in front of you. Oops. You didn't leave enough time. Or even worse, management gets back to you with some "minor" editing changes, adding a full paragraph of narration text. Looks like there's no way you'll be able to fit in all that narration without talking reallyreallyreally fast. Rather than altering the flow of your piece (or having to rerecord), consider instead performing a frame extension. Extending a frame is easy, and can be done anywhere within a clip.

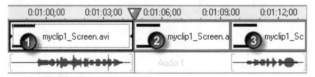

1. The first half of your clip. 2. The extended frame to accommodate the extra narration. 3. The second half of your clip.

I like frame extending because it's completely imperceptible to your audience. In the final video, a frame extension appears to the user as if you simply stopped moving the mouse for a moment to talk about the current feature, and when finished, it's *Okay, all done. Moving on....* Very natural-looking. Also very easy to forget this functionality is there*. Don't. It'll easily become one of the handiest tools in your editing arsenal.

To **extend a frame**, simply follow these steps:

1. Place the seek bar on the frame you'd like to extend by clicking the appropriate spot on the time reference area. This can be anywhere in a clip, not just the beginning or end.

2. Choose **Extend Frame...** from the **Edit** menu.

   or

   Right-click the video clip in the Timeline, and then choose **Extend Frame....**

   or

   Press **Ctrl-E**.

3. In the dialog that appears, choose the number of seconds by which you'd like to extend the frame. This can be any number from 1 to 600.

4. If the frame extended was in the middle of your clip, then the original clip is automatically split in two to make room for the extension.

---

* If you're recording narration with the Voice Narration tool, keep in mind that frame extensions can also be done (more easily in fact) by using the tool's Extend Current Frame feature, which we'll talk about in Chapter 10.

IV: Editing

The extension looks and behaves as its own clip. Once created, you can drag it to any location on the Timeline. Unfortunately, frame extensions cannot be resized the way that other kinds of clips can, so if your timing is off, you must delete the extension and try again.*

Adjusting Clip Speed

You may encounter rare instances where the timing of the entire clip is a bit off. Perhaps you were feeling rushed the day you recorded it, and as a result, *everything* is a bit too fast. I find that this happens often when a client insists on doing the actual screen recordings personally, relying on me to edit and narrate the final video. I'm almost never left with enough time to actually talk.

Or maybe the pacing is a little on the slow side, and you're constantly waiting for an activity to finish, leaving gaping pauses in your narration. It's also possible that you have a pretty standard clip in terms of its pacing, but you'd like to give it a time-lapse effect (either sped up or slowed down).

So what to do? You could edit out a bunch of segments within the clip to speed things up. You could do a bunch of frame extensions to slow things down. You could go back and rerecord the whole clip (possibly with the time-lapse effect engaged). Or you can simply change your **Clip Speed**. Altering the clip speed essentially takes the clip you currently have and speeds up or slows down the whole thing by a certain percentage that you set.

The one drawback to this feature is that the speed-altered clip cannot be previewed in real time. During the preview, the clip will play at its original speed, and you won't actually see the change in velocity until the final video is produced. At this point, it's too late to do anything about it if the timing is still off. Some people are comfortable "flying blind," and this limitation won't bother them. I personally like to know exactly what I'm getting before producing my final video, and the following procedure for changing a clip's speed reflects this personality quirk.

---

* That is, frame extensions of *video* clips cannot be resized. You can perform frame extension on image clips as well, and those extensions *can* be resized. But since an image clip can be drastically resized in either direction, anyway, why would you want to perform a frame extension on it in the first place?

To **alter the speed of a clip** for your final video, follow these easy steps*:

1. Once you've identified the clip you'd like to adjust, **Save** your project.

2. Start a **New Project**, importing the clip into your Clip Bin.

3. Drag the clip onto the Timeline, setting the editing dimensions to the clip's original size.

4. Choose **Clip Speed...** from the **Edit** menu.

   or

   Right-click your clip in the Timeline, and choose **Clip Speed...** from the context menu.

5. The Clip Speed dialog will appear:

   As you can see, you can select a new percentage for your clip. Enter a number less than 100% to slow it down and more than 100% to speed it up. Be careful not to ratchet it up or down too much on the first try — you'd be amazed how much difference a 10% to 20% increase/decrease can make. Once adjusted, the clip's new duration in seconds will appear. This can be handy in situations where the clip absolutely *must* be *x* seconds long.

6. Start the Production Wizard by clicking the **Produce Video As** button ( ) on the Main toolbar. Choose **Custom production settings**, and click **Next**.

7. In the Production Wizard, choose **AVI video** as your file format. Click **Next** to continue.

---

* These steps include procedures we haven't yet covered, such as producing a video. While I've attempted to guide you through this uncharted terrain in a stepwise, tunnel-vision manner, please refer to those portions of the book if you get stuck.

8. In the AVI Encoding Options box, you'll probably want to uncheck the **Encode audio** check box, even if your clip has an audio track. Unlike the Camtasia Recorder's Time-lapse capture feature, adjusting the clip speed will also affect the clip's audio, rendering your voice as either a slow, rumbling growl or a high-pitched chirp, depending on which direction you go. On the other hand, if that's the effect you're going for, then feel free to leave the audio on (but remember to set the audio at master level: PCM, 44.1 kHz, 16 Bit, Mono). The color depth and frame rate are both fine at Automatic. Click **Next** to continue.

9. In the Video Size box, click the **Largest video size** radio button if it is not already selected. Click **Next** to continue.

10. In the Video Options box, make sure all check boxes are unchecked. Click **Next** to continue.

11. In the Marker Options box, make sure all check boxes are unchecked. Click **Next** to continue.

12. In the Produce Video box, enter a new name for your file. I generally keep the file name the same, but add an "SA" (short for "speed-adjusted") tag at the end. For example: MyClipSA.avi. Click the **Browse** button (📷) to put your produced work in the directory of your choice. Make note of where you saved it; you'll need this info when you import it back into your main project. Feel free to clear all the other check boxes in this dialog. Click **Finish**.

13. View the produced file and make sure that the timing is right. Repeat steps 4 to 12 if it's not. Keep in mind that even if you execute the Clip Speed command multiple times, the number you enter is still a percentage of the *original* speed.

14. Reopen your main video project file. No need to save the other project; you won't be coming back to it. Import your speed-adjusted clip into the Clip Bin.

15. Replace the original clip on the Timeline with your speed-adjusted one. Edit as needed.

This procedure, while a bit more complicated, does show an accurate reflection of the video's total running time, and gives you a correct preview of what the speed-adjusted clip will look like within the broader scope of your final video. I've found that it saves time in the long run.

Viewing and Locking Your Tracks

Turning Your Tracks On and Off

Up to this point, we've dealt mainly with the Video track and maybe the Audio 1 track (which is the audio stream of your video files). In addition to your Video track (which includes video, image, and title clip content, and by definition, is *always* on), you have eight other tracks that you can turn on or off as needed. Why would you want to do this? Well, assuming you have content in several of those tracks (in our case, a big assumption, since we haven't covered the special effects of Camtasia Studio in this book as of yet), you can switch off the tracks that don't require your immediate attention and concentrate exclusively on those that do. In addition to freeing up a little screen real estate, turning off a track prevents you from "misclicking" and making inadvertent adjustments to a track that you didn't really want to touch. Also, turning off unused tracks allows for better side-by-side comparison of content in the tracks you're actively working with.

The Timeline with all tracks visible.

Note that when I say "turn on or off," I refer only to the visibility of the track information on your Timeline, *not* to the track's content in your video. In other words, I might turn off my Callouts track to give me a little more space on the Timeline, but my callouts *will* still show up in both the Video Preview and my final video.

When you add content to the Timeline that would reside in a track currently not visible, Camtasia Studio turns it on automatically. Any track can be turned on or off manually, regardless of whether or not it contains any content. Any content inside an "off" track is still there; it's just hidden. To make any needed adjustments, just turn the track back on.

IV: Editing

> This is how you **turn tracks on or off** in Camtasia Studio:
>
> 1. On the Editing toolbar just above the Timeline, click the **Tracks** button.
>
> 2. A drop-down list of tracks will appear, with check marks indicating which of those tracks are currently visible. Click the name of the track you wish to turn on or off.

If you so desire (and have the space), you can give more room to your tracks by clicking and dragging on the **colored border** just above the Editing toolbar. When you're in the correct spot, a dual-headed arrow (↕) will appear. Drag it upward to resize the Tracks area. Note that only the three audio tracks (Audio 1, Audio 2, and PIP Audio) expand very much when sized upward. This is done by design in order to give you a better view of the waveforms inside those tracks. The Video track will also expand by a finite amount to give you a slightly bigger view of the clips' thumbnail images.

Locking Your Tracks

When selecting and cutting out segments, *everything* that falls within that selection gets cut, including video (and its corresponding audio track), markers, special effects, background audio, and any picture-in-picture video. At least by default. This default can be changed.

How does it work? Well, when editing your video, that video's audio track and any special effects currently applied to the video are *always* automatically edited as well. Nothing you can do about it. They're a package deal.

That's *not* necessarily the case with your background audio, captions, and picture-in-picture (PIP) tracks. It's possible that you have your Audio 2 track (which, if you'll recall, can consist of anything from background music to sound effects to post-recording narration) as well as the video and audio tracks of your PIP segments *exactly* synchronized with your screen video, and you therefore *want* any editing you do to the screen video to affect those tracks as well. On the other hand, you might not. You might want to hack and slash your video to little bits, but don't want to see your Audio 2 or PIP tracks hacked to bits along with it. A good example of this is when you have background music in the Audio 2 track. If your video cuts affected the Audio 2 track as well, then the music would suddenly have missing pieces. It would skip over those portions cut by your video edits, with random notes or even whole measures suddenly gone. Suffice it to say, the playback of that lovely concerto you picked out for your video would be somewhat, erm... dis-concert-ing.

This is where the idea of *locking tracks* comes into play. You can lock a track (or group of tracks) to ensure that any editing you do as a whole won't trim out desired content. Take a look at this Timeline, where the Audio 2 track is locked. Here's a before-and-after shot:

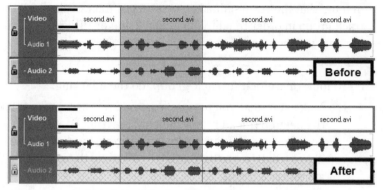

With Audio 2 locked, the video edit does not affect your background music whatsoever.

You see those little locks to the left-hand side of your tracks? These are the track locks. For the purposes of locking, all nine tracks are grouped into four categories:

- **Caption.** As captions are usually tied to your video content, most of the time you'll want to leave this unlocked — if a video segment gets cut, its corresponding captions should generally get the ax as well. But if you plan on keeping all the narration and just assigning it to a new video segment, you'll then want to keep the captioning content safely locked.

- **Video.** This includes your Video track (obviously), as well as Audio 1, Zoom, Quiz, and Callouts. Though the Markers track appears above this group, it too is tied to the Video track.

- **Audio 2.** This track is used exclusively for external audio files. These sound files can consist of just about anything, such as music, sound effects, and post-recording narration. We'll discuss this track in detail when we get to Chapter 10, "Working with Other Media: Audio, PIP, and Title Clips."

- **PIP.** A secondary video stream, either laid over the screen video in a picture-in-picture format or laid out side by side. While designed for the inclusion of real-world video such as a webcam shot of a person's face, this can be just about any video file. The PIP Audio track is much like Audio 1 in the sense that it is exclusively for the video's audio stream. You'll read more about creating and editing PIP material in the next two chapters.

Up to now, I've talked exclusively about turning off the Audio 2 and PIP track groups for the purpose of freely editing the screen video content without trimming the content in those other tracks. But keep in mind that the reverse holds true as well: You can also lock the Video track group in order to edit your Audio 2 and/or PIP content without hurting your screen video.

To **lock or unlock a track group**, do the following:

1. Make sure that you have at least one representative track of the desired track group visible on the Timeline. If not, turn on at least one of the tracks in the group by clicking the **Tracks** button on the Editing toolbar and then choosing the appropriate track.

2. Click the group's lock icon. When locked, the icon will change to a "closed padlock" and the affected tracks will be displayed with a light gray crisscross pattern:

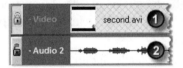

1. Locked. 2. Unlocked.

3. Make any desired edits to the unlocked tracks.

4. If desired, click the lock icon again to unlock.

Fun with Markers

When turning on the various tracks on the Timeline, you probably noticed the Markers track appearing above the main Video track. As I mentioned in Chapter 5, "Recording Your Screen," a marker is a placeholder that marks something noteworthy. Markers can be added both during the recording phase (see Chapter 5 for instructions on how to do this) and here in Camtasia Studio during editing. Markers can be added for any number of reasons, but their general uses in Camtasia Studio fall into three basic categories:

- **To leave a note for yourself.** I call these "breadcrumb markers." Particularly if I'm working on a long-term project where I might not touch the file again for a week or more, I often use markers to remind myself of editing changes that still need to be made. For example, if I need to add a custom callout but don't yet have the graphic image, I'll go to that spot on the Timeline and add a marker that says "Insert *x* custom callout here." When recording, I often add markers to note a new take rather than going through the hassle of stopping and restarting the Recorder. So, when I import my clip into Camtasia Studio and add it to the Timeline, the presence of markers lets me know that I should delete everything up to the most recent marker, as those sections contain takes where I screwed something up.

- **To prepare a table of contents.** There's a wonderful feature in Camtasia Studio that will use your markers to create a navigational menu for your final video. Simply set a marker for each new topic in the video, naming each one appropriately. Then produce your project. After production, the user will see a menu to the left of your video that contains links, the text of which is mined from the various markers' names. If a link is clicked, the user is brought to that exact point in the video where the marker had been placed. You'll learn more about how to create a table of contents in Chapter 12, "The Production Process."

- **To split your video into palatable pieces.** Markers can also be used for designating splits. If you have a particularly long video clip, you can set markers at key points throughout, and then have Camtasia Studio split the video at the various marker points with a single command. Once split, these clips can be reordered or otherwise edited at will.

  Additionally, if you have a reaaaally long project, to the point that exporting it as a single video becomes infeasible, you can have Camtasia Studio split the contents of your Timeline into individual video files according to markers that you set. This is done at production time, and Chapter 12, "The Production Process" explains it all.

So, now that we've discussed just why markers are so useful, let's go over exactly how to perform the various tasks related to marker creation, naming, editing, deletion, etc. If you created markers at record time, they'll automatically appear when you drag the marker-containing clip from the Clip Bin onto the Timeline. In fact, the Markers track will turn on automatically to ensure you don't miss them.

IV: Editing

But remember how I said that you can also **add a marker** right within Camtasia Studio? Here's how to do it:

1. Place the seek bar where you'd like to add the marker by clicking the appropriate spot on the time reference area.

2. Choose **Markers > Add a Marker** from the **Edit** menu.

   or

   Press **Ctrl-M**.

   or

   If the Markers track is visible on your Timeline (feel free to turn it on if it's not), right-click anywhere in the **Markers** track and choose **Add Marker**. Note the marker will be placed at the exact location of the seek bar, *not* at the spot where you right-clicked.

3. The Marker Name dialog opens automatically*. Enter a name into the field. This can be anything, of pretty much any length, though keep in mind that there's a finite amount of tooltip space for reading, so don't go writing the Great American Novel on it. Also, you'll want to keep it to just a few words if using the marker to construct a table of contents, as the text will need to fit in a column next to the video (though with most formats, this text *can* be set to wrap to multiple lines if necessary). Click **OK**.

---

* If you don't like the fact that the Marker Name dialog automatically opens every time you add a marker because it disrupts your "marker-adding groove," you can turn this capability off by going to **Tools > Options**, and then unchecking **Prompt for text when adding Markers** from the **Program** tab.

A marker's name doesn't make much of a difference if you're only using it to split up a great big file into smaller pieces. But it *is* important if you're using the marker as a built-in to-do list to remind yourself of work to be done. And it's really, really important if you're creating markers for a table of contents. After all, the names of your markers are what will be used as your link text.

A marker will be placed at the point of the seek bar. It looks like a little green diamond. If you mouse over the marker, you can find out a little information about it, such as the timing of the marker as well as its name.

Note that you can name/rename a marker at any point by double-clicking it, or by right-clicking and choosing **Set Marker Name**.

Moving, Deleting, and Syncing to Markers

Before we can start executing any high-level commands with our markers, you'll need a few more nuts-and-bolts techniques for manipulating them. Fortunately, your markers are very easily manipulated.

Here are three fun methods of **having your way with markers**:

- **Move 'em.** You can move a marker around by clicking and dragging its diamond anywhere on the Timeline.

- **Delete 'em.** To get rid of a marker, simply click it once and then press the **Delete** key.

    or

    Right-click the marker, and then choose **Delete from Timeline**.

    or

    To get rid of all markers at once, choose **Markers > Remove All Markers** from the **Edit** menu.

- **Sync to 'em.** To sync the seek bar to the exact spot of your marker, simply click on the marker.

    or

    Right-click the marker, and then choose **Move to this Marker** (though frankly, this seems like unnecessary work to me).

In addition to clicking in order to sync the seek bar to a marker, you can actually move it from marker to marker with two special commands: one for moving forward and one for going backward:

Name	Menu Command	Hotkey
Previous Marker	Play > Previous Marker	Ctrl-[
Next Marker	Play > Next Marker	Ctrl-]

These commands will cycle through your markers, meaning that when you hit the last marker and execute the Next Marker command again, it'll go back to the first marker. You can also execute these commands regardless of whether or not the playback head is in motion (though it will stop once you do).

Splitting Up Your Timeline Using Markers

Remember when I said that you can split one or more clips into a bunch of individual clips using your markers? Once you have your markers set up, it can all be done with a single command. Keep in mind that it does this for each and every marker on your Timeline — unfortunately, you cannot simply pick and choose which markers will receive a split and which won't.

What's the benefit of this? Well, if you're working with particularly long clips with a variety of topics in each one, splitting according to your markers will allow you to adjust the order of these topics rather than being stuck with the order in which you recorded it. You can also perform other clip-specific edits such as adjusting the clip speed of one topic, while leaving the others alone.

To **split your Timeline content according to your markers**, do the following:

1. Create all your markers, double-checking each one to ensure that they're all placed exactly where you want them.

2. Choose **Markers > Split at All Markers** from the **Edit** menu.

This procedure effectively creates a series of clips according to your markers. These individual clips behave just as if you had conducted a series of manual splits, allowing you to move them around, perform individual edits, and resize them (both reducing and expanding). I find that creating markers to conduct splits alone doesn't really save you any more time than splitting them manually does, but if you already have the markers in place for another reason, the ability to split at all marker points can be a great help.

Before closing out the section on markers, I want to draw your attention to the fact that the commands for creating a table of contents as well as splitting your Timeline content by markers are both executed during production. We'll discuss these items in detail when we get to Chapter 12, "The Production Process."

Saving Your Work

Saving your video project is a relatively straightforward process. When you save, a project file with the extension .camproj is created. It contains data on the placement and editing of all the material from your original clips. Remember how I said that the files referenced by the project aren't actually altered in any way? This is because the project file keeps track of all the Timeline information and its organization. Every callout, every marker, every *everything* related to your project is somehow tracked in this file.

But the project file isn't the only way of saving your work. You can also export your project to a ZIP format, thus making it ready for travel. You can even save off the Timeline's audio to its own file or save a frame of video as a still image. I'll show you how in the following sections.

Saving a Project

To **save your video project**, do the following:

1. Click the **Save Project** button (💾) on the Main toolbar.

   or

   Choose **Save** from the **File** menu.

   or

   Press **Ctrl-S**.

   or

   Choose **Save As...** from the **File** menu. Whereas the first three options will only present the user with a dialog for choosing a file name and location for the project if the project hadn't been saved previously, Save As... will always bring up this dialog. This will allow you to save off a new version of any project you've saved previously, under a different name and/or location.

2. If saving for the first time (or if executing the Save As... command), the Save As dialog appears. You are prompted to enter a file name as well as specify a directory. This is a standard Windows dialog that will look slightly different depending on your specific operating system.

3. As a housekeeping nicety, you have a drop-down list in your dialog called **Source clips**, which helps you keep your project file and media files nicely bundled together. If you're like me and are always careful about keeping a standard directory for your project and media files, then you can leave it on the default **Keep source clips in current locations.** But if your source clips are located all over the place, you can also opt to move or copy your media files to your project folder. Doing so means better organization and less chance of inadvertently deleting a file that you didn't know still belonged to one of your projects.

4. Once you've navigated to the correct directory and typed in a file name, click **Save**, or choose **Cancel** to exit the dialog without saving your changes.

5. If you have saved previously, choosing any Save option (other than Save As...) will simply write your changes to the current file, and no further action on your part is necessary.

Your video project file contains all the editing data for the external video data files that it references. The project file doesn't actually copy and hold onto any of your video data; otherwise, your project file would be extremely large. The downside of this is that if any of your referenced video files are deleted or moved, your project will be essentially broken. If Camtasia Studio cannot find a file referenced either in the Clip Bin or on the Timeline, it will display the following dialog, asking if you wish to go find it:

Camtasia Studio

Unable to locate file "c:\interactivity\survey.camrec". Would you like to specify its new location?

Yes   No   Cancel

If you choose **Yes**, a dialog will appear that will allow you to navigate to a replacement file. If you merely moved or renamed a file and didn't actually remove it, navigate to and click the appropriate file, and then click **Open**. Your project file will open, and you will notice that the file name reference will change within the project if you had renamed the file.

If, however, you really deleted the file in question, then choose **No**. All references to the file will then disappear from the Clip Bin and/or Timeline. Note that you may have to click through this same dialog twice or more in reference to the same file: once for the Clip Bin and once for the number of times the clip appears on the Timeline (keeping in mind that a split clip technically constitutes two clips).

AutoSave

If you're like me, chances are that when you're in "editing mode," your sole focus is on the task at hand, and paltry details like saving your work just don't occur to you. Then, the unthinkable happens: The application crashes. While TechSmith has put a lot of effort into making the product as stable as possible, no software is completely bug-free, and conflicts on your system could potentially lead to the occasional crash.

Even if you're not exactly diligent about saving, Camtasia Studio will help keep all your hard work safe by autosaving every 10 minutes. If desired, this interval can be set even narrower, and I actually encourage you to do so, as the AutoSave procedure is quick and invisible. Unless you're working on a gargantuan project, you're unlikely to even notice.

To toggle AutoSave or change the interval, go to **Tools > Options…**, and adjust the settings on the **Program** tab. I recommend setting the interval to a maximum of five minutes. When you restart the application and load your project after your crash, a dialog will pop up, telling you that an autosaved version of the project exists and asking if you wish to open it. An answer of Yes will open the autosaved version, and No will revert to the last saved version (and the autosaved version will be gone forever, so make sure you really mean it).

The AutoSave function does not go into effect until you save the project for the first time. It cannot recover untitled projects, so make sure that saving and giving your new project a name is one of the very first things you do.

Creating or Opening a Project

After teaching you how to save off a project, I suppose I'd be remiss in not telling you how to open it again, though I'm confident you'd be clever enough to figure it out all on your own. While I'm at it, I'll also show you how to start a new project from scratch. Since these functions are pretty similar if not identical to every other Windows program you've ever used, I'm not going to spend too much time on it. But let's go through the motions just for the sake of completeness, shall we?

This is how to **open a Camtasia Studio project** file:

1. From the **File** menu, choose **Open Project....**

   or

   Click the **Open Project** button ( ) on the Main toolbar.

   or

   Press **Ctrl-O**.

2. The Open dialog appears. Navigate to the folder that contains your desired project file.

3. Click your project file, and then click **Open**.

If you already have the file's directory open in Windows Explorer, a simple double-click of the file will also open it. Keep in mind that you can open a Camtasia Studio project file (.camproj) created with earlier versions of the software*, but you may need to convert the old file so that Camtasia Studio 5 can read it. You'll see a dialog that looks like this:

If you click **Yes**, Camtasia Studio completes the conversion and opens it as a new .camproj file. The original file is renamed (with the word "_backup" appended to the original name) and preserved, should you need it for archival purposes.

---

* Starting with Camtasia Studio 5, the application can no longer open the old Camtasia Producer (.cam) files that were part of Camtasia Studio 1.0 and earlier (back when the product was simply called Camtasia). If you have an earlier version of Camtasia Studio (versions 2 through 4), you might have luck using it to convert the .cam to an older .camproj file, and then using Camtasia Studio 5 to convert *that* file so that it's usable in version 5.

This process will flawlessly convert any older .camproj file, so any project going as far back as Camtasia Studio 2 can be salvaged. The one thing you'll want to keep in mind, however, is that older .camrec recordings won't be able to take advantage of SmartFocus, as this feature requires metadata from each .camrec that was only introduced in version 5.

This little speed bump aside, I've found the conversion from an old project to a new one to be a relatively quick and trouble-free process. Of course, if you'd rather start all over from scratch, you'll need to create a brand spanking new project.

Here's how to **start a new project** in Camtasia Studio:

1. From the **File** menu, choose **New Project....**

   or

   Click the **New Project** button ( ) on the Main toolbar.

   or

   Press **Ctrl-N**.

2. A new, untitled project is created with nothing in the Clip Bin. Either record the screen or start importing your previously created clips to get started.

Also, don't forget that the Camtasia Studio Welcome dialog you get when starting up Camtasia Studio can help you open a project or start a new one (either by recording content or by helping you bring some pre-existing content into the new project's Clip Bin).

Importing or Exporting a Project

With all those blasted media files that your Camtasia Studio project file has to reference, it goes without saying (though I will, anyway) that a project file doesn't travel particularly well. For example, when putting the project on a CD-ROM to give to a client, port to another computer, or file away for archiving, it's astoundingly easy to forget about a file or two in the process. Even if you managed to keep track of all your clips, other files such as custom callouts could (in fact, probably *would*) go by the wayside.

Fortunately, Camtasia Studio offers a built-in solution to the portability issue. You can quickly and easily export your project to a ZIP file, which includes all elements of your video, including video clips, audio, images, callouts, etc. In addition to conserving file space (it is packed into a ZIP file, after all), your exported project is now a single file that can be easily dropped onto whatever disc, flash drive, etc., you have handy. A special XML file included in the export, called a *manifest*, is used to coordinate all this (e.g., *myfilename.manifest*). The manifest contains a roster of all your project elements, so that Camtasia Studio knows what goes where without having to parse the entire contents of the ZIP file. For example, it's the manifest that tells Camtasia Studio whether an image file is in fact an image clip or actually a custom callout.

Bottom line, this function is a very welcome addition if you ever need to move a project from one computer to another, and its execution is pretty straightforward as well.

This is how to **export a Camtasia Studio project**:

1. Make any needed edits or adjustments to your project, saving the project file after you're finished.

2. From the **File** menu, choose **Export Project as Zip…**.

3. A dialog appears, prompting you to choose a name and location for the ZIP file. You can either enter a file path into the **New zip filename** field or click the **Browse** button (🖻) and navigate to it. At any rate, your ZIP file need not reside in the same directory (or have the same name) as your actual project.

4. If you leave **Include all files from Clip Bin in zip** unchecked, the exporter will ignore any clips sitting in your Clip Bin that haven't yet been added to the Timeline. This does not mean that your exported project won't have any files in its Clip Bin — those clips that have been added to the Timeline will still reside in your zipped project's Clip Bin.

5. Click **OK**. A brief progress dialog appears as the contents of your project are being packed up.

The resulting file can be read with any application that can extract ZIP files, such as WinZip or WinRAR (in fact, Windows XP and Vista have this capability built right into the operating system). However, with Camtasia Studio on the destination computer, unpacking your project is even easier. Camtasia Studio sports a corresponding **Import** feature that can automatically extract everything and even open up the extracted project for you when finished.

This is how we **import a zipped project** back into Camtasia Studio:

1. Place the exported (zipped) file in a location accessible to the destination computer.

2. Open Camtasia Studio. From the **File** menu, choose **Import Zipped Project…**.

3. The Import Zipped Project File dialog appears, with two file path fields that you'll need to fill.

4. In the **Zipped project file to import** field, we need to specify the location of the ZIP file. Either type in the file path directly or click the **Browse** button (⬚) and navigate to it.

5. Next, you'll need to decide where you want your new project to reside. It's advisable to start a new directory just for that project, since the normally high number of files imported can really clutter up a root directory. I mention this because the program defaults to importing your project data directly into your Camtasia Studio directory of your My Documents folder. Even if you want things in the Camtasia Studio folder, it behooves you to add a new folder name onto the end of the file path (e.g., *\myfoldername*). When you click **OK**, it'll ask if you want to create this new folder. Click **Yes**.

6. If you want to dive into your project right away, be sure to leave **Open project after import** checked.

7. You'll get a progress dialog as the file unpacks. Provided the option in step 6 was enabled, your new project will open in Camtasia Studio, ready for editing and production.

Since the exported project is basically just a garden-variety ZIP file, it can also be unpacked (using the Extract function) with any file compression application that supports ZIP, and, of course, pretty much all of them do. But I recommend using Camtasia Studio for importing, just to make sure everything winds up in the right spot (e.g., custom callouts get imported as such, etc.).

IV: Editing

Saving an Individual Video Frame

Should you ever desire to make a screenshot of your video, you don't need to fire up SnagIt and set up all your capture options. You can actually save off a frame of your video as an image file. Why would you want to do this? Here are a few common scenarios:

- You're creating written documentation to go along with your video, and want to spare yourself the extra work of creating screenshots just for the text portion.

- You want to advertise your newly created video on your web site.

- You're assembling a library of video links on your web site, and you want a thumbnail image of each one to accompany the title and description.

- You want your colleague to proof a particular screen, and a static image will do.

Saving a video frame is as easy as it is useful. Here's how it's done:

1. Move the seek bar to the exact frame you want to save, either by clicking a location on the time reference area or by using the various keyboard hotkeys.

2. Choose **Save Frame As...** from the **File** menu.

   or

   Press **Ctrl-F.**

3. A Save As dialog appears, where you must choose a location and file name for your image. By default, you have a pre-filled file name consisting of the project name and time location of that frame within the project (example: *MyProject (Time 0_02_49;15).png*).

4. Also, you need to choose a file type for your image: BMP, GIF, JPG, or PNG. Select the appropriate file type from the drop-down list and click **OK**.

Saving Just the Audio

In addition to saving a frame as a separate image, you can also split off your audio into its own file. This can be useful for importing audio into high-end third-party applications such as Adobe Audition or Sony SoundForge. It's also handy if you want to retain a video's audio track while discarding the video content itself (for example, to attach the same audio to an updated video).

This is how to **save the audio track** as its own file:

1. From the **File** menu, choose **Save Audio As....**

   or

   Press **Ctrl-U**.

2. A Save As dialog appears, prompting you to select a location and file name for your audio file. Do so and then select the type of file you want from the drop-down menu, either WAV (uncompressed and hence high quality, but large) or MP3 (slight quality loss but *much* smaller). Click **Save**, or choose **Cancel** to exit the dialog without saving.

Do keep in mind that executing this command will save all your audio tracks in a single WAV file. There is currently no way of selecting which tracks to save or of splitting tracks into multiple files. The only way around this is to delete or silence the audio segments that you don't want to have in the exported file, save your audio, and then undo the changes to your project until all the audio tracks are restored.

IV: Editing

Summary

The main Camtasia Studio application is where you can edit your base video footage, combining your individual clips into an overall presentation. The interface contains the Clip Bin, for storing your clips until you're ready to include them in your video; the Video Preview area, for getting a sense of what your video will look like; the Task List, for executing commands such as importing clips, adding special effects, and producing your content; and the Timeline/Storyboard, where you can rearrange and otherwise edit your video content.

Here's a (very) condensed version of how to **import and edit your clips** in Camtasia Studio:

1. Launch Camtasia Studio.

2. Execute the **Import Media** command, bringing in all the files you think you'll need on the project. These files will appear in the Clip Bin.

3. To add clips to your final video, drag them from the Clip Bin down onto your Timeline. You can alter their order by clicking and dragging them around the Timeline.

4. Adjust your Project Settings to reflect your planned output, possibly using SmartFocus to scale your original footage down.

5. You can edit out content from your clips by selecting a portion (using the mouse or keyboard) and choosing **Cut Selection**. Alternatively, you can trim the beginnings and endings of clips by clicking and dragging their left- and right-hand borders.

6. More advanced editing techniques, such as splitting the clip into two parts, extending the current frame, altering the speed of a clip, or changing the duration of an image, can be done by placing the seek bar in the appropriate spot and then executing the command.

7. If desired, markers can be added to your project for help in editing or to set up a table of contents. Simply place the seek bar in the right spot and then press **Ctrl-M**. Markers can be moved, renamed, or deleted as needed.

8. Don't forget to save your project frequently. Should you ever need to move your project to another computer, you may do so by using the export and import commands. You may also save a frame of video as a still image or save the audio in your project as a WAV or MP3 file.

Now that we have a handle on basic editing, let's lay in some additional streams of content, such as camera video as well as one or more audio streams, all of which is covered in the next chapter.

Exercises

Up to now, the exercises have been rather general and not geared toward a specific goal. That's about to change. We're going to create an actual video project using prerecorded clips. Our project is a tutorial about Camtasia MenuMaker. Since this project will be continued in subsequent chapters, it's important to save your work.

1. Open Camtasia Studio, and import the different media files from the Chapter 9 media folder on the companion CD into your Clip Bin. Double-click each one to preview it.

2. Drag the seven image/video clips to the Timeline from your Clip Bin, starting with the even-numbered clips, and then the odd-numbered ones.

3. In your Project Settings dialog, set your editing dimensions to Recording Dimensions (688 x 520).

4. After all the clips are on the Timeline, put them in numerical order*.

---

* You wouldn't normally alternate between .camrec and .avi for your captures. I've only done so to give you a little practice at sorting these files out in the Clip Bin and on the Timeline.

5. Check the duration of the image clip. Unless you've played with the settings, the image's length should default to 5 seconds.

6. Change the duration of the image clip to **10** seconds.

7. Drag your **narration.wav** audio clip onto the Timeline. Its duration should match that of your Video track pretty much exactly.

8. In clip 03.avi, there is a disconcerting pause at the end of the clip where nothing is really happening. Trim it out, from both the Audio and Video tracks.

9. Place markers at the beginning of each video clip (the AVI and CAMREC files). Name them thusly:

   - 01.avi: **Choosing a template.**
   - 03.avi: **Adding files.**
   - 04.camrec: **Main Menu properties.**
   - 05.avi: **Testing out your video.**
   - 06.camrec: **Creating your menu.**
   - 07.avi: **Copying your project to CD.**

10. Save your file as **MyProject.camproj**.

Chapter 10

Working with Other Media: Audio, PIP, and Title Clips

Now that you have your various screen video clips assembled and edited to your liking, you've got a good foundation upon which you can build by adding a few additional media streams. Back in the previous chapter, we talked about importing all sorts of different media types for use in your video presentations. While it's true that two of the three items we'll be discussing in this chapter (audio narration and camera video) can also be created during the recording process, to be frank, I find that concentrating on one stream of content at a time yields a much better quality product. This chapter addresses how to create these elements in *post-production*, that is, after recording has taken place. In the case of audio and PIP video, these can be done in post just as if you had created them while recording. You need only to tag along as the Video Preview progresses, recording your camera video and/or audio as you go. Just follow the steps laid out in this chapter, and you'll discover just how easy it is to assemble the "multiest" multimedia presentation on the block.

In Chapter 9, you learned how to use the Import media... command to bring various production elements into your Clip Bin. In this chapter, the focus will be on the remaining three commands in the Add section of your Task List. We'll be chatting about getting the most out of the following supplementary media:

- **Title Clips.** No more having to assemble a title screen using a huge, cumbersome image editing package and then importing it as a still image. Camtasia Studio offers a one-stop workshop for constructing title and ending screens. Add text, adjust the color, and even import a background image.

- **Voice Narration.** This is where you'll find out about the ins and outs of recording and editing quality audio narration to go with your video content. We'll cover both the basic Voice Narration tool and the Camtasia Audio Editor, a separate utility for creating and editing audio. We'll discuss the importing and saving of your audio tracks, and finally, tricks and troubleshooting tips for achieving the best sound possible.

- **Record Camera.** In addition to including a PIP track in your video during the recording process, you have the option of recording camera video after the fact as well. Here, I'll give you the basics of recording video content from a webcam or digital camcorder.

Adding Title Clips

Two of the most essential elements of video production are the opening and closing credits. The opening credits "warm up" the audience by providing a sense of what to expect in the upcoming material. The closing credits tell who's responsible for the work as well as possibly prompt the audience to action by telling them what they can do next. There are, of course, a gazillion variations on these themes. For example, title segments can also be placed in the middle of a video rather than just the beginning and end. And a title screen's content can be just as varied as its timing. Here are just a few ideas about where title screens work well with Camtasia Studio content:

- Placing an introductory screen at the beginning of the video to announce its content.

- Giving sales or contact information at the end of the video.

- Splitting the content into palatable chunks by introducing each new topic or theme with a new title clip.

- Setting up individual case studies or usability studies by introducing each new user's vital statistics.

Essentially, if you need to get a text message across in your video unfettered by other screen content, title clips are the way to go. And with all the formatting options available right within Camtasia Studio, you can easily crank out title screens that are as attractive as they are functional.

To get started with **creating title clips**, do the following:

- From the Add section of your Task List, choose **Title Clips**....

  or

- From the **Edit** menu, choose **Title Clips**....

Either one of these will bring up the Title Clips pane, which looks a bit like this:

As you can see, there are two areas that help us determine what our title clip will look like:

- The Title Clips pane, which lets you specify the text font and formatting, the background, and the clip's name.
- The Video Preview, which allows you to determine the placement of the clip's textual elements.

So, let's **create a title clip**:

1. **Title name.** The first order of business is to give the clip a name, which serves no purpose whatsoever other than as a reminder to yourself when looking over the items in your Clip Bin. Just enter a name into the field that'll help you remember the clip's actual content later on.

2. **Background.** You have two options in selecting the background of your title clip. You can go with a solid color, in which case you need only click the **Color...** button to specify a color from the palette.

or

You can go with a background image, which can be a BMP,
GIF, JPG, or PNG file. Just click the **Image** check box, and
then click the **Browse** button (🖼) to navigate to your
image, choosing **Open** after you've found and selected it.
Either that, or you can actually type the full file path of your
image directly into the corresponding field, but honestly, who
does that?

Now, since the background image will be stretched across
the entire title clip, make sure that the dimensions of your
image file correspond to those of your video's output dimensions as closely as possible, or you might just find that lovely
image stretched beyond recognition like a Sunday comic on a
piece of Silly Putty.

3. **Text.** Once you've got the background taken care of, let's add
    our text. Just click inside the text box and start typing.
    You've got some standard formatting capabilities here. As
    you've probably fired up a word processor application once or
    twice in your life, I'm quite certain that these tools are
    already second nature to most of you. However, to be com-
    plete (this is the *Definitive Guide*, after all), here's a handy
    reference table. I've also thrown in some useful editing com-
    mands, just for kicks.

Name	Button	Hotkey	Notes
Font	Arial ▾	---	Since your callouts are rendered prior to production, you don't have to worry about whether the desired font is on your users' systems.
Font size	36 ▾	---	
Bold	**B**	Ctrl-B	
Italics	*I*	Ctrl-I	
Underline	<u>U</u>	Ctrl-U	

Name	Button	Hotkey	Notes
Color	[ ]▼	---	Lets you change the color of any piece of selected text.
Text Drop Shadow	A	---	Places a gray drop shadow beneath your text.
Align Left	≣	Ctrl-L	The six alignment keys are useful in placing the text so that it's legible and so that it doesn't obscure the background image.
Align Center	≣	---	
Align Right	≣	---	
Align Top	=	---	
Align Vertical Center	=	---	
Align Bottom	=	---	
Select All	---	Ctrl-A	Selects all text for formatting change or deletion.
Copy	---	Ctrl-C	Copies selected text.
Cut	---	Ctrl-X	Cuts selected text.
Paste	---	Ctrl-V	Pastes any text from the clipboard into your text window.

4. **Video Preview.** Notice how the Title Clips pane and the Video Preview work in unison. The preview area is helpful for adjusting exactly where on the title clip you'd like the text to appear. To restrict the text to a particular section of the clip, simply resize the green bounding box by clicking and dragging one of its black handles. This is particularly

important with background images where there may be a portion of the image you don't want obscured by text.

5. Click **OK**. Notice how your brand-new title clip now appears in your Clip Bin. You can preview it at any time by simply double-clicking the clip in your Clip Bin, or by right-clicking it and then choosing **Preview Clip**.

6. To add the clip to your Timeline, right-click it in your Clip Bin, and then choose **Add to Timeline** (or **Add to PIP** if you'd prefer the title clip to appear on your PIP track). It will appear as the last clip on the track.

   or

   Click and drag the clip from your Clip Bin onto the Timeline or PIP track. This option gives you the added flexibility of being able to place the clip wherever on the track your heart desires, not just at the end.

7. As with any static image clip in your project, your title clip can be split or extended. You can also adjust the duration of the clip by right-clicking the instance on the Timeline and choosing **Title Duration....**

The default duration of your title clips can be set anywhere from 1 to 60 seconds. Go to **Tools > Options...**, and then enter a value into the Title clips field in the Default duration (seconds) section.

One of the great things about doing your title clips directly within Camtasia Studio rather than in an image editing application is that your clips stay completely editable. However, I *must* make absolutely clear to you exactly what happened when you dragged that title clip down from the Clip Bin onto the Timeline, as it will have a profound effect on how and where you edit your title clips should you ever decide to make changes.

Perhaps an analogy would be helpful. While in college, I worked in a costume shop, where I learned how to sew and make clothes from patterns. That title clip sitting in your Clip Bin is like a dress pattern. You can use that pattern to make an infinite number of dresses. Each dress, once created, can be custom tailored without changing the original pattern. Likewise, the pattern itself can be altered, meaning that every dress created from it from that point onward will incorporate those new alterations, but the dresses you made *before* you changed the pattern will obviously still sport the older look.

I can put a dozen or more instances of a single title clip onto my Timeline. Once it's on the Timeline, though, it becomes a completely separate entity from that clip currently sitting in the Clip Bin that spawned it. They no longer have *anything* to do with each other. I can make changes to the title clip in the Clip Bin, but any instances of that clip already on the Timeline will be unchanged. Only *new* instances will have the changes. I can also change a single instance on the Timeline, but neither the other "sibling" instances of the clip on the Timeline nor the "parent" clip in the Clip Bin will be touched as a result. Clear as mud? One obvious lesson here is to make absolutely sure the title clip you created is *really* what you want (in terms of both accuracy and design) before you start dragging a hundred instances of it onto the Timeline.

Here's how to **make changes to your title clips**, regardless of where they are:

1. For clips in the Clip Bin, simply right-click the title clip, and choose **Edit Title Clip**.

    or

    For clips on the Timeline, just right-click the desired instance of the title clip on the Timeline, and choose **Edit Title Clip**. Double-clicking the clip works, too.

2. Make the requisite changes, and click **OK**.

If you wish to get rid of the title clip entirely, you may do so the same way you would remove any other clip from your Clip Bin: Simply select it and press **Delete**. Alternatively, right-click the clip and then choose **Remove from Clip Bin**.

Finally, you can get basic information on title clips in your Clip Bin by right-clicking a clip and choosing **Properties…**. You'll see its name, its default width and height (which, by the way, correspond to the editing dimensions you set in the Project Properties dialog), its background image (if set), and the hex value of whatever background color you've chosen.

That's all for title clips. While not as flexible from a design perspective as something produced in Photoshop, for example, these clips have the wonderful advantages of being easily created and edited. This can be a godsend when deadlines are tight. And when altering a particular project to incorporate software updates (possibly months later),

IV: Editing

it's also nice to know that everything you need in order to make changes is right there inside the Camtasia Studio project file.

 The Title Clip feature works great for static title screens, but occasionally it's called for to spice things up by turning an average title screen into an animated extravaganza, complete with flying title text and dancing logos. For this, you'll need to turn to third-party applications. Two such programs, BluffTitler DX9 and WildFX Pro, can more than accommodate that need. Demos of both are included on the companion CD.

Working with Audio

In the previous chapter, I taught you all about how to import media clips, including audio, as well as how to add them to your Timeline for inclusion in your final production. This is fine and dandy if you already have some audio clips lying around that, by some miracle, are perfect sounding and already perfectly cut to the length of your video. Chances are, however, that you're not quite that lucky. This section is sort of a catch-all for all things audio. As you'll soon see, we've got a *lot* of ground to cover:

- We'll start by going over the essentials of recording audio narration using the **Voice Narration** tool.

- We'll talk about how to perform some basic editing of your audio directly on the Timeline.

- Of course, sometimes those tools are insufficient when you need to do something a tad more advanced (such as mixing two audio sources). It's times like these that you'll need to break out the **Camtasia Audio Editor**, and I'll give you the full details on how to use it.

- Finally, I'll give you some tips for getting a good recording from any source (including system sound). If you're having trouble with the logistics of getting your system set up to record sound, you might want to look here first. Appendix C, "Equipment Buyer's Guide," is also a good resource for those who are experiencing poor quality. It discusses the most common microphone setups, and can let you know when it's time to upgrade one or more components.

The Voice Narration Tool

Whether you end up adding voice narration to your video is a matter of personal taste. Some people decide to use captions and/or frequent callouts in lieu of narration, particularly in locked-down corporate environments where not every machine is equipped with a sound card. With my clients and trainees, I always strongly recommend that they narrate their videos. In addition to adding a more personal touch to your content, you've got a whole new stream of information available to you, an ability to engage another of the senses. The multimedia aspect has the capacity to truly draw the user into the video experience. And for vision-impaired users, it may be the primary (or only) way of receiving your information.

Say you do decide that narration would work well for your video. The next logical question is *when* you wish to add it. As I've mentioned earlier in this book, you can do so while you're recording your screen video. Many users of Camtasia Studio prefer to do it this way (I'm told), mainly because there's a certain simplicity in recording everything at once. I find that this system works mainly for quickie tutorials where you're nursing somebody you know through the process of executing a computer task. This is the kind of video where a barrage of awkward pauses and "Ums…" is completely acceptable, since it's likely that only one person is ever going to see it.

For soon-to-be-published tutorials and marketing spots, however, the task of recording everything in one take, while maintaining an acceptable level of polish, becomes a virtual impossibility. You've got to keep one eye on what you're doing with the mouse and keyboard, another eye on the storyboard to know what you should be doing next, another eye on your narration script, and yet another eye on your capture area toolbar to make sure your audio levels are okay. That's a lot of eyes. It therefore behooves you to focus on the screen video aspect at record time, and to narrate your video footage *after* the fact, in post-production.

Fortunately, this is not a complicated thing. When you decide to make an audio recording with Camtasia Studio, you actually have a couple of different options available to you. For one, you've got the Camtasia Audio Editor, which is a separate audio program inside the Camtasia Studio suite of applications. It's a wonderful resource, and we'll be covering it in just a bit.

The **Voice Narration** tool functions just a bit differently. It is embedded into the main Camtasia Studio interface, and with good reason. Its singular purpose is to let you narrate what's going on in your

IV: Editing

video. When you record narration with the Voice Narration tool, your Video Preview is playing back through the Timeline as you go along. During recording, you're simply talking about the various topics as they're happening on-screen. It's an organic process that feels very easy and natural.

So how do we get going? For starters, I recommend performing a first editing pass on your project *prior* to laying in your audio. Why is this? Well, when you add narration with the Voice Narration tool, you're synchronizing that audio with the video content. Keeping things neatly synced then becomes a challenge when you have a lot more editing to do. As I explained in Chapter 9, you have the ability to lock certain tracks so that any editing changes you make don't affect that track. So, if you have an audio track already in place on a video you want to extensively edit, you've got two choices:

■ Leave your audio track unlocked so that everything stays in sync throughout the editing process. Unfortunately, this means being very aware of where the sound waveforms are and only cutting video sections where there are pauses in the narration, or you could find that individual word and sentence fragments have been unintentionally destroyed.

■ Lock the audio track so that it isn't touched when you edit your video. However, keep in mind that cutting out sections of video will knock your audio and video tracks out of sync, forcing you to do some creative audio editing later to resynchronize them.

Either way, editing gets a lot more complicated once you've laid in an audio track. So do yourself a favor and edit the video first, keeping one eye on your script (now that you have an eye to spare) to make sure you're leaving enough room in the video to eventually say what you want to say.

So, you've got a nicely edited video. The final step before recording is to make sure you've got your audio hardware set up correctly. See the end of this section for setup tips, and also be sure to check out Appendix C, "Equipment Buyer's Guide," to see if you're missing any vital components. Now, on to recording your narration...

The first step is to **open the Voice Narration tool**, done thusly:

■ From the Add section of your Task List, choose **Voice Narration....**

or

■ Choose **Voice Narration...** from the **Edit** menu.

The Voice Narration pane appears. Before we actually begin recording, we have a few options to set. Our first choice pertains to which track we want to use, and yes, there *is* a difference between these tracks. The Audio track 1 has historically been reserved for pre-existing audio tracks of AVI files. It's where your audio would be if you recorded the narration during the actual capture. So, if you plan on doing background narration for videos that already have some sound effects in them, you'll want to use your Audio 2 track if you don't wish to overwrite the audio that's already there.

There's another thing about Audio 1 that you should know: It is inescapably tied to your Video track. If you want to edit the Video track, then the sound data in the Audio track 1 is along for the ride. There's no locking, hiding, or otherwise protecting it. They're a package deal. Therefore, pick **Record to audio track 2** if you think you might want to lock it. This is particularly important for background music tracks, since even the slightest edits can (and probably *will*) wreak total havoc on the timing of the music, the results of which are pretty jarring to the ear. As a general rule, I use Audio 1 only for the audio I recorded during capture (usually system sound, keyboard and mouse click sound effects, or PowerPoint audio), thus leaving the Audio 2 track for narration and possibly background music.

 Since the Audio track 1 is tied to your Video track (whatever that track may contain: AVI video, title clips, still images, etc.), keep in mind that the Audio track 2 will be your only option if there's nothing currently on your Video track on the Timeline. So if you immediately head over to the Voice Narration tool upon starting a new project, the Record to audio track 1 button will be grayed out.

Our next set of choices concerns the portions of the audio track we wish to use for recording. Camtasia Studio is kind enough to auto-terminate our recordings based on the parameters that we set here. We've got three options from which to choose:

■ **Until end of selection on timeline.** If you have a particular section of your Timeline selected, this option will only record as far as the right-hand edge of that selection, ensuring that any pre-existing audio outside your selection remains untouched. It's particularly helpful for recording retakes on the Audio track 1, where you've got a sentence that needs to be redone buried inside a bunch of narration you're more or less happy with. You cannot make Timeline selections while in the Voice Narration pane *until* you click this option.

IV: Editing

- **Until end of clip.** This option is especially handy if you're working with Audio track 1, and certain clips already have audio in them that you don't want to disturb. When the playback head reaches the end of the current clip, the recording will stop automatically.

- **Until end of timeline.** Recording won't stop until the end of the last clip in your Video track. When working with Audio track 1, be careful that you don't have any audio in front of the seek bar you want to save, as this option will mow down everything in its path. With Audio track 2, any audio in front of the recording will be pushed to the right if there's not enough space.

Regardless of what you choose, there is one option that can make life much easier if you suddenly find that the amount of planned narration vastly exceeds the length of your video footage. Checking **Auto-extend last video frame while I continue narrating** takes the final frame of the selection, clip, or Timeline (whichever you chose) and automatically extends it while you continue talking. The result is pretty seamless; no one will ever know that the original segment wasn't long enough. Of course, Camtasia Studio also offers a way of doing manual frame extensions while recording audio, and I'll talk about this in a moment.

If you've already got audio anywhere on your Timeline when you set out to record, one option you'll probably want checked is **Mute speakers during recording**. If left unchecked, all sound will be played back during recording. As you can imagine, having other bits of audio blasting from your speakers (and having your mic pick up the ambient sound) while you're trying to record your narration will probably lead to some nasty background artifacts that you really don't want on your narration track. So, what if the sound between your Audio tracks 1 and 2 are supposed to interact, and you therefore *need* to hear what's happening on the other track while you're recording? Leave Mute speakers during recording unchecked, and invest in a good pair of closed-ear headphones. That way, you'll be able to hear the playback of your other track, but your microphone won't. In fact, I generally recommend having an audio setup that allows you to monitor what your mic is picking up, anyway. While it might seem unnecessary (considering that you're already in the same room with your mic), what you hear and what your microphone hears may not be the same thing. When I started monitoring my input, I was able to catch errors and anomalies as soon as they were recorded. I could then quickly correct them. We'll talk more about audio monitoring in Appendix C, "Equipment Buyer's Guide."

The final part of the Voice Narration pane lets you adjust the volume of your mic as well as your audio settings if you haven't already done so. Just speak into the microphone normally while you adjust the accompanying slider. We'll discuss volume adjustment in detail in just a moment.

If you're not seeing any activity *at all* on the volume bar when speaking into the mic, then there's a problem. Address it by clicking the **Audio Setup Wizard...** button. This is the same wizard you adjusted back in Chapter 5 when setting up the audio for recording your initial footage. It's this dialog that lets you choose the device and source from which you want to record.

While you got a look at the Audio Setup Wizard back in Chapter 5, let's do a quick refresher. Here are the basics in terms of choosing the right device and source to record your audio:

- **Audio device.** Your sound card will be listed here, as will any software-based recording devices. If you have an audio interface, it too will be represented here, possibly with multiple listings that correspond to the box's various inputs. USB mics and webcams (if they're audio-enabled) will also be present. Make sure you have your sound card selected if you wish to record system sound.

- **Recording source.** Certain devices (especially sound cards) offer multiple input sources, and this section gives you the chance to select between them. You can pick Microphone, Speaker audio, or both if you want to capture everything. There's also a Manual input selection option for more off-the-wall choices. For example, virtually all sound cards have a microphone port. Many others also sport a line in jack as well, which you could use for recording from an external CD device or your iPod.

- **Input level.** This slider control allows you to set the volume of your currently selected input source. To do this, you'll want to first check your levels by speaking into the microphone.

For the best results, try to keep the peaks of your audio just below the maximum, somewhere orangey red. If the peaks of your audio are consistently maxing out in the red, then some portions of your audio may be *clipped* when digitized, and the result does not sound pretty. Just adjust the slider up or down to find the right level while speaking normally into the microphone. For owners of audio interfaces, keep in mind that most of these devices have their own hardware- and software-based controls for volume, and as such, tweaking the slider may do nothing. Consult your interface's documentation for details on adjusting the recording volume.

   If you don't trust yourself to accurately find the "sweet spot" of your audio volume, consider letting Camtasia Studio do the heavy lifting *for* you. Click **Next**, and you'll be able to automatically set the recording volume by clicking **Auto-Adjust Volume**. You'll be given a brief sentence to read into the mic (though you can probably get away with saying anything you want), and Camtasia Studio adjusts your recording volume based on what the microphone picks up. After soliloquizing your way to an ideal audio level, click **Finish** to lock in your adjustment.

   So, once you've got your source selected and your levels adjusted, it's time to start recording. Pick a quiet time of day and post a sign outside your door that says, "Quiet, please. Recording in progress," or perhaps something a bit surlier depending on how much you like your officemates. Please see the buyer's guide in Appendix C for some good information on setting up your workspace for desirable acoustics.

Now that you have your options set, here's how to actually **record your narration using the Voice Narration tool**:

1. Place your green seek bar at the point in the Timeline you wish to begin recording. If only recording a selection of content or recording until the end of a given clip, make sure you've set the appropriate record option on the Voice Narration pane. If recording to Audio track 2, bear in mind that you are not allowed to record from a spot on your Timeline where recorded content already exists in that track. Delete the old content first, or at least move it out of your way.

2. Click the **Start Recording** button. This will start the playback head in motion, and you will see your video progress in the Video Preview.

3. Speak into the microphone at the appropriate points in your video.

4. If the amount of script exceeds the amount of footage, consider clicking the **Extend Current Frame** button to "pause" the video playback head while you finish talking, and then click **Resume Video Playback** to keep going. In actuality, it stretches out the frame on which you first clicked the button, spawning all the video frames you need in order to finish up your spiel. This extension will appear on the Timeline as a separate clip.

5. At some point, you'll want to stop recording. This can be done either automatically (e.g., at the end of a selection or clip), or manually by clicking the **Stop Recording** button.

6. You'll be prompted to save the recording as a WAV file. Simply navigate to your project folder and specify a file name. Click **Save** to preserve the recording, or **Cancel** if you're not happy with your narration and want to begin again.

7. If you recorded to the Audio 2 track, the WAV file will appear both in your Clip Bin and in the appropriate place on your Timeline, where it can be further edited if desired. If you recorded to the Audio 1 track, the file won't be available as a separate clip in your Clip Bin, as this content gets effectively bound in place on the Audio 1 track.

As for recording over old content, you'll get different behavior depending on which track you've chosen. If you record to Audio track 1 where there's already pre-existing content, the Voice Narration tool will simply record right over the top of it. You'll still be prompted for a new file name, although it will appear on the Timeline as if the changes have simply been merged into the old track.

Keep in mind that the new content is in fact kept in the file you just created. If you recorded over the pre-existing audio track of an AVI file, for example, the sound data in that original file was *not* affected when you recorded over it. Pursuant to Camtasia Studio's nondestructive philosophy, all of these items are tracked by the project file. The media files themselves aren't touched.

With Audio track 2, you cannot record over old content. It's not kosher to place the seek bar in the middle of an existing audio clip and click **Start Recording** — you'll get an error message if you try. You've got to start in a blank spot on that track. So what happens if there are audio clips to the right of your current recording, and you end up exceeding the available empty space by making a lengthy new recording? No, those clips aren't cannibalized; they just get pushed to the right:

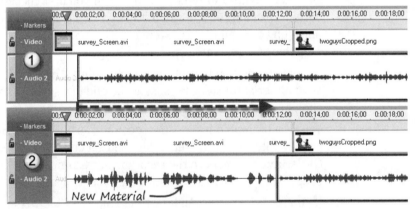

1. My Timeline with a pre-existing audio clip in my second audio track. 2. This clip gets pushed to the right when I record a longer new clip right before it.

If you want to get a better view of your audio waveforms, simply resize the Timeline to give your audio some breathing room:

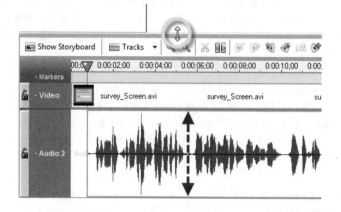

The audio tracks will expand, whereas the others will remain the same height. And of course, using the Zoom tools will do the same thing on the horizontal plane.

The duration of your recorded content is up to you. Each new recording creates an audio file, and this can lead to problems considering that most of us stammer or otherwise mess up from time to time. A full-length video is a *looooonng* way to go without making a mistake. So how do we address this? Some people create a new recording for every sentence, or every clip, or every topical section, while others just throw caution to the wind and try to do the entire video in one take. Both ends of the spectrum have their advantages and disadvantages. The multiple files approach gives you flexibility because you can quickly move clips around and edit them freely without affecting the timing of the other clips (provided you're recording to Audio track 2, that is). However, more files also means more "stuff" to keep track of.

Another option is to record everything at once, saving it as one file, and then split it up and move the parts around during the editing process, which we'll be talking about next.

Basic Editing of Your Audio Tracks

Once you've got some audio clips on your Timeline, they can be edited just like any other series of clips. Again, there are a few differences between the Audio 1 and Audio 2 tracks. Let's talk about these differences for a moment:

The **Audio 1 track** is the counterpart to your Video track. You have no control over the placement and duration of sound clips in your Audio 1 track — the duration and location of an Audio 1 clip exactly mirrors its corresponding video content. All cuts to your Video track will also affect Audio 1, and vice versa. The two tracks are inextricably bound together.

> If your newest recording on the Audio 1 track ends up spanning multiple video clips, Camtasia Studio will split the audio content in the project file, assigning a particular segment to whatever video clip you were on at the time. If you decide later to change the order of your video clips, the audio will be jumbled as well. Keep this in mind if the order of your video segments is still up in the air. If you have a sentence that spans the gap between video clips, the sentence will be cut in two when you change the order!

In a moment, we'll be talking about some "audio only" edits you can perform (such as fades, volume adjustments, and silencing a selection) that won't affect your Video track. But when it comes to the synchronization of the elements in Audio 1 with your video content, every sentence is pretty much glued in place. Your **PIP Audio** track functions very much the same way; it too is tied to its corresponding Video (PIP) track.

The **Audio 2 track** offers a lot of comparative freedom. You can add as many sound clips to your Audio 2 track as you like. You may freely move these tracks around and change their order. Additionally, unlike the clips on your Video track, your clips do not necessarily have to butt right up against one another. You can leave some blank space between clips, making it easy to fine-tune the synchronization of your audio clips to whatever's happening in your video.

Another advantage of the Audio 2 track is that you can leave numerous portions of your clips on the cutting room floor, and it won't affect your Video track (or Audio 1), provided you lock your Video track. Conversely, you can apply the lock to Audio 2, and any video edits won't hurt your narration.

While these are significant differences, there are also some commonalities. Let's now discuss some basic editing techniques you can perform on your sound files, regardless of what track they're in.

Trimming a piece of an audio clip is done the exact same way you do it for video:

1. Make sure that any tracks you do *not* want trimmed are safely locked.

2. On the Timeline, select the section of audio you wish to trim. Remember, with content on the Audio 1 track, any video within that selection also gets the ax.

3. Click the **Cut Selection** button (✂).

   or

   Press **Ctrl-X**.

Unlike the editing of video content, where trimming is basically the one-trick pony of your whole editing arsenal, you've got a few additional techniques you can use to bend your audio content to your will. Camtasia Studio is kind enough to make these tools accessible directly from your toolbar:

From left: Fade In, Fade Out, Volume Up, Volume Down, Replace with Silence, and Audio Enhancements.

Taking advantage of these tools is simple: Just select the content to which you'd like to apply one of these effects, and then click the button to apply the effect.

 Remember that these tools will affect any and every audio track that isn't locked tight. If you're not careful, the execution of that Replace with Silence command you used to stifle a cough might also have just gotten rid of an entire measure of your background music as well as a sentence fragment on your PIP Audio track. Be sure to make judicious use of track locking in order to avoid these difficulties.

These six tools do the following:

- **Fade In.** Begins the selection at 0% volume, and as the selection progresses, gradually and steadily builds up to 100%. The speed of your fade therefore depends on how much material you select.

- **Fade Out.** Essentially the same process, except in reverse. Handy for bringing background music to a close.

- **Volume Up.** This raises the volume of your selection by 25%. Clicking the button multiple times has a cumulative effect. Just be sure not to increase the volume to the point that the sound exceeds 0 dB, where clipping (and therefore distortion) will likely occur.

- **Volume Down.** Clicking this button reduces the volume of your selection by 25%. I'll often use volume reduction to "balance" my tracks, making sure that my background music doesn't overpower my narration, for example.

- **Replace with Silence.** This option reduces the volume of your selection down to 0%. It's excellent for getting rid of clicks, pops, and other annoyances that would otherwise mar a good recording.

- Finally, we come to **Audio Enhancements**. This handy set of tools gives you a tremendous advantage in cleaning up an essentially good but flawed audio track. Let us examine this pane in greater detail.

The Audio Enhancements pane consists of special filters that can really help improve how your audio sounds. With these filters, you can normalize the volume, knock out background noise, and even improve the vocals. Let's begin with the volume.

If you've done some audio recording in the past, you may have noticed that the volume of your recorded material wasn't entirely consistent. This can happen for several reasons. Some people have a natural tendency to trail off as they approach the end of a sentence. Others fail to maintain a consistent distance between their mouth and the microphone. And most of us just have a particular rhythm to our speech where the loudness naturally waxes and wanes. Volume differentiation can also happen when you record different audio segments on different days. The microphone placement and your distance to it probably varied a bit, and the new segment can sound a little different as a result. Camtasia Studio offers a way of overcoming these inconsistencies.

In the section marked Dynamic range control, click **Even out volume levels**. You'll notice that the waveform on your Timeline changes. Depending on the level of normalization you select, this will bring the volume levels of all your narration more in line. Note that you can select between high, medium, and low volume variation, and even select custom values if you're the sort who likes to tweak in order to achieve the best possible outcome. Click the **Show advanced options...** link to adjust the following using the corresponding slider controls:

- **Ratio.** How much compression (increased loudness) gets applied to everything above your established threshold (see below).

- **Threshold (dB).** The threshold is your baseline of how loud the audio should be before Camtasia Studio begins to limit it.

- **Gain (dB).** This setting can increase overall volume by a set amount *after* compression is applied.

These three settings will all change by an incremental amount whenever you adjust the (high/medium/low) volume variation levels, and once you've found a level that you're more or less happy with, you can customize the individual settings from there. And keeping in line with Camtasia Studio's nondestructive policy toward original video and audio footage, all the tools on the Audio Enhancements pane are applied without actually touching the underlying files. This means that you can undo the effect(s) whenever you wish. If you ever want to remove the Dynamic Range control, just uncheck **Even out volume levels**, and you'll find that the original audio has returned in all its glory.

Keep in mind that the Dynamic Range control options, along with the other settings offered by the Audio Enhancements pane, apply changes to *all* audio on your Timeline, regardless of what you have selected, regardless of what track(s) contains the audio, and regardless of whether any (or all) of these tracks is locked. *Everything* will change when you execute an audio enhancement command.

The next section, Background noise removal, is designed to get rid of excess noise in your recording. This tool can target things like the hum of your computer fan and other equipment, distant voices from across the hall, or the sounds of traffic from outside. It does this by silencing everything that falls below a certain decibel level (the noise), while keeping everything above its established decibel level (your narration). There are a couple of ways in which you can help the noise removal tool do its job:

First, you'll need to select whether you want the tool to **Automatically try to detect noise on the timeline** or if you'd rather **Manually select a region of audio with noise but no voice narration.** I generally find the latter more effective, particularly if you recorded in a loud environment where the *noise floor* was high, meaning you have less difference in volume between your signal (the desirable part) and all the noise. Just select a small snippet of your Timeline where you weren't speaking. It doesn't have to be much; the one-second pause between two sentences will work just fine.

Once you're ready, just click **Remove Noise.** The audio waveforms on your Timeline that were once green will suddenly turn maroon. You can preview the changes by playing back your Timeline content per usual. You can do a quick "before and after" comparison by selecting a sample of narration, playing it back, and toggling the **Restore noise** check box to sample the original audio. If you notice certain anomalies with Restore noise enabled (such as the ends of words dropping off), you can reduce the sensitivity of the noise removal tool with the **Adjust sensitivity** slider control.

> While audio enhancement capabilities such as these can employ little tricks to increase the perceived quality of your narration, nothing can take the place of a high-quality original recording, and no amount of waveform manipulation will yield a truly higher-quality file than your original audio. These techniques can do wonders to clean up a good recording, but they cannot salvage a bad one. Therefore, try to avoid the complacent attitude that you can always "fix it in post." A carefully recorded master file may reduce or eliminate the need to apply audio enhancements entirely, and those that are applied will be all the more effective.
>
> Noise reduction is a good example of this. If there's not a lot of noise in the original recording, then the noise removal tool can better target what little there is, while leaving the desirable portions untouched. Also, the noise removal tool has a hard time differentiating background noise that occurs while the narrator is speaking, so while it's a handy tool to have in your arsenal, it does have its limits. So keep it happy by feeding it good, wholesome recordings instead of auditory junk food, and it will serve you well for many years to come.

But we're not finished yet with the audio enhancements. There is a third (somewhat hidden) tool, called **Vocal Enhancements**, that you can bring up by clicking the **Show me more audio options…** link at the bottom of the pane. This tool sports several options, the first of which is vocal optimization. This tool helps remove annoyances like *plosives* (those "popping p" sounds) and *sibilants* ("hissing s" sounds). Since the algorithms it needs to effectively do this are somewhat different for the male vs. the female voice, you'll need to pick the gender of the narrator by clicking the appropriate button.

You also have check boxes for eliminating *clipping* (where part of a loud waveform gets chopped at the 0 dB threshold) and *clicks* (mouse click sounds, microphone rustling, and other assorted fizzles and pops that just shouldn't be there). You can set the sensitivity of the click removal tool by adjusting the accompanying slider.

The Camtasia Audio Editor

While the Voice Narration tool is a well thought-out means of quickly getting some narration into your project, sometimes you need a little more power and flexibility. For example, you might want to:

- Record multiple takes of each sentence without having to save off a new file each time.

- Make use of the clipboard to cut, copy, and paste audio segments.

- Mix your recording with another audio file, such as some music.

In cases like these, **Camtasia Audio Editor*** is the tool you should be using. It is a stand-alone audio editing application that can create audio from scratch as well as weave an audio track into a video or still image file (thus creating an AVI video). It does not tie in with the current open project in Camtasia Studio, so if you want to narrate your video project, you'll either have to edit and then produce it as an AVI so that it can be opened in Camtasia Audio Editor, or simply add audio to the various AVI clips you recorded *before* combining them into a presentation. I know this sounds complicated, but the separation of video and audio editing can in fact work quite nicely to your advantage, and later on, I'm going to show you a couple of different possibilities as to how you can make it happen. For now, though, let's dive right into the nuts and bolts of using the application.

In this section, I'm going to teach you all about using this wonderful utility for narrating your videos. Though I think the Voice Narration tool is exceptional for banging out a quick voice-over on a simple project, it simply doesn't hold up to the rigors of assembling narrated sequences for longer, more polished videos, where higher quality is demanded and multiple retakes are standard.

---

* Included as a free application with Camtasia Studio, the Audio Editor is a next-generation version of TechSmith's legacy DubIt utility.

Let's start with **opening the program**:

- From the **Start** menu, go to **All Programs > Camtasia Studio 5 > Applications**, and finally choose **Camtasia Audio Editor**.

  or

- From within Camtasia Studio, choose **Camtasia Audio Editor** from the **Tools** menu.

  or

- From within Camtasia Studio, choose **Camtasia Audio Editor** from the **Launch other tools** button on your toolbar, which looks like this:

Once you've opened up the application, you're generally greeted with the welcome screen that looks like this:

You're given three options:

- **Create a new audio file.** This starts the main user interface with a blank waveform and five seconds of space on the Timeline. This space will automatically increase to accommodate your audio and video as you record or import files.

- **Edit an existing video, audio, or image file.** An Open dialog will appear, letting you navigate to a file. Your file options include video (AVI), audio (WAV), and still images (BMP, GIF, JPG, PNG).

- **Edit a recent file.** If you've used the Camtasia Audio Editor before, this drop-down list contains all your most recently edited works.

 If you don't want to see this welcome screen in the future, just clear the check box labeled "Show this dialog at startup." Should you ever desire it back, you can activate it again by choosing View > Options... and clicking "Display welcome dialog on startup" on the Program tab.

Now, just as with the Voice Narration tool, it behooves you to first set up your capture device and check your levels. Our first stop is the Audio tab of the Options dialog. If you choose **Options...** from the **View** menu, and then click the **Audio** tab, you'll have a dialog that looks like this:

Here you have a couple of check box options that give you a bit of control over how you record:

- **Allow audio to extend video length** will extend the final frame of your video to accommodate your audio track if the length of your narration ends up exceeding the length of your video.

- **Mute audio while recording** will refrain from playing back any sound currently on the audio track while you're recording, so that the sound coming out of your speakers doesn't feed back into the microphone.

A quick click of the **Audio Setup Wizard...** button will give you the same options for selecting your Audio Capture Device as well as the Audio Capture Source should your capture device support more than one.

> Note that on the Audio tab, as with every tab in your Options dialog, you can choose to return to "factory default" settings by clicking the Default button. Since the Audio Capture Device and Audio Capture Source settings are both taken from the operating system, these are the only two options that are unaffected by clicking this button.

Now, go ahead and exit the dialog. We're going to check our levels next. To the right of your toolbar, you should see a small gauge called **Recording Level:**

Speak into the mic to check your levels. You can adjust the sensitivity of your capture source by clicking the small speaker icon. A slider called **Recording Volume** will appear (which you can also bring up by choosing **View > Recording Volume...**) that you can then adjust to bring your normal speaking voice up to line level (yellow to orange usually, with peaks in the red just below the maximum).

Another thing we might want to do before we start recording is to adjust our audio format and attributes. As I mentioned, you can do this in the Audio Setup Wizard, but to access the dialog more quickly, just choose **Audio Properties...** from the **Edit** menu:

Your default audio format is the TechSmith LAME MP3 encoder at 44.1 kHz, Mono. As I mentioned in Chapter 7, "Recorder Tools Options," I prefer to save my master recordings in an uncompressed (PCM) format. You can always compress and/or downsample later if file size gets to be an issue.

Now that we have the setup particulars out of the way, let's take a look at our standard recording interface:

Here are the various components we'll be working with:

① **Menu bar.** Umm... it's a menu bar. All your various commands are available here.

② **Preview area.** If you open an AVI or still image in the Camtasia Audio Editor, it will display here.

③ **Record and playback controls.** Buttons for recording, playing back, and navigating your file.

④ **Recording Level.** Lets you monitor the pickup of your recording source and adjust its sensitivity accordingly.

⑤ **Audio waveform.** This is a visual representation of your audio sample data. Portions of the waveform can be selected for editing.

⑥ **Seek bar.** This is the starting point of any pasted or mixed-in insertions.

⑦ **Playback head.** The current point in the playback of the file.

⑧ **Waveform edit toolbar.** Commands you can execute on a waveform selection. These include fade, adjust volume, silence or delete selections, zoom, and undo/redo.

⑨ **Position gauge.** Shows both the current elapsed time as well as the total duration of the file.

IV: Editing

Now that you've got a basic orientation to the interface, let's actually record something. You can place the seek bar wherever you want the recording to start, and since this is a new recording, we should probably begin at the beginning.

Here's how to **record your narration** with the Camtasia Audio Editor:

1. If narrating a video or still image, choose **File > Open...** to navigate to the desired file. Click **Open** once you've found and selected it.

2. Click on the Timeline to place the seek bar where you want recording to begin. This is typically only necessary if there's a lengthy pause between the start of the video and the spot where you'll begin the narration (for example, if you plan on adding a musical intro piece).

3. Click the **Record** button (●) to start recording.

   or

   Choose **Record** from the **Edit** menu.

4. Record your narration. You can pause at any time by clicking the **Pause** button (▮▮) or choosing **View > Pause**.

5. At the conclusion of your narration or if (well, probably *when*) you make a mistake, click the **Stop** button (■) or go to **View > Stop**. The waveform image of what you just recorded will appear on your Timeline.

6. If you stopped recording due to a mistake, go back and preview your audio (and I'll show you all the details of navigating your audio coming up next), stopping just before the sentence that contains the error. After you've made sure that the seek bar is placed correctly, repeat steps 3 to 5 to continue (and eventually conclude) your narration.

If you'll recall, I mentioned that image files can also be opened for adding sound. The resulting file is actually an AVI file, with the video portion being entirely consumed by the image. While I don't typically add audio to images during my Camtasia Studio work, I've found the Camtasia Audio Editor to be an incredibly handy stand-alone tool for annotating a picture.

For example, you can send someone a diagram with an audio track explaining its significance. Or add a heartfelt message to a meaningful picture of yourself to share with a loved one. It's great for quickly sharing a "talking picture" with others. Just remember that the software automatically uses the TechSmith Screen Capture Codec (TSCC), so be cognizant of this codec's content and distribution limitations when using the Audio Editor for this purpose.

Navigating Your File

By now, you should have made your first tentative steps toward recording some audio segments. At this point, it will be useful to quickly familiarize ourselves with the accompanying navigational controls, which can help you move through your content with a minimum of fuss. The following table describes the buttons in the record and playback controls area.

Name	Button	Menu	Hotkey	Notes
Record	●	Edit > Record	---	Sets the recording process in motion.
Play the entire file	▶	View > Play All	---	Plays from the beginning of the file, regardless of the current location of the seek bar or playback head.
Play	▷	View > Play	Spacebar	Sets the playback head in motion.
Pause	❚❚	View > Pause	Spacebar	Stops the playback head in place. Choosing Play once more will resume from that point.
Stop	◻	View > Stop	---	This will stop the playback head, returning to the location of the seek bar.
Beginning	◀◀	View > Beginning	Home	This command returns the playback head to the beginning of the file.
Previous Frame	◁	View > Previous Frame	Left Arrow	Moves the seek bar backward by a single frame.

IV: Editing

Name	Button	Menu	Hotkey	Notes
Next Frame	▷	View > Next Frame	Right Arrow	Predictably, this moves your seek bar forward by one frame. This and the Previous Frame command are useful for fine-tuning the location of the seek bar for when you want to resume recording from an exact location.
End	▷|	View > End	End	Knocks your seek bar all the way to the end of the file, which is handy for adding a musical outro.

With the latter four navigational hotkeys, you can also add a selection to the mix by holding down the **Shift** key as you execute them. For example, by pressing **Shift-End**, you'll select everything from the seek bar's current location all the way to the end of your file. Of course, as you've probably already discovered, using the mouse to click and drag a selection works, too, but I find that the keyboard shortcuts (especially Previous Frame and Next Frame) are particularly useful for making precision selections.

A selection is useful not only for specifying which part of your file will be on the "business end" of your next editing command, it's also handy for doing retakes. Say you've got a sentence with some overlapping background noise from outside. Rather than simply placing your seek bar and clicking Record, you first select the errant sentence. This ensures that only that space in your Timeline will be available for recording, and that your recording session will auto-terminate just before the playback head reaches the part of your recording you want to keep.

Now, selecting appropriate content is a lot easier when you're focused on a particular section of your recording rather than seeing a bird's-eye view of the entire file. This is where zooming comes in. When you're zoomed in on some content, a scroll bar appears on the Timeline, just below your waveform area. This scroll bar can be dragged around to reveal other sections of the file. It also helps to resize the application window of the Camtasia Audio Editor to give you a bit more screen real estate to work with. In addition, the following four commands will help you gain a much better view of what you're doing:

Name	Button	Menu	Hotkey	Notes
Zoom to Selection	🔍	View > Selection	---	Takes the current selection and zooms it to take up the full length of your waveform area.
Zoom In	🔍	View > Zoom In	Ctrl-+	Zooms in by a certain percentage, always keeping the seek bar within view.
Zoom Out	🔍	View > Zoom Out	Ctrl-—	Zooms out by a certain percentage.
Zoom to 100%	---	View > Zoom to 100%	---	Makes the entire length of your file visible in the waveform area.

As you may have noticed, the specific commands for selecting and zooming work slightly differently here than they do in the main Camtasia Studio interface, but a bit of practice should have you zipping through your file and selecting its desired portions like a champ. Of course, now that you have a part of your audio selected, what can you do with it? Plenty, as it turns out. Let's therefore move on to the available editing commands.

Editing Your File

Now that we've got some audio on our Timeline, we can manipulate that audio data, such as fading it in or out, controlling volume, and of course, getting rid of sections. Just as with Camtasia Studio, you've got some basic editing commands right on your toolbar. Let's take a look at these in the following table:

Name	Button	Menu	Hotkey	Notes
Increase Volume		Edit > Volume...	---	Increases the volume of your selection. The toolbar button increases the volume by a set amount, whereas the menu item lets you select the level of volume.
Decrease Volume		Edit > Volume...	---	Decreases the volume of your selection.
Fade In		Edit > Fade In...	---	Fades in the volume of the selection. The toolbar button will automatically fade from 0% to 100%, whereas the menu item allows you to set the fade percentage.
Fade Out		Edit > Fade Out...	---	Fades out the volume of the selection.
Replace with Silence		Edit > Replace with Silence	---	Removes the audio within a given selection, replacing it with silence equivalent to the length of the selection.
Insert Silence	---	Edit > Insert Silence...	---	This command lets you inject a given number of seconds to the right of your seek bar, moving the rest of the content over.
Delete the Current Selection		Edit > Delete	Del	Removes the selection, closing the surrounding audio around it. For example, if you have three sentences, and you delete the second one, playback will then move from the first directly to the third with no pause in between.

One interesting thing noted above (and a departure from the way things work in Camtasia Studio) is that selecting a volume or fade command from the menu gives you greater control than simply clicking its corresponding toolbar button. For example, if I select an area and click **Fade Out**, the command happens automatically, fading from full volume down to nothing. If I choose **Edit > Fade Out...**, then I get a dialog that looks like this:

...thus allowing me to set the precise level of fade.

Another freedom given to you by the Camtasia Audio Editor (and not available in Camtasia Studio) is the ability to use your clipboard to move and copy audio content. Say you want to swap the order of two paragraphs. Do you simply rerecord them? Of course not! Just select the first paragraph, cut it, place your seek bar after the second paragraph, and paste. The remaining audio moves over to accommodate your inserted content.

In addition, if you should ever desire that your pasted content *overwrite* whatever's to the right of your seek bar, you can do that as well. The Camtasia Audio Editor actually sports two different Paste commands. The first, called **Paste (Extend)**, pushes the rest of your content over so that nothing gets deleted. This is the "standard" paste function that gets executed when you press **Ctrl-V.** Another function, available only from the Edit menu, is called **Paste (Overlay)**. Executing this command means that when you paste in a selection, a portion of the audio content directly to the right of the seek bar (equivalent in length to your pasted selection) will be replaced. Be careful with this feature, as it's easy to destroy content unintentionally.

Yet another advantage that the Camtasia Audio Editor has over the Voice Narration tool is the ability to insert additional audio files. These commands let you navigate to a WAV file and insert it right into the current Timeline starting at the seek bar's current location. Just as with the Paste commands, you have different options as to how you want the inserted content to interact with what's already there. The following three commands are available exclusively from the Edit menu:

- **Insert Audio File (Extend).** This inserts the chosen audio file into the Timeline, pushing all current content to the right of the seek bar over to make room for the inserted file.

- **Insert Audio File (Overlay).** This inserts the audio file into the Timeline, and anything caught in the path of this new content will be replaced. Keep in mind that the new content will only replace enough of the old stuff to make room for itself. So, if the undesired portions currently sitting to the right of your seek bar are lengthier than the file you're about to insert, you'll want to double-check the end of the file and mop up any remaining unwanted material as necessary.

- **Insert Audio File (Mix).** This inserts the audio file, mixing its content with whatever audio is already present on the Timeline to the right of the seek bar.

The latter command is really exciting, because you can effectively mix two different kinds of content into a single track. For example, if you've got narration, and you want to have a light background music track at the same time, you can effectively combine the two files into a single track, and then import it into your Audio track 2 in Camtasia Studio, thus leaving Audio track 1 in place for system sound and sound effects. It allows you to "cheat" a little, working in different levels of audio that would otherwise exceed Camtasia Studio's track limit. The problem when combining tracks in this manner is that editing then becomes difficult, and should you ever desire to separate the two tracks again, well… forget about it.

I therefore encourage you to follow the procedure I've laid out below if you want to **mix audio data** using the Insert Audio File (Mix) command:

1. Edit your video narration file completely, so that the only step remaining is to add the other audio file. Note the file's duration.

2. Choose **File > Split > Save Audio As…** to save off a separate "clean" copy of your narration.

3. Choose **File > Save** to save your video and audio narration as an AVI.

4. Open and edit the other audio file, making sure that the duration is the same length as that of your AVI. This is done by inserting silence into various portions of the audio clip. The point of this exercise is to have a good sense of how the elements in the two files are going to interact, and as such, it's important that the durations of the files be identical.

5. Choose **File > Split > Save Audio As...** to save off the copy of this file you're going to be inserting.

6. Reopen the AVI file you created in step 3. If necessary, place the seek bar at the location you wish to insert the audio file.

7. Choose **Edit > Insert Audio File (Mix)...** to lay down the new file you created in step 5.

8. Preview your work to make sure that the two sound files match up as expected, and that your video and audio sequences synchronize nicely.

9. Choose **File > Split > Save Audio As...** to save off your custom audio "mix." It is this file you'll be importing back into Camtasia Studio for use in your Audio 2 track.

Since this is above all an audio editing application, there's really nothing here for editing your video. However, one nicety that's included is the ability to extend the length of a video clip or still image to accommodate an extra sentence or two of narration. If you go to add your audio narration and suddenly realize you've left too little room to actually record what you want to say, you can add some video "dead space" to squeeze in the remainder of your audio script.

So, here's how to **extend the length** of your video or still image clip.

1. Open your AVI or image file if you haven't already done so.

2. In the case of an AVI, place your seek bar on the frame of the video you'd like to extend. With still images, the placement doesn't matter.

3. From the **Edit** menu, choose **Extend Frame....**

4. Choose the number of seconds to add to the resulting video's duration, either by entering it directly into the field or by clicking the spinner buttons to the right of the field to increment the duration by one second per click. You may extend a frame by up to 10 minutes (600 seconds). Fractions of seconds may be entered, provided the extension is at least one second long. Click **OK** to continue.

5. You'll see the total duration change on the Position gauge to reflect the extension.

6. Make a note of the location and duration of this extension. You're likely to need this info later when resynchronizing your audio in your Camtasia Studio video project.

Using the Camtasia Audio Editor in Conjunction with Camtasia Studio

So, you've learned how to create and edit audio segments in the Camtasia Audio Editor, but you may be wondering just how to reconcile your editing work here with your video edits within the main Camtasia Studio application. After all, we're in the business of recording audio to augment our *video* content, are we not? So, let me take you through two different models for combining the talents of Camtasia Studio and the Camtasia Audio Editor. This procedure detailed below is actually pretty representative of my own real workflow...

Let me explain how *you too* can **utilize the Camtasia Audio Editor** as part of your preferred process.

1. Open your video project in Camtasia Studio and edit it to your liking, paying particular attention to the timing of elements. It's important to make sure you've got enough space during your video footage to fit in all your narration (and still take a breath or two somewhere in the middle).

2. Produce your video as an AVI file. This file serves only to be fed into the Camtasia Audio Editor so that you can effectively time your narration. You won't need the file for anything after recording the narration.

3. Open the AVI in Camtasia Audio Editor. Record your narration, going back to rerecord segments that didn't turn out well. If you have to extend the video anywhere to accommodate your narration, you may freely do so. However, make a note of both the *duration* and *location* of this extension, as you'll have to do the same thing in your actual video project. Otherwise, your audio will be longer than your combined video when importing the audio file back into your Camtasia Studio project.

4. Save the audio as a WAV file, choosing **File > Split > Save Audio As....**

5. If desired, mix in another audio source (such as background music), and then save a new audio file under a different name by repeating step 4.

6. Go back to Camtasia Studio, importing the audio file you created into the Clip Bin.

7. Add your audio clip to Audio track 2. It appears as a single long track. If you ever need to adjust the order of your video clips, you can use the **Split** command (**Ctrl-D**) to split up your audio track, and then adjust the order of both tracks to make sure that your audio stays with its corresponding video.

8. Save your project, and produce it to whatever format you desire.

This is the way I typically work, as a matter of personal taste. Keep in mind that there's another method that other users employ with success. I don't personally do this because it forces you to only work with AVI clips in Camtasia Studio, thus robbing you of the advantages of the CAMREC format. Plus, there are some additional issues with adding audio to unedited video content. But it *is* another effective way of combining the power of Camtasia Studio with the Camtasia Audio Editor.

This **second method of using Camtasia Audio Editor** in conjunction with Camtasia Studio goes like this:

1. Record your initial clips in Camtasia Studio *as AVI files*. If you have already recorded your footage in CAMREC format, you can break them down and extract the AVIs by launching Camtasia Studio, importing the files into your Clip Bin, and then right-clicking the CAMREC files and choosing **Extract Camrec Contents....**

2. Don't drag anything to the Timeline just yet. However, now that you have all needed files just sitting there in your Clip Bin, it's probably a good idea to **Save** it as a new project so that you don't have to repeat this step later. After saving, go ahead and **Close** the project.

3. Open an AVI file in Camtasia Audio Editor. Record your narration, going back to rerecord segments that didn't turn out well.

4. Save the changes back to the AVI by choosing **File > Save (Ctrl-S)**.

5. Repeat steps 3 and 4 for each individual AVI in your project.

6. Reopen your project file in Camtasia Studio (or start a new one and import your media files if you haven't yet done so). Start dragging clips onto your Timeline. You'll now notice the presence of sound in the Audio 1 track.

7. Edit the project to your liking, being cognizant of where your audio segments are so that you don't inadvertently trim out the middle of a sentence. It helps to zoom in as well as increase the vertical size of your Timeline, so that you can use the actual waveform as a guide.

8. Save and then produce the project to your desired format.

You may be looking at the above procedure and thinking, "It seems weird to add audio narration to video clips that haven't been edited yet. Can't you create the Camtasia Studio project first, make your edits, and *then* add audio to the clips?" Nope. Well, I suppose you *could*, but the results aren't pretty.

If you add an audio stream to one of the AVIs in your project, your audio won't show up in the edited clip on the Timeline when you reopen the Camtasia Studio project. The one exception to this is if you extend either the audio or video in the Audio Editor. In that case, you'll reopen the video project to find that your edited clip does indeed now have sound, but oops! All your edits are suddenly gone.

Recording System Sound

Up to now, you've learned about your various software options for getting your narration into Camtasia Studio. Now we're going to discuss changing the recording source from the microphone to your internal system sound. From PowerPoint presentations to games to Windows alert sounds, sometimes you'll want to record the audio from your computer. This handy guide will help you do just that.

Technique 1: Using Your Sound Card

If your microphone is plugged into your sound card (which it probably is, if you're not using an audio interface), you've likely been using "Microphone" or "Line In" as your audio capture source. It may interest you to know that most modern sound cards offer an input source that "listens" directly to what's happening on the system. Camtasia Studio's Audio Setup Wizard will almost always select the correct source for recording your system sound automatically. Just select your sound card as the Audio device and then choose **Speaker audio (what you hear)** as the Recording source.

If, for some reason, Camtasia Studio does not correctly select the source, you can choose one manually by choosing **Manual input selection** as the Recording source and picking your source for the system sound. Different sound cards call it different things. If your sound card offers one of the following as an audio capture source:

- Mixer
- Mono Mix
- Stereo Mix
- Wave Out
- What U Hear

…then you're in business. What's nice about using your sound card for recording system audio is that everything is happening right on the sound card — you don't even have to buy a cable. In fact, a few sound cards will even let you select multiple sources from which to mix audio.

When exploring all the possible sources offered by your sound card, it's just a matter of selecting each one individually, and then doing a test capture to see if the source is indeed picking up your system sound as expected. I've outlined a testing procedure for you at the end of this section. Once you've got the correct input source selected, recording system sound works just like recording your microphone.

If you're a user of **Windows Vista**, recording directly from your sound card may or may not be an option for you. The drivers put out by the different sound card manufacturers are rather bare-bones at this point. In the case of my system, I did indeed have the ability to record system sound, but for some reason it was listed as an entirely different device rather than a separate source of one device. I have no idea at this point how common this phenomenon is, but I'll go ahead and give you the steps, just in case it helps a few of you:

1. First, choose **Start > Control Panel > Sound**, and select the **Recording** tab. The list of potential recording devices appears.

2. Even if a system sound option is available (we'll call it "Stereo Mix" for the purposes of this discussion, but it could go by another name), it may yet be hidden. Right-click anywhere in the dialog and choose **Show Disabled Devices**. See if Stereo Mix shows up. Even if it does, it might be listed as "Currently unavailable." Let's fix that...

3. If your system is set up like mine, you'll need to first disable the source making use of the device before you can enable Stereo Mix. Right-click the device marked "Working" (probably your microphone), and choose **Disable**.

4. Right-click your Stereo Mix device and choose **Enable**. Click **OK**.

5. Go ahead and bring up Camtasia Studio (or Recorder or Audio Editor), and select the new device in the Audio Setup Wizard. You may have to restart the application in order for the new device setting to be recognized.

Play an MP3 file or movie trailer and see if the Input level meter detects any activity. If it does, you're all set. If not, take heart. We have a few more options to explore....

Technique 2: Total Recorder

If you don't have the hardware setup to record your system sound, you might want to consider a software-based solution. High Criteria, Inc., offers one such solution in the form of their **Total Recorder 6.1** audio capture utility. A demonstration version is included on the companion CD. Total Recorder installs a special driver that works to capture the digital sound directly from the output of your sound card. Aside from Technique 1, this is the only means of recording system sound that preserves the audio in 100% digital form (in other words, no conversion takes place).

Once you've got the application installed, simply run it and click the **Record** button. This puts Total Recorder into "listening" mode, and recording begins when the actual audio does. The only major drawback is that the Camtasia Studio suite of applications cannot utilize the Total Recorder driver — only the Total Recorder application itself can. This means that you'll have to save off a separate audio file, import it into Camtasia Studio along with your recorded video, and then take a moment to resynchronize the two streams. Not a dealbreaker, but a pain nonetheless.

Technique 3: Creative Cabling

So you've tried every potential audio input source that your sound card has, and nothing picks up your sound card's audio. You may also be in a "locked-down" work environment where you aren't allowed to install driver software. In this case, you might need to invest in a cable or two to make the recording of system sound an option for you. The easiest solution is to purchase a single stereo cable with a stereo mini-plug on each end, jacking one end into your line out or headphone port and the other into the microphone port. You'll probably have to adjust both the recording and playback volume settings in your sound control panel, but this is a workable solution. The only inconvenience is having to unplug the cable end every time you want to play back what you've recorded. This problem can be circumvented with the additional purchase of a stereo Y-cable, so that you can plug your "recording cable" and your speakers into your line out port simultaneously. This has the added advantage of actually being able to monitor what you're recording.

Another solution, rather than going from the headphone jack to the microphone port, is to cable from the headphone jack into one of the audio input ports on your preamp, or into your audio interface if you happen to have one (and you *totally* should — see Appendix C for a discussion of this point). This can allow you to *mix* audio content from your speakers with another source (such as a microphone). If using an analog preamp, the output from the preamp would then feed into your sound card.

There is but one drawback to both of the "creative cabling" options. The first two techniques we discussed allow you to record everything digitally. With this technique, however, you're taking a signal destined for loudspeakers (an analog signal), and then re-digitizing it when the signal travels *back* into your sound card by way of the microphone port. This digital to analog to digital conversion will probably mean somewhat poorer quality than you would otherwise have gotten.

Technique 4: Miking the Speaker (Not Recommended)

There is of course one additional "poor man's" solution, namely to set up your microphone next to your speaker. This has the advantage of being able to record your voice and system sound at the same time (though most sound cards will let you do this also). It has the major disadvantage of picking up all other ambient sound in the room, and the sound quality is, well… something akin to a grainy Xerox copy of a vibrant color photograph. I do not recommend this option, but enough people will end up doing it anyway that I may as well teach you how to do it "right."

First off, it's helpful to use an omnidirectional microphone for this purpose, so that your voice and your speaker (or your two speakers, in the case of stereo recording) are picked up equally (see Appendix C for the lowdown on microphone directionality). Also, I find that I can reduce ambient noise on the recording by lowering the recording volume of the mic while increasing the playback volume of the speaker. Finally, if you're recording a stereo source, make sure that the microphone is equidistant from your two speakers so that *both* channels are picked up. You'll be converting a stereo signal to a mono one, but it's a lot easier than separately miking both speakers.

Testing Out Your Settings

If you're testing out audio input sources to see what works for you, or even after you've found what you've needed and are just gearing up to record your session, I strongly recommend performing a brief test to make sure you're picking up system sound okay before committing to a full-length recording.

Just follow these steps to do a quick **10-second sound check**:

1. Make sure you've got the right audio input source selected.

2. Perform an action on your machine that gets some audio cranking out of those speakers. Opening a movie trailer or a music MP3 file will do the trick.

3. Don't forget to enable the **Record Audio** command in Camtasia Recorder.

4. Start the capture, making sure to check your audio levels in the Statistics and Properties area of your Recorder window. If you see movement on the audio levels bar, then you're picking something up.

5. Wait about 10 seconds, and then close whatever sound or video file you opened. You should be hearing nothing but silence at this point.

6. Now, as a final sanity check, stop the recording and preview the clip. Does your recording play back the audio at a volume and quality level that's appropriate?

Provided your sound test works out, then you're ready to roll on a full-length recording. If not, here are a few handy troubleshooting tips you may find useful. These tips apply to recording your microphone as well as your system sound.

If there's *no* sound on your video preview...

- When recording from Camtasia Recorder, make certain that your Record Audio check box is checked. Forgetting to set this option is typically the most common cause of dropping an audio recording.

- Make sure that the correct audio capture device and capture source are set in your Audio Setup Wizard.

- Check to ensure that your Volume slider isn't set to zero.

- Double-check your connections. If capturing microphone audio to your sound card, make sure that the line going from your preamp is plugged into your microphone port as opposed to one of the myriad other jacks on the back of your card.

- If using a preamp (whether analog or digital), double-check the volume dial on the unit itself, making certain that you've adjusted the right dial for the input port in question.

- If using an audio interface, USB headset, or any other microphone with a USB or FireWire connection, check to make sure you have the latest drivers for your unit installed.

If the sound in your preview is muffled, garbled, or just not at the level of quality you expected...

- When recording to Camtasia Recorder or the Camtasia Audio Editor, check your Audio Format settings. Master-quality recordings should have an audio format of **PCM** (uncompressed), with attributes of at least **44.1 kHz, 16 Bit, Mono.**

- It's possible that your recording volume is set too loud, and that clipping is occurring. Camtasia Recorder, Camtasia Audio Editor, and the Voice Narration tool in Camtasia Studio all have a volume unit meter to test out your recording volume. Double-check it to make sure you're not "residing in the red zone." If it's too high, adjust the dial on your preamp/audio interface, or turn down the volume of your capture source in the Audio Setup Wizard.

- One of the links in your audio recording chain (microphone, preamp, sound card, cables) could be malfunctioning, or be of such poor quality that it requires replacement. Swap out one component at a time to see if you can find the culprit. Note that this doesn't always have to be costly. My setup once experienced a sudden onset of horrible *staticitis*, and after nearly ripping out my hair from trying out new components with no change in quality, I finally discovered that the $5 cable going from my preamp to the sound card had become damaged. In this case, a quick trip to Radio Shack had me back in business. If it turns out that one of your components *does* need to be retired, be sure to look at Appendix C, "Equipment Buyer's Guide," for help in finding an acceptable replacement.

Recording Picture-in-Picture (PIP)

As we talked about back in Chapter 5, Camtasia Recorder supports the recording of an additional video stream, typically coming from a webcam or video camcorder (though it can actually be pretty much any video source). However, just as we discussed earlier in this chapter, managing the screen recording alone during your capture is already quite a handful. In the previous section, we talked about how you could postpone the capture of your audio narration until after the initial screen recording was done. Now, you'll learn how to do the same for your PIP track.

> To get starting with recording your camera video, you have to **open the Record Camera pane** in Camtasia Studio, like so:
>
> ■ From the **Edit** menu, choose **Record Camera....**
>
>   or
>
> ■ In your Task List, click **Record Camera...**, located in the Add subsection.

At this point, you're probably noticing something of a similarity between the Record Camera tool and the Voice Narration tool from earlier in the chapter. The functionality of these two utilities is actually remarkably similar. You still need to select a source, choose if/when you want the recording to automatically terminate, etc. The only difference is that this time, we're working with both audio and video, so rather than producing a WAV file, you'll have the audio and video tracks encapsulated into a single WMV file.

The Record Camera pane.

So, we've got three basic sections with which to concern ourselves: Recording duration, Camera, and Audio. Starting with Recording duration, notice that you have the same options as the Voice Narration tool for the automatic termination of your recording:

- **Until end of selection on timeline.** If you have part of the Timeline selected, your PIP capture will only run as long as the selection, after which it will stop and prompt you for the file name. If you have this option selected with *no* selection on the Timeline, the program will capture your camera video until you manually stop it by pressing the Stop Recording button.

- **Until end of clip.** If you have more than one clip on the Video track of your Timeline, the capture will only last until the end of the current clip.

- **Until end of timeline.** If this option is selected, your PIP capture will last as long as there's material in your Video track. This is a good option for making sure that there's no extraneous PIP material that artificially extends the length of your video.

Just as with the Voice Narration tool, you also have a check box called **Auto-extend last video frame** that will help ensure that you never run out of room when recording your camera video segment. The final frame of your screen video (which will obviously vary depending on which of the above duration options you have set) will be extended to make up the extra length.

In the Camera section, you'll have the opportunity to select from your various installed video sources. If you open the drop-down menu, you'll be able to select between your webcam and, say, your TV tuner card, your FireWire-enabled DV camcorder, and your video capture board. As you'll soon discover, everyone will see something different when they open this list because we all have different video devices installed on our machines. So what if a device you're expecting to be there is actually missing from the list? It's usually due to one of the following factors:

- The device isn't currently connected to your computer.

- The device isn't powered up.

- The proper drivers are not installed, or parts of the installation have been somehow corrupted.

If you have selected a valid video device, you should immediately see an image appear in your Preview box. In the case of a webcam, you'll be able to adjust the focus and zoom at this point to get the best quality possible prior to hitting that Start Recording button.

Newer webcams are designed to take advantage of the USB 2.0 standard and the increased bandwidth it affords you. If you're experiencing blurry, laggy video quality with a recently purchased webcam, double-check to make sure it's not plugged into a USB 1.0 hub.

Then, you've got the **Camera Properties...** and **Video Format...** buttons. These buttons both key into settings dialogs determined by the video device software, so again, everyone will see something different (though I've compiled a list of likely possibilities in the section called "The Camera Tab" in Chapter 7). And of course, if you've played around with your settings so much that you completely forgot what you did (and hence, how to undo it), you can always click the **Default** button to go back to your default video capture device. It will also reset everything and reinitialize the video stream, so it's a good button to have if your Preview box gets corrupted for whatever reason.

Now, moving on to the audio side of things: The **Record audio** check box will determine whether or not you desire a PIP audio track, so make sure it's checked if you'll be narrating your PIP video at all. The other settings are essentially pulled right from the Voice Narration tool, so I'll describe them here only briefly:

- **Mute speakers during recording.** Mutes the playback of your sound card so that your mic isn't picking up feedback from your speakers.

- **Audio Setup Wizard....** Lets you choose an audio device as well as select what you want to record, manually selecting a source if necessary. You can also have the system auto-set an optimal recording volume if you're recording from the camera's microphone.

- **Input level.** Allows you to preview the recording volume and adjust the input level slider accordingly.

Let's now get started on **recording a new PIP video**, done just like this:

1. Make sure that you can see a good image of yourself (or whatever you're trying to capture) in the Preview box on the Record Camera pane. Make any focus/position adjustments as necessary.

2. Place your green seek bar at the point in the Timeline you wish to begin recording. If only recording a selection of content or recording until the end of a given clip, make sure you've set the appropriate record option on the Record Camera pane. Keep in mind that you are not allowed to record from a spot on your Timeline where recorded PIP content already exists. Either delete/move the old content first, or start in a different place on the Timeline. If there's already PIP content to the right of your recording, it will be pushed farther over as needed to accommodate your new recording.

3. Click the **Start Recording** button. This will start the playback head in motion, and you will see your video progress in the Video Preview. It might take a second or two for the video device to initialize before the capture starts in earnest.

4. Record your PIP video (and possibly audio) as appropriate.

5. At some point, you'll want to stop recording. This can be done either automatically (at the end of a selection or clip), or manually by clicking the **Stop Recording** button.

6. You'll be prompted to save the recording as a WMV file. Simply navigate to your project folder and specify a file name. Click **Save** to preserve the recording, or **Cancel** if you're not happy with your PIP capture and want to begin again.

IV: Editing

7. If this is to be the first PIP clip on your Timeline, you'll see a dialog that looks like this:

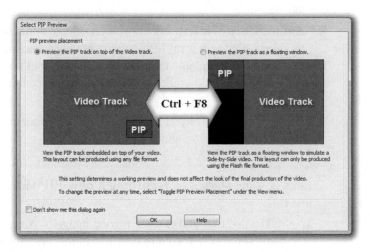

Here you can choose how you want to preview your PIP video within Camtasia Studio. You can view it **on top** of your screen video, simulating what you would see in an actual picture-in-picture video. Your other option is to view the PIP preview **in a separate window** (which can be either floating or docked, based on your preference). Keep in mind that this option is *for previewing purposes only*. It has *no* bearing whatsoever on the actual production. See Chapter 12 for information on choosing an appropriate production layout.

If there's a pre-existing video clip in your Video track, then the WMV file will appear both in your Clip Bin and in the appropriate place on your Timeline. However, PIP tracks need a Video track in order to exist, so if there's nothing on the Video track, your recording will still be saved, but it will only appear in the Clip Bin. You'll need to drag it to the Timeline manually after you've added content to the Video track.

Once you've got the PIP content on the Timeline, it can be edited (or locked for editing) just like any other video content. Your PIP clips can be repositioned simply by clicking and dragging the clip on the Timeline. PIP clips are not visible in Storyboard view.

Now, the audio stream of your PIP clip functions just like the Audio 1 track does — it is tied to the PIP Video track. This audio can be edited using the tools on the Camtasia Studio editing toolbar, but the PIP Audio track cannot be moved separately from its corresponding video. The PIP Video track, in addition to supporting the same editing techniques available to your screen video content, offers a few special editing commands that allow you to control the position of the PIP window as well as fade in and out, add a border or drop shadow, or even hide the PIP window at certain points in your video. We'll be discussing these tools at the beginning of the next chapter, so stay tuned....

Summary

In this chapter, you learned about some of the additional media types available to help you augment your screen video footage. In addition to your Camtasia Recorder captures and still images, you can create special title clips to help you label your content, audio content using either the Voice Narration tool or the Camtasia Audio Editor, and camera video using the Record Camera tool.

Inserting a **title clip** is simple. After choosing **Add Title Clip...**, you must give the clip a name, choose a background color (or image to serve as the background), and then add your text. The text content can be formatted just like you would in any word processing application. Options for changing the font, size, color, and alignment are all represented.

For adding **audio narration** post-recording, you have two options: the Voice Narration tool or the Camtasia Audio Editor. The former is mainly for lending your voice to a quick how-to video where a high degree of polish is neither desired nor expected. The latter is better suited to lengthier, more professional productions. Retakes are easier, and the ability to mix in additional audio files grants you some much appreciated flexibility.

For the **recording of system sound**, you were presented with four options:

- Change the input source of your sound card to "listen" to the system sound rather than your microphone.
- Use Total Recorder to digitally capture the audio signal being processed by your sound card.
- Run a cable from your sound card's output to loop back into its microphone or line in port.
- Position your microphone to record the sound coming from your speakers.

IV: Editing

Finally, we discussed the recording of **picture-in-picture** content. Once you've selected the right video device and set your audio options, adding PIP video to your screen recordings post-capture becomes child's play. You'll learn how to position and otherwise edit this newly recorded content in the next chapter.

Exercises

1. Open your **MyProject.camproj** file from the previous chapter. If you skipped those exercises, you'll find an exported project called MyProject_ch10.zip in this chapter's media folder.

2. In the audio file (somewhere in the clip **06.camrec**), I accidentally coughed into the microphone. Replace the cough with silence.

3. If desired, use the Voice Narration tool to rerecord the narration using your own voice. You'll find the script available in this chapter's media folder (narration.doc).

4. Whether using my narration or your own, optimize the sound using the sound enhancements tools.

5. Create a title clip called **Intro**. Use the file **bkgd.png** from this chapter's media folder as your background image (you might want to copy it to your project directory first). Change the font size to **48 pt.**, and enter the text **Intro to Camtasia MenuMaker**, using a font of your choosing. Place your new clip on the Timeline.

6. Using the Camtasia Audio Editor, record the following piece of narration: **This brief tutorial will give you the basics of creating a CD menu front-end with Camtasia MenuMaker. We'll start by making use of the MenuMaker Wizard.**

7. Once satisfied with the quality of your recording, save it as **intro.wav** and import it into your project's Clip Bin. Drag the clip onto the Timeline, just in front of your narration.wav clip. If needed, adjust the volume to more or less match that of the other clip. Trim out any unneeded pauses.

8. Stretch your **Intro** title clip to approximate the length of your intro.wav sound clip.

9. Create another title clip called **Ending**. Enter this text: **Thanks for watching!** Use the **Align bottom** command to place this text at the bottom of the window. Change the font and size as desired. Once finished, drag the title clip to your Timeline, this time at the end of the presentation.

10. If you have a webcam or camcorder attached to your computer, place your seek bar right at the start of your Ending title clip. Record a PIP clip, using the following piece of narration: **Thank you for watching our training video today about Camtasia MenuMaker. If you haven't already done so, feel free to check out the other tutorials in this series.** Save this file as **PIP.wmv**. It should get added to the Timeline automatically.

11. Adjust the duration of your Ending title clip to reflect the length of the PIP clip. Use the volume tools to adjust the loudness of your PIP clip to match the other two.

12. Save your project.

Chapter 11

Editing Effects

In the first chapter of this unit, you were introduced to the Camtasia Studio interface, and learned both basic and advanced editing techniques for combining your recorded clips and paring them down to get rid of unwanted footage. So, we take a mass of raw clips, with a few gold nuggets buried deep within a mountain of junk, and then we refine refine refine. We end up with a lean, efficient, hard-working video. Well and good. But skillful editing pertains not only to what you take away, but also to what you *add*. In the last chapter, you got the opportunity to fill in some additional content by adding audio and camera video streams, and even title screens. These are important additions, but perhaps not enough to really set your world ablaze. In this chapter, we're going to complete the editing process. You'll learn how to sex up your edited content by adding a variety of special effects for a polished, professional end result.

Not that I'm a fan of implementing special effects for their own sake, mind you. Far from it. As you may have already read in Chapter 6 on Recorder special effects, adding some pizzazz is a great thing to do, but it's also easy to overdo. Haphazardly dumping a sackful of effects into your project stamps the word "amateur" in big, bold letters on your forehead in permanent ink.

However, a smattering of effects, meaningfully and tastefully done, can elevate your work to a more professional level and leave your audience wondering, "Whoa. How'd they do that?"

Keep in mind that all these effects (with the noted exception of transitions) only work in the Timeline view. If you happen to be in the Storyboard view when you choose one of these effects, then the Timeline view will open for you automatically.

To get started down the path to professional productions, look no further than your own Task List.

Take a look at your Edit heading. In this chapter, we'll focus on these six commands. (Yes, I know there are actually *seven*, but I'm excluding Audio enhancements, as we've already covered it.) Before we dive into the details, here's a quick synopsis of each effect and its capabilities.

- **Audio enhancements.** These are the splendid volume normalization, noise reduction, and vocal enhancement tools that we discussed in the previous chapter.

- **Zoom-n-Pan.** Zoom into a window to give your audience a more detailed view. Or zoom out to show your entire screen. Even gently glide from one place on the screen to another with the Pan feature. With Zoom-n-Pan, these Hollywood-style camera effects are a cakewalk. You can even apply SmartFocus to automate most of the process.

- **Callouts (and Flash Hotspots).** Place arrows, callout bubbles, highlights, and even custom graphics all over your video content. You can also add text to each shape, and even make it a clickable hotspot when exporting to Flash.

- **Transitions.** Fades, wipes, and slides are but a few of the tricks you can pull out of your sleeve once you've mastered the art of adding film-like transitions between your scenes.

- **Captions.** Would you like to create captions for your hearing-impaired viewers? How about foreign language subtitles? Captioned videos are a snap to do: Simply type or paste them in your script, set the timing, and you're done.

- **Flash quiz and survey.** Ever create a video, and then wish you could test the viewer's knowledge of what you just covered? Camtasia Studio lets you set up a multiple-choice quiz for SWF or FLV output, specifying such things as the allowed number of tries as well as feedback for right or wrong answers. You can also ask survey questions. If desired, you can even upload results to a learning management system via SCORM or let the user e-mail the results to an address that you specify.

- **Picture-in-Picture (PIP).** We've already learned how to create a PIP video, both during the capture phase as well as after. Well, here you can edit that PIP video content, along with any other video you placed in your PIP track.

Zoom-n-Pan Effects

Have you ever seen a Ken Burns documentary on PBS? His most famous work was an 11-hour long retrospective on the U.S. Civil War, but he's covered a wide variety of topics over his career that look at different aspects of Americana: jazz, baseball, Mark Twain, and the Brooklyn Bridge, to name but a few. Since all of his films focus on historical topics, which often predate the invention of film, he doesn't usually have a lot of raw footage with which to work. Burns is therefore famous for the technique of taking old photographs, drawings, and letters, and then manipulating the camera to slowly zoom in on interesting portions, or to gently pan across a static image to convey a sense of action. Add music, sound effects, and a voice-over or two from a distinguished actor, and you've got yourself one compelling piece of filmmaking.

Camtasia Studio offers you that same level of professionalism for your video footage, whether you (like Burns) are trying to spice up a static image or you're working with actual video. You see, in addition to the stylistic coolness of using the **Zoom-n-Pan** feature, there's a pragmatic aspect to it as well. Many applications are space hogs; they like to take up your entire screen. When it comes to recording these gargantuan windows, you're going to need to find a way to reduce the dimensions of the video window, as people don't typically enjoy looking at a video window that's larger than their entire monitor (the long download times for a file this size are also a real pain). So, if you want to capture everything, you've got two basic choices:

- Scale your clips down to a manageable size when producing. I typically find this option unacceptable for any detail work because of the huge reduction in quality that comes with it. Images become blurry, and text becomes downright unreadable.

- Use Zoom-n-Pan to zoom in on a particular area of the screen, then pan to follow the mouse cursor as it moves about the screen. If you produce at the same dimensions as your zoom, then no quality whatsoever is lost. The one drawback to this method is that it tends to explode the file size if you're panning a lot. Producing to a format that's more tolerant of high-motion video (such as FLV or QuickTime H.264) will alleviate this.

These two methods are not mutually exclusive, mind you, and can be used in conjunction for a wonderful effect. You stay zoomed out to show the full interface of the program, and then zoom in and pan around to demonstrate the details. To see what I mean, take a look at the sample video **zoomnpan.avi** in this chapter's exercise folder on the CD-ROM. Open it now and watch it.

Here's a basic overview of how I did the **Zoom-n-Pan effects** for this quick video about everyone's favorite program:

1. I recorded the video at the dimension **1032 x 780**, which is just large enough to capture all the details of the Camtasia Studio user interface, but too large to keep as my final output size. These dimensions are exactly 1.5 times larger than the planned dimensions of my final video. When experimenting with zooming, always try to keep the proportions of your initial recording the same as your planned output. If you don't, you'll either end up with superfluous background bars (think of a widescreen movie shown on a square TV set) or stretched content (i.e., your video will look like a funhouse mirror reflection of itself).

2. In the editing phase, I started with the video at 100% to show the whole interface, but then zoomed in after a few seconds to **688 x 520**, which is a more manageable size (and will serve as the dimensions of our final video).

3. The zoom started on the top left-hand corner of the screen, but this gets problematic when the focus shifts to portions of the screen outside our direct view (e.g., when I'm dragging clips onto the Timeline in our video). So what to do? Follow that mouse, of course! A quick pan makes this easy work. It's best to follow whatever the cursor is doing, but don't follow too closely by constantly panning. In addition to making your audience seasick, you'll bloat the file size of your video exponentially.

4. At the end of the video, I zoomed back out to show a final shot of the whole screen.

5. When producing this video, I set my screen dimensions to **688 x 520** (though my editing dimensions were set to the original recording dimensions of 1032 x 780). This way, all portions of the video where I was zoomed out to 100% (at 1032 x 780) will be scaled down, but all zoomed content will display full-size, with no quality loss of any kind. We'll cover the act of producing at different window sizes in Chapter 12, "The Production Process."

Of course, zooming is helpful even when you're *not* producing at a smaller size than the original recording. When doing particularly detailed work, there may be instances where you'd want to show the user interface elements of the target application at an even *larger* size than 100%. The Zoom feature shines here as well, but do be careful not to enlarge the video too much, as your content can quickly become blocky and pixelated.

Zooming is great when trying to distinguish among a bunch of look-alike buttons and fields.

Historically, the main problem with Zoom-n-Pan was the sheer amount of time and experience it took to wield the tool effectively. Setting all those zoom points in your video can be a bit tedious, especially if you're not really sure what you're doing. Starting with version 5 of Camtasia Studio, you now have **SmartFocus** at your command. This is a one-click utility that automatically sets relevant zoom-n-pan points throughout your video. When making your captures, the Camtasia Recorder also captures information that will later let SmartFocus work its magic — where you click, where you type, where you move within the capture area. This information is all saved within the .camrec file. While SmartFocus is pretty good about determining where those points should go, it's not perfect, and it's likely that you'll need to do a fair amount of tweaking in order to get them just right. I therefore want you to learn how to set zoom-n-pan points manually first, and we'll then revisit SmartFocus at the end of this section.

So, enough of the conceptual stuff — let's actually get our hands dirty with this feature, starting with **opening the Zoom-n-Pan Properties pane**:

- In the Edit section of your Task List, choose **Zoom-n-Pan....**

  or

- From your **Edit** menu, pick **Zoom-n-Pan....**

IV: Editing

Your Zoom-n-Pan Properties pane opens. To execute your very first zoom, the first thing you'll need to do is place your seek bar at the exact spot in the clip where you want your zoom to go. Keep in mind that your zoom will last only as long as the duration of the current clip. When your clip ends, so does your effect.

Zooming

So, you've got your seek bar on the right spot, yes? To execute the zoom, click the **Add a new keyframe** button (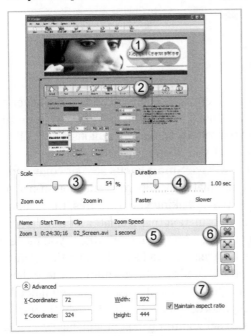). A new zoom point will be added to the keyframe list. At this point, your Zoom-n-Pan Properties pane should look something like this:

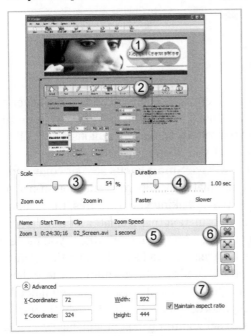

The pane breaks down thusly:

① **Zoom-n-pan preview**, which shows the overall clip, giving you a guide for your zoom.

② **Zoom-n-pan frame.** This adjustable frame lets you select an area to which you want to zoom/pan.

③ **Scale slider.** This is another mechanism for increasing/decreasing the size of the zoom-n-pan frame. You can also enter a value into the percentage field.

④ **Duration slider.** Set the duration of the effect anywhere from zero (instantaneous) to five seconds (extremely slow).

⑤ **Keyframe list.** This area will allow you to view and adjust your zoom-n-pan keyframes.

⑥ **Keyframe tools.** Buttons to add or remove keyframes, expand a keyframe to full size, apply SmartFocus, and access zoom options.

⑦ **Advanced.** These fields allow you to type in the exact size and dimensions of the zoom-n-pan keyframe, which can be rather useful when you want to zoom in to 100% of your desired production size.

The pane may look complicated, but virtually all your options actually fall within three basic parameters: the size of your zoom window, the window's position, and how fast you want the zoom/pan to happen.

We'll start with the basics of **zooming in**:

1. Click the desired frame on the Timeline where you want to *end* your zoom/pan.

2. Click **Add a new keyframe.**

3. In the Zoom-n-Pan Properties pane, you will first need to specify the **Size** of your zoom window. The zoom size can be anything as long as both coordinates fit inside your video's original dimensions; anywhere from full-screen all the way to 2000% magnification. There are four ways in which you can go about setting the size:

   - Adjust the **Scale slider** to zoom in and out.

   - Set the **percentage** by manually entering a value into the corresponding field.

   - In the **Advanced** portion of the pane, manually enter values into the **Width** and **Height** fields to specify the dimensions in pixels. If desired, you can check **Maintain aspect ratio** to retain the same proportions when altering one of the two fields. Uncheck it if you want the proportions of your zoom window to be different (though, again — *not* recommended).

   - Of course, you can also resize the zoom window by clicking and dragging the handles of the green **zoom rectangle**, like so:

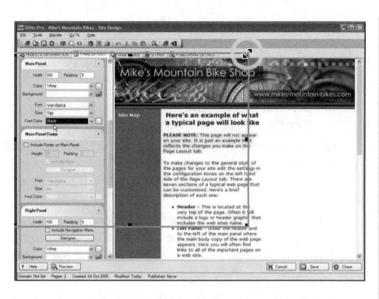

Notice how changes to the zoom rectangle and the Size fields affect each other. You can use this to your advantage: First, position the zoom rectangle roughly where you want it, and then tweak the numbers to make sure you have the details right.

4. Next, we have to set the location of our window. You've got two options here. You can use the **X-Coordinate** and **Y-Coordinate** fields to specify the horizontal (X) and vertical (Y) coordinates, in pixels, from the top-left corner of your screen. If you don't need to be quite that precise, simply click and drag anywhere inside the green zoom frame, and place it anywhere within the video's original dimensions.

5. Finally, you'll need to specify the **Zoom duration**, that is, how quickly you want the zoom to occur. Do you prefer a slow, sweeping movement or a fast close-up? Particularly if file size is a concern for you, you can also instantly close in on the details without the animated zoom effect. It's not sexy, but it gets the job done.

6. Check out the effect in your Video Preview. Does everything look as expected?

7. If you need to change the location of your zoom on the Timeline, just click on the blue diamond that represents your zoom effect to select it, and then click and drag it to a new location on the Timeline.

A Zoom-n-Pan keyframe will remain in effect until the end of the clip, or until the next Zoom-n-Pan keyframe is reached on the Timeline, whichever comes first. If you're zoomed in on one clip and you want this zoom effect to continue into the following clip, you'll need to insert a new, instant zoom effect with the same size and position settings as the first effect at the very beginning of the second clip. Wow, that sentence just read like an *Abbott & Costello* sketch, didn't it? Perhaps a visual would help:

The second Zoom-n-Pan keyframe is a mirror of the first one, and it serves to continue the current zoom level into the next clip.

If ever you need to change a zoom effect, a double-click on its icon (◆) in the Zoom track on your Timeline will bring up its Zoom-n-Pan Properties pane for you to edit at any time.

The triangular-shaped ramp attached to this clip symbolizes the clip's zoom speed. It will help you better gauge the exact point on your Timeline the zoom will begin as well as when the zoom/pan animation finishes. The ramp will be longer, shorter, or nonexistent based on the zoom speed you chose*.

Panning

Of course, zooming in on an object is just half of the equation. Once you're zoomed in, you're focused on just a small portion of the screen, and ignoring the rest. However, this small area of focus can still be moved around, which is what **panning** is all about. It's like having a flashlight in a darkened room. You can only see a small part of the room at a time, but the rest of it is still there, and can be discovered simply by casting the beam in another direction.

---

* If your zoom begins or ends close to the beginning/end of the clip that contains it, the duration of the fade effect will auto-scale based on those constraints.

Panning the focus to the remotest corners of your capture area can be accomplished thusly:

1. Create a **zoom effect** for the clip in question. Since panning requires working with a smaller space than the entire capture area, this first step is a necessity. Click **OK** to return to the Zoom-n-Pan Properties pane.

2. Move the Timeline's seek bar to a point later in the clip where you want to pan. You should be placing the seek bar at the exact moment on the Timeline where you want the pan animation to *end*.

3. Click the **Add a new keyframe** button. A new Zoom-n-Pan point appears on your Timeline. Camtasia Studio remembers the size and location of your last zoom effect, and this is a good baseline for doing your pan effects, which you'll want to keep exclusively horizontal or vertical for the most part. A diagonal pan where both the vertical and horizontal position coordinates change, especially coupled with a corresponding shift to the size, tends to look a little wonky and unprofessional.

4. Change the field values or drag the green zoom rectangle to reflect the desired position.

5. Set the **Duration**. For pan effects, I would discourage you from setting the slider all the way to the left unless you're really worried about file size. Instantly panning to another part of the screen (especially if you're only moving the position a short distance) can be somewhat disconcerting to the viewer.

Of course, as implied above, you can also change the zoom size during a pan for a zoom/pan combination effect. However, you'll need to keep in mind a basic rule of graphic design. For these kinds of effects to work well (actually, for *any* kind of zoom or pan effect to work), you'll need a stark contrast in size and/or position between the beginning and end of the effect. Subtly panning over by just a few pixels is visually off-putting — it makes your audience wonder if you actually meant to do it. Suddenly, they're no longer focused on your content, but rather on your skill with Zoom-n-Pan. Special effects like these are there to augment the *content*; they shouldn't be drawing undue attention to themselves. I know it sounds like a paradox, but the more dramatic the visual change, the less likely your viewers will raise an eyebrow at it.

Managing Your Zoom-n-Pan Effects

Now that we've figured out how to add zoom and pan effects to our videos, let's learn a few general housekeeping practices that will facilitate our working with them. Check out the Keyframe list on the Zoom-n-Pan Properties pane:

Name	Start Time	Clip	Zoom Speed
Zoom 2	0:05:10;26	Cutaways.wmv	5 seconds
Zoom 1	0:19:13;29	01new_Screen.avi	5 seconds
Zoom 3	0:19:40;08	01new_Screen.avi	1 second
Zoom 4	0:20:55;09	02_Screen.avi	1.75 seconds
Zoom 5	0:21:19;06	02_Screen.avi	Instant

If you've been following along while reading, then you should already have at least a couple of entries. You've got the following information at your fingertips:

- **Name.** You're given a generic name for each effect (Zoom 1, Zoom 2, etc.), but you can rename each one if desired by clicking twice (slower than a double-click) anywhere on the item's line.

- **Start Time.** This is the point of time in which the zoom/pan effect will "arrive at its final destination," *not* when the zoom/pan animation begins.

- **Clip.** The video clip to which the animation is applied.

- **Zoom Speed.** The amount of time, in seconds, it takes for the effect to happen.

Of course, if ever you need to change an effect, it's incredibly easy to do so. Just reopen the item's Zoom-n-Pan Properties pane.

You can **open any pre-existing Zoom-n-Pan keyframe** by executing one of the following steps:

- Double-click on the **Zoom point**, located on the Zoom track on your Timeline.

 or

- Click an item in the Keyframe list from within the Zoom-n-Pan Properties pane.

Once you've got the specific effect open, just make any editing changes as needed.

If you look next to the Keyframe list, you'll notice a column of buttons that will help in the creation, removal, and maintenance of Zoom-n-Pan effects. Let's take a look:

 Going in order from top to bottom: Add a new keyframe, Remove the selected keyframe(s), Expand the selected keyframe(s) to full-screen, Apply SmartFocus to entire timeline, and Open zoom options.

We've already discussed how to add effects, and removing unwanted ones is just as easy. To delete an individual item, select it in the table on your Zoom-n-Pan Properties pane, and either click the **Remove the selected keyframe(s)** button ( ) or simply press the **Delete** key, confirming with **Yes** when the "Are you sure?" dialog pops up. Keep in mind that you can make use of the Shift and Ctrl keys to select multiple keyframes for a single deletion.

The next button in the toolbar, **Expand the selected keyframe(s) to full-screen**, provides an easy way of alternating between a zoomed-in position and zooming all the way back out to show the entire interface. Say you just set a 320 x 240 zoom point. You want the next keyframe to zoom all the way back out to the clip's original 800 x 600 dimensions. Adding the next keyframe will give you a zoom point of the same size and dimensions as your last one, namely 320 x 240. But one click of this button will make it full-size. Yes, you could do it manually, but the button's single-click simplicity means saved time, especially if you want to zoom out multiple keyframes at once, as this tool also supports multiple keyframe selections.

SmartFocus is important enough to merit its own section, so we'll be talking about it in just a moment. The final toolbar button opens up additional zoom options. It's the same as choosing **Options...** from the **Tools** menu, and then clicking the **Zoom** tab. In it, we see four options...

■ **Apply Zoom-n-Pan hints.** When enabled, this option shows the audience a green rectangle around the area they'll be zooming into when the zoom begins. It provides a visual cue whenever you're about to zoom in on a section of your capture area.

- **Limit SmartFocus keyframes to editing dimensions.** When you select editing dimensions in the Project Settings dialog, this setting explicitly instructs SmartFocus to only zoom in as far as those editing dimensions. This means that, at a maximum, the audience will view content at 100% its original capture size, but never magnified.

- **Show zoom rectangles in Preview Window.** Checking this box will change the way your Video Preview shows the zoom. Rather than showing the zoom effect as the audience would see it, checking this option gives you a better overview of the included zoom content within the broader scope of the video's original dimensions.

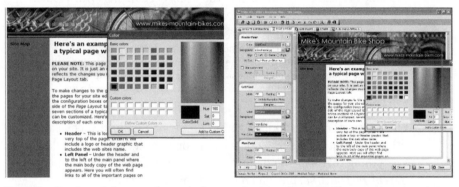

The Video Preview of the same frame is shown twice here, first with Show zoom rectangles disabled, and then with it enabled.

As you can see, it looks very similar to the zoom rectangle window on the Zoom-n-Pan Properties pane. Note that this effect is only visible in the Video Preview when the Zoom-n-Pan Properties pane is up. If you exit Zoom-n-Pan mode entirely, then the Video Preview will revert to behaving as if the Show zoom rectangles option were disabled. I don't personally use this feature very often, but in segments with a lot of mouse activity, I often find it handy when planning my zoom/pan effects so that I can better track the mouse cursor.

- **Default duration (seconds).** This slider sets the standard duration for all new Zoom-n-Pan effects.

Click **OK** when you're happy. Now, let's move on to the details of the SmartFocus tool that you first saw back in Chapter 9.

SmartFocus

When discussing zooming and panning techniques in this chapter, I gave you guidelines for drilling down on sections of interest within your overall capture area, and for moving that focus around so that you could follow all the action happening on your screen. For complicated tutorials, it can be very detailed work. Arduous. Time-consuming. The opposite of what we need if we're under a deadline.

SmartFocus aims to resolve that. During the capture stage, the Camtasia Recorder is collecting metadata about the action happening within the capture area: things like the active window, text entry, mouse position, etc. All this information gets saved right along with the other capture streams inside the .camrec, starting with version 5.

 Keep in mind that you need to have .camrec selected as your file format in order to capture the information that SmartFocus needs to do its job. AVI won't cut it. Additionally, since the Camtasia Recorder only started capturing this metadata with Camtasia Studio 5, .camrec files captured with earlier versions won't have this information either, and SmartFocus won't work on them.

When SmartFocus is applied within Camtasia Studio, a special algorithm automatically sets Zoom-n-Pan points based on its knowledge of everything that happened during the capture. SmartFocus applies to the *entire Timeline*; bits and pieces cannot be selected.

> To **apply SmartFocus**, do one of the following:
> - Click the **Apply SmartFocus** button (🔍 Apply SmartFocus) on the Timeline toolbar.
> - Click the **Apply SmartFocus to the entire timeline** button (🔍) from the Zoom-n-Pan Properties pane.
> - Choose **Edit > Timeline > Apply SmartFocus**.

SmartFocus then lays in appropriate Zoom-n-Pan keyframes. These can be adjusted, added to, or removed just like any other, using the techniques we already discussed. It's likely that you're going to need to make some adjustments — the algorithm, while good, doesn't have ESP. It'll follow the basic action on the screen, but for a truly professional result, make sure you clean it up by hand. Also, keep in mind that there are a few caveats for using SmartFocus where it might not always work, or at least not work as expected:

- As I mentioned, SmartFocus only works with clips recorded in .camrec format with Camtasia Studio 5 or later. AVI files and CAMREC files captured in earlier versions are taboo.

- Each clip needs to be at least 30 seconds in length. SmartFocus won't bother with clips that are shorter than this.

- The editing dimensions have to be smaller than the original capture area. Otherwise, there's no need to zoom at all.

- Don't use the Zoom-n-Pan features of the Camtasia Recorder. If the Zoom property in your Recorder's Statistics pane shows anything other than 100%, no keyframes will be generated. The same thing happens if you use Recorder to pan the capture area (whether by dragging the capture area or by using AutoPan).

- SmartFocus only works when the mouse cursor is present inside the capture area. If your mouse cursor is outside the capture area for longer than five seconds, SmartFocus turns itself off until the cursor returns.

- In rare cases, SmartFocus might not work where there's simply too much happening in the capture area at once; erratic mouse activity, animations, and other sweeping changes might cause this to happen.

These trivialities aside, SmartFocus can shave a lot of time off preparing a project for smaller distribution, even for those who are well-versed in zooming and panning. Simply click, tweak, and produce.

Callouts and Flash Hotspots

As you've probably already discovered while recording your own creations, you can pack an awful lot of material into a relatively small video window. Thus far in this chapter, you've learned how to zoom in on your content and pan around to shift the attention to various parts of the capture area. But sometimes this focus isn't enough, and you'll want to annotate what you're showing. This is where *callouts* come in.

Imagine, if you will, an invisible layer (made of cellophane, or perhaps some equally transparent substance crafted by a higher alien intelligence) placed over the top of your video window, to which any number of static visual elements (arrows, bubble callouts, graphics, etc.) can be glued. If you want to draw attention to a particular area of the screen or post some kind of text signage, simply add a callout.

Callouts appear over the top of your video for whatever period of time you specify.

Callouts were available in the earliest versions of Camtasia, later combining with Flash hotspots into a single mechanism. *Flash hotspots* are clickable areas of your video that allow you to temporarily halt playback ("Click here to continue"), move to a different section of the video ("Click here to find out more about this feature"), or even jump to a web URL ("Click here to visit us online"). Camtasia Studio lets you not only set up a transparent hotspot, but also assign hotspot interactivity to any pre-existing callout. If you know you want to make a callout clickable, this saves you the added step of installing a separate hotspot layer on top of it.

Camtasia Studio offers a whole library of preinstalled callouts for you to use in your creations, but you can also import any graphic image for use as a custom callout. We'll be tackling the built-in callouts first, but not to worry — we'll address adding your own custom images to your pool of callouts before the chapter is out.

Before we can do anything, though, we must first instruct Camtasia Studio that we'd like to **add a callout** and specify where we'd like it to go.

1. Enter the Callouts pane by choosing **Callouts...** from the Edit section of the Task List.

    or

    Choose **Callouts...** from the **Edit** menu.

2. Place your seek bar in the Timeline where you want the callout to appear.

3. In the Callouts pane, click **Add Callout**.

A callout will be added to the Timeline, which you should be seeing right in your Callouts track:

Additionally, you'll see the actual callout in your Video Preview:

The added callout appears in your Video Preview, where you can easily place and size it relative to the other information on your screen.

Finally, you'll also have access to a host of options for tweaking your callout on the Callout Properties pane:

The available choices on the Callout Properties pane are divided into three sections: Shape, Text, and Properties.

Whenever you add a new callout, notice that the callout begins wherever you placed your seek bar on the Timeline and then stops after a given period of time (five seconds by default). If your callouts typically tend to run longer or shorter than that, you can change the default length of the callout by choosing **Tools > Options...** (Program tab), and then changing the value of the **Callouts** field in the section called Default Duration.

Defining the Callout's Shape

Now that we've got a callout on the Timeline, we're going to tweak it using the settings in the Callout Properties pane. The first thing we'll need to do is specify its *shape*. Click the drop-down arrow next to **Callout type**, and you'll see that you can change the current callout to one of 14 different types. You've got boxes, arrows, and callout bubbles (some filled with a color, others with no fill), and you've even got a few "special" callouts to which I'd like to draw your attention:

- **Highlight Rectangle.** This is a solid block of semi-transparent color that you can use as a sort of virtual highlighter pen, marking things of interest on the screen.

- **Transparent Hotspot.** While all callouts can now have a hotspot attached to them, this is an invisible box you can use if there's a portion of the actual video footage you wish to make clickable.

- **Text Callout.** This callout is also invisible, save for the text that you enter. Note that you can add text to *any* callout, even your custom ones. Use this one if you want text and nothing else.

- **Blur Callout.** Speaking of text, you may occasionally be recording windows that contain sensitive bits of text you'd rather your audience not be able to see. I'm talking about things like passwords, account numbers, salary figures, and the like. This callout will blur anything underneath it, thus rendering it illegible.

One cool thing about the various callout types is that each one remembers all the settings from the last time it was used. Whenever you add a new callout of the same type, it will retain all the properties of the last one (though these can of course be subsequently altered). This is really handy if you're inserting, for example, a series of filled rounded rectangle callouts throughout your video, and you want to maintain consistency in terms of size, position, coloring, etc.

Once you've picked a callout type, you'll next need to choose an **orientation**, which is essentially the direction your callout is facing.

Shape

Callout type: [Arrow icon] Arrow ▾ Custom Callouts...

[row of four arrow orientation icons]

Fill Color... [ ]   Border Color... [■]   Restore Shape Defaults

☐ Make Flash hotspot   Flash Hotspot Properties...

There are four orientation possibilities for this arrow callout, but for some callout types, you'll have as many as eight.

Simply click the desired orientation, and the callout will be automatically updated in the Video Preview. In fact, *any* changes you make are updated in real time, so you'll always be able to see exactly what you're getting whenever you make a change.

Next, we need to give our callout some color. You've got two buttons for this: **Fill Color** and **Border Color**. Note that one or both of these may be grayed out depending on the callout type. Simply click the button, and choose a color from the corresponding palette that opens.

Believe it or not, your custom callouts actually *can* be colored using these two color buttons. Whether or not you'll actually achieve a desirable effect depends heavily on the image type. Two-tone GIF images recolor a lot better than photographic JPGs with millions of colors.

Of course, if you've really made a mess of things while playing around with the various settings, there's a handy reset button called **Restore Shape Defaults** that will bring back that shape's "factory defaults." Note that this affects not only your Shape options, but also *all* properties of the callout.

Adding a Flash Hotspot

One cool aspect of callouts is the ability to take any callout and make it clickable. To take advantage of this, you'll need to produce your video in a format that supports some degree of interactivity, so only users of SWF and FLV output need apply. In fact, I strongly encourage you to check out these two formats *anyway* if you haven't already done so, as they both have other strong merits that make them major assets in your file format arsenal. Take a peek at Chapter 12 for more info on all the formats. So, if management has stipulated that another output format be used (or if you think you're too cool for school and don't wish to heed my advice), then you may freely skip this section. The rest of you, follow me...

Here's the general procedure for **adding a Flash hotspot callout**:

1. Add a new callout as you normally would and tweak it to your liking.

2. While on the Callout Properties pane, click the check box for **Make Flash hotspot** (for the Transparent hotspot callout type, it will be checked automatically).

3. The **Flash Hotspot Properties...** button will become active. Click it.

4. The Flash Hotspot Properties dialog will open. At the top of the dialog, you'll have a check box option called **Pause at end of callout**. If this option is checked, then the playback head will actually stop at the conclusion of the callout to await instructions from the user. It's a good option if you're using callouts to set internal navigation in your video (e.g., "Click here to repeat this section" or "Click here to continue"). If you want the hotspot to be optional (such as making a URL in your video clickable), then clear this check box.

5. Now it's time to choose the **Action** associated with clicking the hotspot. You've got four choices:

   ■ **Click to continue.** The playback head simply resumes as if it had never been stopped. This option is only available if you've opted to pause at the end of the callout.

   ■ **Go to frame at time.** You can direct the audience to a specific part of your video, down to the hour, minute, second, and centisecond.

   ■ **Go to marker.** If you've specified markers for all your important sections, then they'll be listed in the Go to marker drop-down list, complete with time and name (if given).

   ■ **Jump to URL.** This is a powerful option that will let your audience access web sites directly from your video. If you don't want the video window to be replaced by the new URL, then make sure that **Open URL in new browser window** is checked. The Jump to URL option will accept pretty much any valid web URL, including mailto links, so if you want to add a "Click here to e-mail us" link to your callout, it's easy to do so (e.g., mailto:joeschmo@xyz.com).

6. Click **OK** to confirm your choices and set the hotspot.

Remember what I said about your hotspots only playing nice with SWF and FLV (hence the reason they call them *Flash* hotspots)? If you start producing in a different format, you'll get a warning message telling you that your callouts won't be interactive, and what a pity that would be.

Adding Text

You've probably noticed by now that several of your callout types, such as rectangle, bubble, notepad, etc., look as though they were designed to hold some kind of textual message. Well, friends, you can add text to any callout you've got (even custom ones). You've got all kinds of great uses for text-based callouts, including:

- Special instructions to your audience
- Supplementary information on your topic (think VH1's "Pop-Up Video")
- A dialogue bubble for your PIP image or a static image of someone
- Captioning a piece of narration (This has been mostly supplanted by the Captions feature, which we'll talk more about later in this chapter.)
- Quickly titling a segment without having to do a full title clip
- A small text callout, consisting of only asterisks or some other placeholder character, for blocking out sensitive information in your video

Adding text to a pre-existing callout is actually rather simple. Everything happens right here in the Text section of your Callout Properties pane:

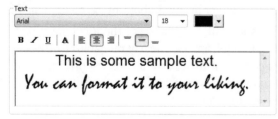

IV: Editing

The first thing to do is simply to click in the big text field and start typing. Words will start to appear over your callout in the Video Preview. Once it's there, you've got all the standard formatting options. Check out the section called "Adding Title Clips" in Chapter 10 if there are any editing commands you're unsure of.

 If importing text from other applications, note that your basic clipboard hotkeys (Ctrl-C, Ctrl-X, and Ctrl-V) all work just fine. (*Secret tip:* You can actually paste tables onto your callouts from any word processing or spreadsheet application. Just try to get the sizing right *prior* to copying and pasting the table. If you need to resize things in Camtasia Studio, the text will resize just fine, but the table itself will not.)

Adjusting the Callout's Properties

Now that you've got the desired message on your callout, it's time to do a little fine-tuning regarding how it's displayed. If you look in the Properties section on your Callout Properties pane, you've got a few miscellaneous options:

- **Fade in.** When introduced, the callout will gradually fade in rather than simply "popping" onto the screen. Unfortunately, you cannot control the speed of this fade effect.

- **Fade out.** Same thing, except it happens on the callout's exit.

- **Add drop shadow.** This adds an eye-catching shadow effect to the callout. It is available for every callout type except Text callouts (this includes custom callouts).

- **3D edge.** Checking this box adds a special three-dimensional effect to your callout.

- **Size callout to text.** This is a dandy option for automatically resizing your callout to accommodate your ever-expanding text as you type. It saves you from the back-and-forth hassle of "type, resize, type, resize, etc." You cannot manually adjust the width or height of your callout when this feature is enabled.

- **Keep aspect ratio.** If you plan on resizing the callout, checking this box first will lock the callout's aspect ratio so that the shape's width and height will resize proportionately. It helps avoid that neat "Silly Putty" effect brought about by careless resizing.

- **Opacity.** This slider allows you to set the level of visibility for your callout, ranging from 1% (nearly invisible) to 100% (totally opaque). You can use it to achieve a cool, semi-transparent effect, though this can increase your file size, so use it sparingly if bandwidth is an issue for you.

Finally, you have the ability to numerically adjust both the size and position of your callout using the Width/Height and X/Y fields, respectively. You can make use of these fields or simply click and drag the callout inside your Video Preview (or perform some combination of the two).

To recap, this is how we **move a callout**:

■ In the Video Preview, click and hold the mouse cursor anywhere inside the callout's green border, and drag to a new location.

or

■ In the Properties section of the Callout Properties pane, adjust the **X** and **Y** fields to indicate the number of pixels to the right and downward from the upper left-hand corner of the video window you'd like the lower right-hand corner of your callout to be.

And you can also **resize your callout** in one of two ways:

1. In the Properties section of the Callout Properties pane, click the **Keep aspect ratio** check box if you'd like your sizing changes to maintain the callout's original dimensions.

2. In the Video Preview, click and hold the mouse cursor on one of the eight black resizing squares on the callout's green border. Drag one of the squares to size the callout up or down.

or

In the Properties section of the Callout Properties pane, adjust the **Width** and **Height** fields to indicate the number of pixels wide and/or high you'd like your callout to be. If your Keep aspect ratio check box is checked, then the other field will automatically self-adjust after you've altered one of these fields.

Adding Custom Callouts

Arrows and dialogue bubbles are all well and good, but what about when you want to slap your corporate logo or individual portraits of your management team onto your video? Can you add those elements as callouts? Yes, you can. If you look toward the top of the Callout Properties pane, you'll notice a button we haven't talked about yet: **Custom Callouts....** Give this button a click to open the Custom Callout Manager dialog:

You'll start out with a list window of custom callouts (which should be empty if you haven't yet added any callouts on your own). Let's remedy this by adding a custom callout or two.

You can **start your own library of custom callouts** by following these easy steps:

1. From the Custom Callout Manager dialog, click the button labeled **New Custom Callout....**

2. An Open dialog will appear, prompting you to navigate to an image. You can choose from BMP, GIF, JPG, and PNG images. This chapter's folder on the companion CD has a few images for your use if you don't have anything else handy. Select your image and click **Open.**

3. The callout name and file name will appear in the Custom callout list window. Certain details about your callout, including its file path and dimensions, will appear in the corresponding fields. Custom callouts are automatically saved inside a special Custom Callouts folder, which can be found inside your Camtasia Studio folder within My Documents.

4. Your callout is given the default name "Custom Callout." Feel free to alter the Description field to give your callout a name that's a bit more descriptive and interesting.

Those are the basics of adding a custom callout. Any time you wish to remove a callout from the list, simply click the callout's name in the Custom callout list, and then click the **Remove Selected Callout** button. Of course, if you really want a lot of control, there are a few advanced options with which you'll want to familiarize yourself.

If the callout is designed to contain text, then the **Text indent** fields will let you specify margins for your custom callout so that nothing important in the image gets obscured. Take a look at these two "picket sign" callouts:

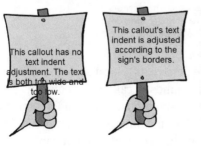

The first callout has no Text indent adjustments, whereas the second one makes use of Text indent to shift the text up so that it corresponds with the actual sign.

So how do we accomplish this? Well, the values of these fields represent the number of pixels *inward* from the left, right, top, and bottom you'd like your text to be. In the preview of your custom callout, the red box indicates the acceptable area for text, and the dimensions of this box will change automatically as you adjust the four Text indent fields.

The next set of options has to do with how the image is scaled. All custom callouts are *raster images*, pictures that are made up of lots and lots of pixels. Unlike vector images, which are not comprised of pixels but rather rendered mathematical calculations, raster images do not scale particularly well, as seen in the following example:

Left, an image at original size. Right, the same image blown up (notice the blocky pixelated effect).

Camtasia Studio has a special method of scaling certain callouts called **Vector grow** to help circumvent the problem of scaling up your custom callouts. Note that this system doesn't actually vectorize your callouts, but rather allows them to scale with no loss in quality by fundamentally changing the way the image is scaled. When you click Vector grow, you are given the opportunity to choose a one-pixel wide column (X-Coordinate) and a one-pixel tall row (Y-Coordinate) that will repeat themselves over and over as the image is scaled up. The rest of the image won't change in scale at all. These coordinates are represented by green lines in your callout's image preview.

The same image from before, this time blown up with Vector grow in effect. As you can see, the corners are actually the same size as before.

Of course, there are a couple of caveats. Because of the nature of this scaling technique, only certain kinds of callouts need apply. First, the image needs to be more or less symmetrical. Second, rectangular shapes tend to fare better than round ones, since circles tend to become rounded rectangles as they're stretched outward:

The Vector grow feature doesn't care for circles. My smiley face just got a little blockheaded.

As for those images that don't fare so well under Vector grow, just try to import the image at a size that would best represent its real-world usage within Camtasia Studio. After all, resizing your callout as little as possible will always yield better quality results.

Now that you've got a custom callout or two, you might be wondering how you actually add them to your project. The answer is simple: the same way that you add all your other callouts. If you take a peek now at your Callout type drop-down list, you may have a surprise in store if you scroll down a ways... yep, there's your custom callout. All the same orientation choices, callout properties, and yes, coloring options, apply to your custom callouts in addition to your regular ones. So feel free to play around to see what neat (if unintentional) effects come about as a result. Remember, if you mess things up beyond all recognition, a simple click of the **Restore Shape Defaults** button will put it all right again.

If you have a video with a lot of keyboard hotkeys or shortcuts, you may want to display those keyboard combinations on-screen at the right moment. Callouts are ideal for this. You could always use a standard text callout, but that's a tad boring. Fortunately, Alan over at AlanWho.com has released a set of high-quality keyboard icons for each and every key on a standard 104-key keyboard. He was kind enough to include PNG versions of each key so that you can import them as custom callouts. They're free to use and distribute, so I've placed them in this chapter's media folder on your disc. Enjoy!

Transitions

If you've followed the advice in this book thus far, then your recordings have yielded a number of clips that you have then managed to slap together in Camtasia Studio and edit to your liking. As mentioned earlier in the text, trying to record everything in one take is not only a waste of time, it yields a boring result. Films and television programs are made up of multiple shots, organized into scenes, and your videos should be as well. When putting your scenes together, sometimes the best method of introducing the new scene is simply by "cutting over" to it abruptly. Sometimes not. As with film and TV, Camtasia Studio offers fades, wipes, and even more complex ways of moving from the end of one scene to the beginning of another. These gaps are called *transitions*, and the stylistic effects you can insert during transitions can help bring your production to a new level of professionalism, provided you limit yourself to a few such effects per video (this is another one of those features that's notoriously easy to overdo).

To **get started with transitions**, simply do the following:

- In the Task List under Edit, choose **Transitions....**

or

- Choose **Transitions...** from the **Edit** menu.

Notice that you're now in Storyboard view. This is the default view for adding transitions. If you started in Timeline view, you'll be taken back there upon conclusion of your "transitioning duties." You only need two things in order to add a transition: the clip you're transitioning *from* and the clip you're transitioning *to*. So, if you don't have at least two clips present in Ye Olde Storyboarde, head on back to your Clip Bin and import some more.

Adding a Transition

Okay, now let's take a look at the available transitions. You've got a library of 25 of them at your disposal — they're listed in alphabetical order in the Transitions pane. To see what a given transition will look like in action, just double-click it. The Video Preview will show one still image transitioning into another. In order to see how the given transition will work with the actual content, you'll need to add that transition to your Storyboard.

Here's how to go about **adding a transition effect**:

1. Make sure you have at least two clips on your Storyboard.
2. Select a transition from the Transitions pane list.
3. Click and drag the chosen transition effect from the list to the small transition box that rests between your two clips.

This box represents the transition between these clips, and it looks like this:

A small plus sign (+) will appear next to your mouse cursor when you drag a transition effect onto a transition box.

Release the mouse button to assign the transition effect to those clips.

or

Right-click the desired transition effect. You will receive a context menu asking where you'd like the transition effect placed:

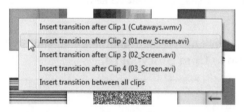

Select your desired location by left-clicking it. The transition effect will appear in the appropriate transition box.

4. A graphical representation of the transition effect is now visible within the transition box. You can now preview the effect by clicking the **Play** button in your Video Preview. You can go back and preview your effect at any time by clicking the effect in your transition box, and then playing back the preview.

5. How was the timing of the transition? Too fast? Too slow? You can adjust the timing of your transition by right-clicking the transition effect inside the transition box and choosing a duration for the effect, from one second (quickest) to five seconds (slowest).

6. Repeat this process for other pairs of clips as desired.

IV: Editing

If you want to adjust the default timing of your transitions, you can easily do so by choosing **Tools > Options...** and entering a new value into the Transitions default duration field on the Program tab. Any integer from 1 to 5 will work; 3 is the factory default.

Changing Your Mind

Obviously, you are *not* stuck with your first choice if you decide it doesn't work with the content. To replace the transition effect, simply add a new one to the same spot, and it will replace the first one. Another option you have for replacing a transition is to right-click the transition box, and then select a new transition effect from the **Change Transition** submenu.

Of course, if you'd rather **delete the transition effect** entirely, you've got a couple of options for doing so:

- Select the transition effect by clicking inside the transition box. Press the **Delete** key.

  or

- Right-click inside the transition box, and then choose **Remove from Storyboard**.

A Few Parting Words about Using Transitions

Transition effects place a professional piece of eye candy between your clips, and people really seem to like them due to their "Wow!" factor. As such, the temptation may be strong to place a transition between each and every pair of clips, preferably different ones to show off all the cool effects you have at your disposal. This is a bad idea. Transitions should be used sparingly. I personally only use them when doing so communicates meaning. For example, the Radial Wipe effect is one of my personal favorites because it's reminiscent of the hands of a clock. As such, I'll often employ it between two "before and after" clips to convey the passage of time. I could give you other examples, but the bottom line is this: Never use a transition effect just because you can. Make sure there's stylistic and/or communicative intent behind your choice.

Of course, sometimes the motivation for adding a transition effect is the simple desire to cover up a mistake. Hey, it happens to me, too. I've often had multiple clips that were supposed to flow seamlessly into one another, only to discover that the beginning of my new clip placed the mouse cursor completely on the other side of the screen. Or, I forgot to reset the location of a window or other screen object correctly, and now there's a disconcerting "jump" between clips. In cases like these, a well-placed transition effect can sometimes really come to your rescue. Other times, it's even more conspicuous than simply cutting over to the new clip and hoping people don't notice. It's always worth a try as a last resort prior to rerecording.

Keep in mind that most transitions only work well when the end of the first clip and the beginning of the second have radically different content. For transitioning between two nearly identical screens, the following transitions work well: Cube Rotate, Fade Through Black, Flip, Glow, Page Turn, Peel, Pixelate, and Roll.

Of course, do understand that all these transitions can take a serious toll on your file size, depending on the output format you've chosen. For those formats that are very forgiving of high-motion video, such as Flash FLV and QuickTime H.264, you can add a flurry of transitions without it having too large an impact on your hard drive space. For most other formats, you'll need to be a little more conservative: Go for fewer effects of shorter duration. Some transitions compress better than others, so feel free to experiment.

Captions

I once had a client who wanted their training videos captioned for their hearing-impaired customers. There were approximately 10 videos, totaling roughly an hour of content. At that point, I had to implement these captions using the Callouts feature discussed earlier in this chapter. Callouts are wonderful for adding dialogue bubbles, labeled arrows, or a random graphic to your video, but using them for captioning was a terribly laborious process.

If only I'd had the Captions feature available to me at the time, I could have saved myself hours of effort and frustration. Not only are captions a terrific addition to your video content arsenal (particularly if a lot of your viewers are hearing impaired or have a low proficiency in English), but they're ridiculously easy to do. Simply add your text narration, sync the text with your audio, and you're all set up to deliver your video with glorious captions. It's not a long process, either — once you get the hang of timing out your captions, it should only take

you as long as the running time of your video, as you're literally synchronizing the captions as you watch.

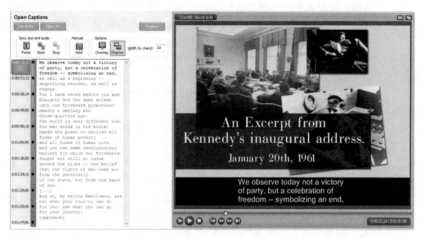

As you paste in your narration text and sync it with the audio, you'll be able to
monitor your captions right inside your Video Preview.

A lot of attention is being paid to video captioning these days due to
the Section 508 laws, which require federal agencies and departments
(and depending on the state, some state entities as well) to make some
basic accessibility provisions for people with disabilities. For these
organizations, all videos and multimedia titles need to be appropriately
captioned. If you work for the U.S. federal government, or if you plan
on using Camtasia Studio to create a product (and the U.S. government
is a potential target market for you), it would behoove you to research
the basics of Section 508 compliance. Please check out
www.section508.gov for more information.

For all video formats except Flash, Camtasia Studio employs what
is known as *open captioning*, meaning that the added captions are
always visible to everybody. Unlike closed captioning, they cannot be
turned on/off as needed. These captions are in fact "burned into" your
final video. The application can either superimpose them over your
video content, or extend the vertical length of your video window so
that the captions appear in their own black box, just below the actual
video content.

Flash users, however, have the ability to add closed captions to
their work. When playing the file back in their browsers, they'll be
able to view the captions, or not, simply by clicking the appropriate
button.

To get started down the road of captioning our narration, we first have to **open the Open Captions pane** in Camtasia Studio, which is accomplished thusly:

- Choose **Captions...** from the **Edit** menu.

  or

- In the Task List, choose **Captions...** from the Edit subsection.

  or

- If you have any pre-existing captions on the Timeline, double-click one. The Open Captions pane will appear, starting right with the caption you selected.

If this is your first time bringing up the Open Captions pane, a tip screen will appear. Read through it if desired, and then close it to continue.

Adding Narration Text

If you followed the above procedure, the Open Captions pane should be open. Now it's time to insert your narration text. The easiest way to add the corresponding text to audio narration you record on the fly is to view your video in small chunks using the Video Preview and type the transcription into the text window as you go. Of course, things are even simpler if you had the foresight to narrate your video from a script (yet another reason to script everything ahead of time!). Just open your original source document, copy your entire script, and then paste it into the text window using the Paste button, which is in the Sync text and audio section of the Open Captions pane, and looks like this: ⊞

To recap, here's how to **add narration text to create your captions:**

1. Make sure the Open Captions pane is visible.

2. Move the seek bar on your Timeline to the point where your narration starts, presumably near the beginning of the video.

3. If importing text from a pre-existing script, select and copy the entire text in your source file.

4. Return to Camtasia Studio, and then click the **Paste** button,
    located just above the narration text box.

    or

    If creating a new script from scratch, scan through the video
    using the controls on the Video Preview pane. Transcribe the
    audio as you go by clicking in the text box and typing your
    caption content.

5. Perform any needed editing to remove superfluous text.

The first caption is automatically inserted at the point where you
placed your seek bar. Since Camtasia Studio displays three lines of
caption content at a time, the first three lines of your script should be
colored black. The rest of your text will be colored red, meaning that
this text has not yet been assigned to a *caption point* (a point on the
Timeline where a caption appears). Caption points are symbolized by
small blue dots, and appear on your Timeline in a special Caption
track, like so:

Notice that you'll have a bit o' text from the first line next to each caption point on the Timeline to help you get your bearings (it's easier to
see when you're zoomed in). Currently, you only have one caption
point on your Timeline. Poor little guy looks lonely, doesn't he? Let's
give him a few friends by adding some more caption points. This can
be accomplished by one of two methods: **With the Sync text and
audio tools** or **manually.**

Synchronizing Your Caption Content

The first method of synchronizing your captions, and by far the simplest, is to utilize the Sync text and audio commands. This will play through the video, and will allow you to click the first word of each caption block (the three-line block of text that belongs to every caption) as it appears in the voice-over narration. Every time you click, a new caption point appears on your Timeline.

This is how to **synchronize captions to your audio:**

1. Make sure you've inserted all needed text and edited it appropriately, so that it mirrors your audio track. I also insert carriage returns at appropriate spots to make sure that the captions don't break in awkward places. I've listed a few tips for formatting your captions in a separate guide at the end of this section.

2. If you've been scrolling around in your video, move your seek bar back to the beginning of your video.

3. Press the **Start** button, located just above your caption text window. The video will begin to play back.

4. Mouse over the text in your caption text window. See how the mouse cursor changed to a pointing hand? Proceed to the first word on the fourth line (i.e., the first red word). When you come to that word in your audio narration, click it. That second block of caption text will be synchronized with the narration. Congratulations, you just created your second caption point.

5. Repeat the process for each new three-line block of text. A new *caption point* will be automatically added every three lines. Of course, it doesn't always have to be three lines. You can also click to create a one-line or two-line caption block if it'll help improve the flow. I always try to avoid *widow* and *orphan* text blocks, those little one-liners that make up the very beginning or tail end of a particular thought. For example, if I'm captioning a sentence comprised of four lines total, I'll usually do two blocks of two lines each, as opposed to a three-line block and then a one-line orphan on the next block.

IV: Editing

6. Feel free to pause the action by clicking the **Pause** button (which toggles between Play and Pause). Simply click **Play** to resume, and the playback continues right where it left off. When finished, or if you need to stop for an extended period, clicking the **Stop** button will conclude that session.

If you ever want to resume a stopped session, simply place the seek bar where you want to start, and then click **Start**. You'll get a dialog that looks like this:

Sync Text and Audio

Where would you like to begin syncing your text and audio?

○ Start at beginning of Timeline and remove all existing caption points

○ Start at current caption and remove subsequent caption points

OK   Cancel   Help

The first option will completely wipe out all your previous captions and kick you back to the start of your video. With this selection, you're essentially telling Camtasia Studio, "I want to start all over again." The second option only wipes out any captions located *after* your current spot on the Timeline. You can start at your most recent caption and continue onward, or you can backtrack a bit if your last few captions weren't quite right.

Of course, you've probably figured out by now that you don't even need audio narration to insert captions. If you just want to use captions alone, you may freely do so. Simply sync the captions to the actions in the video itself rather than to the audio commentary. It's certainly possible to do this, but for the sake of accessibility, I don't recommend it. If you take out the audio portion, then it's your *sight*-impaired viewers who are left out in the cold. While it's often tempting to remove the audio due to file size considerations, there's just no real replacement for a professionally delivered voice-over.

Manual Addition and Organization of Caption Points

As cool as the Sync text and audio tools are, if you demand greater precision (or if you just have poor reflexes), you can add a caption point manually. Manual control is also handy for those occasional situations where the narration is sparse, and you simply want to jump to those specific points in the video rather than wading through the whole thing. Just click a word, click the spot on the Timeline corresponding to that word, and pair them together by clicking **Add**.

Need more detail? This is the drill for **manually adding your caption points**:

1. Place the seek bar at the exact point on your Timeline where you want your new caption to start. The sound waveform in your audio track(s) can be a handy guide for getting the placement right. Feel free to zoom in for greater precision.

2. Click in your caption text window at the *beginning* of the first word in your desired caption. The placement of your cursor is important. If you've clicked in the middle of a word, the word will be split in two, and the caption block will begin with the second half of that word.

3. Click the **Add** button in the section labeled Manual on the Open Captions pane.

4. A caption point will appear both at the designated spot on your Timeline and next to your specified caption block. For the caption point in your text window, on the left-hand side you'll see the exact point in the video's running time that the caption will appear.

Adding to the fun is the fact that your caption points are not set in stone. No sir, not by any stretch. Simply click and hold on one to see what I mean. The selected caption point turns a lovely shade of cyan. In this manner, your caption points can be dragged around, both on the Timeline and in the caption text window, though these each serve different purposes:

- **Timeline caption points.** Dragging a caption point here changes the time at which that caption is introduced. You can make subtle adjustments to the timing of your captions in this way. You can't go

IV: Editing

hog-wild, though. You cannot drag to reorder captions, nor can you come within one second of any adjacent caption.

Your caption points require a certain amount of elbow room. The DCMP (Described and Captioned Media Program, the federal program that oversees captioning for the hearing impaired) recommends that all captions remain on the screen for at least two seconds. Camtasia Studio is a bit more flexible, allowing a bare minimum of one second from the point a caption is introduced to the point that it's replaced by the next caption. One nicety is the program's ability to intelligently give you the space you need. If you place a caption a little too close to the one that came before it (< one second), Camtasia Studio will nudge your current caption over by a set amount (five seconds, provided there's not another caption in its way, in which case it may be less). If you try to insert a caption between two pre-existing captions that are already less than two seconds apart it simply can't comply, and you'll get an error message.

- **Text window caption points.** These caption points can also be dragged about, with dramatically different results. If you click and hold on these caption points, notice that a horizontal line appears in your text window:

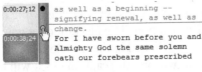

Drag your caption point to choose what text to include in your caption.

This line shows exactly what is included in the current caption point. While Camtasia Studio sections off your captions into three lines by default, you can place your caption points to include one, two, or three lines of text. Three's the maximum. If you try to rope in more, you'll end up with more of the dreaded red text, and you'll need to move the next caption point upward to help take up the slack.

Keep in mind that a caption will remain on the screen until the next caption comes in. If you have breaks in your video that don't have any audio commentary, and you don't want the most recent caption to linger on through 30 seconds of silence, you can take it off the screen by manually inserting a blank caption point:

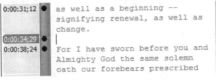

Just place your mouse cursor right at the beginning of the second caption block (the caption you want to appear *after* the pause). Then click **Add**. A blank caption point appears. Note that you might have to adjust the timing afterward to get it just right.

Likewise, you can also edit the text itself to change the amount you'll see on each line. For example, the DCMP recommends that every new sentence start on its own line. Just place your cursor in the appropriate spot, press **Enter**, and then adjust the caption point if necessary. As another example, you may occasionally find that you have odd breaks where a phrase is broken up into two different caption blocks, thus obscuring the meaning. Feel free to get in there and move that text around. Of course, it does facilitate the process if you do it sooner rather than later. That way, you'll only have to lay down the caption points once, rather than needing to juggle them around because you made all kinds of text edits after the fact.

However, now that we've added all the captions, the next issue that naturally comes up is how in the world we can delete one should the need arise. Fortunately for us, this too is rather straightforward. Simply right-click on one of your caption points (whether in the text window or on your Timeline). It presents you with three removal options:

- **Delete Caption and Text.** This option not only gets rid of a particular caption point, but also the text block associated with it. It's useful if you ended up striking a phrase in your audio narration, and this change never made it back into the script file for whatever reason.

- **Delete Caption Point Only.** This removes only your caption point. The text block that was formerly part of the caption point will remain intact, and you'll probably need to shift some of your other caption points around to get this text included in your captioning again.

- **Delete All Captions and Text.** This is another "do-over" option that gets rid of *everything*. Don't fret about accidentally wiping out all your hard work, though — for this option, you'll get a friendly dialog box that asks you if you're absolutely sure. Choose wisely.

Captioning Options

After adding and editing all our script text and its corresponding caption points, it's now time to point out a few additional options that help specify how and when the captions get displayed. While advanced formatting and placement options are not offered (yet), there are a couple of nice formatting choices that are left up to you. Check out the controls in the Options section of your Open Captions pane.

As you can see here, we've got some choices to make. Fortunately, they're pretty simple ones.

Overlay

The Overlay toggle button will let you determine whether the caption is laid over the actual video content (always at the bottom of the window) or whether the caption will appear in its own box. Here are examples of each:

This caption makes use of the Overlay option. It appears right over the top of your actual video.

The Overlay option is off. The caption appears below the video in a black box.

With Overlay disabled, the vertical height of your video will be extended to accommodate the captioning text box. In other words, your actual video won't be shrunk down in any way to make room for the caption box, so you needn't worry about that. Overlaying the captions doesn't increase your video dimensions at all.

Keep in mind that the text is always white, and the font is always Arial. For overlaid text, the text will have a black outline around it (useful when dealing with white backgrounds). For the overlay-abstainers, the caption box is always black (even if you've selected another color for your video's background). Keep this in mind when designing the look of your video project.

It's important to note that the Overlay button only works for open caption formats, that is, all formats *except* for Flash (SWF and FLV). For Flash videos, closed captioning is in effect, and the Overlay setting does nothing.

Display

The job of the Display toggle button is simple: It allows you to choose whether you want to include captions in your video. *Come again?* you're probably saying. *Why do I need this? What was the point of this whole section if not to include captions in my video?*

Well, friends, in the creation of your video project, depending on the demand from your audience and/or the decisions from the boardroom, you may find yourself in the position of having to create two versions of your video, one captioned and one not. Rather than forcing you to maintain two separate project files, this handy button will let you toggle the presence of captions in your video, while maintaining the actual data should you need it again. This setting is also reflected in your video's preview, so if you're working with captions and wondering why they're not being displayed, your troubleshooting should begin with this option.

Width (in chars)

As you've probably figured out, the Width option specifies the maximum number of characters in each line of your caption block. It can accept any value from 20 to 100. Though it can be tempting to squeeze more information onto one line, I strongly urge you to resist. The setting of 32 characters per line has been the standard since closed captioning was introduced back in 1980, and with good reason. You don't want to overwhelm your viewer with captions to the point that they ignore the video. Keep in mind that the longer you make your line, the smaller it will appear in the video. That said, if you have a compelling reason for increasing line length, it's comforting to know you have the option.

Formatting Tips for Captions

To help you in achieving better captions for your Meisterwerk-in-progress, I've compiled a short list of tips for formatting them. Most of these are borrowed from the Described and Captioned Media Program (DCMP), a program of the National Association of the Deaf (NAD). These folks compile an annual Captioning Key* to aid aspiring captioneers (which is sort of like a *mouseketeer*, but without the dorky caps or Annette Funicello). If you'd like a more detailed series of guidelines, feel free to check them out. At any rate, I hope these are helpful to you:

- All captions should be left aligned.

- If a phrase is repeated (i.e., "Move it slowly. Move it slowly."), then the second line should be indented a couple of spaces.

- The standard 32 characters per line is strongly recommended.

- If sound effects are used, you might want to caption the sound in parentheses or brackets, especially if it's critical to the meaning.

- Every sentence should begin on a new line unless the sentences are short and thematically related (e.g., "This is it! My greatest discovery!").

- Additionally, line breaks should be done in as commonsensical a way as possible so as not to obscure meaning. Try not to break up prepositional phrases, noun phrases, verb phrases, names, or titles. Try to start conjunctions (and, or, etc.) on the following line.

- The words-per-minute that the user is required to read should never exceed 160. You want to caption as close to verbatim as possible, but if the rate at which the narrator is speaking precludes that (which would obviously never happen with videos narrated by *you*, but let's assume for argument's sake that some random fast-talking colleague did your voice-over), you may need to "tighten up" the commentary. Shorten the captioning just enough to get it under 160 wpm. One exception: You should never do any editing on famous quotes, poems, or song lyrics.

---

* At the time of this writing, the 2007 version of the Captioning Key was available here: www.cfv.org/caai/nadh7.pdf.

- On a related note, try to keep each caption on-screen for at least two seconds.

- There's no need to caption information that is already shown on-screen, such as a callout.

That's it for captions. When finished captioning your video, clicking the **Finished** button at the top of the Open Captions pane will take you back to the main Camtasia Studio interface.

Flash Quiz and Survey Creation

While I always thought educational television was a great idea in theory, something always bothered me that I'd been unable to put my finger on until just recently. The tube is a one-way medium. It cannot solicit feedback. It cannot test your knowledge. It offers no real way of interacting with the content. With the rapid adoption of "smarter" home entertainment devices like TiVos and Media Center PCs, however, this lack of interaction could soon be but a memory.

And so it goes with screen video content. Earlier in the chapter, we covered Flash hotspots as a way of adding a bit of interactivity to any SWF or FLV video you create. The Flash Quiz and Survey functions go way beyond the simple clicking of a button or two. You can now actually ask your viewers a series of questions in the form of multiple-choice, fill-in-the-blank, or short-answer items. If desired, you can also choose to receive the results, either to your learning management system (or LMS) via SCORM or by having the viewer e-mail their results to you. If you're not part of a larger organization that uses an LMS or content management system, then e-mailed results are the way to go.

Quizzes and surveys are administered very much the same way, with only a couple of exceptions. For example, with surveys, grades/scores are not tallied, as the questions are for information collection only. On a related note, surveys offer *short answer* as a viable question format, which is not a suitable format for quizzes that automatically score answers. The computer is just not smart enough to tell a correct sentence from an incorrect one. You can add a short-answer question to a quiz, but you'll have to grade it manually.

In short, quizzes are excellent for making sure that your audience is actually retaining the information you're trying to get across. With surveys, the roles are actually reversed, as you're placing the audience

IV: Editing

in the role of teacher, helping you acquire knowledge you didn't have before. While this feature is still a bit young to offer anything fancy like ordinal scales, surveys do give you the basic tools needed to get inside the heads of your users and gain valuable insights as a result.

We'll explore both of these possibilities by **entering the Flash Quiz and Survey Manager** pane within Camtasia Studio:

- In the Edit section of your Task List, click **Flash Quiz and Survey....**

  or

- Choose **Flash Quiz...** from the **Edit** menu.

Flash Quiz and Survey Manager

| Assist Me | Show Me | | | Finished |

Quiz/Survey	Time

Move Up
Move Down

Edit...
Delete
Delete All
Preview

Create Quizzes and Surveys

Add Quiz...

Add Survey...

Add a Question to Selected Quiz or Survey...

As you can see, the Flash Quiz and Survey Manager pane looks pretty bare right now. Currently, your only available options are Add Quiz or Add Survey. These features are designed to be extremely flexible — you can add multiple questions for each quiz/survey, and multiple quizzes/surveys for each video. If you end up deciding to give your viewers the option of sending their results via e-mail, one nice thing is that all results from all quizzes and surveys will be amalgamated in a single message that the viewer can send upon conclusion of the video, rather than firing off multiple messages.

As there are a few fundamental differences between quiz and survey creation, let us begin with quizzes.

Adding a quiz is actually a pretty straightforward procedure. Here's how:

1. Move your seek bar to the exact location on your Timeline where you'd like your quiz to appear.

2. Click the **Add Quiz...** link in the Flash Quiz and Survey Manager pane.

3. The Quiz Appearance and Feedback dialog appears. Enter a name for your quiz in the **Quiz name** field.

4. In the **Answer numbering** drop-down list, you can choose alphabetical or numeric ordering, or no ordering scheme.

5. The next section, titled **Quiz feedback**, gives you a couple of options regarding how you want the viewers to receive feedback. Checking **Include these questions in quiz score** includes the actual questions on the quiz's score sheet. Enabling **Display feedback when questions are answered** means that your viewers will be able to see, immediately upon answering a question, whether the answer was right or wrong. If disabled, they won't know how they did until the end of the quiz.

6. Additionally, it's easy to customize the feedback text for correct and incorrect answers (though these can be individualized on a per-question basis, if desired). If, instead of "Incorrect," you'd rather the words "Wrong! Loser!" appear when the user misses a question, just type it in here.

7. Finally, you can specify what action should be taken when the user provides an incorrect response. You've got two options:

   - You can **continue** right on to the next item, or proceed with the rest of the video if this is the final question.

   - You can **jump** to a specified point in the video by entering the appropriate time in hours, minutes, and seconds. This is handy for taking the viewer back to review the exact segment in the video that covers the question missed.

8. Click **OK** to continue. The program ushers you right into creating your first question.

9. You'll be presented with the Question Type dialog. It asks if your question should be **Multiple Choice**, **Fill in the blank**, or **Short answer (not scored)**. Click the appropriate radio button, and then choose **OK** to continue.

So, now we have our first quiz set up. If you look on the Timeline, you can see a blue diamond that represents your quiz in the Quiz track:

 This little guy means you've got a quiz at that point in your Timeline.

When you create your final video in SWF or FLV format, the video playback will come to a halt when reaching this point on the Timeline so that the viewer can take the quiz. When finished with the final question, playback will continue from that point as if nothing had ever happened. The one exception to this is if you set the action for the **If incorrect** field to **Jump to time**. In the event that the viewer uses up all their allotted attempts to correctly answer a question, the video file reroutes the playback to the point in time you specified.

Multiple-Choice Questions

Where we proceed from here depends on which question type you chose. Let's cover these in turn, starting with multiple choice.

Here's the "right answer" for **designing a multiple-choice question**:

1. If you chose **Multiple Choice** from the Question Type dialog, then the Multiple Choice Question pane will appear. The Quiz Name is shown in gray (since you cannot edit the name from this pane). Notice how a basic quiz screen bearing the name of your quiz appears in the Video Preview.

2. In the **Question** field, type or paste in your question. There are no menu choices or toolbar buttons for executing the paste function, but the standard paste hotkey (**Ctrl-V**) works just fine. Keep in mind that when making any edits to the question or answers, it generally takes a few seconds for the new content to update in your Video Preview, so don't panic if you don't see the changes right away. Also, depending on question length, you may want to move the first line of the question down a line or two in order to make the screen content more balanced, thereby improving the aesthetics.

3. To insert your first answer, click in the **Answers** window where it says "<Type an answer choice here>." To move on to the next answer, click the **Add** button, or simply press the

Enter key. Your first answer will appear in the preview window, using the ordering scheme you specified when first creating the quiz. To change any answer, simply click on it twice.

4. Create your other answers. You can add as many potential answers as you wish. Click the check box next to the correct answer so that the system can provide appropriate feedback as well as do an accurate tally of correct answers for results reporting. The feedback for each item will appear to the right of the answer, like so:

This is what your multiple-choice question will look like, provided you didn't change the default feedback labels when creating the quiz.

5. To remove any of your answers, select it and then click the **Delete** button. The answer choices will always be presented in the order you see in the Answers window, but you can manually alter the order by clicking an item, and then clicking the **Move Up** and **Move Down** buttons as appropriate.

So, those are the basics of creating a multiple-choice question. But what if you'd like to change the appearance or feedback just for this question alone? For example, can you alter how the answer choices are numbered, display customized feedback for correct and incorrect responses, exclude this question from the quiz score, or even have question-related branching (e.g., have the playback jump to a particular time if the answer was incorrect)? Indeed you can. Give a click on the **Appearance and Feedback...** button, located just below the Answers window. The following dialog will appear:

For each question, you can simply go with the default, or you can forge a new path.

By default, each question is set to **Use quiz defaults**, meaning that it simply follows whatever you specified for the quiz in general. However, if you want to change the appearance of this specific question, or if you'd like to deliver custom feedback for this question, then choose instead **Customize this question**. The rest of the dialog will then become editable, and you can make your changes at will. Click **OK** to lock in your changes, or **Cancel** if you've changed your mind.

At this point you may be asking yourself, "*Self,* doing customized feedback for each question is a nice touch, but what if I want to give comprehensive, ultra-customized feedback for each and every answer of a given question?" Yes, that would come in handy, wouldn't it? Not only could you tell the person whether their response was right or wrong, but you could explain *why* it was right or wrong, citing specific examples that can actually lead to a deeper understanding of the material.

Fortunately, Camtasia Studio has you covered. If you wish to customize an answer's feedback, simply click the answer to select it, and then click the **Edit...** button, located to the right of the Answers window. The Edit Answer Details dialog appears, which looks something like this:

If desired, you can change the text of the answer in the **Answer** field. To enter customized feedback for this item, just click the **Customize this answer** button. Here in the Edit Answer Details dialog, you can specify both a custom **Feedback** (or just leave it on the default if desired) as well as the **Details** that clarify exactly why the answer was right or wrong.

Though the Video Preview gives you a strong sense of how the quiz question will look and behave, there will come a point where you'll obviously want to test it out. Fortunately, Camtasia Studio doesn't make you produce the entire video just to examine your one question. Clicking the **Preview** button will open your question in the default web browser on your system, so that you can actually select answers and view feedback. It's a great way to do a final sanity check just before production.

Fill-in-the-Blank Questions

If you click **OK**, then all changes to your question will be saved, and you'll be spit back out (*ptooey!*) onto the Flash Quiz and Survey Manager pane (clicking the **Save question and return to the manager** link at the bottom of the question pane will do the same thing). Now we have some actual content in the quiz management window, specifically the name of a quiz, and one multiple-choice question underneath it. We'll talk about quiz management in a little bit, but for now I want to launch right into creating a fill-in-the-blank style question. The procedure is remarkably similar to the multiple-choice format, so you'll get the hang of it in no time at all.

So, here's how we "fill in" the requisite information to **create a fill-in-the-blank question:**

1. From the Flash Quiz and Survey Manager pane, click **Add a Question to Selected Quiz or Survey...** (assuming for now that you're *not* starting a brand-new quiz).

   or

   From any question pane, click the link marked **Save question and add another question**.

2. In the Question Type dialog that appears, choose **Fill in the blank**. Click **OK**.

3. Type in your question. If it is a true "fill-in" style question, you can hit the underscore key (_) a few times to create an underlined "blank."

4. Press the **Tab** key or click the first line in the **List of acceptable answers** field to select that line for editing. Type in the correct answer.

5. If more than one correct answer exists, pressing **Enter** or clicking the **Add** button will add subsequent lines for giving additional acceptable responses. You may enter as many correct answers as you wish.

6. If you want to change any of the defaults you set when first creating the quiz, click the **Appearance and Feedback...** button.

7. Just as with multiple-choice questions, you can test out your question by clicking **Preview**. The viewer simply needs to click in the answer box and type a response, which can be submitted by either clicking the **Submit** button or hitting the **Enter** key.

8. When finished, click **OK**, located at the top of the pane, to save the question and return to the Flash Quiz and Survey Manager pane.

Keep in mind that the answers given are *not* case-sensitive, so there's no need to add every possible case combination to the list of acceptable answers. For example, if you've given "PowerPoint" as a correct answer, the video will also accept "Powerpoint," "powerpoint," etc. However, alternate spellings, synonyms, and different forms of the same word will all need to have an individual answer attached, so try to spend a little time on each question to make sure you've thought of every conceivable word (or word combination) that might be correct. If you want to be a really nice person, you might even think about adding some common misspellings of the right answers to your list. After all, you're probably trying to test your audience's knowledge of the *material*, not their spelling prowess.

Short-Answer Questions

Short-answer questions were new to Camtasia Studio 4, meant mainly to augment its new survey capabilities, which we'll be looking at in a sec. Short-answer questions can also be added to quizzes; they just won't be scored by the system. For these questions, there are simply too many variables for the computer to be able to tell a right answer from a wrong one. This shouldn't discourage you from using them, of course. As you'll later discover, it's possible to receive all answers by e-mail, or to your learning management system via SCORM. The short-answer portions can then be graded by hand.

Here's how to **add a short-answer question** to your quiz or survey:

1. From the Flash Quiz and Survey Manager pane, click **Add a Question to Selected Quiz or Survey...** (assuming for now that you're *not* starting a brand-new quiz).

   or

   From any question pane, click the link marked **Save question and add another question**.

2. In the Question Type dialog that appears, choose **Short answer (not scored)**. Click **OK**.

3. Type your question into the **Question** field.

4. As this question type isn't scored, there's no immediate feedback to provide. By default, the system tells the user "Thank you," whenever the user submits a response. As always, you can customize this response by clicking the **Appearance and Feedback...** button.

5. Click the **Preview** button to see what your question will look like.

Collecting Survey Data

Now that quizzes are well-covered, let's discuss *surveys* for a moment. Most of what you'll encounter when creating a survey mirrors that of quiz creation. The biggest difference is that survey material isn't scored, regardless of question type. This means that if you have quiz and survey material present in the same video, the survey questions are discounted entirely when computing the final grade or score. It also means that feedback options (beyond the basic "Thank you") are disabled when the question is part of a survey.

To **add a survey** to your video, here's what you do:

1. Move your seek bar to the exact location on your Timeline where you'd like your survey to appear.

2. Click the **Add Survey...** link in the Flash Quiz and Survey Manager pane.

3. The Survey Appearance and Feedback dialog appears. Enter a name for your survey in the **Survey Name** field.

4. Under **Appearance**, choose how you want your responses numbered: numerically, alphabetically, or no numbering at all.

5. Under **Survey feedback**, check whether you'd like any feedback displayed whenever the user clicks the Submit button. If so, you can freely replace the default "Thank you" with anything you wish. Click **OK** to continue.

That's essentially all there is to it. Just as with quizzes, you can add as many questions as you like. You can also customize the feedback on a per-question (using the Appearance and Feedback... button) or even on a per-answer (using the Edit... button) basis, though you typically require this level of granularity more with quizzes than with surveys.

Here are a couple of additional tips I've found handy when developing survey forms with Camtasia Studio: First, make sure one of your questions asks for a name or ID number if you want to be able to identify that particular viewer later. Also, use multiple-choice questions for true/false or yes/no style questions as well as questions that ask users to choose the best or most desirable option from a series of choices. Unfortunately, Camtasia Studio doesn't currently support allowing the viewer to pick more than one item from the list.

Keep in mind that Camtasia Studio is still in the early stages of its Quiz and Survey implementation. Expect these features to grow more robust as the product develops. In the meantime, though, those with more complex quizzing needs can turn to a product from Articulate (www.articulate.com) called Quizmaker. With it, you can set up interesting exercises like drag-n-drop matching, word bank questions, sequencing tasks, and survey items such as Likert scale questions and essay questions, among others. Using the End action feature of Camtasia Studio's Flash output, you can rig your SWF/FLV video, at its conclusion, to launch the web page of your Articulate quiz for a nearly flawless user experience.

The Art of Quiz and Survey Management

Okay, so it's not really an art — Camtasia Studio actually makes the management of quizzes and surveys in your video a pretty uncomplicated affair. As I mentioned, each video can carry on its back as many quizzes/surveys (and questions therein) as you want. The ability to add multiple quizzes and surveys within a video is actually quite powerful. It allows you to test intermittently throughout the presentation instead of leaving everything for the end. This is useful when dealing with a longer video.

One nice technique involving multiple quizzes is to use them for reading your questions aloud. I once had a project where the questions were part of the narration. At the end of each narrated question, I inserted a one-question quiz that repeated the question in writing (and obviously required them to answer). The client appreciated that their viewers had the ability to *listen* to the questions prior to making a response.

Adding another quiz or survey follows the same procedure as adding the first one. Just make sure that your seek bar is in the right location on your Timeline. Of course, even if you goof and put it in the wrong section of your video, remedying this is as simple as dragging the icon that represents your quiz/survey to a new location on the Quiz track of your Timeline:

You'll find that your quizzes and surveys are easily moved about with a single click-and-drag maneuver. Quizzes are represented by diamonds, and surveys by circles.

As you've probably already noticed, the insertion point of your quiz/survey is plainly listed in the Flash Quiz and Survey Manager pane, just to the right of its name. This updates automatically if you move a quiz on the Timeline.

Okay, we've already gone over the options for adding a quiz or survey. The obvious counterpart is *deletion*, which we have not yet covered. You've got two basic options here:

- **Delete.** Simply click a question to select it, and then click this button to be rid of it. If you select the *overall* quiz or survey, then the entire thing (along with all questions contained therein) will be gone. For whole quiz or survey deletion, you'll get one of those "Are you sure?" dialogs that accompanies most major computing decisions. Click **Yes** if you are indeed sure.

- And speaking of big decisions, you also have the option to **Delete all.** As the name suggests, this is the "big red button" command that nukes *all* your quizzes and surveys as well as all their corresponding questions, effectively taking you back to square one. Don't use it lightly.

At any rate, now that you have a bunch of quizzes and surveys at your disposal (hopefully you have at least a couple left after experimenting with those Delete commands…), you may be curious to know how to go back in and edit something you've already done. One method is to click on the desired object to select it, and then choose **Edit….** An even easier method is to simply double-click the desired object. You'll see different things depending on what you selected. If you chose an individual quiz/survey question, that question's pane will pop up, enabling you to add responses, change the question, etc. If you chose a main quiz or survey heading, then you'll see its overall **Appearance and Feedback** dialog.

Finally, just as with the individual question panes, the **Preview** button is available to test out your work. If you have a single question selected, then Camtasia Studio will preview only that one question. If you have a quiz or survey selected, then you'll be able to preview *every* question in that quiz or survey.

Also, please understand that you will *not* be able to test out your quiz or survey by casually browsing your video in the Video Preview. While previewing the video, you'll instead get a placeholder graphic for your quiz or survey, and you'll be prompted to click the **Play** button in order to resume playback*. Also, keep in mind that the Flash Player's default security settings can often prevent quizzes and surveys from running when the SWF or FLV file is played back locally (meaning from your hard drive and not from a web server).

---

* If desired, you can disable the placeholder graphic in the Video Preview by choosing **Tools > Options**, and then clearing the check box for **Show quiz placeholder** in the **Program** tab.

Of course, we still haven't discussed exactly how you can receive feedback on your quiz or survey material once you *do* publish it. This is handled when actually producing your project. We'll discuss how we can have the results of quizzes and surveys sent to our learning management systems (LMS) and even to our very own e-mail inboxes when we get to Chapter 12, "The Production Process."

Picture-in-Picture (PIP) Editing

Starting with version 3, Camtasia Studio offered the ability to include a *second* video stream to augment your screen video footage. This was mainly done with the purpose of letting you use a webcam so that your target audience could actually see your face as you walked them through the intricacies of your software. This video stream would appear in a window within the main screen recording (hence the term **picture-in-picture**, or **PIP**).

But that's only the beginning, folks. You can place pretty much whatever you like inside your PIP track. You can, of course, insert a view of your face, but you can also use an action shot that thematically relates to the screen content. And who says that your PIP material has to be camera video at all? Perhaps you'd like to remind users of a previous talking point without leaving the current screen. Or maybe you want to do a zoomed close-up of a particular toolbar while still maintaining a view of the full user interface. By making use of screen video for *both* streams, you can accomplish both of the above goals with ease.

A bit later, Camtasia Studio included an additional convenience for those users who produce Flash (SWF and FLV) video files: the ability to lay out the two video streams in a side-by-side formation rather than superimposing one over the other. This way, you can ensure that nothing in your screen video will get obscured by another video window. This choice between two layout formats provides a lot of flexibility.

Up to now, our discussions of picture-in-picture video have focused mainly on creating it and importing it into Camtasia Studio. In this section, we'll cast the spotlight on Camtasia Studio's special editing options for PIP. Now you can select and cut material out of your PIP track just as you would with your screen video track. However, the application offers additional tools that augment the inherent "PIP-ness" of your camera video, and that's what we're going to explore. But before we do that, let's talk about previewing our PIP track and how this affects the editing process.

The PIP Preview

If you've been reading this book straight through rather than flipping around (which I realize is probably unlikely), then you've already discovered the various methods by which you can add video to your PIP track. To recap, it's typically done in one of the following three ways:

- You were recording PIP at the same time as your screen video, and both tracks were automatically added to the Timeline when you chose to edit your work in Camtasia Studio (Chapters 5 and 8).

- You imported all your screen video and camera video clips into the Clip Bin, and then dragged the intended PIP clips down onto the PIP track manually (Chapter 9).

- You created PIP video using the Record Camera tool, and it was added to the Timeline automatically upon saving (Chapter 10).

No matter what method is used to "christen" your PIP track, once you've got a clip down there, the **Select PIP Preview** dialog is going to appear:

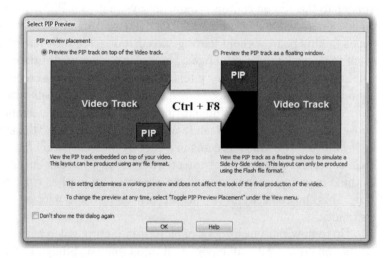

You've therefore got two choices as to how you want to display your PIP content while working in Camtasia Studio:

- **Preview the PIP track on top of the Video track.** This is a true "picture-in-picture" setup. The contents of the PIP track will actually display in a small window inside your Video Preview where your screen video is shown.

- **Preview the PIP track as a floating window.** This option allows you to view your PIP content separate from your Video track in a side-by-side formation. It can be shown in either a floating window or docked beneath your Clip Bin.

Regardless of which option you pick initially, you can always toggle back and forth between these two views by choosing **View > Toggle PIP Preview Placement**, or simply by pressing **Ctrl-F8**. If you opted for a side-by-side view, you can dock/undock this window at any time by clicking the button in the top right-hand corner of the preview window:

Now, pay close attention, as this next point is really, really important: *Whatever option you choose has ZERO bearing on how the produced file will ultimately look*. These preview choices are exactly that, for previewing your work. All your actual production-related decisions are made whilst traversing the Production Wizard dialog, which we'll talk about in the next unit. That said, your preview mode *does* have an impact on the PIP editing choices you have at your disposal. So while you may freely flip back and forth between preview modes as much as you like, it would probably behoove you to maintain the PIP preview that resembles your planned output.

Editing Your PIP Video

Once you have a video clip or two in the PIP track of your Timeline, you can trim this content just as you would your screen video. All your basic editing commands still work. You can size down the video's borders or cut from the middle to trim unwanted segments out of your clip. You can split your clips into individual sections, which can actually be quite useful for your PIP content, as we'll see in a moment. You cannot, unfortunately, perform a couple of the more advanced commands such as extending a frame or altering the clip speed (though I've honestly never missed them).

Things really get interesting when we get into the editing tools designed exclusively for PIP clips. Keep in mind that the current preview mode will affect your available choices. For example, if you're previewing your PIP track in side-by-side view, you won't have options for the size and placement of your PIP window, since the size of your side-by-side video will be determined in the Production Wizard.

But first things first. Let's actually **open a PIP clip for editing**:

1. From the **Edit** menu, choose **Picture-in-Picture (PIP)....**

   or

   Under Edit in your Task List, click **Picture-in-Picture (PIP)....**

2. You'll see a list of your PIP clips on the table of your Picture-in-Picture pane. Double-click one of your clips.

   or

   Click to select one of your clips, and then click **Modify selected PIP clip** to open it.

   An alternate way of opening your PIP clip for editing (and perhaps the easiest) is to simply double-click it from the PIP track of your Timeline. It's certainly the most direct route — you can skip step 1 of the above procedure entirely.

In addition to showing all the PIP clips on your Timeline and giving you the option of opening one, the Picture-in-Picture (PIP) pane also lets you do a little housecleaning:

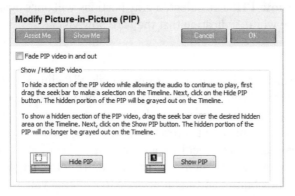

You have options here to **Remove selected PIP clip**, which gets rid of the clip you just clicked, or **Remove all PIP clips**, which clears your PIP track in one fell swoop. Of course, you can also trash a clip the traditional way, by clicking it in your Timeline and then pressing **Delete**.

Now, let's talk about the Modify Picture-in-Picture pane, and the editing choices located therein. I'm going to split this part into two sections, since you'll be seeing two very different dialog panes depending on the current preview mode.

Editing the Side-by-Side Preview

Since the side-by-side view of your PIP content is quite a bit more static than the actual picture-in-picture view, you've got considerably fewer options governing the window's appearance:

But the side-by-side view does offer a couple of variables we can adjust, the first of which is **Fade PIP video in and out**. When this

IV: Editing

option is checked, you have a nice effect of fading in from black when the PIP clip is introduced, and then fading to black again when it ends. And yes, the background color is *always* black, unless you specify a background image for your PIP window, which we'll discuss in the next chapter.

The next section, **Show/Hide PIP video,** is very handy for those situations where you don't necessarily want to show your face the entire time, but do want your PIP audio narration to carry through the entire length of the clip. To accomplish this, you'll need to blank out the sections in which you don't want the PIP video to be visible. It's like taking a bottle of Wite-Out (or in this case, Black-Out), and painting over portions of your PIP Video track. And it's really easy to do.

This is how you **hide portions of your PIP video,** and how you can make it **reappear:**

1. Navigate to the Modify Picture-in-Picture (PIP) pane if you're not already there.

2. Select a portion of your Timeline that coincides with the part of your PIP track you want to hide. Don't worry about locking other tracks, as this command applies *only* to your PIP track.

3. Click the **Hide PIP** button. The hidden portion of your PIP track will now display in gray:

4. To make any portion of your hidden PIP content visible again, select all or part of the hidden (grayed out) material, and click **Show PIP.** The selected gray portions will once again become white, indicating that they are now visible.

You can have as many hidden portions in a single PIP clip as you want. Keep in mind that if you have **Fade PIP video in and out** checked, it will fade in or out at every point your PIP content is shown or hidden. Of course, if you simply don't care about preserving the PIP audio, you can accomplish the same effect by splitting your PIP content into separate clips and then moving them around on your Timeline. However, I really like the flexibility that the Show/Hide tool affords you in terms of easily bringing hidden content back.

If you intend on transitioning your PIP content in and out over the duration of the video, you might want to try out a program called Visual Communicator from Serious Magic (www.seriousmagic.com). It too offers picture-in-picture effects, but with a large library of cool transition effects as well as the ability to *chroma key* your PIP video (meaning that you can digitally place a still or moving image behind your "talking head" in the video). I occasionally use VC to augment Camtasia Studio when I need to add a little "PIP pizzazz." A demo is available on the companion CD.

Next, let's talk about the somewhat broader range of editing options available for picture-in-picture editing. Remember that the options you're shown on the Modify Picture-in-Picture (PIP) pane are reflective of the preview mode you've chosen. So, if you enter this pane only to discover that you're in the wrong mode, you first have to cancel back to the main interface (where your Clip Bin is located), toggle the PIP preview by pressing **Ctrl-F8**, and then re-enter the Modify Picture-in-Picture (PIP) pane.

Editing the Picture-in-Picture Preview

If you enter the Modify Picture-in-Picture (PIP) pane while in Picture-in-Picture Preview mode, things now look a bit different:

Modify Picture-in-Picture (PIP)

When producing your video using a Flash Side-by-Side template for the PIP, only the Show/Hide and Fade In/Out options will be applied to the completed video. Other properties that you choose here are only applied to the PIP when using a template other than Flash Side-by-Side.

| Assist Me | Show Me | | Cancel | OK |

Properties

Opacity: 100 %

☑ Include border   Color... ■   Width: 320   X: 704

☑ Fade PIP video in and out   Height: 240   Y: 528

☑ Drop shadow   Shadow direction: Bottom-Right ▼

Show / Hide PIP video

To hide a section of the PIP video while allowing the audio to continue to play, first drag the seek bar to make a selection on the Timeline. Next, click on the Hide PIP button. The hidden portion of the PIP will be grayed out on the Timeline.

To show a hidden section of the PIP video, drag the seek bar over the desired hidden area on the Timeline. Next, click on the Show PIP button. The hidden portion of the PIP will no longer be grayed out on the Timeline.

[ ] Hide PIP   [■] Show PIP

Notice that you have the same options as before for fading the PIP video in and out as well as for showing/hiding portions of the video. But we also have some formatting choices regarding the size, location, and appearance of your PIP video that only make sense in a true picture-in-picture format.

Since the PIP window will be appearing over the top of your screen video, you're going to want to adjust its size and position within the window in such a way as not to obscure anything important. So that's where we'll begin.

Here's how to **change the size and location of your PIP window** within your Video Preview:

1. Open the Modify Picture-in-Picture (PIP) pane while in Picture-in-Picture Preview mode. If necessary, click to place the seek bar over a portion of the PIP clip that isn't hidden. You should see a green rectangle in your Video Preview that contains the current frame of your PIP track:

2. To adjust the clip's location inside your screen video window, click and hold anywhere inside the green rectangle, and then drag it to a new location.

   or

   For more precise placement, adjust the **X** and **Y** coordinate fields on the Modify Picture-in-Picture (PIP) pane. These coordinates represent the upper left-hand corner of your PIP window.

3. To alter the size of your PIP clip, click and hold on any of the black squares located around the border of the green rectangle, and drag to increase or reduce the window's size. Note that the window's aspect ratio is automatically maintained.

   or

Enter values for **Width** and **Height** into the corresponding fields on the Modify Picture-in-Picture (PIP) pane. These values are measured in pixels. Note that the window's aspect ratio is *not* automatically maintained, so be careful not to stretch your PIP video content into a funhouse mirror reflection of itself. If you do so accidentally, resizing it in the Video Preview will snap it back into proportion.

Note that changing the size and position of your PIP window in this manner changes it for the *entire* PIP clip in question. So what if you want the size or position (or any of the other formatting elements) of your clip to change at some point, for example to move out of the way of some important screen content? Simple. Split it up into separate clips. Just remember to lock your other tracks first (unless, of course, you want the split to happen there, too). Once that's done, each clip in the PIP track can have its properties adjusted individually.

In addition to sizing, you can dress up the appearance of your PIP window with a few additional options. To wit:

- **Opacity.** This slider will let you set the opacity of your PIP window anywhere from 1% (nearly invisible) to 100% (fully opaque). You can use this tool to make your PIP window semi-transparent, which, in addition to being a nice effect, gives the user a partial view of the content that's underneath the PIP window.

- **Include border.** Lets you specify whether you want a colored border to appear around your PIP window. The border is a couple of pixels wide (the width is not editable). Click the **Color...** button to choose the border's color.

- **Drop shadow.** Check this box to place a drop shadow just outside your box to give the PIP window a somewhat three-dimensional quality. You can even choose the direction of the shadow. In the **Shadow direction** drop-down list, simply pick any of the four corners of your PIP window for the shadow effect.

Now, as I've mentioned, most of the settings in this dialog pertain to Picture-in-Picture Preview mode. If you end up producing a side-by-side video after tweaking all these options, note that the Fade PIP video in and out and the Show/Hide PIP video options will still be honored, but everything else will be ignored. Of course, the project file will still maintain the settings regardless of how you produce, so if you ever do decide to produce in a picture-in-picture format, you won't have to start over from scratch.

So that's the scoop on editing your PIP video. In the next chapter, you'll come full circle by learning how to produce those PIP segments (and all your other effects) as part of your final video.

Summary

When it comes to spicing up your freshly edited footage with special effects, you needn't look any further than the Edit section of your Task List, as this chapter focused exclusively on exactly these supersexy effects (excepting Audio enhancements). Here's a tightly condensed summation of each:

- **Zoom-n-Pan.** If you want to show the details of a particular window or toolbar more closely, it's easy to zoom in for a closer look. While zoomed in, Camtasia Studio makes it a snap to pan around to reveal other areas of the recording area. You can manage your zoom and pan effects on the Zoom-n-Pan Properties pane within Camtasia Studio. SmartFocus helps automate the process, automatically generating zoom and pan points that you can then tweak to your liking.

- **Callouts and Flash Hotspots.** Callouts are an excellent means of "marking up" a video by superimposing text and graphics on top of it. For Flash videos, you can even add a bit of interactivity by making your callouts clickable. These can be formatted with a variety of colors and effects. You have a library of pre-installed callouts available to you, and you can add as many custom callouts as you like.

- **Transitions.** These special effects provide a smooth and appealing means of moving from one clip to the next. Adding a transition is as simple as dragging one onto your Storyboard. You can easily change/remove them later as well as set the transitions' duration. Remember that transitions look gaudy if overdone, so try to exercise restraint.

- **Captions.** Camtasia Studio now sports both open and (for Flash videos) closed captioning, allowing your nonnative language speaking or hearing-impaired audience to have better access to your content. The process is fairly automatic. Just type or paste your script into the text window, and then play through your video, paying attention to the narration. Simply click on each narrative segment as it's being spoken to synchronize the text with the audio. Additionally, you have a few formatting options such as character width and whether you'd like the captions superimposed over the video.

- **Flash Quiz and Survey.** For those who produce their videos in Flash (SWF and FLV), Camtasia Studio offers multiple-choice, fill-in-the-blank, and short-answer questions to test your viewers' knowledge or solicit their feedback. Feedback can be general; it can also be custom-tailored to the current question, or even to an individual response. The user's score (or survey data, as the case may be) can then be uploaded to a learning management system via SCORM or automatically sent to a specified e-mail address.

- **Picture-in-Picture (PIP).** With some new video footage in your PIP track, you learned how to perform various editing effects for both side-by-side and floating PIP video. In addition to setting up the preview to your liking and cutting out unwanted portions, you have access to special PIP-only editing commands. Specify when you would like the PIP image hidden or shown. Choose the window's size and position. Even format your PIP window with fades, borders, and drop shadows.

Exercises

1. Open your **MyProject.camproj** file from the previous chapter. If you skipped those exercises, you'll find an exported project in a zipped file called MyProject_ch11.zip in this chapter's media folder.

2. In your 05.avi clip, zoom in on the **Test Menu** command just as it's being clicked, and then zoom back out to show the menu that opens.

3. Add a Flash hotspot callout to your 02.jpg clip that states **Click here to download more MenuMaker templates**. Link it to the following URL: http://www.techsmith.com/camtasia/accessories/mmtemplates.asp.

4. Add a **Radial Wipe** transition between your 06.camrec and 07.avi files to indicate that time has passed in production. Feel free to experiment with other transitions if desired. Note that you may need to split and move parts of your audio narration in order to keep it in sync with your video. Don't forget to lock the Video track, or that content will be split as well.

5. From this chapter's media folder, import **CD.png** as a custom callout. Insert this callout during 07.avi, where the narration says **Now you're ready to burn to CD- or DVD-ROM using your favorite burning application**.

6. In this chapter's media folder, you'll find a file called narration.doc that contains the entire narration script for the video. Use the Captions feature to turn this text into captions for your video.

7. Between your 07.avi clip and your ending title clip, add a quiz to test users' knowledge of the material covered. The questions can be multiple-choice, fill-in-the-blank, short-answer, or any combination thereof. They should obviously be related to the content, but can otherwise be anything you desire. Here are a few to use as a jumping-off point:

   ■ Where can you change the dimensions of your menu?

   ■ True or false? You can set up your navigation menu to run automatically upon insertion of the CD.

   ■ Camtasia MenuMaker is to CD-ROM what Camtasia _____ is to the web.

8. If you don't own a camcorder or webcam, and thus weren't able to create a PIP clip in the previous chapter, feel free to use the PIP.wmv clip located in this chapter's media folder. Import this file into your Clip Bin, and then add it your Timeline to coincide with your ending title clip.

9. If needed, toggle your **PIP Preview Placement** to display your PIP window inside your Video Preview. Change the size and location of your PIP video to fill up a good portion of the title clip while keeping all your "Thank you..." text in plain view. Give the PIP window a colored border as well as a drop shadow.

10. Save your project.

EXTRA CREDIT:

Start a new project, and import **SmartFocus.camproj** into the Clip Bin and onto the Timeline. You're going to want to deliver this video to a mobile audience (320 x 240). Apply SmartFocus to this clip. You'll notice that some of the zoom points are less than ideal. Tweak it to your liking.

Now, try again (whether using SmartFocus or manual control) with editing dimensions of 688 x 520. In this chapter's exercise folder, check out the zoomnpan.avi file if you haven't already to see how I tackled this one. Turn back to page 312 for a full description of what I did here.

EXTRALIFE

by Scott Johnson

Sharing Your Videos with Others

All our efforts up to now have focused on planning, creating, and refining our content. However, this content cannot exist in a vacuum (well, I suppose it *could*, but then it would get all dusty). Regardless of the hours spent creating your masterpiece, if you cannot share it easily and efficiently with other people, preferably the *right* people, then all that work was for nothing.

The chapters in this unit will help you gain a grasp of distributing your work. There is no single correct way of doing this. So much depends on your content and on your audience that I cannot give you a simple, unified blueprint for getting your videos into the right hands, much as I'd like to. Fortunately, Camtasia Studio arms you with an array of flexible distribution options. So, no matter what the confines of your own professional environment, you're sure to have at least one effective way of sharing your work, and probably several.

The five chapters of this unit are as follows:

- **Chapter 12: The Production Process.** This is where you'll learn how to take your video project and produce it in a format that others can view.

- **Chapter 13: CD-based Videos with Camtasia MenuMaker.** If your goal is to create a CD- or DVD-ROM of your videos, know that Camtasia MenuMaker can help you create an attractive, functional front-end menu, and in this chapter, I'll show you how.

- **Chapter 14: Web-based Videos with Camtasia Theater.** If the preference is for web distribution, but you still want to have the fancy menu navigation of a CD, then Camtasia Theater is the tool for you.

- **Chapter 15: Other Output Options.** In this chapter, I'll show you some supplementary tools for helping you share your work: Batch Production, Pack and Show, and the Camtasia Player.

- **Chapter 16: Post-Production Customization.** With some know-how and a bit of light coding, you'll learn how to customize almost every aspect of your final production.

Chapter 12

The Production Process

After recording all your segments with the Camtasia Recorder and editing it all in Camtasia Studio, you have one final step in creating a fully functioning, stand-alone video. It's time to take your edited footage and produce it in a file format that best suits your audience and your content. In this chapter, you're going to take all the different elements and process them into a seamless, sweet-smelling package. Along the way, you'll be making choices that will affect the size, aesthetics, and functionality of your presentation, and it's the job of this chapter to help you navigate through this maze of dialog choices so that you have an end product you're happy with.

This chapter is split into four sections:

- **Recommend My Production Settings.** The simplified Production Wizard essentially asks you a series of questions about your content and how you want to share it, and then *poof!* selects all your production options for you. As it's a very handy tool for the novice, I'll give you the dime tour, but you'll really get your hands dirty with...

- **Common Production Elements.** This section identifies the common elements of all the file formats, letting you in on what choices are available to you during the process. Production dialog screens common to all file formats are covered in detail within this section, including Video Size, Video Options, Marker Options, and the Produce Video screen.

- **The File Formats.** In your Production Wizard dialog, you have nine file formats from which to choose (well, actually 10, as SWF and FLV are two distinct formats). I'll explain all the options available for each of the available file formats and, more importantly, exactly why you'd want to use the format in question. In this section, the encoding options for each of the file types are discussed.

- **Production Presets**. This section teaches you the ins and outs of creating, editing, and using customized production presets. Just select your production options once, and you can use them forever. No muss, no fuss.

The first section applies only to people who are brand new to producing and possibly intimidated by all the options. The second section is for all y'all, covering choices you'll need to make regardless of what the video's file type is going to be. As for the third, I expect that people will want to read up on the specific file format in which they want to produce, and you won't hurt my feelings if you ignore the rest. Of course, if you aren't sure what file format you need, it would be helpful to at least read the first few paragraphs written about each file format so that you can make an educated decision (though I do give a brief summary of each at the start of the section). The fourth and final section, while not essential to producing, will save you time if you plan on producing a number of videos in a consistent format. By creating a preset, you won't have to muck around with specifying your file settings each and every time. Preset creation is a good skill to have. Regardless of what path you'll take, we all start at the same place. We have to tell Camtasia Studio that we want to produce.

Production of your video is accomplished thusly:
- From the **File** menu, choose **Produce Video As....**

  or
- Press **Ctrl-P.**

  or
- Click the **Produce Video As** button ( ) on your toolbar.

  or
- Click **Produce Video as...** in the Produce submenu of your Task List.

You'll end up on the Production Wizard dialog. You now have a variety of options from which to choose. Let's discuss them. We're going to skip over the Production Presets section for now, and begin with Recommend my production settings.

Recommend My Production Settings

Welcome to the beginner's tour in video production. If you're the type of person who would prefer not to get bogged down in the technical details of selecting codecs, choosing an optimal frame rate, or deciding what your audio sample rate should be, then the simplified Production Wizard is just for you. To get started down this road, simply choose **Recommend my production settings**, and then click **Next**.

Since different file types and settings are better suited for certain kinds of video, the wizard will ask you a few quick questions about how you plan on distributing your videos as well as what kind of content you have. This is to help you arrive at the best possible production settings for your purposes.

Distribution Method

Your first stop on this trip is choosing the method of distribution; in other words, how you'll get your videos into the hands of your audience.

Camtasia Studio can help come up with the proper file format based on the chosen distribution method. For example, SWF files are ideal for the web, while AVIs work better for DVD.

In terms of distribution method, you've got the following six choices:

- **Web.** Choose this option if you want to upload your production to a web server for your audience to view online. Choosing the web as a distribution format has the distinct advantage of being readily changeable and correctable. If you burn a CD-ROM or distribute a DVD, correcting any errata or otherwise updating your video content is troublesome and expensive. While distribution on the web carries with it obvious bandwidth restrictions, high-speed Internet access is now cheaper and more accessible than ever before. Even my mom has it. And with Camtasia Studio, it's a snap to create low-bandwidth versions of your videos to appease those poor souls who are still stuck on dial-up. No matter which group you're trying to reach, your file format is likely to be SWF or FLV.

- **E-mail.** Click here if you want to send your video as an e-mail attachment. This is handy for sending a quick "how-to" video to a colleague. The keys to a successful video attachment are small file size and immediate accessibility on the other end, without the person needing to mess around with acquiring the right codec or player. As such, WMV is the format of choice, giving you both the aforementioned advantages while at the same time packing it all into a single handy file.

- **CD.** This option is best if you want to burn your files to a CD-ROM or DVD-ROM disc. Putting your content on these discs is advantageous in a couple of ways. First, they're relatively high capacity, meaning that you can pack a lot of content onto a single disc, and they're really still the way to go if ultra high-quality video and audio are a must for you. They also overcome all bandwidth restrictions your audience might have — in fact, users don't even need net access to view your stuff. You'll be producing as an AVI, WMV, SWF, or FLV file (depending on the presence of Flash hotspots and/or full-motion video).

- **DVD-ready.** This option will give you a pristine AVI video for importing into your favorite DVD authoring application. (Yes, you do need another program to create DVDs for viewing on console televisions.) Even if you have an authoring program at your disposal, keep in mind that DVD creation does come with its share of headaches. To help remedy them, I've provided a brief tutorial on producing content for DVD in the AVI section of this chapter. For the time being, I recommend that you *not* choose this option, and instead follow the tutorial if you're interested in making DVDs.

- **Hard drive or other.** This is a catch-all "other" choice that I suspect most people use for putting videos out on their corporate network drives, a purpose well-served by this option. This will give you a high-quality AVI, WMV, SWF, or FLV file (depending on the presence of Flash hotspots and/or full-motion video) that you can store on any local drive. Then, if you want to share it with your colleagues, e-mail them a link to your video rather than attaching it to the actual message. It's cleaner, puts less stress on your corporate network, and allows you to do lengthier, more elaborate videos.

- **iPod or iTunes.** This option will produce a file suitable for viewing on a video iPod. Even without an iPod, the produced M4V file will be viewable with either the QuickTime Player or on iTunes. Because it's optimized for viewing on the iPod, however, the video dimensions will automatically be 320 x 240. If outputting to iPod, I strongly recommend that you first set the editing dimensions to 320 x 240, and engage SmartFocus to zoom in on your content so that you don't lose clarity. If you plan on using Camtasia Studio for video podcasting, then this is the choice for you.

One additional nicety is the ability to produce other types of "extra" content while producing your main video. This is a boon to university professors and others who wish to release their tutorials as podcasts. You can choose **Create MP3 File** to add an audio file or **Create iPod File** for those with video iPods. This is particularly nice if you end up choosing a format that can be embedded into a web page. When the user goes to your content page, they're automatically presented with all options bundled into a single splash screen:

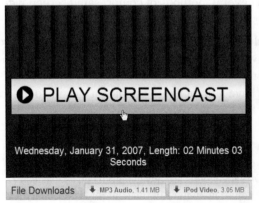

Each screen is automatically stamped with the date of production as well as the length, and the corresponding downloadables are clearly marked with the file size, so that your audience can quickly determine whether it will fit on their portable devices. They can click to play the main presentation, or right-click the MP3 Audio or iPod Video links to download the content appropriate for their players.

Once you've made your choice, go ahead and click **Next**.

Content Type

With the noted exception of DVD-ready and iPod/iTunes*, for every distribution method, you'll next have to specify what kind of content your video project contains. This allows Camtasia Studio to get a somewhat better handle on the specific file format and audio format it should be using.

The Content Type screen.

This screen has two sections: Video content and Audio content. In the **Video content** section, you have three check boxes:

- **My video includes screen recording.** Check this box if any of your clips contain footage of recorded applications. If this is to be the only box checked, then you're in luck, since Camtasia Studio has developed several methods of compressing screen video data into small file sizes.

- **My video includes PIP or full motion video.** If you've got real-world camera video in your production (imported high-motion clips, picture-in-picture), check this box. You may also want to check it if you have a lot of photographic images in your screen videos.

---

* By definition, DVD-ready videos are always produced as lossless 720 x 480 AVI files, and therefore no inquiry of the content type, quality level, or video dimensions is necessary. iPod video is always 320 x 240.

- **My video includes a PowerPoint recording**. Since PowerPoint recordings are likely to (a) have been recorded full-screen, and are therefore quite large, and (b) contain lots of animations and photographic content, Camtasia Studio encodes it as if it were a full-motion video. If your PowerPoint presentation was recorded in a window rather than full-screen, and doesn't sport lots of photos or animated effects, then you can probably get away with *not* clicking this option.

Now that the video portion is out of the way, we come to **Audio content**, which contains two check boxes. If your project has no audio, you can obviously leave both unchecked. Your options are as follows:

- **My audio includes voice narration**. If you have any audio track of you (or someone else) speaking, check this box.

- **My audio includes music or sound effects**. If you have a background music track, mouse click and keyboard sounds from the Camtasia Recorder, or other miscellaneous sound effects, click here.

What's the point of specifying the content? Well, in answering the video-related questions, Camtasia Studio determines the proper file format. Within each file format, there are often multiple possible methods for encoding the audio. Some of these audio codecs are better suited to the human voice, others excel at music, while still others are passable at both. Once you've checked the boxes that best reflect the content of your clips, go ahead and click **Next** to move onward.

Video Quality, Screen Dimensions, and Audio Quality

After clicking the **Next** button, the next screen you will reach (at least you will if you didn't check DVD-ready or iPod/iTunes) presents you with a slider bar that represents the **video's quality**.

The slider works like any other slider control you've ever used — simply click and hold on the slider to drag it to the desired location on the spectrum. Likewise, you can click anywhere on the line, and the slider will jump one step closer to your mouse cursor.

File size versus video quality

Which is more important to you: file size or video quality?

Smaller file;
lower video quality

Better video quality;
larger file size

On this screen, you can drag the slider to specify the overall quality level as well as change your screen dimensions.

So, we're back to that classic conundrum of pristine quality (and a gigantic footprint) vs. small files (and a blurry mess). I'd love to give you some sage advice about the ideal setting, but it's dependent on so many factors, and only you and the other decision-makers in your organization know what's best for your purposes. Here are a few questions to ask yourself that might help you refine your thinking, and thereby choose the best settings for your content and your audience:

■ Does the software that you're recording have a dense user interface? You know the type I'm talking about: lots of tiny buttons and fields and intricate graphics. Will losing a little detail completely lose the understanding of your audience?

■ And speaking of your audience, how many of them are on low-bandwidth Internet connections? If you've never investigated this, you should. You might just be designing videos for a small subset of your users.

■ How old is your audience? Young eyes are much better equipped to deal with slightly blurry details and graphic artifacts than is the senior set. If your company is dedicated to accessibility in the design of your software and your web site, then a super-crisp video might just be worth the increased load time. And this consideration isn't limited to the elderly, of course — *all* your visually impaired users will thank you.

■ Of course, if your clips consist mainly of simple diagrams, clip art, and title screens with large block text, then your audience probably isn't missing a lot of information if you decide to go low quality.

■ Is it worth it to your organization to create multiple videos for different bandwidth levels? The batch production capabilities of Camtasia Studio significantly reduce the time and effort required to do this. You can read all about batch production in Chapter 15, "Other Output Options."

Your eyes make the best judge. When experimenting with different quality settings, try producing multiple times at different quality levels, naming each new video something different so that you can do a side-by-side comparison*. Sometimes it's amazing how much file space you can save with no perceptible drop in quality. Other times, the quality drop-off is so severe that no amount of bandwidth savings is worth it.

Next, we come to the **Video dimensions** section. Here, you're first shown the **Original video dimensions**, meaning the dimensions of the largest clip in your project (largest in terms of dimension). Next, you're shown the proposed **Final video dimensions**, which are the dimensions at which your video will actually be produced.

Video dimensions

Original video dimensions: 640x480 pixels

Final video dimensions: 640x480 pixels

Would you like to change your final video dimensions?

Yes. Change Dimensions...

Here you can influence how large your final video will be.

If Camtasia Studio decides that Flash is the best option for you, then the Video dimensions section will be supplanted by the **Flash Templates** screen. Please see the section on SWF/FLV production later in this chapter for full details on the sizing and template selection options offered on this screen.

Now, for distribution methods where file size is an issue (web and e-mail), the final dimensions are likely to be smaller than the originals if you recorded at a decent size. For CD and hard drive distribution, it will probably be the same as the original size, and for DVD distribution, it will always be 720 x 480, and there's nothing you can do about it (in fact, you won't even see this screen). The same goes for iPod video, which is always 320 x 240.

---

* The use of Camtasia Studio's preview feature makes this a cinch, and I'll show you how to create production previews later in this chapter.

If you're unhappy with them, you can **change the proposed final dimensions** thusly:

1. Click the button labeled **Yes. Change Dimensions....**

2. The **Video Dimensions - Preview** dialog will appear, and you will see a preview of your video window at the specified dimensions.

Your preview window. The window depicts the first frame of the first clip in your project.

You can change the dimensions by clicking and dragging one of the video window's handles (those tiny black squares that surround the window).

or

In the **Final video dimensions** drop-down list, choose a new set of dimensions.

3. Click **OK** to accept the change, or **Cancel** to exit the dialog without changing.

Keep in mind that you won't be able to exactly specify the final dimensions; you can only choose from an incremental series of dimensions. For more freedom in specifying your video's dimensions, you'll have to leave the simplified Production Wizard behind.

If your project includes audio, then the next screen* you'll come to will sport a slider for your **audio quality**. It's pretty much identical to the one you used to choose the level of video quality. Again, the setting will depend on your needs. For example, is the narration very dense and detailed? Who is your audience? Are there a lot of nonnative speakers of your language? This is but a sample of the many things you'll need to consider when deciding whether it's a good idea to skimp on sound quality.

Settling on Standards

All this talk of setting quality levels brings up a related point, and now's as good a time as any to talk about it. When training clients on the use of Camtasia Studio, I'm occasionally asked, "Daniel, now that we're trained on using Camtasia Studio, management is on us to come up with a set of standards for us to apply to every video we make. You know, things like video dimensions, codecs, quality level, and so forth. Do you have any recommendations for us?"

I sure do. Here's my official recommendation for all of you, free of charge: **Avoid standardization at all costs**. In coming up with a series of set-in-stone rules, you remove the ability of the video creator (that's you) to make choices that will enhance the video based on knowledge of the target audience, the subject matter, or the goal of the presentation. For example, dictating 320 x 240 as the sole acceptable set of video dimensions might make sense for quick web tutorials in your Knowledge Base, but what happens when someone wants to do a flashy, DVD-based marketing promo? By limiting your freedom to do what is in the best interest of the *production*, you're virtually guaranteeing an end product that's completely free of any innovation, with technical specs that could be grossly inappropriate for the content.

Of course, keep in mind that being anti-standardization doesn't mean I'm against *consistency*. I believe it is only professional and appropriate that all videos within a given project share the same video dimensions, color scheme, audio settings, etc. My point is that all settings should be designed to augment the project in question rather than adhere to some overriding,

---

* If producing to SWF or FLV, then the Audio quality screen will actually come *before* the Flash Templates screen.

arbitrary set of standards. Of course, I realize that the decisions regarding the adoption of standards do not typically rest with the people who are actually making the videos. In this case, try to exert whatever influence you have to convince management about the evils of company-wide video standards. If you think it'll help, you're welcome to refer them to an "industry expert" (me), and I'll do my best to win them over.

Multiple File Production

If you're producing to CD or DVD, then the next screen offers to split your project into multiple files. If you happen to have a longer project, it might be wise to split it into a few different files. Provided you've created some markers in your production, you can use these markers as the automatic split points.

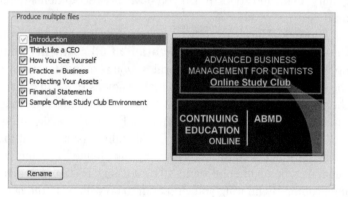

To make use of this function, simply check those markers where you'd like a split to occur. Each checked marker will become its own file, numbered sequentially along with your save name (i.e., MyProject-0, MyProject-1, etc.).

Saving Your Production

For all output media, you'll need to specify a file name and location for your project. The next screen in the Production Wizard will prompt you for this information.

Simply give your production a name, and then choose a directory in which the file(s) should be placed. To select a production folder, either click the **Browse** button, type in a file path directly, or just choose from among the recently used production folders by clicking the drop-down arrow. Note that you also have the option to **Organize produced files into sub-folders**, and since a few of the potential output types can actually produce several files, it's helpful to keep this option checked.

After clicking **Next**, you're presented with the final screen of the simplified Production Wizard, where you'll be able to view a summary of all the settings that the wizard has chosen for you.

If you're unhappy with anything you see on this screen, you may have the option of changing it by clicking the **Modify Settings...** button. This will lead to dialogs where you can fine-tune the encoding options as well as the video size options of your production. We'll be covering both of those dialogs in the upcoming section, so feel free to flip ahead a page or two if you run into any problems.

Even with the use of the Modify Settings… button, some settings (such as marker options, SCORM reporting, HTML embedding, etc.) simply cannot be adjusted with the simplified Production Wizard. To achieve a finer level of detail in your production choices, you'll need to use the classic Production Wizard, where you first specify a file format, and the rest of your choices flow from there. Starting with the very next section, you'll learn how to tame this dizzying array of options. First, we'll look at the screens and settings that are common to all file formats, and then we'll drill down on the formats themselves. There's a good reason why this is the longest chapter in the book; some of the choices are pretty nebulous. But once you've read through the rest of the chapter, I guarantee you'll have a solid sense of what formats and settings will work best for *your* production.

Common Production Elements

Okay, so you've taken a bunch of raw screen footage and then edited the pants off it, adding everything from callouts to markers to an additional audio track. What other options do you have left that will affect the look and feel of your final video? Plenty, as it turns out. Producing a video is all about taking that edited footage and then making choices that will have a profound effect on the final video's size and quality. While the various file formats have very fundamental differences, there are some basic commonalities about the kinds of decisions you'll need to make along the way.

Encoding Options

The first choice after selecting a file format typically involves picking how you want the file *encoded*, that is, the algorithm you'll use to compress that file down to an itty-bitty size while retaining as much of the video's quality as possible. The encoding options vary greatly according to the individual file type, and we'll therefore discuss the encoding options in the next section, when we talk about the various file formats in more detail.

Video Size Options

While the Encoding Options screen will manifest itself in different ways for the various file formats, your Video Size screen will remain constant for almost all video output formats*. This screen consists of two sections. The first section, **Video size**, will let you determine the dimensions of the final video as well as influence how your content is displayed within them.

Video size	
◯ Largest video size:	800x600
◯ Preset video sizes:	720x480 (TV/DVD) ▾
◯ Standard video size:	80x60 ▾
◉ Custom size:	
Width: 640	☑ Maintain aspect ratio
Height: 480	
Background Color... ■	
Warning: Changing the size of the video will degrade the image quality in the resulting video.	
File size	
☐ Disable Callout fade effects to reduce file size	
☐ Use Instant Zoom-n-Pan speed to reduce file size	

The Video Size screen.

In principle, this is very simple. You set a width and a height, and the final output conforms to those dimensions. In practice, with images and clips of often varying sizes, things can get weird if you don't know what you're doing.

For example, say you set your video dimensions to 640 x 480. Any included clips that are *larger* than those dimensions (that you haven't zoomed in on during editing) are scaled down. For clips that are *smaller* than the set dimensions, one of two things happen, based on your Project Settings. Say you're working with clips that have an original size of 320 x 240, and your editing dimensions were also 320 x 240. If you produce at 640 x 480 at this point, those small clips will be blown up to four times their original size, thus taking up the entire video window.

---

* Two exceptions: iPod video size cannot be adjusted at all, whereas SWF/FLV does allow you to specify the video's dimensions, but only from the Flash Templates dialog.

However, if you set your editing dimensions to 640 x 480, then the video preview will show the original 320 x 240 clips in their original small size, centered inside a large black border to take up the rest of the 640 x 480 space. And this is also what your final output will look like if you actually produce at 640 x 480. While the latter option is of minimal real-world value, there are occasions when placing a border around your video content is useful, for example when preparing content for DVD (more on this in a bit). Keep in mind that you can adjust the color of that border by clicking the **Background Color...** button. This background color will also show for larger clips that have been scaled down to fit your specified dimensions, but are either too tall or too short to fit exactly, thus leaving solid-colored bars at either the sides or the top and bottom of your window. To avoid this, use an image editing program to crop the image so its proportions are the same as your production dimensions.

On this screen, it's important to remember the settings you chose in the Project Settings when editing your work. Nine times out of ten, you'll want the video size to be exactly the same as your editing dimensions. It avoids surprises and helps ensure that your final production will look exactly as you remember.

The second section, **File size**, will let you check boxes to temporarily disable callout fade effects and/or use zoom-n-pan effects in an effort to get your file size down. It's a nice "quick fix" if you find that your final file size just isn't acceptable. If you have a lot of callouts and zoom-n-pan effects, it's also an easy way to make high- and low-bandwidth versions of the same video without having to maintain separate versions of the same project.

Video Options

Another screen that is present for most file types is Video Options. This screen consists of a series of (usually) four miscellaneous options that affect your video in different ways. Depending on the file format chosen, these may appear in a different order, or even not at all.

The Video Options screen.

Video Info

If you click the **Options...** button in the Video info section, you'll have access to a dialog that lets you add supplementary meta-information about your video that can be accessed by others:

As you can see, you have three tabs:

- **Project Information.** General info about the video project. Where this information actually appears depends on the file format you've chosen. For some formats, it appears at the bottom of your video in ticker-tape style. In other formats, it's a bit better hidden. Animated GIF files don't preserve this information at all.

- **Author Information.** Allows you to take credit for this project. You can include contributors, add contact information, and even specify which person in your organization manages the rights to its content. Both Author Information and Project Information are based on the Dublin Core Metadata Initiative, and allow users to search on any of this information when trying to find your video online.

- **iTunes Information.** These fields supply the appropriate information for setting up an iTunes feed. If you plan on using your produced video/audio for podcasting, this is essential information. Of course, it also means that you have to produce to a format accepted by iTunes (M4V, MOV, or MP3 audio) as well as post your video to a site and set up an RSS feed*.

Keep in mind that the Project Information dialog can be accessed *at any time* (not just during production) by choosing **Project Information...** from the **File** menu.

Watermarks

As mentioned in Chapter 6, "Special Effects of the Camtasia Recorder," watermarks are images that you can stamp onto a video. Usually a corporate logo or product icon, a watermark allows you to "brand" your content. Why would you want to do this? Here are a few reasons:

- You want to protect your content's copyright, preventing others from passing off your video as their own.
- You want your audience to associate your videos with your name or logo, thus building your corporate or product brand.
- You want to mark sensitive video content as confidential or classified.

While you can add a watermark directly to your individual video clips in the Camtasia Recorder, it is far preferable to insert your watermarks here instead. If you burn a watermark into your clips with the Recorder, it's pretty much there forever. With Camtasia Studio, on the other hand, you may change or remove the watermark at will — just produce a new version of your video.

To add a watermark to your final presentation, you simply enable the **Include watermark** check box, and then click **Options...** to choose the watermark image as well as to set the size, location, and formatting of the watermark to your liking. As this dialog is an exact copy of the Watermark tab in the Camtasia Recorder Effects Options dialog, please refer to that section of Chapter 6 for more info on tweaking these options.

---

* Details on creating your own RSS feeds are available at http://www.apple.com/itunes/store/podcaststechspecs.html.

SCORM Reporting

For those who routinely work with a learning management system (LMS), it's good to know that Camtasia Studio supports the uploading of your video content as a lesson module. It packages your video for online distribution through a method called SCORM, short for Shareable Content Object Reference Model, which is a special standard for deploying e-learning content over a network (be it the web or a corporate intranet). It allows your web-based lesson to "talk" to your LMS, regardless of which one you use. SCORM is the standard used to deploy these learning modules, and can be set up to track learner progress. It can allow you, the instructor, to "direct" the learner in a way that you cannot with standard HTML, because you can set up a special branching order of modules. For example, if a student completes module X, the system then knows to serve up module Y next, and so on.

Keep in mind that SCORM presumes the use of a learning management system that will serve up all these modules. There are lots of LMS packages out there, of varying capabilities and price ranges. There are even some open-source (read: *free*) LMS systems that are actually quite good. I'm particularly fond of Moodle (www.moodle.org). If you have the task of setting up any kind of online course, whether or not you plan on utilizing Camtasia Studio videos, I strongly urge you to look at the various LMS options, as they can save you from having to design everything from scratch.

But assuming you *do* want to use CS videos with your course, let's turn back to SCORM so that we can learn how to package them up. The first step is obviously to enable SCORM in the Reporting section of the Video Options screen by clicking the **SCORM** check box. However, if you're producing to SWF or FLV *and* you have a quiz or survey somewhere on your Timeline, the Reporting section of this screen will look slightly different:

Quiz and Survey Reporting

Current reporting options:
Report score using SCORM
Produce both zip file and unzipped files
Quiz Feedback is shown

Options...

You can still get to the SCORM-related options by clicking **Options...**, and then choosing **Report score using SCORM**. Don't worry about the rest of those quizzing options for now — I'll tell you all about them (as well as the quizzing-specific implications of SCORM) when we discuss the details of the SWF and FLV formats later in the chapter.

No matter what format you're producing to, the next thing we'll need to do is set up a *SCORM manifest*, which is a special XML file that lists the components of your SCORM package (in this case, your video content). This manifest sets up the structure of the module, informing the LMS how you want the module delivered.

To create the SCORM manifest for your video content, choose **Options...** (or **SCORM Options...** from the Quiz and Survey Reporting Options dialog if you've got a quiz) to open the **Manifest Options** dialog.

Let's talk about the various fields that need filling in here:

- **Identifier.** This is the ID number that uniquely identifies this manifest. You've got one inserted by default, but you can change it if you want. The only rule here is that it can't be blank or have spaces (Camtasia Studio will automatically convert any spaces it finds to underscore (_) characters).

- **Title.** This is the title of the e-learning course.

- **Description.** Enter a description of your course here.

- **Subject.** This is the subject of your course.

- **Version.** This is the SCORM version number. Choose the one best supported by your LMS.

- **Duration.** The duration of your video. This field is not editable.

- **Language.** The two-letter code (ISO 639-1) of the language used in the video. The default is *en* (English).

- **Lesson information.** Enter the title of your lesson here.

- **SCORM Package options.** Here you have the option of having your module packed into a ZIP file, produced unzipped, or both. Choose whatever option your LMS likes. If supported, uploading everything in a single ZIP file is a lot cleaner.

 Keep in mind that SCORM support in Camtasia Studio is pretty basic. In terms of tracking user progress, the module is checked off as complete the moment the user opens the video. It needn't be viewed all the way through.

HTML

By checking **Embed Video into HTML**, you're telling Camtasia Studio that you'd like your file inserted into a web page for viewing online. It saves you the effort of creating the page manually and then inserting your video. If you click the **Options...** button in this section, you have a few additional related options:

- **Alignment**. Place the video window on the left side, center, or right side of the page.

- **Show Play Controls**. Determines whether the user will have a control bar for playing back your video. It is *on* by default. Keep in mind that suspending the control bar can really detract from the viewing experience, so don't clear this check box unless you really mean it. Also note that an animated GIF file will have no control bar regardless of whether this option is checked.

- **Start Video Playing**. Leaving this box checked means that the video will automatically start playing as soon as it loads. Unchecking it will open the video in paused mode. The user will have to click Play in order to start the playback. Leaving both Start Video Playing *and* Show Play Controls unchecked is not recommended.

Keep in mind that Flash (SWF/FLV) videos don't sport this option, as all Flash videos *must* be embedded into a web page.

Marker Options

For almost all file formats, the next screen you'll come to in the Production Wizard is Marker Options. iPod/iTunes is the lone rebel. The animated GIF format has an abbreviated version of this screen because it can't offer a table of contents, and the Flash version is a bit truncated because its marker names never wrap. Beyond that, this screen looks exactly the same for all file formats:

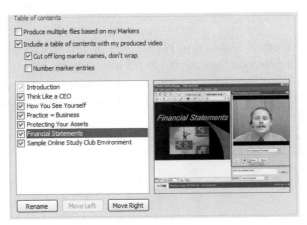

The Marker Options screen.

Now, in order to make good use of this screen, you're going to need some markers on the Timeline. You can technically produce a **table of contents** (or **TOC**) with only the default "Introduction" marker that corresponds to the beginning of your video, but if you're going to bother offering a TOC at all, why not make it a bit more useful than that? If you need help on adding markers in Camtasia Studio, check out "Fun with Markers" in Chapter 9, "Working with Camtasia Studio."

Okay, now that we've added (and hopefully named) a few markers, notice how they appear in the list window, directly next to a preview image. If you didn't name your markers (or you want to change one of the names you'd previously given), just click the marker, and then click the **Rename** button, or simply click twice on the marker name. Note that the preview image is tied to each individual marker, so use it to help you if you can't remember what the marker was supposed to be for. If you still can't figure it out, you'll have to exit the wizard screen and go find it on the Timeline. That's why I generally find it helpful to name your markers *before* producing.

Let us now talk about those four check boxes sitting above the marker list on this screen:

- **Produce multiple files based on my Markers.** This powerful command actually tells Camtasia Studio to slice up your project into individual files. It's useful for a particularly long project. Each marker will signify the beginning of a new file. The file names of these video files will carry whatever name you decide to give the final output, along with a number (MyVideo-0.avi, MyVideo-1.avi, MyVideo-2.avi, etc.)

- **Include a table of contents with my produced video.** Checking this option shows your video with a clickable table of contents. That's right, friends: A single click of this button will use your markers to create an instant web-based navigation menu that looks something like this:

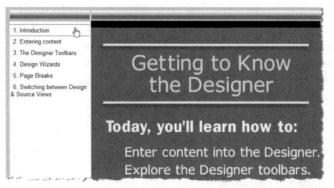

Just click a link, and you'll be instantly transported to that point in your video.

Just keep in mind that your video will need to be embedded in an actual web page for this option to work, so if you haven't yet checked **Embed Video into HTML** from the previous screen, the program will gently remind you to do so. Along with your video files and corresponding HTML page, you may also end up with some JPG images in your output folder that comprise the border graphics of your menu and video (though this depends on file type).

- **Cut off long marker names, don't wrap.** Here's a handy tip for those of you who put five full sentences in each of your marker names (and you know who you are). If you don't want to bother shortening them for your table of contents, and you definitely don't want them ruining the aesthetics of your menu by having each item wrap onto 10 lines, try checking this option. With it checked, every marker name will take up exactly one line, trailing off into an ellipsis (...). Just make sure you "front-load" your marker names with all the important information at the beginning. Otherwise, no one will know what this cut-off marker name is supposed to signify*.

---

* If producing to Flash, your TOC items can only take up one line each. You will not see this option.

- **Number marker entries.** If the order of marker items is of particular importance, you can have Camtasia Studio number the items on your TOC automatically.

One cool thing about your table of contents is that you can set up an outline-style hierarchy of menu items. Camtasia Studio supports up to seven full layers of nesting, so that you can categorize to your heart's content. Simply select the menu item and then click **Move Right** to increase its indent or **Move Left** to decrease it (alternatively, you can use the left and right arrow keys). Just bear in mind that your menu items are always numbered sequentially, regardless of whether (or how) they're nested. So if your main heading is number 1., then its two subheadings will be 2. and 3., etc.

Finally, if there are markers you'd rather not have included in the file splitting and/or table of contents *at all*, you can remove them by unchecking the box next to the marker's name. Note that this doesn't remove the marker from your Timeline; it just removes it from split/TOC consideration when producing. Also, keep in mind that you cannot disable any marker that has nested markers underneath it, so plan accordingly.

Produce Video

Okay, congratulate yourselves: This is the final step for all output types. The Produce Video screen allows you to specify the name and location for your output file(s) as well as see at a glance all the files that will be produced. Additionally, it allows you to set several post-production options.

Output file

Production name:

iTunes

Folder:

E:\Users\Daniel\Desktop

☑ Organize produced files into sub-folders

Post production options

☑ Show production results   ☑ Play video after production

Upload to the internet

☑ Upload video to Screencast.com   ☐ Upload video by FTP

TechSmith
SCREENCAST.COM.   What is Screencast.com?

These files will be created upon production:
Folder:
    E:\Users\Daniel\Desktop\iTunes\
Files:
    iTunes.zip
    iTunes.swf
    iTunes_iPod.m4v
    iTunes_config.xml
    iTunes_controller.swf
    iTunes_preload.swf
    iTunes.html

First, enter an appropriate name for your video output in the **Production name** field. Notice at the bottom of the screen how all the files in your final output will take on this name as their root. Next, we have to choose a location for your produced files. You've got three options here:

■ You can enter a file path directly into the **Folder** field.

■ You can click the **Folder** field's drop-down arrow to display and choose from a list of recent production locations.

■ You can click the **Browse** button (📂) to browse for a directory. You can also enter a file name here, which will subsequently appear in the Production name field when the **Save** button is clicked.

Now, one option you have is to push your produced content into a subfolder of your selected directory so that it doesn't get all cluttered by the (potentially many) files that get produced. Just click the check box marked **Organize produced files into sub-folders**, and upon production, Camtasia Studio will create a special folder, bearing the production name you specified, where it will place all your files. Otherwise, they'll all go right into the directory you chose, where they can conceivably get mixed in with the files already present in that folder.

If you've chosen to embed your video into an HTML file *and* you're producing to a format other than SWF/FLV or iPod/iTunes, a media folder (e.g., myVideo_media) will be automatically created where all production files *except* the HTML file are placed. It just makes things cleaner.

The above items are all the information Camtasia Studio needs to begin producing your file. However, you have a few **Post production options** you can check that may help enhance your workflow. Let's talk about them:

- **Show production results.** When this option is checked, you'll get a dialog with some handy stats as soon as production has completed:

Included is a useful rundown of the files created, the file size and dimensions of the content, and a summary of all the production options you chose. I find it particularly useful for quickly eyeballing the overall file size to make sure it's small enough for web distribution. I strongly recommend keeping this option checked.

- **Play video after production.** This option will automatically open the default media player for your chosen file type (or your default web browser if you chose to embed the content into an HTML page) upon the completion of production. This way, you can immediately have a look at what was produced to make sure that there aren't any glaring errors or omissions. It's a helpful means of doing a quick sanity check, just to make sure things are copacetic before blasting your content out into the world.

- **Upload video to Screencast.com.** In an effort to make online distribution as hassle-free as possible for its customers, Tech-Smith Corp. has a special service called Screencast.com. This is a service aimed at storing and sharing your screencasts. When choosing to produce with this option enabled, Camtasia Studio may first warn you about using a format other than ExpressShow SWF:

While SWF is often the most economical format for online delivery, there are advantages and disadvantages to it that you'll learn about later in the chapter. Feel free to ignore this warning if you know that SWF is an inappropriate choice for your content.

As you proceed, Camtasia Studio will prompt you for your Screencast.com login information.

As you can see, you have links to sign up for a free trial or purchase an account right from this dialog. Once you've taken care of the particulars, you're free to start uploading content.

After production (and after clearing the Production Results dialog if you opted to see it), you'll be prompted to continue with uploading your video to the service. Click **Yes**, and you'll be able to view the progress as the file uploads*. Upon completion, you're presented with a special dialog that contains the project's URL:

---

* If you'd prefer to have the video automatically upload to Screencast.com *without* prompting you first, just choose **Options...** from the **Tools** menu, and on the **Screencast.com** tab, choose **Automatically upload to Screencast.com after my production is finished.**

You can choose **Copy** for pasting the video's URL into an e-mail address if you want to share with others. There's even object code you can copy for embedding into a blog or other content page. Click **Launch URL** to instantly view your project page on Screencast.com. As the content owner, the page you'll see will be very different from that of your audience. You'll be able to:

- Set permissions for viewing your video.
- Upload additional supporting media files.
- Send out invitations for others to view your content.
- Add/edit the video's metadata.
- Organize your video projects into distinct collections, and set up RSS feeds for those collections.

You get a free 30-day trial of the service, and once that's over, you can continue by paying a monthly or yearly fee, and at the time of this writing, several tiers of storage and bandwidth are available according to your expected usage, starting at just seven bucks a month.

Even if you already pay for web file hosting, the features collected here are particularly useful for Camtasia Studio users. If you want to set up a separate space for hosting your videos, I strongly urge you to consider picking up a subscription (or at least giving the free trial a whirl). For shooting out a quick tutorial to colleagues or showing a work-in-progress to a client, there really is no easier way of sharing your work online.

- **Upload video by FTP.** If you already have a trusted file hosting solution, you'll be pleased to know that Camtasia Studio doesn't lock you into using Screencast.com if you want to easily upload your content. With this option, you can upload to any server that supports transfer via FTP. When you start the production process, you're prompted for your server's FTP settings:

Just choose a server name, a file path to your desired directory, and a port (usually 21), and then enter your login details below. You can save this information as a profile so that you needn't enter it every time. Previously saved profiles are available from the drop-down list at the top of the dialog.

You don't need to actually produce in order to upload to FTP or Screencast.com. Camtasia Studio can serve as a vehicle for uploading *any* supported media file(s). Just choose **File > Upload To**, and then select either **Screencast.com** or **FTP**. An Open dialog will appear, where you'll be able to navigate to the files you want to upload.

At any rate, once you're ready to produce, click **Finish**. You'll see a progress dialog that looks like this:

The amount of time it takes to produce a video can run anywhere from a few seconds to many, many hours. Depending on the file type and the media streams you've included in your project, there can potentially be *numerous* steps in the production process. Each step has its own progress bar, shown alongside the bar signifying the total production progress. The amount of time needed for each step is equally varied, according to the complexity of the content, the length of your video, and of course, the processing power of your machine. Your average three- to five-minute tutorial video should typically only take a few minutes to produce with a garden-variety PC.

Provided you checked **Play video after production** on the Produce Video screen, your web browser or media player will launch to play the file. If you checked **Show production results**, they'll show up in a window at the end of the production process. You'll even have a button for saving off your recently used production options as a *production preset* for future use (more on this near the end of this chapter) as well as a button for gaining instant access to the production folder where your newly created files are stored. Click **Finish**, and if you opted to upload via Screencast.com or FTP, you're likely to be asked at this point whether you wish to proceed with the upload. If everything looks as expected, choose **Yes.**

Production Preview

But what if you have a very lengthy video, and you just want to do a quick sanity check to make sure that your settings are correct? Do you go through the hassle of producing the whole thing? Of course not! This is where production preview comes in. Regardless of whether you choose the simplified or standard Production Wizard, in the lower left-hand corner of any of the production settings screens you'll see a small drop-down list called **Preview:**

You're given two options. The first, **Preview Current Settings**, lets you produce the first 30 seconds* of your video so that you can quickly proof the dimensions, compression, audio, and other settings as they currently stand in the wizard. Alternatively, you can bring up the **Production Preview Manager,** which is a fantastic tool for helping you generate and compare multiple previews, letting you easily contrast video dimensions, audio quality, compression settings, etc.

---

* Keep in mind that you can customize the length of your previews (from 10 to 60 seconds) by choosing **Tools > Options…**, and adjusting the **Production Previews** duration field.

So how does it work? Well, every preview you create is stored in a folder called Production Previews, located in your default Camtasia Studio directory. This lets you play back any preview you've already done as well as do a side-by-side comparison between two project previews. It also lets you reuse settings from the preview of another project with your current project. To get started, first select the project you wish to work on from the drop-down list at the top of the dialog; a list of previews you've created for that project will appear. When you select a preview, its details pop up in a separate pane. Once you settle on a particular preview, you can:

- **Play Selected Preview.** This opens the selected preview video using the media player (or web browser) that corresponds to the video's file format. Camtasia Studio maintains every preview you ever create unless you consciously delete it.

- **Delete.** After creating an endless stream of previews for a multitude of projects, things can tend to get a little cluttered over time. Just select the preview and click **Delete** to remove it. When you delete every preview in a given project, that project will be removed from the drop-down list.

- **Compare Setting Details...** This command will open a special dialog allowing you to compare the settings of two different previews, side by side. It's only available when two previews are selected (use **Ctrl** to perform multiple selections).

- **Use These Settings.** You can use the settings from any pre-existing preview (including from other projects) to create a new preview for the current project.

The File Formats

Okay, together we've explored the Production Wizard, and have basically gone start to finish on producing your first video. The stuff that's been left out of the conversation thus far pertains to the individual file formats themselves. This section has two parts (or subsections, if you will). First, I'm going to give a quick summary of each of the nine file formats and why you might want to use each one. If you're not sure which format you need at this point, this is where you should be looking *first*.

Then, I'll go into much greater detail on each file type, giving you a play-by-play on all the various dialog options. Some of these dialogs can get pretty specific, and you won't need to know most of it in order to effectively output to the file type in question. But I'll take you through it all anyway, so that those of you who wish to micro-tweak your settings can do so. Since my assumption is that you'll be flipping straight to the file format that interests you and bypassing the rest, bear in mind that there is a fair amount of redundant information in this section.

File Formats: The Condensed Version

Before diving into the minutiae of each format's compression settings, I felt it best to give you a high-level overview of all of them so that you can do a quick comparison without needing to flip pages until your fingers fall off.

Adobe Flash (SWF/FLV)

Flash is a cross-platform video format that plays with the Flash Player, currently installed on the vast majority of the world's computers because of its ubiquity as an animation format.

- **The good.** Enjoys extremely wide distribution. Supports interactivity with the user. The introduction of Flash video (FLV) makes high-quality, high-motion video a reality. Fans of the picture-in-picture feature can now enjoy side-by-side video.

- **The bad.** The Flash Player's lack of keyboard control makes it a poor choice for visually impaired users. Also, the Flash security settings can occasionally get in the way of playback from a local drive. Beyond that, not much....

- **The bottom line.** Its universal presence in your users' browser windows plus its interactive features (hotspots, quizzes) make this format king of the web.

Windows Media Video (WMV)

Windows Media Video is the current video streaming format from Microsoft. Camtasia Studio produces picture-in-picture files in this format. Files can be streamed over the web or played locally with Windows Media Player.

- **The good.** Excellent for high-motion video, and its ubiquity as a Microsoft format means that everyone (in the Windows world, at least) can access it. Small file sizes.

- **The bad.** Quality, while decent, can't compare to a lossless format like TSCC. Tweaking its settings requires an understanding of the concept of *bandwidth*. Its file type cannot be readily converted.

- **The bottom line.** Small size and universal availability make this format ideal for conservative, locked-down corporate settings where user-installed software is strictly forbidden.

QuickTime Movie (MOV)

Apple QuickTime is a cross-platform media format capable of high-quality video. It plays on the QuickTime Player.

- **The good.** This format is a good olive branch to extend to the Mac users in your audience, whose QuickTime player software cannot read TSCC-encoded AVI files without the aid of the TechSmith Ensharpen encoder. QuickTime codecs like TechSmith Ensharpen and H.264 offer excellent quality.

- **The bad.** Not all Windows users have QuickTime installed, and your audience may skip the video altogether rather than download yet another media player*.

---

* Note that this has become less of an issue in recent years with the success of the iPod and its corresponding iTunes software, which cleverly integrates QuickTime as part of its structure.

- **The bottom line.** QuickTime's Mac-centric history makes it the ideal method for cross-platform delivery, and the newer H.264 codec gives you the best of both worlds in terms of high motion and screen detail, all at a very reasonable file size cost.

AVI Video

AVI (short for Audio Video Interleave) files are produced natively by the Camtasia Recorder. These files can play back in almost all media players, including Windows Media Player and the Camtasia Player (discussed in Chapter 15, "Other Output Options").

- **The good.** AVIs encoded with the TechSmith Screen Capture Codec are completely lossless. AVI is also pretty much the industry standard, so if you ever need to import your video into a high-end editing application or DVD authoring tool, you could do so.
- **The bad.** There are distribution issues with AVI, as the TSCC codec is not installed on most people's machines. Other codecs are universally available, but then the quality suffers. The TSCC codec also chokes on copious amounts of high-motion video, such as real-world camera video.
- **The bottom line.** AVI, while not at all suited for the web, is still the way to go for showing videos on CD-ROM and DVD in all their lossless glory.

iPod/iTunes (M4V)

Starting with version 4, Camtasia Studio can now produce video content in M4V format, which can play in iTunes as well as on the video iPod.

- **The good.** Camtasia Studio videos can finally fit in your pocket! Portability and excellent quality combine to give your users a viable option for enjoying your content on the go.
- **The bad.** The small resolution of the iPod at 320 x 240 pixels necessitates a lot of zooming and panning in order to retain good quality.
- **The bottom line.** While MOV videos are better suited when dealing with iTunes alone, for video iPod compatibility, this is the format you should be choosing.

MP3 Audio

This is an audio-only format. In the last 10 years, MP3 has come to be synonymous with highly compressed, yet high-quality, sound files. It can be credited with bringing about the digital download revolution, opening up a whole new world of music distribution.

- **The good.** For content where the visuals aren't of much importance, going audio-only can yield a substantial file size savings.

- **The bad.** Um, well… there's no video stream. So if you're into that sort of thing, this is a bad choice.

- **The bottom line.** An excellent add-on option for taking your lectures on the road. Only a small fraction of portable media devices out there are video iPods, and thus by offering an MP3 in addition to your video, your content is assured a much broader distribution.

RealMedia (RM)

This streaming media format from Real plays in the RealPlayer media player (and in web pages with the Real plug-in).

- **The good.** Small file sizes. Particularly good audio compression. Its SureStream technology lets you create a single file for several connection speeds.

- **The bad.** A bloated, advertising-laden footprint and some questionable marketing practices have turned off many users to the RealPlayer media player.

- **The bottom line.** A solid choice for streaming web videos, though some users may refuse to install the player in order to view your content.

Camtasia for RealPlayer (CAMV)

These special Camtasia-specific RealPlayer files can be streamed over the web or played back locally. It is better suited for the latter.

- **The good.** Completely lossless video quality.

- **The bad.** Requires both the RealPlayer media player and an Internet connection, as the Camtasia for RealPlayer plug-in will need to be downloaded upon first use. Compression carries the same disadvantages regarding high-motion video as a TSCC-encoded AVI.

- **The bottom line.** A reasonable solution if your goal is to stream lossless content.

Animated GIF Image (GIF)

It's the standard animated GIF you see as banner links in web page headers.

- **The good.** Small file size. It's also completely ubiquitous (anyone with a web browser can play it).

- **The bad.** You're limited to 256 colors, small dimensions, and a limited running time (usually no longer than 20 to 30 seconds).

- **The bottom line.** It's a neat option for efficiently creating eye-catching web banner graphics. I also use it for inserting quick screen animations into my PowerPoint presentations.

Adobe Flash (SWF/FLV)

Now that you've gotten the quickie file type fly-by, it's time to dig into the details of each file type, starting with Flash. Back in December of 1996, a small six-person company named FutureWave sold their animation software (then called FutureSplash Animator) to Macromedia, Inc. In the decade that followed, that little animation utility became a juggernaut, and the Flash Player is now installed on over 500 million PCs. It is one of the most widely distributed pieces of software in the world, its place further cemented with Macromedia's acquisition by larger rival Adobe Systems. The SWF format (originally meaning "Shockwave Flash," and then "reassigned" to mean "small web file") is employed by animators around the world to bring web banners, slide shows, and cartoons to life. Utilizing predominantly vector-based artwork, you could use their tool to concoct a pretty snazzy online presentation weighing in at under 50 K. In addition to the Flash authoring system, other third-party tools began to offer exporting to SWF as a means to leverage the ubiquity of the Flash Player. Nowadays, many applications can create Flash* content files.

With the introduction of Macromedia Flash MX, the authoring system began to support real-world video, an Achilles' heel of the SWF format. While not (potentially) lossless like SWF, the FLV (short for "Flash Video") file format provides exceptional quality even at lower bandwidths, and takes advantage of the omnipresent Flash Player.

---

* The term "Flash" has become homogenized to potentially mean the authoring system, the media player, the project file, or the produced content files. To eliminate confusion, I'll do my best to be specific rather than referring to everything simply as "Flash."

Additionally, both SWF and FLV offer one major advantage over all the other formats currently supported by Camtasia Studio, namely *interactivity*. Since Flash videos are designed to accept feedback from the user in the form of buttons, text fields, and the like, TechSmith is increasingly incorporating these interactive elements into Camtasia Studio. In Unit IV, "Editing within Camtasia Studio," you learned about creating clickable Flash hotspots as well as soliciting feedback from your users by way of the Quiz and Survey feature. Further layers of interactivity are likely to be added as the product matures.

In addition to the interactive elements, Flash production also offers increased flexibility over other outputs, such as the side-by-side PIP layout, multiple encoding options for different kinds of content, custom loading screens, and more direct control over the aesthetics of your control bar. We'll be discussing all these things in this section.

Flash Templates

The Flash Templates screen is your first set of options after choosing Flash (SWF/FLV) in the Production Wizard. It allows you to select a layout (thus choosing which media streams are included in your final video). This is done by picking a **Template**. You may have as many as nine templates available, depending on whether there are any markers or PIP content on your Timeline.

The Flash Templates screen. The chosen template will determine the presence of the various media elements as well as the layout of those elements.

Note that there are a couple of "special case" templates that deserve a mention here:

■ Two **ExpressShow** templates were added in Camtasia Studio 5 to address concerns about the ever-expanding number of accessory files required for playback. ExpressShow packs the video into a single SWF file for easy embedding into a blog or other web page. In addition to single-file simplicity, there are a few other neat things about this template. To wit:

■ Each ExpressShow video shows a clickable YouTube-esque still frame at the beginning:

Just click to start your ExpressShow video...

 Keep in mind that even though the video is paused at the beginning, it is still loading in the background. So, if you embed it into a web page, the video does download (and consumes bandwidth) on every page view. In Chapter 16, I'll show you a technique for embedding that only loads the video when the user clicks on it.

■ The ExpressShow control bar, in addition to giving you the standard volume control, About button, and elapsed/total runtime view, also gives you a new **Fullscreen** button (⊞) that will expand the video to take up the entire screen. Users can press **Esc** to exit Fullscreen mode.

- The ExpressShow with TOC template can display the table of contents on the left-hand side of the video, on the right, or even floating on top of the video. For floating TOCs, the window can be toggled with an added button on the control bar ( ). And all three TOC types have a couple of extra tricks up their sleeves, like the ability to add an image over the TOC, or to give it a headline:

Here's a floativng TOC extolling the benefits of *me*, complete with image and headline.

- Unlike other templates, where you're forced to use the branded Camtasia Studio screen, the ExpressShow **About box** can be fully customized. I'll show you how a bit later on.

Now, a few caveats. First, ExpressShow is for SWF files only (no FLVs), so content like full-motion video that isn't appropriate for SWF won't work in an ExpressShow. This also means that PIP is out. For the aesthetics, you're limited to the Onyx theme (more on themes in a moment). Also, since all effects and settings are "baked into" one SWF file, this means that any post-production tweaking of your video is virtually impossible.

These items notwithstanding, if you're looking for an attractive way of posting a screen video to your blog or web site, ExpressShow might just be the answer you've been looking for.

- **Legacy SWF** template. In setting up support for high-motion video capabilities, callouts with hotspots, picture-in-picture, and quizzes and surveys, TechSmith was forced to make some pretty radical changes to its Flash output technology. Camtasia Theater, a special utility for combining multiple SWF videos, does not yet support this new architecture (at least not officially — we'll also discuss an unfinished version of Theater that *does* when we cover Theater in Chapter 14). For those who really want to create SWFs that are compatible with the official release of Camtasia Theater, TechSmith has included a special template called Legacy SWF output. It adheres to the older technology standards, and as such, it works with earlier versions of the Flash Player as well as plays nice with Camtasia Theater.

Here are a few details about this output to bear in mind:

- Legacy SWFs are not compatible with quizzes and surveys.
- These SWFs only offer a very basic control bar (only Play, Pause, and Stop). You also have the option of having *no* control bar, for example when creating video content for use with Camtasia Theater (which offers its own control bar for your videos).
- No side-by-side video is allowed (or FLV video of any kind). In fact, your PIP track will be ignored entirely.
- No preload movie will be included.
- You cannot build a table of contents with Camtasia Studio (though you *can* do so in Camtasia Theater).

In the future, Camtasia Theater is likely to be officially updated to overcome these stark limitations. Even after that happens, Legacy SWF output can still serve as a viable means of reaching those audiences that use an iteration of Flash Player prior to version 7.

Moving right along, you also have the ability to affect the aesthetics of your control bar from the Flash Templates screen. In the **Theme** drop-down list, you currently have four different display options for your controller (ExpressShow users are limited to Onyx). The Preview will change to reflect your choice. Functionally, these four are the same; just pick the one you think looks best.

Notice that the Production Wizard has placed a plethora of size information at your fingertips, including the proposed size of the video and PIP window (if applicable), the control bar, and finally, the total dimensions. In the **Fit in** drop-down list, you can choose from the video's original size, the most recently chosen custom size, or a series of standard sizes. If you desire even greater control, click **Change Dimensions...**, which will bring up the Video Dimensions - Preview dialog.

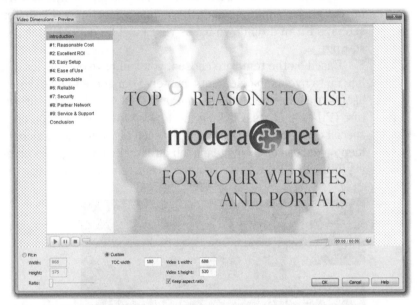

The Video Dimensions Preview provides much better control over your video's dimensions, and is particularly recommended if you're dealing with a TOC or side-by-side PIP content.

You can choose the **Fit in** option, specifying the maximum total width and height. It's useful if you plan on having other content on the same web page, and you absolutely *must* squish the video media to fit within a designated amount of space. Just enter a value (in pixels) into one or both of the fields. For Side-by-Side templates, there's even a **Ratio** slider bar for quickly setting the distribution between the two sides. I prefer the **Custom** option, as it allows you to exactly specify the width and height of your screen video (and your side-by-side PIP window, if applicable). The **Keep aspect ratio** button is checked by default, so the Width will automatically self-adjust if you enter a new value into the Height field, and vice versa.

Remember that screen video content, especially text, doesn't size down particularly well. So, if at all possible, try to keep the dimensions of your screen video at their original size. If you recorded a full-screen video, you may want to consider SmartFocus (or manual Zoom-n-Pan) as an option rather than scaling everything down. You'll only see a small window of the video's original content at any one time, but you'll be able to view that small window with perfect clarity. Just keep in mind that this can really bloat the file size, especially when producing to SWF.

Once you have the sizes adjusted to your liking, clicking **OK** will lock in your choice and remember these dimensions in the Flash Template screen's **Fit in** drop-down list as your most recent user-defined setting.

Based on the template chosen, you will have options for controlling up to five media elements, namely your screen video, your control bar, your audio, your table of contents (TOC), and any picture-in-picture (PIP) elements. Clicking the **Flash Options...** button opens a special dialog that contains a tab for each of the included media elements. You can also open each tab directly by clicking the corresponding link in the Preview area of the Flash Templates screen:

Clicking here will directly open my PIP tab so that I can adjust its options.

Let's discuss each of these in turn.

Video Options

The **Video** tab is all about the compression of your screen video. You can choose the format, frame rate, and other options. Take a peek:

The $10,000 question on this tab is: SWF or FLV? Simply click the radio button of your desired format, and the section of the tab that corresponds to that format will then be accessible. Here are a few key points in helping you decide between the two:

- SWF is mainly for videos that are shorter in length. Due to the way the format is structured, there can be audio/video syncing issues with longer videos. Additionally, the longer a video is, the more memory it consumes on the user's system. If the user doesn't have a lot of free memory to begin with, the video could stop playing entirely. Also, SWF does have a limit to the number of frames a single video can contain (16,000, in case you were wondering).

- SWF offers a great degree of flexibility in terms of how it compresses information. Its default (PNG-based) compression mechanism is completely lossless. However, if there are some high-color elements in your video such as photographic or gradient content, you can switch to lossy (a mixture of PNG- and JPEG-based) compression to get a smaller file.

- FLV is for longer videos that have a lot of motion. Real-world camera videos, PowerPoint files with lots of animation, and other high-motion clips look great and compress well in FLV. It isn't lossless, but the quality is quite acceptable even at a reasonably low bitrate — even screen text looks crisp, with few if any *artifacts* (weird blurry sections in your video window).

- Because of its ability to handle high-motion video, FLV is usually the format you should go with when creating a video with PIP. Well, at least with overlaid or "true" PIP it's the way to go. Side-by-side PIP creates its own file for the PIP portion (which is *always* FLV), meaning that you're free to choose SWF for the actual screen video, if that's the appropriate choice for the content.

There are no hard-and-fast rules here, particularly with PowerPoint files. If there's a doubt in your mind as to which format to choose, you may want to try using that Preview command to create three individual snippets of your project (in FLV, lossless SWF, and lossy SWF). Look at them individually, and then choose the best combination of file size and quality. I'm often surprised at the results.

No matter which file format you go with, you'll still have some choices to make regarding how that format is compressed. Let's start with **SWF**. There are a few controls with which you'll want to familiarize yourself:

- **Colors.** Choose either 16-bit or 32-bit color depth. The Automatic setting will choose the color depth of the original clips. If the color depth is mixed, it will opt for the higher number of colors so that no color information is lost.

- **Frame rate.** Enter the desired frame rate of the finished output. You can take this number down to save on file size, although the resulting video may be choppier. Cranking up the frame rate above the level of the original will give you no additional quality. It's akin to making a photocopy. The copy machine only has the material of the original page to work with, and as a result, the quality of the copy will never be better than the original.

- **Use JPEG compression.** When unchecked, the frames used by Camtasia Studio to make up your SWF video are compiled using PNG compression, which is lossless, meaning that your video will retain perfect quality. If your video content comprises lots of varying colors (photos, gradients, etc.) rather than solid blocks of color, you might want to try checking this option. When enabled, Camtasia Studio compresses each delta frame *twice* (for a discussion of key frames and delta frames, see Chapter 7), once with PNG compression (lossless) and once with JPEG compression (lossy). It inserts the smaller of the two into your final video.

  The result is a video of very acceptable quality, with the potential of being much smaller in size. This size vs. quality differential is at least partly controlled by you. You can set the relative quality level by either dragging the quality slider or typing a percentage into the corresponding text field. Low quality = smaller size, high quality = larger size. It all depends on the needs of the project. If you're willing to put up with lossy compression, you might want to start somewhere in the middle of the spectrum, produce a test preview of your video, and then adjust up or down as needed.

Moving on to the **FLV** format, you will note that the controls are somewhat different. You still have the ability to choose a **Frame rate**, but there are some other options requiring further explanation:

- **Max bitrate.** This represents the amount of information (in kilobits) that can be contained in one second of video. The higher the number, the better the quality (and the larger the file size). The default is 300 KB/sec, which is adequate for most uses. You need to be very concerned about this number if uploading the FLV to the Flash Communication Server for "true streaming," since setting a bitrate higher than the user's connection speed can lead to numerous interruptions in playback. However, Camtasia Studio's FLV output is set up to allow for *progressive download*, which is similar to streaming in the sense that the video begins to play very quickly, but the content is actually downloaded, not streamed. Bitrate is not as critical an issue in these situations.

- **Key frame rate.** The frequency in which key frames appear in your video. *Key frames* are complete pictures of your video image that don't rely on any frames before it (for a complete discussion, see Chapter 7, "Recorder Tools Options"). One note specific to the Flash Player: Users can only seek to key frames when zipping around on the Timeline, so the more key frames you include, the more exact their seeking will be. However, the inclusion of more key frames (lower key frame rate) can also lead to larger file sizes.

- **Bitrate control.** This determines how Camtasia Studio manages the maximum bitrate you just set. You've got three options. Constant bitrate means that the same amount of bits will be allocated to compress a given amount of content, no matter what that content is. This is typically the preferred control method for streaming video, but can lead to problems with progressively downloaded video files (which is how our FLV output is set up to work). If the bitrate is constant, then it may not allocate enough bits for complex portions, while wasting too many bits on the simple parts. Variable bitrate makes more sense in this case, because Camtasia Studio will analyze the content's complexity and allocate its given bits more intelligently, thus yielding more consistent quality. It can do this in either one or two passes. 1-Pass means that Camtasia

Studio analyzes *and* compresses the material at the same time. 2-Pass divides these tasks into separate steps, thereby compressing the material more efficiently. 2-Pass compression can yield smaller files, but takes nearly double the time to produce.

■ **Video quality.** Another quality vs. file size slider, going from 10% to 100%. This is a logarithmic scale, so you'll see a much bigger difference in quality when jumping from 90% to 100% than you would if moving from 60% to 70%. The default of 80% works well for most uses.

One final option you can tweak, regardless of your chosen format, is...

■ **Background Color.** When adding clips of various dimensions to your Timeline, Camtasia Studio will place a smaller clip (at its original size) in the center of the larger playback area, as opposed to scaling it up. The rest of the screen area is filled up by the color you specify here.

Since it only works with SWF, the Video tab for ExpressShow templates is greatly simplified. Additionally, it sports a check box called **Compressed SWF (recommended)**, which can compress your ExpressShow video even further using the zlib compression library. Unless you're averse to small files, there's really no reason to turn it off.

PIP Options

This tab lets you stipulate how your PIP video is going to be compressed. You may or may not actually *see* the **PIP** tab. Two conditions must first be met:

1. You have to have at least one clip on the PIP track of your Timeline.

2. In the Flash Templates screen, you will need to have chosen one of the two templates that include side-by-side video.

If you're doing a standard ("overlay") PIP video, these options do not apply, and are not available to you. This is because Camtasia Studio automatically produces the screen video and overlay PIP content as *one* video, and hence only one set of compression settings is needed.

When doing a side-by-side video, however, you can actually choose different compression settings for each component, since they'll remain two separate files. Have a look at the options here:

Now, considering that we've already visited the Video tab, the options at the top of *this* tab (in the area labeled **FLV**) should already look very familiar to you. Yep, the side-by-side PIP window always gets compressed as an FLV, and you have the same compression options as with an FLV screen video.

The one other option you have is called **Background Image**. Predictably, this option shows a chosen background image wherever you have hidden chunks of the PIP video (see the previous chapter for more info on showing/hiding PIP content). Just enter a file path or click the **Browse** button to open the **Select Image File** dialog. You can choose from the standard supported image formats (BMP, GIF, JPG, PNG). The image will be scaled automatically, but you might want to make sure that its aspect ratio is more or less comparable to that of your PIP image. If you choose to have no background image, then the side-by-side PIP window will simply go black when the PIP video is hidden.

Audio Options

Compared with the various video options, the **Audio** tab is relatively simple. This tab is available to you only if there's something on any of your Timeline's audio tracks (Audio 1, Audio 2, PIP Audio).

As you can see, you've got four settings. First, there's the check box to **Encode audio**. You're free to uncheck it if you do *not* wish your recorded audio to be part of your final presentation. However, assuming that you knew what you were doing when you placed that audio on the Timeline, I'm figuring you probably *do* want to include said audio, so let's talk about how we can compress it.

So, next you'll need to choose an **Audio format**. You've got two or three choices:

- **Uncompressed.** Keeps your audio completely compression-free. Considering that you're probably producing for the web, this option is *not* recommended.

- **MP3.** The most popular option for SWF/FLV audio compression, and with good reason. It offers strong compression and excellent quality for both music and the spoken word. When in doubt, choose MP3.

- **ADPCM.** A speech codec that is only available with SWF. If producing to FLV (or including a side-by-side PIP window), this option won't be listed.

For the format you've selected, open the **Audio attributes** drop-down list to select the level of compression. The attributes are discussed in detail in Chapter 7, but here's a quick summary:

- **Sample rate.** Measured in kilohertz (kHz), this is the number of samples taken of the sound you're recording per second.

- **Bit rate.** The number of possible amplitude levels used to encode your audio. An 8-bit compression offers 256 levels, where 16-bit gives you 65,536 levels. Some codecs (e.g., ADPCM) can use an even lower bit rate.

- **Mono vs. Stereo.** If you've only recorded from one microphone, make sure you select *mono*.

The attributes settings will also give you a sense of how much bandwidth one second of audio will take up, measured in either kilobits (1,000 bits) or kilobytes (1,000 bytes, or 8,000 bits).

Finally, **Positioning** controls are included to set the default volume level during playback. You can either adjust the slider or manually type a value into the percentage field.

Table of Contents Options

The **Table of Contents** tab is where you select the markers for inclusion in your video's menu navigation. It is only visible if you've selected one of the three templates that make use of a TOC. If you've already produced a video in any format other than Flash, you'll notice that the options are similar to part of the Production Wizard's Marker Options screen. The Table of Contents tab looks like this:

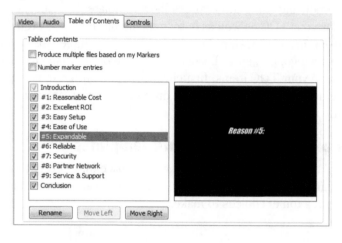

Your marker names are listed in the box on the left-hand side of the dialog, and on the right is a thumbnail image of the video content appearing at the selected marker's location. If there are certain markers you'd rather not include in the TOC, such as miscellaneous note markers, simply uncheck them in your marker list, and they will not appear in your menu navigation.

If the length of your video is unwieldy, it may be useful to split your file into small chunks so that the viewer isn't faced with preloading a large portion of it at once. In that event, choose **Produce multiple files based on my Markers**. You'll end up with a series of Flash videos instead of one long one. In addition to more evenly distributing the preload times, it's also a handy way of circumventing the SWF format's 16,000-frame limit. Additionally, if the sequential order of your TOC items is important, you can have those items automatically numbered by clicking **Number marker entries**.

Just as with the Marker Options screen, you have buttons to help you assemble your navigation. **Rename** lets you assign a new name (and hence new link text) to the currently selected marker. In addition, you can utilize the **Move Left** and **Move Right** buttons to nest topics inside one another to create subtopics (again, the left and right arrow keys will work just as well). The cool thing about nested lists in the Flash Player is that the user can expand/contract main topic headings (by clicking the accompanying +/– symbol) so that they don't have to view the entire list at once. This can be a major advantage, particularly for PowerPoint recordings, where there may be 100 or more markers (presuming one for every slide).

Bear in mind that there are a few additional settings for this tab when producing using the ExpressShow template. You can specify a **Title** for your TOC as well as determine its placement: **Fixed-Left**, **Fixed-Right**, or **Floating**. Finally, you have an **Image file name** field to select a logo, presenter headshot, or some other image to appear just above your TOC items. Just click the Open button to navigate to it, type in the file path, or click the drop-down arrow for a list of recently used images.

Controls Options — Standard Templates

Finally, the **Controls** tab is your personal space for altering the aesthetics and functionality of your video's control bar. As you can see, we've got a ton of choices to make:

Let's first talk about how the controller bar *looks*. These tools are all in the Playback controls section of the tab. You have the ability to alter the following:

■ **Show about box.** Checking this option will place a button on the control bar (▣) that brings up a special box with file stats and any other information you care to include:

The About box has two tabs: **About** and **File Info**. As you can see on the Controls tab of the Flash Options dialog, you have a small field for entering text. You can type anything you wish, and here are a few ideas:

■ General info about the video

■ The author's name

■ Copyright information

■ Contact information (phone, e-mail, web address, etc.)

You've got up to eight full lines of content to fill in as desired, and it will all appear on the About tab. The File Info tab displays a few handy stats about the video, such as the **File URL**, **File Size**, and **File Duration** (in frames).

■ **Show duration.** Shows the video's total duration (in seconds).

■ **Show elapsed time.** Shows the exact point of the playback head in time, so that the user knows exactly how much time has passed. I recommend keeping both this *and* Show duration checked so that your audience can tell at a glance how long they've been watching and how far they have to go on the current video.

■ **Display format.** Here you can choose how you want the various time elements displayed. Just click the drop-down button and select an option. Here's a quick guide to your options:

■ The capital letters **HH**, **MM**, and **SS** represent the number of hours, minutes, and seconds, respectively, that are present in the elapsed time or duration.

■ The lowercase letters **h**, **m**, and **s** are the actual acronyms for these time elements.

For example, if your video has a duration of 4 minutes and 17 seconds, and you select **HH:MM:SS**, the display would read **00:04:17**. If you selected **MMm SSs**, it would read **04m 17s**. If both Show elapsed time and Show duration are checked, then your format selection affects them both — there's no way to select a different format for each.

■ **Controller Color...** Click to choose a color for your control bar from the palette. The chosen color will be displayed right on the Controller Color... button.

■ **Captions initially visible.** If you have captions on the Timeline, this check box determines whether or not the closed captions bar is initially visible during playback. As always, it can be toggled with the Captions button on the user's control bar.

Enough about the aesthetics, though. Let's get into tinkering with the functionality of the playback. All these options are corralled in the Flash actions part of the tab. Get a load of what you can do:

- **Pause at start.** When unchecked, the video will begin to play immediately upon loading (or as soon as the chosen preload threshold is reached — more on that in a sec). Otherwise, it will start in paused mode, thereby requiring the user to click the Play button before playback actually begins.

- **Allow resizing.** This option will allow SWF videos to be resized if desired when viewed inside the actual Flash Player application. Unfortunately, it's very likely that you'll be showing off your SWF file inside a web page, in which case checking this option has no effect whatsoever. Additionally, giving the user the option to scale your content will probably have a rather negative effect on its quality. While I'm generally a fan of always giving the user a choice, in this particular case I tend to recommend keeping this option *unchecked*.

- **Show loading movie.** This handy option will open a small file (usually a SWF, but it can be a static image file as well) while your main video is loading. It usually sports a little animation so that the users have something to watch, and hopefully somewhere the word "Loading..." will appear to let them know they should keep waiting for the good stuff. Observe:

This loading movie plasters my blatant advertising on a cost-conscious client's video, thus meriting them a discount.

Camtasia Studio includes several stock loading movies by default, or if you happen to be Flash-inclined, you can make your own. Just for fun, I have included a few loading movies in this chapter's folder on the companion CD. Feel free to check them out for ideas, or even use them in your own projects. (I doubt you'll want to use my branded corporate one, but I've included a couple of more generic loading movies as well.) I included their corresponding

FLA files, so that you can edit them if you wish. We'll talk more about creating and editing loading movies in Chapter 16.

Once you've checked **Show loading movie**, the **Loading Movie...** button will become available. Click it, and a whole new dialog of options will appear:

Here are the options you'll have:

- **Match loading movie size to main movie size.** Checking this option blows up your loading movie to match the dimensions of your main video. Since it's vector-based, Flash will scale up your loading video with perfect quality. I personally find that this option makes the loading movie too obtrusive, but others appreciate having the loading movie and main video be the same size.

- **Loading movie URL.** You have several methods at your disposal for choosing a loading movie. You can type in a file path, or even a web URL if the file already exists on a web server somewhere. Clicking this field's drop-down arrow will reveal the most recently used loading movie (very handy if you have a few that you use over and over). Finally, you can click the **Browse** button to find the file locally. If you select a local file, it will end up being included in your production folder with the rest of the produced media files.

- **Percent of main movie to preload.** This is where you can stipulate that a certain percentage of the video file be downloaded into the user's cache *before* it begins to play. The goal is to ensure that enough of the video gets stored locally to ensure an interruption-free viewing once the video gets going, and this percentage is going to vary based on the video's projected file size as well as your assessment of your audience's average connection speed. If I'm creating a short, flashy (read: high-motion) marketing video, then I'll crank the preload time up to at least 50% to avoid a lag in the middle of my important message. If it's a lengthy tutorial, then I might take it down as low as 10%, figuring that the rest of the file will load as the user is watching.

- **Minimum preload movie display time.** The number in this field represents the minimum number of seconds that the preload movie will display before it disappears and the main attraction begins. It's particularly important for someone like me who puts branded content onto the loading screen, and wants to make sure that the audience has adequate time to process it before moving on. Also, once the video has been downloaded into the user's cache, not setting a minimum means that subsequent viewings would show the preload movie for a fraction of a second — it would be on and off the screen quicker than a subliminal message.

Keep in mind that this is just a *minimum* — for some users, it may take even longer to reach your chosen preload percentage. It all depends on their connection speeds and the size of your video.

To help you reduce clutter, you may want to produce a single preload movie for all your video files. Upload it to an easily accessible location on your web server, and then link to that URL whenever you produce a new SWF/FLV video.

- **End action.** Finally, you have options for telling the video how to behave once it reaches the end of its content. Choose **Stop** to have the video stop on the last frame. This is useful if you put contact details or other sales information at the end of your video, and would like it to remain on the screen. Clicking **Go to first frame** does just that; it returns you to the title screen (assuming you included one) at the beginning of the video. And **Jump to URL** automatically takes the user to a web page of your choosing. It could be a product sales page, a web site that gives further information, or a media page that lists other videos they might want to see. There are limitless possibilities here.

Now, let's talk about the controls for the nonstandard templates. For the *Legacy SWF ouput* template, there are no themes. You are given the choice between a very basic control bar and no control at all. Even with the basic control bar, there's no About box, no elapsed/total duration view, and no captions. You therefore have no settings for these elements. For *ExpressShow*, its Controls tab differs so much from that of the standard templates that it really requires its own section…

Controls Options — ExpressShow Templates

Due to its unique control scheme, About box customization, and additional display options, the Controls tab for ExpressShow is really an entirely separate animal. Let's take a look at these highly adaptable controls:

Under **Playback controls**, you have the same **Pause at start** and **Captions initially visible** commands that you enjoyed with the standard template Controls tab. The next few check boxes are where things get interesting:

- **Allow resizing** will let you adjust the size of the video within the Flash Player. This option does *not* work if you've got the video embedded in a web page. As I've mentioned several times already, screen video doesn't always look particularly good when scaled, so I'd opt for turning this one off.

- Checking **Camtasia Studio context menu** will display two additional line items when the user right-clicks on the video window to view the contextual menu:

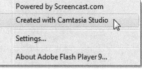

As you can see, the user can click on **Powered by Screencast.com** or **Created with Camtasia Studio** to find out more about these tools.

- As mentioned earlier when we were first talking about ExpressShow, **Full screen option** places a button on the user's control bar that can blow up the video to full screen size. This works regardless of whether it's a stand-alone file or embedded in a web page. The user can toggle fullscreen mode using this button. Pressing **Esc** to exit fullscreen mode is also an option.

Next, you have a check box to **Show About Box,** just like with the standard templates. But unlike the standard templates, virtually every aspect of the ExpressShow About box is customizable. To explore these settings, just click the **Options...** button.

This dialog is split into four sections: Size, Title bar options, About tab options, and Info tab options. Let's explore each in turn:

- First off, it's a rather simple matter to control the size of the box itself. Just enter appropriate values into the **Width** and **Height** fields.

- Next, you can place a couple of items into the About box's title bar. Just type out a **Title,** and you can even browse to add a small **Image,** like so:

My sweet new About box, complete with custom size, title, and icon image.

Just keep in mind that the image needs to be *really* small, or it won't be recognizable after the scaling required to make it fit.

■ The ExpressShow About tab is much more flexible than its standard template counterpart. You can enter lines of **Display text** just like always, but you also have the option of using an **Image** file instead. Just make sure that the size of the About box is big enough to accommodate your image.

■ The Info tab has historically been used to display a few vital stats about your video, including file name, size, and duration. If you leave these options alone, it will continue doing just that. But you can also check to **Display Info tab by default**, meaning that Info, and not About, is the first information the user sees. Perhaps you have no use for showing the vital stats of the file, and would rather simply enter custom text information (essentially giving you a second About tab). Your text would then display *instead of* the default stats, not in addition to them.

Click **OK** when finished.

Next, we have the Start and End Screen customizations. The **Start screen text** appears just below your still image's screen reflection on the start screen. The text can be anything from copyright info to additional instructions to the video's title. If desired, you can include a **Start screen icon** image just to the right of it. For the end of the video, your chosen **End screen icon** will be placed on top of the video window, just above the Replay button.

Finally, you can alter the same End actions you've come to know from the standard template types, with one exception. When checking **Jump to URL**, you haven't traditionally had any say regarding how the new URL appears. With ExpressShow videos, you have four choices:

■ **_self** launches the URL inside the current frame of the current window, effectively replacing your video.

■ **_blank** starts up a brand-new window for the URL.

■ **_parent** launches the URL in the parent of the video's window, that is, the window that spawned the video. If there isn't one, then it launches in the current frame, the same as if you had chosen _self.

■ **_top** launches the URL in the top browser frame. If the video is already at the top, then it's the same as if you had chosen _self.

Quiz and Survey Reporting Options

If you've been paying attention, then you know that one of the main advantages of the Flash format is its interactivity. One manifestation of this interactivity in Camtasia Studio is the ability to add quizzing/survey content and have the results reported back to you. When looking at the **Video Options** screen within the Production Wizard, you can click a special **Options...** button to specify exactly how you'd like those results delivered:

The options in the **Quiz and Survey Reporting Options** dialog are as follows:

- **No Reporting.** Pretty self-explanatory. No results are reported to you.

- **Report score using SCORM.** If uploading the content to your LMS, choose this option. You can specify the SCORM-related details by clicking **SCORM Options...** (please see our discussion of SCORM in an earlier section of this chapter). Your LMS will track the scores of all students who complete the quiz.

- **Report results through e-mail.** For those who don't use learning management systems, Camtasia Studio offers a simpler way of getting feedback. Just specify an e-mail address. You can choose whether you want the score visible to the recipient through use of the **Include score in e-mail** check box. When reaching the end of the video (after the quiz), the user is presented with an **Answers Summary** form:

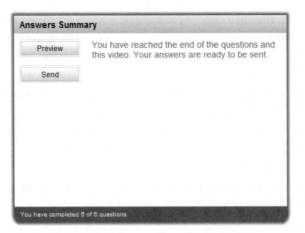

My end-of-video Answers Summary. If viewing an
ExpressShow, this dialog will look slightly different.

They can click **Preview** to view the content of the message, or
simply click **Send** to bring up the pre-addressed message in the
user's e-mail client application. E-mailing is not automatic; the
user must opt to send the quiz results.

If your recipient e-mail address has not yet been determined (or
if the recipient depends on the user, for example if every employee
needs to send the results to their immediate supervisor), you can
leave the **E-mail address** field blank, and the user will be charged
with addressing the message appropriately.

- **Disable Quiz Feedback.** It's helpful to check this option when
  doing a survey, as opposed to a quiz. You can thus disable any feedback messages popping up. Leaving it unchecked will cause the
  appropriate "correct" or "incorrect" feedback to pop up as soon as
  the user submits a response.

Flash File Structure

Due to the modular components of the two Flash output formats, their
file structure is a bit more complex than Camtasia Studio's other output formats. Let's clarify the various components that make up your
video. Depending on your project and the production options you've
chosen, you'll potentially see a multitude of production files. Here's a
quick list just to give you a sense of which file does what as well as
how they interact:

- **Main video file.** This is a SWF or FLV file (depending on your
  choice in the Production Wizard) that contains the actual video.

- **HTML file.** This file serves as the container of the media files for viewing in a web page, and it contains code to help automate the detection of Flash in your web browser. It is produced automatically.

- **Controller file (*_controller.swf).** This SWF file contains the playback controller.

- **Preload move file (*_preload.swf).** Provided you opted to include it, this is the preload movie that displays while the main video is loading.

- **Side-by-side video file (*_PIP.flv).** This FLV file contains your PIP video content. It is only needed when side-by-side PIP video is employed.

- **SWF object file (swfobject.js).** This JavaScript file is responsible for detecting the Flash version on the user's machine. If an appropriate version of Flash Player is detected, it also contains the embedding script for writing out the object and embed tags.

- **Random JavaScript code (*.js).** This is a catch-all file that contains production-dependent scripting, appropriate routing of movie reference arguments, and handling of SCORM content (including quizzes and surveys).

- **Flash CSS Template file (FlashTemplate.css).** Contains formatting and other style information.

- **No Flash Player background graphic (*_nofp_bg.gif).** This is a graphic used for your video's Flash Player detection.

If you opted to produce an **iPod video (M4V)** or **MP3** file, you'll see these in the production directory as well, along with the Flash and graphic files that make up the download front-end menu for those materials.

Finally, you've got the **Configuration file (*_config.xml).** This file is the glue that holds the rest of it together. It is a central repository of information that contains most of the options you set while traversing the Production Wizard. You won't see this file (actually, you won't see *most* of these files) when producing using ExpressShow, since all this information gets packed into a single SWF. While this can certainly make things easier, there is one advantage to keeping production information outside of the encoded video — you can edit and format certain production settings long *after* production has occurred. I'll teach you how to do this in Chapter 16, "Post-Production Customization."

Windows Media Streaming Video (WMV)

Windows Media Video is the proprietary streaming video format partially developed by Microsoft. As such, these files can be read by Microsoft's universally available Windows Media Player (Windows and Macintosh), as well as by some third-party media players that support other platforms. This format can be read natively by Pocket PC devices, and is the sole output format for Windows Movie Maker, Microsoft's consumer-level video editing application. While not a very editing-friendly format, Camtasia Studio can import WMV files for inclusion in a project.

The obvious advantage to carrying the Microsoft name is the fact that everything needed to play back these videos (at least for Windows users) is included in the operating system. This makes WMV the ideal format when producing videos in a "locked-down" corporate environment where the IT department doesn't trust the rest of the staff to manage their computers effectively. In these settings, the ability to install software is disabled, and users have to make do with what they've been provided by IT. Since Windows Media Player is a part of Windows, there are fewer distribution problems with WMV, provided of course that all your users are on Windows-based machines.

Another reason "big corporate" likes WMV is that this distribution can be a bit better controlled when used in conjunction with Windows Media Server. Because it's a streaming format, a copy of the video is *not* downloaded locally when viewed online from a streaming server. While not bulletproof, this is a bit more secure than non-streaming formats. Of course, when placed on a regular web server, WMV files offer what is known as *progressive download*. This carries most of the same advantages as actual streaming (easy, fast-starting online video), except that the content is actually downloaded. In short, WMV shines in locked-down environments, producing small, universally readable, and reasonably secure files at a good quality level.

And speaking of quality, another advantage of the WMV format is that the image quality is easily adjustable. First off, WMV tolerates high-motion video content extremely well. While its Windows Media Video Screen video codec carries many of the same drawbacks (and advantages) as the TSCC AVI codec, there are other, more flexible video codecs for WMV for handling the high-motion stuff. Additionally, you can create very small-sized (albeit low-quality) versions for users on a dial-up connection, and near-perfect quality versions for those with T1 broadband connections. And in this section, you'll learn how to adapt your WMV output for *any* audience and content.

Windows Media Encoding Options

After choosing WMV in the Production Wizard, you'll be presented with the Windows Media Encoding Options screen, which looks like this:

The level of encoding is chosen by picking a production profile from the Profiles drop-down list. If you look toward the bottom of the dialog, one rather important option you'll want to keep checked is **Add index to file (to enable seeking within the file)**. If left unchecked, your users will not be able to navigate the video by means of the scrubber bar. If they click and drag the bar, it will simply snap right back to its original place like a rubber band the moment they release the mouse button. As people are now used to having seek functionality, keeping the option checked will save your users a lot of time and frustration.

After selecting a profile from the list, some general info about the profile will probably appear in the Description box, and the Details box will contain all the technical details of your profile. If you're in a tinkering sort of mood, these settings can be adjusted. Therefore, please allow me to take a minute to demystify a few of these items so that you'll at least have a sense of what you're doing:

- **Video (or Audio) encoding mode.** There are two basic modes: VBR and CBR. Variable Bit Rate (VBR) encoding means that the bit rate will fluctuate depending on how complex the data is at that particular point. More bits get devoted to complex sections and fewer bits to the simpler ones, thus improving the overall quality. It's useful for videos that will be stored locally or progressively downloaded. Constant Bit Rate (CBR) keeps the video's bit rate consistent, and it will stream better as a result. So use CBR if you plan on broadcasting your videos from a streaming server. All the profiles introduced by Camtasia Studio are CBR profiles.

- **Video (or Audio) bit rate.** This is the number of bits per second (usually measured in kilobits (Kbps)) that will stream from your server to the user's computer. A higher number means better quality, and only those on broadband connections can handle it. A lower number indicates a video that can stream well over low-bandwidth connections (possibly even dial-up), but quality will suffer as a result. You will also see a listing called **Audience** that will tell you the total bandwidth requirements (video + audio) for that profile. For streaming, your users' download capabilities must meet or exceed this bit rate in order to smoothly play your video.

- **Audio codec.** The current iteration of the Windows Media Encoder offers the **Windows Media Audio 9 codec**, and it has several versions from which to choose:

  - **Windows Media Audio 9.** The standard codec offers a sample rate of either 44.1 or 48.0 kHz and 16 bits. CD quality can be obtained on a spectrum from 64 to 192 Kbps. Its support of VBR can mean even smaller files with higher quality.

  - **Windows Media Audio 9 Professional.** Includes options for 5.1 channel or even 7.1 channel sound with up to 24-bit/96 kHz fidelity. Since Camtasia Studio cannot take advantage of these enhancements, this codec has little real-world use for our purposes.

  - **Windows Media Audio 9 Voice.** Targets the narrower frequency range of the human voice and is designed for speech content. Unlike a lot of other speech codecs, however, this one handles musical/mixed content admirably as well. Best for low-bandwidth connections.

- **Audio format.** These are the attributes applied to the currently selected audio codec, such as a target bit rate, sample rate, and whether it's encoding mono vs. stereo. You can learn more about audio attributes in Chapter 7.

- **Video codec.** Though you may see some older codec versions, Windows Media Video 9 is the current version. Just as with the audio codec, this video codec comes in several flavors, all of which are compatible with Windows Media Player v7 and above:
  - **Windows Media Video 9.** The standard codec, supporting a wide range of bit rates. Also offers downloadable content with two-pass and VBR recording.
  - **Windows Media Video 9 Advanced Profile.** The same advantages as the first, plus support for interlaced video content. For our purposes, this is unnecessary unless you have imported some interlaced real-world video into your project, such as DV video from a digital camcorder.
  - **Windows Media Video 9 Screen.** Excels at screen video, with large blocks of a single color and minimal background changes. Automatically switches between lossy and lossless compression based on the data's complexity.
  - **Windows Media Video 9 Image Version 2.** Used to "video-ize" still images by using zooms, pans, and crossfades. Not useful for our purposes.
  - **Windows Media Video 7.** While this is an older version of the codec, I mention it here because it offers faster encoding than its next-generation brethren, which can be advantageous if you're in a hurry.
- **Video size.** The dimensions of the video. This can either be **Same as video input** or some other specified dimension. I strongly recommend the former. If otherwise specified, it will override the video dimensions set in your Production Wizard, at least for the actual content. For example, if you have a Video size setting here of 320 x 240, but your setting on the Video Size screen of the wizard states 640 x 480, you'll end up with a small window of content inside a larger window with a black background (regardless of your Background Color setting). It's best to leave this setting alone and instead use the Production Wizard to adjust the video's dimensions.
- **Frame rate.** The number of frames per second at which the video will play. The Camtasia Studio profiles typically play back from 3 to 10 fps, depending on quality level (see Chapter 7 for a more detailed explanation of the frame rate).

- **Key frame.** This lists the interval at which a key frame is inserted. Key frames offer a "complete picture" of your video image. The frames between each key frame, called *delta frames*, are of poor quality (usually a blur of motion). The lower the interval number (and hence the more key frames), the better the image quality. Typically, you would use more key frames for video with a generally consistent background (like screen video and "talking head" camera videos), and fewer key frames with "real-world" camera content (such as a sporting event). For more information on key frames and delta frames, see Chapter 7, "Recorder Tools Options."

- **Image quality.** This number, based on a scale from 0 to 100, is a mark of the video image clarity. Lower numbers result in a smoother video image, while higher numbers indicate a clearer image. Increasing the clarity can have an effect on the frame rate.

- **Buffer size.** The number of seconds in which your video content will be stored prior to encoding. A larger buffer size requires more memory, but yields better quality. The default buffer size is five seconds; for our purposes, there's really no reason to change it.

Editing Your Profiles

But how do we actually change these settings? Just select a particular profile, and then click the **Edit...** button. Note that your Camtasia Studio profiles cannot be edited in this way — more on that in a minute. Since the dialog that opens is technically a Windows Media Encoder screen and is therefore not actually part of Camtasia Studio, I'm only going to gloss over it. One thing you're apt to notice (at least with CBR profiles) is that the term "edit" is a misnomer, as you're actually starting from scratch. After choosing the encoding mode and codec for your desired streams (video, audio, or both), click the **Add...** button to add a target bit rate. After doing so, a tab bearing that bit rate will appear, and you'll be able to set the rest of your options on that tab.

If you don't relish the idea of coming up with all new settings and would rather work from a "pattern," you actually *can* make use of those Camtasia Studio profiles, tweaking them to your liking and storing them in a custom profile.

To do this, we're going to have to **import a profile's settings**, which is done thusly:

1. Back on the Windows Media Encoding Options screen in the Camtasia Studio Production Wizard, click **Manage....**

2. Choose **New...** to start a new custom profile.

3. Click the **Import...** button.

4. Browse to Camtasia Studio's collection of Windows Media profiles. Unless you changed the default install directory, it is probably located here:

   C:\Program Files\TechSmith\Camtasia Studio 5\Windows Media Profiles.

5. Select your desired Windows Media Encoder (.prx) profile, and then choose **Open**.

6. Adjust your settings as desired. To avoid confusing it with the stock Camtasia Studio profile from whence it originated, I'd also recommend renaming the profile.

QuickTime (MOV)

QuickTime is a video and multimedia format introduced back in 1991 by Apple Computer, a full year before Microsoft launched Video for Windows. This newfound ability to play video clips on the personal computer was a watershed moment in the history of computing. While Apple did outsource the creation of a Windows version fairly early on to help fuel the acceptance of the format, QuickTime was traditionally a decidedly Mac-oriented technology. However, its adoption in the Windows world was bolstered several years later by two major events:

■ George Lucas' decision to use QuickTime exclusively for the trailers to his much-anticipated (though ultimately disappointing) *Star Wars, Episode I: The Phantom Menace*.

■ Apple's decision to integrate QuickTime technology into its now ubiquitous iTunes player. You can download QuickTime separately from iTunes, but not the other way around.

As such, distribution in the QuickTime format is no longer the crapshoot it once was. Additionally, thanks to the presence of several high-quality compression algorithms that are available for the QuickTime format (such as H.264 and TechSmith Ensharpen), you don't have to compromise on your video's quality either.

One other distinction is that the MOV file format was designed as a container of sorts for all manner of content and meta-information. It can support things like multiple audio tracks, subtitle tracks, video effect filters, and video masking, among others. Camtasia Studio does not yet take full advantage of the format's versatility, though you *can* currently apply effect filters, a feature that's not available with any other file format. In a moment, I'll show you how.

QuickTime Encoding Options

In order to produce QuickTime videos with Camtasia Studio, you will first need to have QuickTime installed. The Pro version costs $29.99, and while I can recommend this version heartily as an essential part of my video editing toolset, you'll probably only need the Basic version, which is free. Make sure you specify to include the QuickTime Authoring component during installation. When it's time to produce, select **MOV - QuickTime movie**, and click **Next** to specify your encoding options. You'll actually find the **QuickTime Encoding Options** screen pretty bare compared to the other formats:

You've got the details of the current settings, all right, but if you want to actually change anything, you'll need to click the **QuickTime Options...** button. Once you click this button, virtually all of the options are part of the Apple QuickTime software package, *not* Camtasia Studio. We'll be talking about these settings only as they relate to your production capability in Camtasia Studio. Some settings will be covered in detail, others merely glossed over, and a few won't be discussed at all. Please consult your Apple QuickTime documentation if you have further questions about any of these options. Additionally, keep in mind that this section was prepared based on the most current version of QuickTime at the time of writing (7.2). If you have an earlier (or later) version, your dialogs may look somewhat different. So, now that we have the disclaimer out of the way, let's dig in.

The QuickTime **Movie Settings** dialog contains settings for the video, audio, and streaming capabilities of your project.

As you can see, there's a check box next to each element that can be turned on or off. When on, you'll see the details of the current settings, and some additional options buttons will appear. Starting with the **Video** section, a click of the **Settings...** button will get you to your actual compression settings:

At the top of the dialog, you'll be able to choose the codec from the **Compression Type** drop-down list. There are many codecs supported by QuickTime, but there's really no sense in covering them all, as most aren't useful for our needs here. So allow me to save you some legwork and just give the skinny on the Camtasia Studio "top three":

- **TechSmith Ensharpen.** Yes, the people who developed lossless screen video compression for AVI have developed a similar solution for QuickTime. It is *the* choice for perfect-quality screen video, albeit at a cost. It handles high-motion video poorly, and its decompressor is not distributed with the QuickTime Player by default, necessitating that the user download and install it separately (though this is free). TechSmith sells the Ensharpen codec as a stand-alone QuickTime compression solution, but anyone who purchases Camtasia Studio gets Ensharpen for Windows bundled in for free.

- **H.264.** A high-compression video codec that is ideal for high-motion video, offering both amazing quality and small file size. While not lossless, its ability to pack astounding detail into such tiny files represents a major leap forward in compression technology. In many countries, H.264 has been approved or is pending approval for use in high-definition broadcast television, and it is a component in both main contenders' iterations of the next-gen DVD format (HD-DVD and Blu-ray). This codec is only supported in QuickTime 7, thus requiring an update for users of previous versions.

- **Sorenson Video 3.** Prior to the arrival of QuickTime 7 and H.264, Sorenson 3 was the most often-utilized codec in the QuickTime arsenal, and with good reason. Its wide array of compression options and good tolerance of high-motion video made it highly versatile. A solid choice for full-motion video, especially if your audience hasn't yet upgraded to version 7 of QuickTime.

Below Compression Type, the dialog is divided into four sections. What you see here (particularly in the Compressor quarter) will vary based on the codec selected. The four sections of this dialog are as follows:

- **Motion.** Allows you to set the number of frames per second (**Frame Rate**). Choosing a lower rate than the one at which you recorded will reduce the file size, but may result in some choppiness. Provided that the selected codec makes use of *frame differencing* to compress its video frames, you can also set the number of key frames. This can be **Automatic** (using the key frame rate of the original video), **Every *x* frames**, or **All** if you want to have *every* frame be a key frame (not recommended). For more information on frame rates and key frames, check out Chapter 7, "Recorder Tools Options."

One final option available in a select few (most recent) codecs, such as H.264, is **Frame Reordering**, which can result in compression improvements. If you read the section on key frames in Chapter 7, then you know that you can have key frames as well as *delta frames* (intermediate frames whose content depends on the frame before it). Some codecs such as H.264 make use of a *third* type, called *bi-directional frames* (or *B-frames*), that can predict a frame's content by referencing frames that come both before *and* after it. These frames generally require fewer bits than the former two frame types, thus enhancing compression.

- **Data Rate.** If you decide to stream your QuickTime movie instead of setting it up as a progressive download, these settings allow you to specify the bit rate (in kilobits per second) that will stream from the server to the user's computer. The larger the data rate allowance, the higher your video's quality. The **Data Rate** can either be set to **Automatic** (influenced by the Compressor Quality setting) or given a limit in kilobits*. Some codecs will also allow you to select the file's **optimization** between web streaming, CD/DVD-ROM storage, and download.

- **Compressor.** The options located in this section vary tremendously with the kind of codec you're using. Here's a quickie rundown of some of the settings you may run across:

  - **Depth.** The number of colors in your video's available palette.

  - **Compression.** A numbered spectrum that allows you to choose between better compression, therefore smaller file size, and faster compression, therefore reduced production time.

  - **Quality.** A slider that allows you to choose between small file size on the low end and best quality on the high end. This can also have an effect on the file's bit rate when streaming.

  - **Encoding.** For compression using a variable bit rate (VBR), this setting will let you select the number of encoding passes. Rather than maintaining a constant bit rate (CBR) that will keep the bit stream consistent (which makes for better streaming), VBR first analyzes the material, dedicating more bits to the complex sections, while not wasting bits on

---

* When assigning a bit rate, keep in mind that this represents the *total* maximum bit rate for the file, including audio.

the simpler parts. **Single-pass** encoding analyzes and compresses the data in a single step, while **Multi-pass** divides the analysis and encoding into two different steps. This helps encode the data more efficiently, but also takes twice as long.

- **Options.** Certain codecs have a special button called **Options…** that takes the user to a special proprietary dialog in which additional settings can be viewed and adjusted.

- **Preview.** This is a small image of the Camtasia Studio icon, which offers a small preview of how using the chosen compressor at its current settings would affect the appearance of a graphic image. It's not terribly useful, but it should help you catch any glaring errors (such as mistakenly setting your color depth to grayscale) before you waste time producing a video you'll ultimately discard.

Wow, you'd think after all those adjustments that we'd be just about finished with the video end of things. Not quite, though. QuickTime offers a little-used feature called **Filters** that can do some pretty wacky stuff with your video. If you click on the **Filter…** button, you can choose from a series of Photoshop-style filters that apply to the entire video. Put old-style film noise on clips to give them a "vintage" feel. Sharpen the edges of your video picture. Or turn everything pink by adjusting the RGB balance. It's well beyond the scope of this book (and apparently beyond the scope of QuickTime's own documentation) to talk about all the filters and their various settings, but I encourage you to experiment to help you get a sense of the possibilities. The only real downer is that filter effects always apply to the *entire* video — you can't target individual sections.

As for the **Size…** button that follows, I strongly suggest you leave it alone. The Video Size screen of the Camtasia Studio Production Wizard offers much more comprehensive sizing options, and adjusting the size in two different dialogs can only lead to problems.

Compared to the whirlwind of video options in QuickTime, your sound settings are pretty subdued:

Clicking the **Settings...** button under Sound gives you a few basic fields to fill in:

- **Compressor.** The audio codec you're using to compress the sound. Some of the common choices are detailed below.

- **Rate.** Runs from 8.0 to 48.0 kHz (in Camtasia Studio), and refers to the number of *samples* (little snapshots) taken of a digital waveform.

- **Size.** The bit depth indicates the number of volume levels used to represent sound. You can choose between 8-bit (256 levels) and 16-bit (65,536 levels). 16-bit is generally preferable regardless of the codec used.

- **Mono vs. Stereo.** Mono recordings play identical content from both speakers, whereas stereo attempts to mimic the spatial location of sound by playing different content from each of the two speakers. In almost every case, you'll want to choose mono.

- **Options....** Certain codecs have additional options dialogs they offer. For example, with the QDesign Music 2 codec, you can specify a target bitrate.

The quality of your sound is largely determined by the audio codec you use to compress the sound data. Here are the choices I would typically recommend:

- **MPEG-4.** MPEG-4 utilizes *Advanced Audio Coding* (AAC). It is the one truly excellent QuickTime codec for voice, music, and sound effects alike. If you're compressing your audio at all, this will be your codec 99.9% of the time.

- **None.** While typically a setting used only for authoring, you may want to leave the audio data completely uncompressed if not distributing the files online (e.g., using CD- or DVD-ROM).

- **QDesign Music 2.** This codec was the best general-use codec out there when introduced back in 1999. To this day, it remains a solid choice for mixed (voice/music) content, but tends to have phasing issues when used for speech alone. Purely instrumental music is particularly good.

- **Qualcomm PureVoice.** This is a speech codec designed by QUALCOMM. It's a QuickTime version of their PCS digital phone codec. Sound quality is acceptable for voice narration but like fingernails on a chalkboard for anything else.

Back in the Movie Settings dialog, your next option is **Prepare for Internet Streaming**. If you plan on delivering this file online, I recommend keeping this option checked. When enabled, you have two (well, technically three) options for delivery: progressive download and true streaming. Here's how it breaks down:

- **Fast Start.** With the Fast Start option enabled, you can deliver QuickTime content from any standard web server. This is *not* actual streaming, but rather a technique called *progressive download*. True streaming video requires the use of a streaming server (which can be quite expensive), and the video stream is broadcast to the user's machine without actually storing the video file there. With progressive download, the video is actually downloaded rather than streamed, but it will begin playing while the download is still in progress. This gives all the "instant access" benefits of streaming, but without the overhead of setting up a special streaming server.

- **Fast Start — Compressed Header.** All QuickTime files contain a *header*, which is special information located within the file that describes the file's contents. With both of the "Fast Start" options, QuickTime places this header right at the front of the file, so that the player has all the information it needs to start playing the file right away. Compressing the header stores this meta-information with fewer bits, meaning that the actual content can start even faster. This is the generally recommended option if you and your users will be downloading your content over the Internet.

- **Hinted Streaming.** When Apple adopted streaming technology for use in QuickTime, it decided against rebuilding QuickTime from the ground up to accommodate this new technology, opting instead to create a special track (called a Hint track) that would give the streaming server the info it needed in order to stream the video file. People with sensitive content love streaming because the content isn't actually downloaded, thereby allowing better (but not bulletproof) control of distribution. It's akin to sending out a broadcast TV signal. Determined people can capture the content with a VCR or TiVo, but most will simply watch. After viewing your streaming video, there's usually no trace that they ever saw your video, except for perhaps a small *reference movie*, which is a small video that references your streaming video. It's handy for e-mailing video content to someone, because the size of the reference file is so small.

 If you do plan on streaming your videos in QuickTime, remember to only use web-enabled video codecs (such as H.264 or Sorenson) and audio codecs (AAC, QUALCOMM PureVoice, QDesign). Some compressors, such as Ensharpen, are not designed to be streamed.

At any rate, choose **Hinted Streaming** to create a file for upload to a streaming server. The **Settings…** button contains detailed settings regarding packet size, duration, etc. It's best to leave these settings on their respective defaults unless you know otherwise. Many of these options require specialized knowledge of your video and audio codecs' capabilities as well as the technical constraints of the network.

AVI

AVI (Audio Video Interleave) is a video file format created by Microsoft. It combines video frames and waveform audio in alternating interleaved pieces. AVI files adhere to the Resource Interchange File Format (RIFF), which gives the file the ability to store meta-information about its own content, such as duration, video dimensions, etc. As such, it's a stand-alone file that requires no other supplementary files in order to work (at most, you'll get an HTML file if you checked Embed Video into HTML). This format has been around since 1992, and is still the most popular video file format in existence.

Because of their ubiquity, these files can play in almost any media player, including Windows Media Player and the Camtasia Player. They can also be readily embedded into any HTML document for playback online using the Windows Media Player plug-in. Additionally, it's the format of choice for video editing applications. In fact, AVI is the format in which Camtasia Recorder encodes all your captured screen video clips*.

That said, AVI files that are encoded with the TechSmith Screen Capture Codec do have a distribution issue. Since Windows doesn't come with TSCC installed, you can't necessarily rely on your audience to have the codec on their end to decode your content. The codec is freely downloadable from the TechSmith web site, but if you'd rather not trouble your users with downloading and installing something prior to watching your video, there are a couple of other ways around it. Please see Chapter 15, "Other Output Options," for a full discussion.

---

* Even if you captured to the CAMREC format, the actual screen video file is still encoded as an AVI inside the CAMREC container file.

AVI Encoding Options

When producing to AVI in Camtasia Studio, the Encoding Options screen looks like this:

In terms of video encoding, you first have options for setting the number of **Colors** as well as the **Frame rate**. We discussed these items in detail back in Chapter 7, "Recorder Tools Options," but here's a quick recap: The color depth refers to the number of available colors in the video's color palette. You can save a little on file size (depending on the video codec) by ratcheting this down a bit. The frame rate is the number of frames per second at which the video displays. More frames per second equates to smoother video. Fewer frames per second takes up less file space.

> Remember that cranking the frame rate up above the rate at which your clips were originally captured doesn't buy you anything in terms of playback smoothness.

Both of these options default to **Automatic**, meaning that the program will find the highest color depth and frame rate of all the clips on your Timeline, and will produce the entire project at those settings. Note that Camtasia Studio will use the lowest settings possible without losing any color or frame information. For example, if you recorded all your clips in a combination of 8-bit (256 colors) and 16-bit color, the Automatic setting will produce everything at 16-bit, as opposed to 8-bit (some color information lost) or 32-bit (superfluous). You can, of course, manually set these options by choosing a value from their drop-down lists (or in the case of Frame rate, enter any integer from 1 to 30).

Video Compression

Back in Chapter 7, we discussed the merits and drawbacks of the default codec for capturing video, namely the TechSmith Screen Capture Codec (TSCC). In almost all recording situations (games and CAD applications being the general exceptions), TSCC is the only codec you need for capture. The codec playing field opens up tremendously on the production end. You may have photographic content or high-motion elements in your video, thus negating TSCC as an appropriate choice if you don't want your video file to take up half your hard drive space.

To examine the list of codecs you have at your disposal, simply click the **Video Compression...** button. Open up the drop-down list labeled Compressor. Everyone's list will be different depending on the codecs they have installed. Here's the current state of mine:

At this point, the TechSmith Screen Capture Codec is already well-covered ground. Here are a few other video codecs you may find on your system.

- **MPEG-4.** You'll see a lot of different names for the various flavors of this codec, from DivX to Xvid to 3ivx. It's a lossy codec designed to play real-world (high-motion) video well. This is probably the best choice for videos that have tons of photographic or camera video content.

- **Indeo 5.10.** Decent quality, but now nearly obsolete. Compression is so-so, and the video dimensions must be divisible by four to avoid quality issues.

- **Cinepak.** This is one of the very first multiplatform AVI codecs, and was originally developed for playing small movies on 386 machines. It excels at decoding video on machines with *very* slow CPUs, but beyond that, has little to recommend it nowadays.

- **Microsoft Video 1.** This video codec from Microsoft hasn't been updated in nearly 15 years. It may have been cutting edge in its day, but its now comparatively weak compression, poor quality, and lack of data rate control make MV1 a poor choice.

- **Full Frames (Uncompressed).** This is exactly what it sounds like — no compression whatsoever takes place. The files are enormous and unwieldy. If you want a lossless solution, opt for TSCC first. Even for high-motion video, the files are likely to be much, much smaller.

Audio Compression

Now let's move on to the audio side of the equation. As you'll see, it's a fairly important side, since audio can easily comprise up to 90% of your overall file size if you're not careful. The first thing you need to do is decide whether you want to include an audio stream at all. If you have no narration or sound effects, then clear the check box for **Encode audio.** If you leave it checked, then you will effectively be encoding a long stretch of pure silence, which can consume up to 187 kilobytes per second of your video's duration. That's a rather hefty price to pay for "dead air," so make sure this box is cleared if you have no audio in your project.

The next option determines whether you want the audio *interleaved*, that is, having the video and audio streams stored in alternating pieces in the file. Turning this option off can speed up the production time, but I don't typically recommend it, especially if the file may end up getting stored on a slower storage device like CD-ROM or ZIP disk. To be on the safe side, I recommend leaving the **Interleave audio every [...]** box checked. The interleave rate determines how tightly the "strands" of your video and audio streams are woven together. It defaults to every second, and that's quite acceptable for most playback devices. If you envision your videos being played on older, slower machines with legacy CD-ROM drives, you might want to crank the rate up to every frame (also called *full interleave*) to ensure smooth playback.

Now, let's pick ourselves out an audio codec. If you click the **Audio Format...** button, you'll be able to select a new Format (codec) as well as that codec's Attributes from a drop-down list.

You may recall that I promoted capturing your audio with PCM (pulse code modulation, also known as "uncompressed"), at 44.1 kHz, 16 Bit, Mono. Regardless of the codec chosen, you'll have options for at least two of these three attributes. While we discussed these in detail back in Chapter 7, here's a quick rundown of these attributes:

- **Sample rate.** Runs from 8.0 to 48.0 kHz (in Camtasia Studio), and refers to the number of samples (little snapshots) taken of a digital waveform.

- **Bit depth.** The number of volume levels used to represent sound. For PCM, you can choose between 8-bit (256 levels) and 16-bit (65,536 levels), but some other codecs may offer an even lower number of bits. 16-bit is generally preferable regardless of the codec used.

- **Mono vs. Stereo.** Mono recordings play identical content from both speakers, whereas stereo attempts to mimic the spatial location of sound by playing different content from each of the two speakers. In almost every case, you'll want to choose mono.

Provided all your files will still fit, I encourage you to maintain the aforementioned audio settings when creating a "master" AVI for archival purposes, and when producing to CD- or DVD-ROM where file space isn't at a premium. If producing an AVI for the web or e-mail, we will need to examine other codecs to help get the file size down. Here are the others I typically recommend:

- **MPEG Layer-3.** This audio format has been popularized by the digital music scene. It offers very good compression of music and (to a somewhat lesser extent) voice, with minimal loss in quality. If you have mixed content (voice, music, sound f/x), then MPEG Layer-3 is a strong candidate, but truthfully, it has since been supplanted by...

- **MPEG Layer-3 (TechSmith LAME).** This is TechSmith's version of the open-source LAME MP3 codec. In case you were wondering, LAME is a recursive acronym for **LAME A**in't an **MP3 E**ncoder, which in its current iteration isn't actually true. It is, in fact, currently the best encoder out there for attaining high-quality MP3 sound for voice, music, and sound effects alike. Its quality/file size ratio is so impressive that the Camtasia Recorder now encodes to MP3 LAME by default instead of PCM.

- **CCITT A-Law and μ-Law.** Developed to compress analog signals for digital telecommunications systems, these codecs offer telephone-quality audio for *voice* recordings. They're a terrible choice for music. They compress sound data by intelligently reducing the dynamic range of the human voice. Functionally, there's no appreciable difference between these two codecs — A-Law is employed primarily in Europe, while μ-Law (pronounced *mew*-Law) is the standard in the U.S. and Japan.

This Audio Format dialog has an extra ability you may find handy. If you take a look at the **Name** drop-down list, you'll see that you have several premade audio profiles available for your use. You can also create your own. This is extremely helpful if you utilize a particular set of audio options consistently. Just set up your Format and Attributes as desired, and then click **Save As....** You'll be prompted for a name, and when you click **OK**, the profile is saved and available for your use whenever you like. To get rid of one you don't need, just choose the profile and then click **Remove**.

Prepping Your Videos for DVD Output

While all of the Camtasia Studio file formats are great for reaching a computer-savvy audience, you might find your users are better served by being able to pop a DVD into their players and watch your content on a television. If it's your wish to export your video project for display on a standard DVD player, you'll be able to do so, provided you have a separate DVD authoring program and a little know-how. This DVD mini-guide is designed to give you just that.

First off, understand that converting from a computer (digital, based on pixel resolution) to a television (still predominantly analog, based on numbers of lines) standard has its share of quality issues. Most DVD authoring programs do a reasonably good job of converting digitized video into a color signal that can be read by the television standard of your target audience (NTSC for the U.S. and Japan; SECAM for France, Russia, and parts of Africa; and PAL for pretty much everywhere else).

The first thing to do, therefore, is to use Camtasia Studio to give that authoring program as "clean" (high quality) a source as we can, which means producing an AVI encoded with TSCC. We need AVI so that the authoring program can easily import it; we need TSCC because it's lossless. Since 720 x 480 is the standard dimension for producing DVD content*, those are the dimensions at which Camtasia Studio will ultimately produce in order to avoid distortion.

But there's a snag. Keep in mind that many televisions tend to "trim" the outside edges of their content. If you're not careful, this can mean that important content in your video won't actually be visible on the user's television if it strays too far from the center. So, you've got two choices when recording your videos:

---

* 720 x 480 is the digital standard resolution for DVDs in North America and Japan, which use the NTSC standard. If producing a DVD for a European audience, you should instead choose 720 x 576 to adhere to the PAL digital standard resolution.

- Keep all the important stuff (especially text) away from the periphery of the recording window so that it's not at risk of being trimmed off.

or

- Establish a "safe zone" where *all* content appears in a smaller window, surrounded by black background space to make up the rest of the 720 x 480 dimensions. I typically use 558 x 440, but this is not set in stone — you're welcome to take these dimensions as a baseline and then experiment with the aspect ratio to better fit your content and the DVD standards of your country.

The final stumbling block is that you'll need a DVD authoring application of some kind to take your AVI file(s) and create a disc that's actually playable on a console DVD player. Camtasia Studio won't do this for you. Fortunately, there are a number of choices out there ranging from low-end consumer packages (CyberLink PowerProducer, Ulead DVD MovieFactory) to versatile prosumer/professional solutions (Adobe Encore DVD, Sonic Scenarist). Prices run from as low as $50 all the way to $20,000, so you'll need to find the right mix of features, learning curve, and cost.

So, to **make your content DVD-friendly**, try the following:

1. Record your videos at 558 x 440 (or similar), using TSCC for your video stream and master-quality PCM for the audio. Make sure *all* your videos are the exact same size. Import them into Camtasia Studio.

2. When the Project Settings dialog appears, choose **720 x 480** as your editing dimensions, and click **OK**. At this point, you should see your content in the preview window, with a black border around it.

3. After editing, click the **Produce video as...** link to produce your final project as an AVI.

4. On the Video Size screen in your Production Wizard, choose **720 x 480 (TV/DVD)** from the Preset video sizes drop-down list if producing for a North American or Japanese audience (where the NTSC standard for DVD prevails).

or

If you live in a region where PAL is the supported standard for DVD, choose instead **720 x 576** from the Standard video size drop-down list.

5. Make sure that **Background color** is **black**.

6. Produce your final video, then import that video into the DVD authoring tool of your choice.

7. Set the aesthetics and menu options as allowed by your authoring program. Produce and burn the DVD.

iPod/iTunes (M4V)

The Apple iPod is the most successful portable media player to date. It was introduced back in 2001, and at the time of this writing, over 100 million of these little devices have been sold to consumers worldwide. The iPod's combination of style and usability won over legions of fans, including those well-entrenched in the PC camp. Today, well over half the portable media players on this planet bear the Apple logo. Not bad for a company that was fighting for its very survival just a decade ago.

The iPod began as an audio-only device. When color screens became cost-effective to produce, Apple introduced photo capability in its 2004 product line. In 2005, they rolled out the fifth-generation iPod, which brought video to the device. The latest iterations include support for video games and limited PDA-style functionality (calendar, contacts, etc.). And of course, the iPhone takes all the above and adds a web browser, e-mail, and phone capabilities. Apple sold a million units in under three months.

iPod/iTunes Encoding Options

Camtasia Studio supports M4V file output, encoding the video stream as H.264 and the audio stream as AAC (MPEG-4 audio). You can encode one of these little gems either as a stand-alone file or as an "accessory file," to augment your main (full-sized) video. Whether on its own or with a friend, the iPod/iTunes encoding options here are simpler than for any other output type. Other than the ability to add metadata to your file in the form of the Video info dialog, you only have one setting with which to concern yourself: **iPod bandwidth.** This is a drop-down list for you to choose low, medium, or high quality for your file. Because MPEG-4 is a lossy codec, choosing low may introduce visual artifacts that are absent from the higher-quality versions, but you'll end up with the smallest possible file size. The audio doesn't change; its settings always remain AAC 44.1 kHz, 16 Bit, Stereo. Truthfully, there's not really much of a quality differential on the video side, either; the low setting still looks great.

The video size is automatically set to 320 x 240, which is the dimension of the iPod screen. For the reality of your video creation, this is going to mean one of two things:

- Camtasia Studio is going to scale your video *way* down to fit these dimensions. That's bad news for screen video; graphics will be fuzzy and virtually all text will be pretty much illegible. It's not a bad way to go for PowerPoint presentations, however, especially if you remember to keep all the text on your slides nice and large. If producing the iPod video as an adjunct to a larger video, this micro-scaled version is what you're going to end up with. On the upside, this method requires the least effort.

- Or you could do things the harder way, which means using the zoom and pan tools to follow the action all over the screen, sticking to your moving mouse cursor like white on rice. Of course, 320 x 240 is a rather small space to work with, and if the action moves around a lot, you could end up making your audience seasick. In fact, these small dimensions probably won't even capture the entire window of most alert dialogs, let alone their corresponding application windows. The upside of this technique is all the screen video detail is there in its full-sized glory, and looks perfect.

 If you plan on producing iPod videos for exclusive display on an iPhone or a television (either by attaching your iPod via an AV cable or through the AppleTV console), you'll get much better resolution by producing your content to a 640 x 480 MOV file, and then using QuickTime Pro to convert the file for the iPod/iPhone.

As you can see, which technique you use depends heavily on the content. Also, please bear in mind that if you want to produce content that's compatible with *iTunes* (and not necessarily the video *iPod*), then a QuickTime MOV file is always an available option. That way, you can produce your video at full size. You only really need the iPod/iTunes production option when you want your content to be *portable*. Speaking of which, if you want to reach a much broader audience-on-the-go, then it may be time to consider producing an audio-only file, which we'll be talking about next.

MP3 Audio

Starting around 1995 (perhaps not coincidentally the same year the World Wide Web began to take off in popularity), MP3 files began circulating the ether in great numbers. The format's appeal stemmed from its inherent ability to tightly compress large amounts of sound information into small files, yet retain fidelity by discarding only those portions that are less audible to the human ear. While the technology has since improved, with formats such as Ogg Vorbis and AAC offering higher quality sound at the same or lower bandwidth, MP3 remains the most popular digital audio standard in existence.

This new method of accessing music by download represented a substantial change in how music and other audio was distributed, and gave rise to the upheaval that accompanies any major paradigm shift (record stores closing, record companies up in arms, etc.). While initially the domain of illegal file swapping, digital downloads gained mainstream acceptance when the record companies finally got with the times and green-lighted various online music distributors, beginning with iTunes.

And what started as a music revolution gradually shifted to other audio presentations — lectures, panel discussions, and call-in radio shows could all be recorded to MP3 files for dissemination online. Thanks to the growing popularity of Real Simple Syndication (RSS), anyone with a mic, a computer, and a net connection could become a broadcaster, whose periodic musings would reach the ears of anyone who bothered to subscribe. Podcasting was born.

While iPod video represents the ideal in enjoying portable Camtasia Studio content, the reality is that the video iPod represents but a tiny fraction of portable media devices, most of which are audio-only. As a content creator, it stands to reason that you should try to reach these individuals. Of course, it's ideally suited to certain kinds of content only. For example, software tutorials really need that video stream in order to make sense. But for other videos, such as university lectures and marketing demonstrations, the audio may be able to stand on its own. If you know you want to create an MP3 audio file from your video, try to be cognizant of that fact beforehand, when you're writing your narration. Always ask yourself, "Can this be understood without the video portion to back it up?" This is actually a good exercise, anyway, as it will allow those with visual impairments to get the most out of your video material.

MP3 Audio Encoding Options

MP3, like the iPod/iTunes encoding, can be created either as a supplement to a video presentation or as a stand-alone main attraction. Either way, you'll be able to adjust the meta-information (which is particularly important for podcasting) as well as choose the level of encoding by setting the **Bit rate**. Since MP3 is a lossy standard, you have a wide range of choices in attaining a target file size. Just choose an appropriate bit rate from the drop-down list. The exact setting will depend on the length of the material as well as where your disposition falls in the larger files vs. crappy quality debate. My recommendation (if going for quality over small size) is 44.1 kHz, Mono (especially if there's no music), and 96 kBits/second. That's only 720 K (less than a megabyte) per minute of high-quality sound. This is obviously better suited to a five-minute demo than a 45-minute lecture. But with a little experimentation (don't forget to make use of that Preview command!), you'll find acceptable quality at a file size you can live with.

RealMedia Streaming Video (RM)

Originally starting out as Progressive Networks in 1993 (and debuting its RealAudio tool in 1995), RealNetworks has been hailed as a leading force in the development of streaming technology as well as reviled for its shady marketing practices. Love 'em or hate 'em, the RealVideo component of their constantly updated media player suite has been a mainstay of video streaming since 1997.

RealVideo is typically joined to a RealAudio component, and packaged as a single RealMedia (RM) file. RealMedia is a *streaming* technology, which means that it can be accessed in one of two ways:

- **Stream.** If you have access to a streaming server (in the case of RM files, a technology called Helix Server), you can set up your content for true streaming. You can think of streaming as something one "tunes into" (such as a TV or radio broadcast) as opposed to something one owns and plays back at their leisure (such as a CD or DVD). This makes streaming ideal for live content. It's also handy for organizations that are protective of their content and the way it's distributed. Because a file that plays from a streaming server can't be downloaded, you can decide what content is available to your audience and when.

    RealNetworks has employed a protocol called RTSP (short for Real Time Streaming Protocol) to aid in the playback control of video and audio content. This protocol allows the client (your audience) to issue commands to the streaming server (the place where your RM files are stored), enabling VCR-like command functions (play, pause, etc.) as well as the ability to perform time-based access of the content (e.g., jumping right to Chapter 3 of an audio book).

■ **Download.** RealMedia content can also be run from a standard web server, which is called *progressive download*. This method downloads the video content into the user's cache, and the video can start playback while the download is still in progress. While this carries with it a few minor drawbacks (no parallel clip synchronization, no live broadcasting), it does sport the main advantage of true streaming, which is (nearly) instant access to video content. As soon as just enough of the video downloads to get you started, it will play, and then download the rest as you go. Because of the expense and technical headaches of setting up a streaming server, this is the option most of you will probably go for.

RealMedia Encoding Options

So, let's now talk about how we encode RealMedia content within Camtasia Studio. After choosing **RM - RealMedia Streaming media** as the desired output method in the Production Wizard, you'll come to the RealMedia Encoding Options screen:

The first decision you have to make is whether you want your video produced as a **SureStream** or just a single-rate file. You may only choose the former if you'll be uploading the file(s) to a RealServer G2 compatible streaming server (such as Helix Server). SureStream technology allows you to produce a single file that can be served at many different connection speeds. You see, when producing your content, you'll choose a **Target audience**. With this audience in mind, Camtasia Studio produces a media file at a given *bitrate* (number of kilobits per second), which is the rate that the data flows from server to client. The higher the bitrate, the better the video's quality, although people on slower connections won't be able to view your high-bitrate content. The video's bitrate simply exceeds their connection speed, and as a result, they can't view it.

This is where SureStream comes in. With it, you can select *multiple* target audiences, effectively producing several of the same video sequences (at different bitrates) and then packaging them into one file. When viewed online by the client, the server automatically selects the highest playback bitrate that the client can handle. Now, this technique can produce some very large files (depending on how many target audiences you select), but you will then be able to include users who wouldn't have otherwise had the connection capacity to see your video.

With **Single rate** video, you can only select *one* target audience, but you also have the advantage of playing back the content from any web server. A streaming server needn't be installed. So, if you don't have access to Helix Server (or if you're not sure, which probably means you don't), this is likely to be the best option for you.

Next, you'll need to choose an **Audio format**. RealAudio actually makes use of several audio codecs. The codec and its attributes will be auto-selected for you based on the type of audio content you have. Just choose an option from the drop-down list. Note that you can also choose **No Audio** if there's nothing in any of your audio tracks.

Now that the audio is taken care of, it's time to choose the **Video quality**. RealMedia only uses a single video codec to encode its video stream. This codec used to be based on H.263, but RealNetworks has since moved to a proprietary encoder. Just as with the Audio format, you've got a list of descriptive options in the corresponding drop-down list. Just choose the option that best represents your content, and you're good to go.

Before moving on, though, there are a couple of check boxes that have a dramatic effect on how your video is encoded. The **2-pass encoding** option analyzes and encodes your data in two separate steps (as opposed to one). This both increases the quality and can also reduce the file size, but splitting the encoding into two steps comes at the cost of increased production time. It's a recommended option unless you're really running up against a deadline (or you're just a generally impatient human being).

Finally, you have the option to encode your video with **Variable bit rate (VBR) encoding**. This means that all the little bits in your video will be parceled out intelligently, with more bits being dedicated to the complex portions of the video, and fewer bits going to the simpler sections where there's not a lot of motion or change. While the default option, Constant bitrate (CBR) encoding, is generally better suited for streaming, VBR can produce better quality. Just keep in mind that VBR-encoded files may take longer to buffer before they can start playing, which means a disconcerting delay for the user. And for those who are broadcasting their content from a streaming server, a sudden spike in bitrate due to fast motion or scene changes could end up exceeding the user's connection speed, thus resulting in an interruption in playback. You might want to forgo this option if you're streaming a video that has a lot of high-motion elements.

Camtasia Studio always remembers your most recently used settings. However, should you ever decide to return to the recommended "factory defaults," just click the **Default** button.

As far as playback of your content is concerned, you can produce a lone RM file and then link to it, so that the RealPlayer media player will open upon accessing it. Or you can embed the content into an HTML page (selectable from the wizard's Video Options screen), although doing so creates a lot of files. You'll have the RM file itself as well as the HTML file, a web style sheet (CSS), a JavaScript file (JS), and a number of image files that help to comprise the playback environment on the web page. Make sure you upload *everything* to ensure that the video displays correctly.

Camtasia for RealPlayer (CAMV)

Several years ago, TechSmith partnered with RealNetworks to deliver a lossless screen video solution to the RealMedia platform. Out of that partnership came the Camtasia for RealPlayer (CAMV) file format. These files are designed to play back pretty much exclusively in the RealPlayer media player. For the advantages and drawbacks of this media player, please view the previous section on the RealMedia (RM) streaming format.

Like the RealMedia format, CAMV files can be either streamed or progressively downloaded. *Streaming* a file means that it's broadcast, like a television or radio transmission. No files are left on the user's machine after viewing. This is of great benefit to those who want to better control the distribution of the content, since videos can't just be downloaded and otherwise disseminated to other people who have no business viewing them. You'll need a streaming server, such as Helix Server, in order to deliver true streaming. With *progressive download*, you only require a garden-variety web server. And downloaded files still enjoy the "streaming" advantage of instant gratification, as the video will begin to play very quickly, usually just a few seconds after the user clicks the "watch video" link.

That said, CAMV files are typically better suited to local and intranet delivery than distribution on the web. You see, *unlike* the RealMedia format, CAMV files are completely lossless, meaning that there's no loss in video quality whatsoever. In fact, the CAMV file format is really nothing more than an AVI encoded with the TechSmith Screen Capture Codec (TSCC) that subsequently had its extension renamed to ".camv." Lossless encoding works best for content with stable backgrounds, not much motion, and no photographic elements or color gradients. Even if you adhere to those guidelines, AVI files are just not as suitable for the web as some of the other file formats like SWF, FLV, or WMV. The one advantage a web-bound CAMV file can offer over a pure AVI is that the CAMV decoder resides on Real's servers, and should auto-download for your users the first time they try to access your content, thus reducing or eliminating any distribution problems. Even so, I'd be hard-pressed to recommend CAMV for Internet distribution.

Camtasia RealPlayer Plugin Encoding Options

If you choose **CAMV - Camtasia for RealPlayer streaming media** as your output method, you'll next come to the Camtasia RealPlayer Plugin Encoding Options screen:

This will allow you to do things like choose a target audience as well as set video and audio options. Let's begin with the **Target audience** section. Provided you've done your homework and know a little something about who's actually accessing your content, then you probably have a reasonably good idea as to their average connection speed. Go ahead and choose a target audience from the options that are listed in the dialog (displayed in order from lowest to highest bitrate).

The *bitrate* is the number of bits per second that travel from the streaming server to the client (audience). Every target audience has a corresponding target bitrate. For example, if you ignored my advice about not putting CAMV files on the web, and want to optimize the content for viewing on a 56 K modem, then the content will typically be streamed at 34 Kbps (kilobits per second). You can also create higher bandwidth versions for those with speedier connections, and for local playback, you can probably get away with choosing the highest bandwidth settings. TechSmith has specified certain bitrate defaults for each target audience, but these can be adjusted by clicking the **Target Bitrate Settings...** button.

Simply select an audience from the **Target Audience** drop-down list, and its current **Target Bitrate** will appear. Keep in mind that this is the total bitrate for both your video *and* audio. You can adjust this field as desired, but I generally find it best to stick with the default values, which are all plainly visible just below the field. Clicking the **Restore Defaults** button sets all target audiences back to their default values. Click **OK** when finished.

Also, bear in mind that the bitrate for your audio can be adjusted separately. For example, if you're willing to let the audio quality take a hit in order to secure a better picture at a particular bitrate, you can do so. Just click the **Audio Target Settings...** button. The dialog that appears is remarkably detailed:

For each target audience, you've got different compression settings for four different kinds of audio (Voice Only, Voice with Background Music, Music, and Stereo Music). For each one, select a bitrate setting from the drop-down list. To help you make a more educated choice, let me clarify a couple of the terms you'll encounter:

- **RA8.** This uses the RealAudio8 (ATRAC3) audio codec. It is a stereo-only codec, which you probably don't need.

- **High-response.** Specializes in capturing high-frequency audio data (such as a flute or a high-pitched female voice).

Don't forget that any bitrate you set gets subtracted from the total available bandwidth set in your Target Bitrate Settings dialog, so double-check to make sure you've got enough room left over for the video stream. And just as with the Target Bitrate Settings, you have a **Restore Defaults** button that takes everything back to the factory-installed settings.

Meanwhile, back on your Camtasia RealPlayer Plugin Encoding Options screen, you have a few more options to set before you can move on. In the section labeled **Video options**, you can adjust the following:

- **Colors.** This specifies the number of colors in the video's available palette. 16-bit (65,536 colors) is the default, meaning that little if any color information will be lost from your original video clips. You can also take the color depth down to 12-bit (4,096 colors) or 9-bit (512 colors).

- **Frame rate.** The number of frames per second at which the video plays back. This can be set to Automatic (maintaining the highest frame rate among the video clips in your project), or you can choose a different rate from the drop-down list.

- **Keyframe rate.** Specifies how often the encoder inserts a key frame into the video. For a full discussion of frame rate and key frames, see Chapter 7, "Recorder Tools Options."

For the audio side of things, simply choose an audio type from one of the four **Audio format** listings (or select **No Audio** if your video doesn't contain any). The compression options are taken from whatever is specified in the Target Audience Settings dialog's Audio tab for that particular target audience and audio format.

Finally, you'll need to specify a **Preroll** length, which is the number of seconds that RealPlayer will buffer your video before it begins to play. If you want to ratchet up the target bitrate a little to reduce the number of dropped frames, you can add to the preroll to help compensate. Just keep in mind that the higher your preroll, the more you're testing the patience of your audience.

At this point, you're probably thinking, "Wait a second. If I can produce a video for a 28 K modem target audience, how can that video *possibly* be lossless? There's gotta be a catch." Well, actually, there is. The Camtasia RealPlayer plug-in reduces the bandwidth by dropping frames, meaning that you won't be seeing the fluid playback at lower bitrates that you would normally experience. Provided you check **Show production results** on the wizard's Produce Video screen, you'll be shown exactly how many frames were dropped. In extreme cases (like our 28 K modem example), the final output will probably end up looking more like a slide show of image stills rather than an actual motion picture, which is part of the reason CAMV files are ill-suited for the web.

Of course, if you absolutely *must* create CAMV content for a low-bandwidth audience, there are a number of things you can do. The biggest one is to be really careful not to include any high-motion, high-color video content in your project. Recording at smaller video dimensions helps a lot as well. Some additional techniques include:

- **Bumping up the target bitrate.** Be careful about this one if you're broadcasting the content from a streaming server. If you increase the target bitrate beyond your audience's download capacity, you'll be in trouble. As I mentioned, you can help offset this by increasing the preroll.

- **Decreasing your audio bitrate,** thus lending more of the overall bits to your video stream. Obviously, your audio quality will suffer as a result.

- **Decreasing the frame rate.**

- **Decreasing the number of colors.**

Producing to this format creates a number of files. You'll have a CAMV file for the video stream, an RM (RealMedia) file for the audio stream, and a SMIL (pronounced "smile") file for synchronizing the two streams. This is the file that users will need to double-click (as opposed to CAMV or RM) to play back your video locally. And of course, you'll get an HTML file if you opted to embed your video in a web page.

Animated GIF File (GIF)

The GIF (Graphics Interchange Format) file format was introduced in 1987 by CompuServe Corporation. Due to its excellent lossless compression, GIF quickly became a mainstay of the Internet, and has still not yet been replaced by PNG (Portable Network Graphics) as the most popular lossless image format on the web. The only caveat with GIF is that it's limited to a palette of 256 colors.

Unlike most image formats, GIF also supports frame animation. Most of the advertising banners and other animated windows you see on the web these days are either SWF or animated GIF. As versatile as it is, GIF does have a few limitations:

- Because it must be completely downloaded before playback can begin, GIF animations are best for brief segments of less than one minute in length.

- You cannot include an audio stream.

- You only have 256 colors to work with.

If used appropriately, animated GIFs made with Camtasia Studio are wonderful. I've used Camtasia Studio to create web banners as well as brief animated segments for my PowerPoint presentations. Since embedded AVIs tend to have horrible scaling issues in PowerPoint, using animated GIFs instead can help overcome this limitation.

Animated GIF File Encoding Options

So, let's get busy with the **Animated GIF Encoding Options** screen. Since we don't have a lot of audio and compression options to contend with, this one is comparatively simple:

All the details of your current setup are plainly listed at the bottom of the dialog. The options available for you to adjust are:

- **Colors.** This is the number of colors to be used in the palette, from 2-bit (4 colors) to 8-bit (256 colors). **Automatic** will use the color depth that most closely corresponds to your clip's number of colors, which is pretty much always 256 colors.

- **Frame rate.** Here you can adjust the number of frames per second. Again, **Automatic** will try to approximate the clip's current frame rate, but when producing to animated GIF, it's generally best to reduce the frame rate somewhat.

- **Loop indefinitely** vs. **Play** *x* **time(s).** This specifies the number of times to play through the animation.

- **Optimized palette.** This option intelligently compiles the palette for the image based on the colors in your video project. This produces a superior-quality image.

- **Fixed Palette.** This uses the same color palette each time rather than optimizing the palette from the content. This is typically only useful if targeting users who are still using 256-color desktops (which is practically nobody at this point).

- **Include Windows colors.** This option keeps the "standard" 20 Windows colors as part of the palette, regardless of whether you've chosen an optimized or fixed palette. As these colors help to comprise a lot of screen objects (such as windows), I recommend keeping this option checked.

- **Dithered color reduction.** This option simulates a larger color palette by combining two or more colors to produce the effect of a new color. For screen recording, this is useful if capturing color gradients (one color smoothly transitioning into another) so that your content doesn't show a disconcerting banding effect.

If embedding an animated GIF into PowerPoint 2003 or 2007, be sure to set the Play x time(s) field to the number of times you wish the GIF to play *plus one*. For example, if you set this field to "2," then PowerPoint will play it through only once. Don't ask me why. Earlier versions of PowerPoint don't appear to have this problem.

Custom Production Presets

As you've been able to tell by reading (or skimming) through this chapter, there are an unbelievable number of settings available to you when producing your final video. To help you cut down on the sheer number of choices you have to make, TechSmith came up with a neat addition called custom production presets. If you're planning on using a particular set of production options relatively often, you can save these settings under a name of your choosing, and then just call them up whenever it's time to produce. They also give you a few stock options to which you *always* have access, to wit:

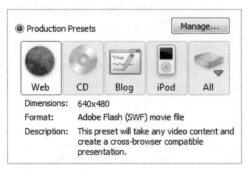

Your production presets. Any custom presets you created will be available in the **All** drop-down list.

Suddenly, with just a couple of clicks, you have everything set up just how you like it. Additionally, these presets can be used in conjunction with Camtasia Studio's Batch Production feature, letting you use that preset on several projects or videos at once — more on this in Chapter 15, "Other Output Options."

To get started **building your custom production preset**, do the following:

1. On the main Production Wizard screen, choose **Production Presets**.

2. You'll have a drop-down list available with the names of all your custom presets. Since you probably haven't created any yet, it's likely to only contain the default presets. Let's remedy that by clicking the **Manage...** button.

3. The Manage Production Presets dialog appears. Click **New....**

4. Enter a new **Preset name** and corresponding **Description**, and then choose a **Video file format.** Click **Next.**

5. Based on the file format you chose, you'll have the same series of options as if you'd selected the file format from the main Production Wizard screen. Just set your options accordingly, clicking **Next** to move on to the next screen of options.

6. When all your options have been selected, you'll be taken back to the Manage Production Presets dialog, where you'll see your new preset in the Production Presets drop-down list. The currently selected preset's information will be clearly displayed in the lower half of the dialog. At this point, you can add a **New** preset, **Edit** an existing one, or **Remove** any preset you no longer need.

7. Click **Close** to exit the dialog and use your new preset.

Remember that you can also save a particular set of production options as a preset. On the Production Results screen (at the end of a production), choose **Create Production Preset....** Give it a name and description, and you're done!

Summary

In this chapter, I showed you two very different methods of producing your edited project into a form that could be viewed by others. **Recommend my production settings** chooses the file format and settings based on the project's content and its desired output medium. Your other option is to choose all format and options settings **manually.**

If you'd rather specify everything manually, you need to consider the following:

■ How do you want to distribute the video? CD-ROM? E-mail? Web? If delivering over the Internet, would you rather have the content streamed or downloaded?

■ Does your video have high-color, high-motion components, or is it mostly screen video? This will have an effect on the compression method you choose.

- What are the constraints of your audience in terms of connection speeds and the kinds of media players they can use?

- How should you size your video for best visibility? Make sure you consider those members of your target audience with low-resolution monitors.

- Would your audience benefit by the inclusion of interactive components, such as quizzes and hotspots?

Once you have your settings chosen, don't forget to create a custom preset if you plan on using those settings often. This will not only be a boon to the internal consistency of your projects, but it's a real time-saver as well.

Exercises

1. Reopen your project from the previous chapter. If you skipped those exercises, there's a completed version of this project (MyProject_ch12.zip) in this chapter's media folder that you can import.

2. Produce your project as a **Flash SWF file** using the One Video with PIP and TOC template. Select **Use JPEG Compression** at **80%**. Choose whatever control bar you think looks best.

3. View a 30-second sample of your video using the Preview feature. Does everything look and behave as expected?

4. Add a preload movie to your video, using one of the sample preloaders located in this chapter's media folder. While still on the Controls tab, add some appropriate text to the About box.

5. Add a watermark to your video. You can use either the default watermark or the watermark.png image supplied to you in this chapter's media folder. Adjust the size, position, and formatting of the watermark to your liking.

6. If you created a quiz for this video, set up the video to report the results to your e-mail address.

7. On the Produce Video screen, check **Upload video to Screencast.com**, set up a trial account, and once production is complete, finish your upload to view it online. Using the service, send an invitation to someone else to view your work.

8. After producing your first video, go back and produce it again (or at least preview) using FLV. How does the quality and file size compare? Try a few other video formats.

9. Try producing the video into a mobile format (iPod, MP3). What challenges would you face in adapting this content for mobile devices?

10. Try producing your content using an ExpressShow format if you haven't already. Be sure to try out all the special customization options that go along with ExpressShow.

Chapter 13

CD-based Videos with Camtasia MenuMaker

While the development of Camtasia Studio has focused more on web deployment in recent years, output to CD-ROM or DVD-ROM remains the best way to deliver your videos with exceptional image and sound quality. With Camtasia MenuMaker, you can:

- Assemble your videos into one cohesive package
- Better control exactly how these videos are displayed
- Create an attractive front-end menu that autoloads upon insertion of the disc

In this chapter, we'll discuss all the juicy details of using this component of Camtasia Studio to create a world-class CD-ROM to distribute to your audience. We'll cover the entire process — from selecting a template and adding files to adjusting the look and functionality of your menu and testing and exporting it. But before we get ahead of ourselves, let's start with getting the program open.

You can **open Camtasia MenuMaker** in one of four ways:

- Choose **Start > All Programs > Camtasia Studio 5 > Applications > Camtasia MenuMaker**.
- From within Camtasia Studio or the Camtasia Recorder, select **Camtasia MenuMaker** from the **Tools** menu.
- From within Camtasia Studio, click the **Launch other tools** button on the Main toolbar, and then select **Camtasia MenuMaker**.

■ From within Camtasia Studio, choose **Create CD menu...** from the Task List, under the heading Produce.

Now that we've opened Camtasia MenuMaker, the main interface window appears, along with a special dialog that asks how we want to begin. Since MenuMaker is project-based, we're given options for either opening a menu we've made or creating a new one from scratch.

MenuMaker's Welcome dialog. If desired, this dialog can be turned off by unchecking the box at the bottom of the window. You can always turn it back on by choosing Tools > Options... from the main MenuMaker interface, and then checking Display welcome dialog on startup.

The options are as follows:

■ **Create a new project using the Wizard.** This will allow you to choose from a multitude of pre-existing templates, add your files, and give the menu a title before you're thrust into the main user interface.

■ **Create a new project (Advanced).** Actually, there's not too much distinction between this and the previous option. You're brought to a special dialog where you can select a template as well as give your menu a name. The only critical difference is that you aren't actually given the option of adding any files until you're working within the main user interface.

■ **Open an existing project.** Just like it sounds. A dialog opens that lets you browse for your project file (example: myfile.cmmp).

■ **Open a recent project.** Selecting this option activates a drop-down list, in which your last four most recent projects appear.

Simply select the project you want and then click **OK** to open that project. Note that you also have access to the last four most recent projects under the File menu, available in the main user interface window, which we'll come to in a bit.

Getting Started with a New Project

Let's start by using the wizard to create our first project. If you haven't yet left the Welcome dialog, simply select **Create a new project using the Wizard**, and click **OK**. If you're already in MenuMaker's main user interface, go to the **File** menu and choose **New...**, where you'll be given an opportunity to choose the wizard.

Once you've chosen to create a new project using the wizard, the first wizard dialog asks us to choose our template. It consists of a Templates window where we choose the template, and a Preview window that shows us what the selected template actually looks like. The dialog looks something like this:

You may notice that I have a lot more templates available to me than appear in *your* template window. This is because TechSmith provides a vast downloadable library of Camtasia MenuMaker templates for your use, absolutely free. These templates are currently available for download on TechSmith's web site*. The swanky new templates can be downloaded either collectively (careful, though: there are a great many

---

* At the time of this writing, the templates are available here:
http://www.techsmith.com/camtasia/accessories/mmtemplates.asp.

templates here, and the file size is *very* large) or as individual themed collections. I highly recommend picking them up.

To pick a template, simply click its corresponding folder to open it, and then click on the template name. A preview of that template will appear in the Preview window. Keep in mind that a template isn't just a background image (though that's all you'll see in the preview), but also a color scheme, and in some cases custom sounds and cursors (though these add to the template's file size). Can you create your own custom templates? You bet, and I'll show you how later on in this chapter.

Before continuing, make sure you're *very* happy with your template. While you can always pick another template from within the main user interface, a brand-new project is started whenever you do, so it is impossible to switch templates on a project in progress and retain all your work (don't ask me why). Once you're actively working in your project, you're basically married to the template you've selected, so choose wisely. Note that you can always return to the Choose Template screen while still in the wizard by clicking the Back button to page back through the screens.

Once you've found the template that best suits your project, just click **Next** and you'll move on to the Choose Files screen, where you can pick the files that will be included as part of your project. Just click the **Add Files...** button, and a dialog opens that will let you browse for all the files you want included. Once you've selected your file(s) and clicked **OK**, it appears in the dialog's files window. You can also include files from different directories in your project with zero problems.

Note that your options here aren't limited to AVI video files. You can add just about any kind of file you can think of, including videos, images, audio, or documents. Just keep in mind that your audience is going to need the appropriate application to open whatever file you want to add, and unless you're working in a corporate environment where everyone in the company has access to the same software, you cannot simply assume that your entire audience will have Microsoft Word on their machines, for example. So please be wary of adding files in formats that need costly, proprietary software in order to open them. If a particular file format has a free viewer application, you may wish to include it as part of your menu, or at least provide a link to download it (more on how to do this later).

One handy feature of the Choose Files screen is that it keeps a running tally of the disk space needed by the project at the bottom of the window. This is useful for determining whether all your desired files are actually going to fit on a single CD-ROM or DVD-ROM. You can easily see if you're going to go over the limit of the media format you've chosen, and if so, you can pare down the number of files, further compress your files (in the case of audio or video), or plan to split your content onto multiple discs. This total includes the file size of everything you've included in your project, including the menu itself.

If you wish to remove a file you've added, a simple click of the **Delete File** button will make it go away. Likewise, you can change the order of your items in a couple of different ways. The first way is with the Move buttons. Just click on the item you want to move. You can select multiple items by clicking and dragging. Then click **Move Up** to move your item(s) one step closer to the top of your list. **Move Down** obviously moves things in the opposite direction.

The second way to change the order of your items is by clicking one of the two Sort buttons. Clicking **Sort By Name** will put all your files in alphabetical order. **Sort By Type** will sort items by their individual file types. AVI files get paired with other AVIs, WAV files with other WAVs, Word documents with all the other DOC files, etc. Sorting by file type also puts the files in alphabetical order, just grouped by file type. You can obviously tweak the order to your liking by using the aforementioned Move buttons. Please keep in mind that the files you've added will all display on the main menu. If you have a lot of files you need to place in your menu, it may behoove you to create submenus for each chapter or file type rather than include everything on the main menu. More on how to do this later in the chapter. Once you're happy with the main menu contents, click **Next** to move forward to the third and final screen, Enter Title.

Here you're prompted to pick a title for your menu. This title will appear in the title bar of your finished menu, provide the file name of your menu's executable, and be the default file name for both your project file and the folder that contains your final menu (though these can be easily changed). That's all there is to it! Simply enter a title and click **Finished**.

Before we move on to working in our main user interface, I should at least mention the other method of starting a new project, **Create a new project (Advanced)**. It's really not that different from the wizard, except for two things:

- The options for picking both a template and a menu name are combined into a single dialog. Now you have everything on one screen, and getting a project started is more streamlined.

- The step for adding files is absent. It's often useful to skip this step if you want to start your menu but don't necessarily have all your files assembled just yet. Also, you may be unsure of how you want your menu laid out. For example, if you think you might want a menu with submenus rather than everything massed together in a single menu, it's a good idea to hold off on adding your files.

Regardless of whether or not you use the wizard, you needn't sweat too much over the project creation dialogs. They're only there to get things started for you. With the exception of choosing a template, all your decisions in these dialogs can be altered in Camtasia MenuMaker's main user interface, which we'll talk about next.

MenuMaker's Main User Interface

Once you've gone through the project creation dialogs, you'll end up inside MenuMaker's main interface window. In it, you've got a view of what your menu will probably look like, complete with a background image as well as your menu items displayed in a List Box. Additionally, you have:

- A menu bar that contains all your editing functions
- A toolbar for accessing the most often-used functions more quickly
- A status bar at the bottom of the window. When you hover the mouse over a toolbar button, a small tip will appear in this area that explains what the button does.

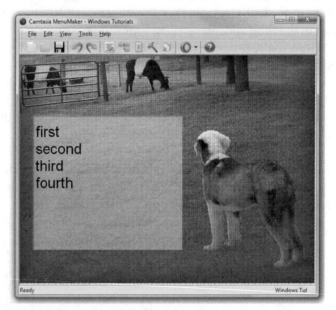

The Camtasia MenuMaker main UI.

We'll discuss the different menu items as they come up in the menu creation process, but to whet your appetite about the kinds of capabilities you can expect from this handy program, here's a quick rundown of the functions on the Camtasia **MenuMaker toolbar**, in order from left to right:

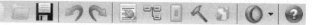

- **New Project.** Creates a new MenuMaker project.
- **Open Project.** Opens a pre-existing MenuMaker project.
- **Save Project.** Saves the current project.
- **Undo.** Oops! I didn't mean to do that.
- **Redo.** Oh, wait. I meant to do it after all.
- **Edit Menu Properties.** Brings up a dialog that allows you to add files, manage your submenus, and alter the look and feel of your menu.
- **Toggle Map View.** A click of this button will place you in Map view, which gives you a hierarchical view of your main menu and all your submenus. This is the ideal place to manage your submenus. Multiple clicks of this button will toggle you back and forth between Map view and the main screen.
- **Test Menu.** This tool will quickly give you a clickable sample of your menu without your actually having to build it first.
- **Create Menu.** This assembles all the pieces of your menu into one folder, including media files, menu data, and an autorun file (if desired). Once created, all you have to do is burn the folder's contents onto a CD-ROM, and you're good to go.
- **Wizard.** When clicked, MenuMaker asks if you wish to save the current project, and then creates a new project based on the wizard.
- **Launch other tools.** This provides a drop-down list from which you can instantly navigate to the other tools in the Camtasia Studio suite of applications.
- **Camtasia MenuMaker help.** This launches the help file.

 If you'd like the toolbar to display the name of each tool along with the graphic, a larger version of the toolbar is available that has this information. From the **View** menu, choose **Show Large Toolbar Buttons**.

The wizard does a pretty reasonable job of assembling all the essential elements of your menu, and if your navigation needs are simple, you may be able to go straight to the testing and final creation of your menu without any further tweaking. But what would be the fun in that? We're going to move on to discuss the Main Menu Properties dialog, where you can add files and submenus, and choose from a wide variety of options to alter the look and feel of your menu. But first, let's talk briefly about the menu's List Box.

The **List Box** is where all your menu items are displayed on the menu screen. Every menu item gets its own line, and if the number of menu items exceeds the amount of space that the List Box has to offer, small arrow bars will appear at the top and/or bottom of the box as needed to let you scroll through the entire list of items. It looks like this:

second
third
fourth
fifth
sixth
seventh
eighth

The user can scroll through a list of 40+ items, even if the box only has enough space to display seven at a time.

The size, color, opacity, and location of the List Box are all determined by the template you've chosen. The box can be transparent, opaque, or somewhere in between, and it comes in a glorious array of colors. And yes, all of these items can be changed. The two properties that can be directly manipulated from the main screen are the List Box's **size** and **location**. This works just like PowerPoint or any other vector-based graphics program you've ever seen. Click and hold over the box, and then drag it around to move it. To resize, click and hold one of the box's eight handles (those little black boxes that dot its border), and drag to expand or shrink the box.

Main Menu Properties

Of course, there are other ways to change the appearance and contents of your List Box. This is done in the **Main Menu Properties** dialog, which contains four or five tabs, depending on whether you're in a submenu.

There are a number of ways to **open the Main Menu Properties dialog**:

- Click the **Edit Menu Properties** button on the toolbar. This will open the dialog box on the General properties tab.

or

- The Edit menu will allow you to not only open the Main Menu Properties dialog, but actually choose which tab you wish to open. Click the **Edit** menu, and then choose **General Properties, Cursor Properties, List Properties, Menu Content,** or **Button Properties** (the latter can only be opened from a submenu).

    or

- Double-click the **List Box.** This will open the dialog box on the List properties tab.

Let's tackle the tabs on this dialog in order, starting with General.

General Properties Tab

As the name implies, the **General** tab contains some basic settings for how your menu will ultimately look. It contains three sections:

- **Menu title.** Remember giving your menu a name back when you first started your new menu project? Well, here's where you can edit the title you entered.

- **Background.** This section contains information and settings about the background image used in your menu.

- **Size.** The dimensions of your menu, measured in pixels. There are fields for Width and Height. The default size of your menu is specified in the template. Note that the dimensions of your menu need not match the dimensions of your video content.

While the first and third sections are pretty self-explanatory, the second section, Background, merits some further explanation. First, you have a field that shows the path of the image file you're using. If the file comes from a template, the field will be pointing to a temp directory, as Camtasia MenuMaker must first unpack the image from the template file that contains it. Of course, you may also select a different image to serve as your background. Simply click the **Open** button, located directly to the right of the Image file field, to open a dialog where you can browse for a new image file. MenuMaker will accept GIFs, bitmaps (BMP), and JPEGs (JPG).

Once you've settled on an image for your background, you'll want to specify a layout. Note that this option is only important if the dimensions of your menu exceed those of your image file. If they do, you'll need to instruct MenuMaker as to how to use this image in filling up the dimensions of the menu. You've got three options here:

- **Center,** which displays the background image at its normal dimensions, centered in the middle of the menu screen.

- **Stretch,** which takes the image and stretches it out to fit the dimensions of your menu. Image quality may degrade considerably if the dimensions of your background image are significantly smaller than the dimensions of your menu. If this is the case for you, you can always select...

- **Tile,** which takes the background image at its usual dimensions and repeats the image to fill up the menu window. This works best for images with very small dimensions.

If you chose the Center option (and the image is smaller than your menu), you need to choose a background color for the space of the menu that is not taken up by your background image. Simply click the **Background color** drop-down list to select that color from a palette of 48 colors, or choose **More Colors...** to create your own custom background color using HSL or RGB values.

Cursor Properties Tab

When creating your menu, it helps to design a uniform theme that carries throughout the entire presentation. This presentation starts with your menu, not your videos. After all, the menu is the first thing your audience is going to see. While an appropriate background image can really help establish this theme, there are additional visual and audio elements to aid you. The **Cursor** tab sports the ability to set a custom cursor as well as sounds for a mouse click and for the mouse hovering over a menu item.

The **Cursor file** field lets you enter a path to a custom cursor. This custom cursor will appear instead of a browser-like "pointed finger" whenever hovering over a menu item. Custom cursors are great for creating a cohesive theme. For example, say you've got a series of videos on the iPAQ personal digital assistant. You might try using a custom cursor in the shape of a stylus to help take your PDA-themed menu to the next level. While subtle, it is a nice touch, provided your cursor isn't so unwieldy as to inhibit functionality.

You can use any cursor file on your system, and the cursor will be packaged into your menu. You can either type the path directly into the field or click the **Open** button (🖼) to its right, which allows you to browse for the file. Camtasia MenuMaker can use both static cursors (.cur) and animated ones (.ani). So where do you get additional cursors? There are a number of software packages (such as IconWorkshop from Axialis, a demo of which is on the companion CD) that allow you to create a cursor from scratch, but if you wish to experiment with this feature right now, Windows generally has a number of default cursors. In Windows Explorer, access the drive that contains your operating system (usually C:), and then go to **Windows > Cursors**, and you should have plenty of cursors to play with.

In the **Sounds** section of the tab, we actually have two fields: **Mouse click** and **Mouse hover**. Setting an audio file in the Mouse click field will play that sound whenever the user clicks on a menu item. For Mouse hover, the corresponding file will play whenever the user places their mouse cursor over a clickable menu item. While setting a custom cursor is mostly a stylistic choice for subtly augmenting the theme of your menu, setting sounds for clicking and hovering actually enhances the usability of your menu by providing audio feedback. A mouse hover sound lets the user know that the text they're hovering on is actually clickable and not just static text. And a mouse click sound confirms that the user has actually selected something, which is particularly useful if you have larger videos that may take several seconds to open.

You set the audio file for these options in the same manner as setting the custom cursor, by either typing in a path or clicking the **Open** button to browse for it. However, with the Sounds fields you also have a **Play** button ( ) that will allow you to test out your file. Note that only WAV files (.wav) are supported. Try to keep these files to less than a second in length, as longer sounds either will be cut off as you hover from menu item to menu item or, in the case of a mouse click sound, can overlap with an opened video's audio track.

List Properties Tab

While the Sounds options can help you provide audio feedback for the user's actions, visual feedback is also quite handy. Let's move on to the **List** tab for a way to provide this feedback, and to decide exactly how our List Box will look in general. This tab has three sections: Text, Frame, and Position.

The **Text** section lets you set the text color of your menu items as well as their alignment inside the List Box. As with a web browser, we can instruct MenuMaker to use different text colors for menu items that have a mouse cursor hovering over them or for items that the user has already visited. These color settings are inherited from the template you selected, but they are fully customizable. We have three settings for a menu item's text color:

- **Normal color.** This is the standard color for your menu text. When your menu opens, all items will appear in this color.

- **Visited color.** Menu items that have already been clicked on will display in this color.

- **Highlighted color.** This is the color for a menu item that currently has the user's mouse cursor hovering over it.

To change one or more of these colors, simply click its corresponding drop-down box and select a color from the palette, or choose **More Colors...** to choose a custom color. In this section, you can also choose how you want the menu items in your List Box aligned. Just click the **Default Alignment** drop-down list and choose **Left**, **Center**, or **Right**. Note that this only changes what the alignment of the menu *defaults* to. You can manually adjust the alignment of each menu item as needed, which we'll talk about in detail when we get to the Content tab.

When looking over your main menu screen, you probably noticed that your list of menu items was encapsulated in a List Box. Now that we've discussed how to change the appearance of your text, it's time to customize the look of the box itself, called the *frame*. You can adjust the appearance of your frame in three ways. Use the **Frame** section to set the background color, opacity, and frame style.

The **Background color** field lets you choose the color of your frame. After selecting a background color, you may notice that the color in the dialog is darker than it appears in the actual menu. This is because the opacity of the frame is adjustable by using the **Blend effect** slider. Just click and hold on the slider, and then slide it to the desired point on the opacity spectrum, which runs from **Transparent** (completely invisible) to **Opaque** (completely solid). The text color of your List Box won't be affected at all by this option. Setting it all the way to opaque will show the actual color you selected, but if you make the frame totally opaque, make sure that there's enough contrast between this color and the text colors you selected to ensure legibility.

Finally, you have the option of choosing a border for your frame, using the **Frame style** drop-down list. You have five options:

- **None.** No border.
- **Bump.** This places a thin raised border around your frame.
- **Etched.** This gives your frame border a slightly sunken-in look.
- **Raised.** This option creates the illusion of the entire frame being slightly raised off the menu background, almost like a button.
- **Sunken.** This option creates the illusion of the entire frame being sunken below the menu background, almost like a pressed button.

The third section, **Position (pixels)**, gives you a way to numerically specify the exact size and location of the frame on your menu. It contains four fields. The **Left** and **Top** fields define the upper left-hand corner of your frame. For example, a value of 20 in the Left field means that the left-hand edge of the frame will start 20 pixels to the right of the menu background's left-hand edge. Meanwhile, the **Width** and **Height** fields give the frame its size. Personally, I find it much easier to simply move and resize my frame on the main menu screen by clicking and dragging on the frame (or its corresponding resize handles). But it's really useful if you want true precision in stipulating the location and size of your frame. For example, say you have a series of submenus in addition to your main menu. You just moved and resized the frame in your main menu, and you want the frames in all your submenus to be uniform with it. Simply note the location and size of your main menu frame, and then type this information into the Position fields of all your submenus.

Content Properties Tab

Now that we've tailored the appearance of the List Box to our liking, it's time to fill it up with content, and the place to do that is the **Content** tab. This is where all the magic happens. The tabs we've talked about up to now have sported some cool ways of customizing your menu, but they're mostly window dressing. Without the actual links, however, there would be no menu. So let's get down to business and add some content. If you started this project using the wizard, you probably already have some content in here. If not, we'll remedy that in short order. This tab has three basic sections: the toolbars, the content list, and the file fields. Let's tackle these each in turn.

At the top of the tab, you'll notice two toolbars: the Main toolbar and the Formatting toolbar. The **Main toolbar** looks like this:

The first four tools are all about adding items. If you followed the wizard, you already have some experience with the first tool, **Add files.** Clicking it will open a dialog allowing you to browse to pretty much any file you've got. Select your file(s) and click **OK**, and it appears in your content list. But files aren't the only kind of menu item that MenuMaker can handle. The next three tools will let you add other elements:

- **Add web address.** This will allow you to enter a web URL. When browsing your menu, a click on one of these links will open the person's default web browser and navigate to the page you've chosen.

- **Add static text.** This lets you create a menu item that is there for informational purposes only. It is not clickable.

- **Add submenu.** Sometimes you'll have so many menu items that sticking them on a single menu page becomes infeasible. Clicking this button will create a brand-new menu that is linked to the current one. Upon clicking, you're prompted for a submenu name, and the link on your current menu (as well as the submenu itself) is created. We'll talk more about submenus later in this chapter.

The next two tools in your arsenal pertain to the removal of items you've added. The first, **Delete Selected Items**, gets rid of any menu items selected in the content list. Note that you can select multiple items using all the standard Windows conventions for multiple selection (e.g., click and drag, Ctrl-click, etc.). If you want to chuck everything and start all over from scratch, then use **Delete All Items**, which does exactly what it says. Snip, gone. At least it gives you a warning to make sure you really meant to do it.

Now that you've added some items (as well as trimmed any fat), you may be wondering just how one can change the order of these items. Clicking and dragging won't work; that just selects multiple files. This is where our next two tools come in. Just like in the wizard, the **Move Up** and **Move Down** tools take whatever files you selected and shifts them upward (or downward) line by line. And yes, multiple files can be moved at once. Of course, if you have a great many items, you might just want to sort them and be done with it. You've got two options here. **Sort Items Alphabetically** puts all your menu items in alphabetical order, while **Sort Items by Type** first sorts your items by file type, and then places the individual items in alphabetical order within each type. If you clicked one of these two buttons, any new items added will be sorted automatically.

If you do not specify a sort order, then MenuMaker (for some unknown reason that defies all logic) places the new item just *above* your current position on the list. So, if you already know the order in which you want to place your items, it's best to add them from the bottom up, at least if you don't want to get *very* well-acquainted with the Move Up and Move Down tools.

Finally, we come to the **Edit Parameters** tool, which lets you add command line parameters to the file in question (some applications call these parameters *switches*). These parameters are little codes that tell the application exactly how you want the file opened. Every application has different parameters that they support, so if you don't know exactly what application the end user will employ to open your file, it's generally best to leave this button alone. For our purposes, however, it's a great tool to use in conjunction with Camtasia Player, since we can instruct MenuMaker to package Camtasia Player with our menu, and to use only that program when playing back our AVI files. To take advantage of parameters, simply click the Edit Parameters tool and then type your parameters into the text field that appears.

Now, we can globally set most of Camtasia Player's parameters in our Project Properties dialog (more on that later). But if you don't want all your files to open exactly the same way (e.g., you want one file to repeat over and over until closed, another file to play in full-screen mode, etc.), then you can set those parameters here. For a full list of Camtasia Player's available command line parameters, please see the section on the Camtasia Player in Chapter 15, "Other Output Options."

Next, let's talk about our Formatting toolbar. These options affect how the text is displayed in the List Box, and each menu item can be formatted individually (or as a group, if doing a multiple selection). These tools are designed to help you custom-tailor the formatting of single items, as they override the default settings chosen in the Project Properties dialog (for font, font style, and font size) and in the List tab of the Main Menu Properties dialog (for alignment). After changing some settings on the Formatting toolbar, if you decide to add a new item, that item will still adhere to the project and menu defaults. So, here's a look at our **Formatting toolbar:**

■ **Font.** This drop-down list allows you to select from all fonts on your system. Keep in mind that fonts aren't packaged or otherwise rendered in Camtasia MenuMaker, so you may wish to stick with the more standard fonts to avoid problems on the viewer's end.

- **Font size.** This determines the point size of your text. Click to select one of the standard sizes from the drop-down list, or type in any whole number for a custom size.

- **Font style.** Three buttons control the font style: **bold**, *italic*, and underline. These are toggle buttons; clicking the button again will turn the effect off. Note that these styles can be combined.

- **Alignment.** Left-, center-, or right-justify your text. This trumps the default setting for text alignment on the List tab.

Below these toolbars, we of course see the **content list**, which displays all the files, web links, static text, and submenus we've added. There are three additional fields that appear below the content list that bear mentioning. Every menu item has the following two fields:

- **Name.** This is the name of the menu item. File menu items pull this information from the file name, web links from the URL, static text from itself, and submenus from the name you typed in. In all cases, this name is fully editable. Simply select the errant text in this field and type a replacement.

- **Tooltip.** This is the text that will appear in a little yellow box when the user hovers the mouse cursor over a particular menu item. This text can be anything you wish. By default, your videos are assigned the tooltip "Watch this movie." Of course, the default tooltip is contextual for each kind of menu item, even among files ("View this document," "Listen to this audio file," etc.).

Depending on the kind of menu item you're working with, you may also see one of these fields:

- **File name** (files only). This is the path of the file you're including in the menu. Unfortunately, this path is not editable; you cannot simply point to another file by typing in the path. This means that if your MenuMaker project file is somewhat older and the files it references have been moved or renamed since you last opened it, you'll have to remove the menu item and create a new one in its place.

- **Web address** (web links only). This field defines the URL of the web page you want to link to. It is fully editable, so if the page gets moved, you can type a new address in the field.

And don't forget: You have an **Approximate disk space...** readout at the bottom of this dialog, which can help you determine if your file space requirements are going to exceed the capacity of your media. Always check it before executing the Create Menu... command.

Button Properties Tab

At last we've come to the fifth and final tab in the Main Menu Properties dialog, **Button**. What's that you say? You don't have a fifth tab? Well, friends, that's because this tab is specific to submenus, so we actually have to *be* in a submenu in order to see it.

No worries, though. Here's how to **navigate to one of your submenus**:

1. If you haven't already done so, create a submenu on the **Content** tab of your Main Menu Properties dialog. Click **OK** to return to the main screen.

2. Ctrl-click on the menu item for your submenu.

   or

   Click the **Toggle Map View** button ( ) to enter Map view. Double-click one of your submenus.

3. Open your **Submenu Properties** dialog.

4. Click the **Button** tab.

The Button tab is split into two nearly identical sections, with the same settings for each of two optional (but recommended) navigation buttons. You have the **Back button**, which will take the user back to the current submenu's parent menu (one level up), and the **Home button**, which takes the user all the way back to the main menu. These two buttons, combined with the submenu-type menu items, comprise MenuMaker's navigation structure. Each of the two sections on this tab contains the following elements:

- **Show Back** (or **Home**) **Button.** These check boxes determine whether the buttons for Back or Home are displayed.

- **Button.** This drop-down list displays several graphics you can use for your button. In addition to five "back" buttons and five "home" buttons, MenuMaker also includes five "up" buttons, in case you'd rather use that metaphor to signify a return to the parent menu.

- **Tooltip.** A brief phrase that indicates what the button does. This text will appear in a small yellow tooltip box when the user hovers over one of your buttons for a second or two. The default values here are completely editable.

- **Left position** and **Top position.** These two values govern the placement of your button, and are measured in pixels away from the top and left edges. For example, a top position of 400 means that you want the top of the button to be 400 pixels down from the upper edge of your menu. While it's usually easier to simply click and drag these buttons around on the main screen to place them, assigning numerical values is often useful for lining these two buttons up on a vertical or horizontal axis.

- **Preview.** A full-size image of what the button would look like at the current settings. It updates in real time.

- **Colorize button.** When checked, this option allows you to color your button.

- **Color 1** and **Color 2.** A drop-down palette of colors for your button. Color 1 stipulates the border color, while Color 2 determines the fill color.

These settings not only affect the current submenu, but also set the default for any subsequent submenus that branch off from it, which you can then alter to your heart's content if you want it to be different. And then any submenus created from *that* submenu would inherit *its* settings, and so on.

For all the options in the Main Menu Properties dialog, you can **view the changes made on all tabs** *without* having to exit the dialog. Just follow these easy steps:

1. If you have adequate space on the desktop, drag your Main Menu Properties dialog out of the way so that you can see as much of your main menu screen as possible.

2. Make whatever changes to the menu properties you wish.

3. Click the **Apply** button at the bottom of the dialog. Your changes will automatically update on the main menu screen. Note that not all changes (e.g., custom cursors, among others) will be visible without first testing the menu. We'll discuss menu testing later in this chapter.

So, in this section you've learned all about how to manipulate the look, feel, and content of your menu using the Main Menu Properties dialog, including how to adjust the buttons of your submenus. In the next section, we'll talk more about submenus, including how to organize them using the Map view.

Submenus and the Map View

Submenus are wonderful not only for separating large sections of menu items into palatable chunks, but also for splitting these elements thematically. With the exception of the actual menu items, all of the submenu's properties are inherited from its parent. However, every submenu has its own set of menu properties, which can be individually manipulated apart from the other menu screens. In other words, each submenu can look drastically different from the main menu, complete with a different background image, different sounds and cursors, different text formatting, and of course different menu items.

Unlike all the other menu items on your menu screens, the submenu items can be navigated on the main screen while still in Edit mode. Simply Ctrl-click on the submenu name to go to that submenu. To navigate backward, Ctrl-click on one of the navigation buttons (provided you haven't disabled them): **Back** to go up one level to the parent menu and **Home** to return to the main menu. However, this is not the only way to navigate between your various menus. One easy method is to use the **Map view**.

You can **access the Map view** in one of the following two ways:

- From the **View** menu, choose **Map View**.

  or

- Click the **Toggle Map View** button.

Keep in mind that either of these options can be toggled; simply repeat the step to exit Map view when finished.

Map view is laid out to give you a broad overview of your submenu hierarchy. Your main menu and all your submenus are visible, and the relationships between menus are easy to spot. The Map view looks like this:

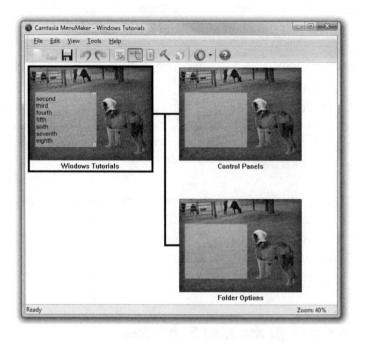

Viewing Your Menus in Map View

If your needs are simple, the default view of your submenu map may be all you need, but as the number of files increases, so does your need to have a little extra real estate in order to fit everything on one screen. You have three options for sizing the menu boxes to your liking: **Zoom in** (Ctrl-Plus), **Zoom out** (Ctrl-Minus), and **Zoom to Fit** (Ctrl-F9), which gives you the largest possible size while still fitting everything on one screen. In addition to the keyboard shortcuts, these commands can all be accessed on the View menu. The Zoom percentage will show in the right-hand corner of the status bar.

When you first enter Map view, you'll notice a black border around the menu from which you accessed this view. A single click on a menu box will shift the selection, whereas a double-click will open that menu in the standard view.

In addition, you can use Map view to instantly access any of the tabs of the current menu's Main Menu Properties dialog.

Getting to a tab from your Map view is done in one of the following two ways:

1. In Map view, click the menu whose properties you want to adjust.

2. In the **Edit** menu, choose one of the following options: **General Properties**, **Cursor Properties**, **List Properties**, **Menu Content**, or **Button Properties** (the latter is disabled if the main menu is selected).

   or

1. In Map view, right-click the menu whose properties you want to adjust.

2. Choose one of the menu's properties tabs from the context menu that appears.

Adding and Removing Submenus

If you've read this far, you probably already know that submenu-type menu items can be added or removed on the Content tab of the Main Menu Properties dialog. What you may not know is that the Map view, in addition to offering a great view of your menu structure, also lets you add and remove submenus at will.

There are two ways to **add or remove submenus**:

1. In Map view, click the menu from which you want your new submenu to branch (for adding) or the menu you want to delete (for removal).

2. In the **Edit** menu, choose **Insert submenu** or **Delete this submenu** as appropriate. These menu options are grayed out when not in Map view.

   or

1. In Map view, right-click the menu from which you want your new submenu to branch (for adding) or the menu you want to delete (for removal).

2. Choose **Insert submenu** or **Delete this submenu**, as appropriate, from the context menu that appears.

Note that the Delete this submenu option is disabled when the main menu is selected, as it's impossible to delete this menu. Whenever adding a new submenu, it appears with a line drawn from its parent so that you can easily see the relationship between menus. Unfortunately, there's no way to drag these menu boxes around to shift the hierarchy of submenus. However, there is a way to redistribute the actual content of your menus, and you'll learn how in the following section.

Moving Content between Menus

Especially if you started your Camtasia MenuMaker project using the wizard, you may have created your project with *all* your menu items on your main menu. When entering the main screen for the first time, it's possible you discovered that your menu was a bit too crowded for all these items, and that the creation of some submenus was in order. Does that mean all the time you spent picking out your files in the wizard was wasted, and that you need to start over from scratch with your submenus? Luckily, no. There's a special tool, available only from the Map view, that lets you shift your menu item content from one menu to another. It's called the **Project Content** dialog, and it looks something like this:

Menu items can be moved both within and between menus in the Project Content dialog.

Here's a quick guide for **moving your menu items around** with the Project Content dialog:

1. In Map view, choose **Project Content...** from the **Edit** menu. The Project Content dialog appears.

2. Select the item you want to move by clicking on it. You can select multiple items by Ctrl-clicking on them.

3. Click and hold over your selection, then drag the item(s) to the new location. Each submenu listing will highlight as you mouse over it. When the desired submenu is highlighted, release the mouse button to place your item(s).

or

Click the **Up** (↑) or **Down** (↓) buttons located above the menu item list to move your selected item(s) line by line, and menu by menu, until the item(s) is in the desired location.

4. Click **OK** to exit the dialog.

With the exception of submenu-type menu items (whose location is obviously set by the submenu hierarchy), all menu items can be moved in this way. In addition to moving content *between* your menus, this dialog also is a great alternate way to change the order of your menu items *within* a particular menu. Another cool aspect of this dialog is that the menu thumbnails in your Map view update automatically as you're moving things around, so provided you're zoomed in close enough to read your menu text, you can get a real-time view of how your changes are affecting what the user is going to see.

Project Properties

In visiting the Main Menu Properties dialog, we learned that we have a multitude of settings for adjusting the look, feel, and content of our menus. We also discovered that we can define an entirely different set of properties for each and every menu. But Camtasia MenuMaker has another dialog containing *global* settings for your menu structure, meaning that these settings affect the entire project. This dialog is called **Project Properties**, and can be accessed from the File menu.

The Project Properties dialog, where preferences that affect the entire project can be set.

The Project Properties dialog contains three sections: Preferences, Display, and Resources.

Project Preferences

The **Preferences** section contains two check boxes that control how the menu and its AVI files are presented:

- **Start menu automatically when CD-ROM is inserted.** Checking this option will include an autorun.inf file with the project that instructs the operating system to run a particular program (in this case, your menu executable) upon insertion of the disc. This is pretty standard on most multimedia CD-ROMs and program installation discs, and prevents the user from having to search around on the disc in order to launch your menu. Unless you have a compelling reason to disable it, it's best to keep this setting enabled.

- **Use Camtasia Player for AVI files.** When you check this box, MenuMaker will package a copy of Camtasia Player on your disc as well as ensure that any AVI files on your menu will open specifically in Camtasia Player. For more about the benefits of using this handy AVI player, please see the section on the Camtasia Player in Chapter 15, "Other Output Options." If you have AVI files in your project, I *strongly* recommend keeping this feature enabled.

When you check the Use Camtasia Player for AVI files box, notice that a button marked **Options...** becomes available. This will open the Camtasia Player Options dialog, allowing you to set a wide variety of preferences pertaining to exactly how you want Camtasia Player to handle your AVI files. Here's a quick breakdown of these preferences:

- **Start playing automatically.** When checked, Camtasia Player begins playing your AVI file as soon as it loads, as opposed to starting the file in paused mode.

- **Exit after playing video.** As soon as the video concludes, the file closes. While a bit cleaner than leaving the file open, it also means that if the users want to go back and rewatch part of the file, they have to click the corresponding menu item again.

- **Repeat video until closed.** This option effectively puts your video in an "infinite loop," playing it over and over again until the user finally closes it.

- **Stay on last frame.** By default, the playback head returns to the first frame of the video upon reaching the end of the file. Checking this option will force it to remain on the final frame. This is handy for when you've attached an ending title screen with your URL and other contact information.

- **Always on top.** If checked, your videos will always be on top of all the other windows on your desktop, regardless of which window has the focus.

- **Play in maximized mode.** This automatically maximizes the Camtasia Player window immediately upon opening the video. If the user's screen resolution is greater than the dimensions of your video, your video will be surrounded by a colored background that takes up the rest of the screen.

- **Play in fullscreen mode.** Your video will play full screen. If the user's screen resolution is greater than the dimensions of your video, your video will be surrounded by a colored background that takes up the rest of the screen. The video's title bar, menu bar, toolbar, and status bar will all disappear.

- **No title bar.** This option opens your video without a title bar. When coupled with the option No dragging by video area, the user will be unable to move the video window.

- **No menu bar.** Ditto, except this time it's the menu bar that gets the ax.

- **No tool bar.** You get the idea. Careful with this one, though. The toolbar is where your video's scrubber bar and other navigational controls are located.

- **No status bar.** This bar shows the video's playback status as well as its elapsed running time and total duration. Click here to get rid of it.

- **No dragging by video area.** Normally, the user can move the window not only by clicking and dragging the title bar, but also by dragging from anywhere in the main video window. This option disables that capability.

- **Background color.** When in maximized or full-screen modes, you're going to see a background color if the dimensions of your video are smaller than the resolution of the user's monitor. This option allows you to choose this color from a palette. Just click the drop-down arrow and select a color.

Note that these options affect *all* the videos in your project, but if you want a different option for one or two of your videos, you can set parameters for that menu item on the Content tab of your Main Menu Properties dialog (see that section for details). Also, while you're not able to set different presets in the Camtasia Player Options dialog (like you can in Camtasia Studio's Audio Format dialog, for example), you can save one custom configuration for these settings if you have particular settings you use all the time. Just check off your items and then hit the **Save as Default** button. If you have a special project where these options need to change, a simple click of the **Load Default** button upon conclusion will bring back all your old settings.

Display Preferences

Now that we've set up how our videos will be displayed, it's time to specify the display properties of the menu itself. The **Display** section of this dialog will let you set the display mode as well as the default font for your menu items.

The **Display mode** option lets you select from two methods of displaying your menu:

- **Window**, which places the menu in a window on your desktop. Your task bar and possibly other windows and desktop icons will still be visible.

- **Full screen**, which places the menu window on a solid-colored background. The color of this background can be selected using the **Desktop color** drop-down control. Unlike full-screen mode for your videos, the menu still technically displays in its own window, only this time the menu window is sitting upon a background that covers everything else.

Your other option in this section is the **Default Font...** button. Clicking this button will bring up a dialog that lets you select the font, font style, and size for your menu items. Plus, you've got a handy Sample field to see just what your default will look like, and for menus with non-Western language characters, you can select any script supported by the font you've chosen. Any new menu items will display using the font information specified here, but pre-existing menu items won't change. To change the font settings for individual menu settings, please see the section called "Content Properties Tab" earlier in this chapter.

Remember that Camtasia MenuMaker does not package your fonts with your menu, nor does it render these fonts in any way. If you specify a font that the user doesn't have installed, the menu program will use a substitute, which probably won't look at all the way you intended. It is therefore advisable to use only the fonts that come with Windows.

Resources Preferences

In order to add a final stylistic touch to your menus, you have a few additional file resources you can add in the **Resources** section. These are nothing critical, but are nice effects that can give your project a little extra something if done subtly. You can specify a file for a custom icon, startup sound, and exit sound, either by typing in a path or by clicking the **Open** button (🖿) and browsing to it. Let's tackle these each in turn:

- **Icon file.** When creating your menu, you have the option of choosing a custom icon for your menu executable that fits your content stylistically. There are numerous royalty-free icon files (.ico) available online, or you can create your own with a program like Axialis IconWorkshop (www.axialis.com), which is the most comprehensive icon creation utility I've ever seen. I've been nice enough to include a trial version of this software on the companion CD-ROM, so go install it and start crankin' out those icons. Camtasia Menu-Maker can then assign your newly created icon to your menu's program icon, rather than using its own stock icon (which, by the way, looks like this: ◉).

- **Startup sound.** When the menu first opens, you can use this option to play a WAV file containing intro music or instructions. This field also has a **Play** button (◁) that will let you sample your sound.

- **Exit sound.** The same kind of deal, except that the audio file plays when the user clicks to exit the menu. This file can be a musical exit, a "thanks for watching" message, or even sales information such as a toll-free number to call. Keep it short and to the point, though; people tend not to like it when their windows don't quickly close when thus commanded.

Project and Template Files

Remember to save often when working on your project. All your settings are encapsulated in a special MenuMaker project file (.cmmp). As with any other Windows document, if saving for the first time, you'll be prompted to choose a file name and location. Subsequent saves will assume you want to save over the top of this file.

You can **save your work** in a number of ways:

- Click the **Save** button ( ) on the MenuMaker toolbar.
- Use the keyboard shortcut **Ctrl-S**.
- Choose **File > Save Project**. If you wish to save your project under a new file name or location, choose instead **Save Project As....**

Another way to save your work is to save your settings as a template file (.cmmtpl). Doing so will save all your project properties and main menu properties settings, but won't save any of the actual content. This creates a convenient starting point from which you can assemble subsequent menus. If you know you're going to create a lot of menus with the same general look and feel (such as when a project is going to span multiple discs), it's a good idea to create a template so that you're not having to constantly reinvent the wheel. This template will show up with all your other templates whenever you create a new project.

To save your template, simply choose **Save as Template...** from the **File** menu, and you'll be prompted for a name. Enter a name, and the template will be automatically saved in the template directory. This directory is stipulated in MenuMaker's Options dialog.

To **change the default template directory**, do the following:

1. In the **Tools** menu, choose **Options....**
2. In the field called **Select template folder**, enter the path of the folder you wish to use, or click the **Open** button to browse for the appropriate folder.

The Final Step: Testing and Creating Your Menu

If you've read this far, you've learned how to create your main menu and submenus as well as choose their look and function. Now you're ready to do one final test run before taking it prime time. You can use the **Test Menu** command to do this, which takes all the settings in your Main Menu Properties and Project Properties dialogs into account, so you end up with a very accurate view of what your audience will experience.

> There are a couple of different methods for **testing your menus**:
> - From the **File** menu, choose **Test Menu**....
> - Click the **Test Menu** icon ( ) on your toolbar.

I recommend testing out your menus thoroughly before bothering to create the real deal. Click on each and every menu item and check out every submenu to make sure everything works as expected. Remember, the menu creation process entails pulling together all your different file elements and saving them in one place, which means that both time and file space get expended every time you do it. Do make sure the menu is problem-free ahead of time.

Menu Creation

Now that you've extensively tested your menu, it's time to create it. This final step packages all your file-type menu items, menu executable, autorun file (if desired), icons, and audio files into one central place where it can finally be burned onto a CD-ROM, ready for duplication and eventual distribution to your audience. Fortunately, since you've already done most of the work, the creation process is pretty painless.

Other than testing, the one other thing you must do prior to creating your menu is to check the Content tab of the Main Menu Properties dialog of any of your menu screens. At the bottom of this tab, the **Approximate disk space used by Project** is displayed. Make *absolutely certain* that whatever media you'll be using has adequate space for your project.

To **create your menu**, just do the following:

1. Click the **Create Menu** button (🔨) on the toolbar.

   or

   From the **File** menu, choose **Create Menu....**

2. The **Camtasia MenuMaker Wizard** will appear. In it, you can specify a directory in which to place your new project folder, either by typing in a path or by clicking the **Open** button to browse for the directory. Then type in a folder name. This field will already be populated with the name you gave your menu, but you can change it at will.

3. Click **Next**, and you'll be prompted to confirm the creation of the folder if it doesn't already exist. Click **OK**. Of course, if you *have* already created a menu under that name, then you'll get a dialog asking if you want to overwrite it. Click **Yes.**

4. At this point you'll have a wait, the length of which depends on the quantity and size of the files you're compiling. Once done, the wizard will finish, with a final screen asking if you would like this new folder opened for you automatically. If you leave this option checked and then click **Finish**, your menu will appear in Windows Explorer, ready to burn to your media. Unfortunately, Camtasia MenuMaker does not sport any built-in burning capabilities as of yet, but just about any CD-ROM creation tool should work just fine. Remember to include the *contents* of your exported menu folder, and *not* the folder itself. Also, be certain to include *everything*, including all subfolders; otherwise, the menu will not work. Once the burn process is complete, you're done! The disc is ready to ship off to a friend or to a production house for mass duplication.

Just because your menu tested out well using MenuMaker's Test Menu feature doesn't mean your testing duties are over. After creation, test the created menu by opening the project's executable (.exe) to make sure *everything* is working. After you burn your disc, be certain to test the disc on a couple of different machines. Does the disc autorun work okay? Does the menu (and your videos, for that matter) display as intended at different monitor resolutions? Is the playback hiccup-free on slower drives? While testing can be time-consuming depending on the amount of content, it costs far less time, money, and hassle to ensure that things are working properly *before* you pay for duplication services and send a million of these discs out into the world. So test early, test often, and then rest assured that your audience is viewing your content exactly as you intended.

Summary

If it's your intention to produce your content for delivery on CD- or DVD-ROM, Camtasia MenuMaker can let you quickly and easily create a front-end menu for it.

Here's the easiest way of **creating a menu with MenuMaker**:

1. Create a new project using the wizard.

2. In the wizard, you'll be able to select a template, add the files you wish to have accessible in your menu, and give the menu a title.

3. In the Main Menu Properties dialog, you'll be able to alter the formatting of your menu as well as add additional links and content.

4. If you need to split up your navigation into smaller chunks, Camtasia MenuMaker lets you create submenus.

5. Be sure to test your menu to make sure everything's in good working order.

6. After everything's been tested, simply produce your project, and then burn those files to CD or DVD with any disc burning application.

Now that we've learned how to create CD-based navigation, we'll be talking about a web-based solution for the same thing. It's called Camtasia Theater, which is the subject of our next chapter.

Exercises

1. Provided you've done the exercises up to this point, you should now have a video about MenuMaker, complete with a Flash hotspot that takes you to a download page with more MenuMaker templates. Let's take advantage of this. Go to the template download page and install some (or all) of the additional templates.

2. Start a new MenuMaker project using a template of your choosing. Add a few AVI files that you've created while working on your projects thus far.

3. Add a mouse click and mouse hover sound. If needed, feel free to pull the click.wav and hover.wav files from this chapter's media folder.

4. Alter the color and alignment options of your text to suit your taste.

5. Add some static text to your menu. Then add a blank line (hint: empty static text line). Finally, include a web URL of your choosing.

6. Test your menu. Does everything work as expected?

Chapter 14

Web-based Videos with Camtasia Theater

While still very often used when the highest quality is called for, CD-ROM based videos are increasingly giving way to web-delivered content. In recent years, increases in bandwidth, coupled with advances in compression technology, have given rise to an exponential increase in video content available online. As we discussed in Chapter 12, "The Production Process," there are several file formats supported by Camtasia Studio that work for web output, but the one most recommended for screen video (at least if your videos don't have a camera video component) is Macromedia Flash (SWF). Theater was designed specifically for SWF files.

Unfortunately, Theater has been somewhat neglected compared with the Camtasia Studio application, and it is now in dire need of a makeover. People who wish to use Theater should be aware of the following:

- It does not currently support the inclusion of Flash video (FLV) files.
- It does not support the addition of quiz or survey content in your SWF files.
- As mentioned in Chapter 12, the playback controller of a SWF file produced with Camtasia Studio is no longer compatible with Theater. All your SWF files should be produced using the Legacy template if you plan on using Theater. Otherwise, any Flash hotspots that are part of your project will be broken.

TechSmith is aware of this gap in functionality, and plans on officially updating Theater soon. In the meantime, they have a partial (read: unsupported) solution called Theater06, which is included on the book's companion CD. It addresses the above limitations and contains a few additional surprises to boot. I'll tell you more about Theater06 at the end of the chapter.

Part of the appeal of SWF as an output format for your videos is interactivity. Camtasia Theater is an application that uses the SWF file format to create an *interactive menu* that appears next to the video screen in your browser window, letting you string a series of videos together into one cohesive presentation. While not supporting the wide range of presentation options offered in Camtasia MenuMaker, Theater allows you to assemble your videos under one navigational menu and, if desired, can even proceed from one video to the next with no action required on the part of the user. Its ever-present menu list gives your web audience an easy way to jump from video to video. This menu gives your viewers total control over which segments they want to watch, and is therefore ideal for the web, where bandwidth is at a premium. So, without further ado, let's open up Camtasia Theater and explore its many capabilities.

To **open Camtasia Theater**, please do one of the following:

- Choose **Start > All Programs > Camtasia Studio 5 > Camtasia Theater.**

  or

- From within Camtasia Studio, Camtasia Recorder, or Camtasia MenuMaker, choose **Camtasia Theater** from the **Tools** menu.

  or

- From within Camtasia Studio or Camtasia MenuMaker, click the **Launch other tools** toolbar button and choose **Camtasia Theater.**

  or

- From within Camtasia Studio, choose **Create web menu...** from the Produce section of the Task List.

You are started off with a new Theater document, a blank canvas waiting to be filled with your SWF files. The menu bar consists of only two menus: File and Help. The **Help** menu is obviously for finding answers if you run into problems, as well as getting technical support, checking for upgrades, etc. The **File** menu allows for the management of your Camtasia Theater projects. It contains the following options:

- **New** (Ctrl-N), for starting over with a brand-new Theater project.
- **Open...** (Ctrl-O), for opening a project you already saved.
- **Save/Save as...** (Ctrl-S), which saves your current work as a Camtasia Theater project (.camthtr). Remember to save early and

V: Sharing

often. Save as... allows you to select a file name and location, and it is the only save option available for a new project. Note that these options merely save the work you've done in Camtasia Theater so that it can be edited at a later date. It does *not* compile your project for presentation. For this, we need...

■ **Export Flash Menu** (Ctrl-E). Once you've added all desired SWF files and set any additional options, this button compiles your project with all SWF videos and menu navigation in one folder, ready for posting to your web site.

But we're getting ahead of ourselves. First, we need to actually put some content here if we want Camtasia Theater to create a menu out of it. Fortunately, this isn't tough. As you can see in the main Theater interface, we have two tabs: Menu and Controls. The former lets us add our files and determine what the menu looks like, and the latter takes care of the control bar details such as the appearance of the controller and the selection of a preload movie (if desired). Let's examine what each of these tabs has to offer.

Menu Tab

Your **Menu** tab is where you determine things like font, color, and size of your menu items as well as specify what videos are going to be part of your menu. It is divided into three basic sections: General Properties, Colors, and Menu List.

General Properties

In the **General Properties** section, you probably want to start off by giving your menu a name. Note that this is the name of your overall presentation, not an individual component thereof. Simply type a name into the **Menu title** field. Upon production, the folder and file names of your project data will derive from the text you enter here. While the menu name can be pretty much anything you want, non-IE browsers tend to have issues with accented characters (e.g., *ñ, ö, á*, etc.), so you might want to keep this in mind when naming your menu. Take a look at the finished menu here:

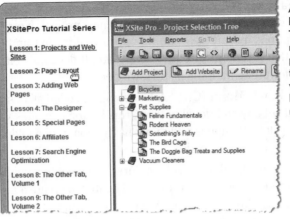

A menu created by Camtasia Theater. The menu can be placed either to the left of your video (as shown here) or to the right.

As you can see, you've got your menu title at the top, with the individual menu items listed beneath. You can adjust the font size for both the title and the menu items. Just click the **Menu title font size** or the **Menu item font size** drop-down arrow to select an appropriate size. As there's no preview, settling on a size can be tricky, and you may have to produce multiple menus before you're happy with the result. Keep in mind that your menu area is pretty narrow, so if you have lengthy title names, it's probably best to keep the font size small.

Also note that your menu needn't necessarily display to the left of the video area. You can change the **Menu alignment** by clicking on the drop-down arrow and choosing your desired alignment: left or right. This is more than merely an aesthetic choice. If your videos have large dimensions and you want to be sure that your menu isn't clipped at smaller monitor resolutions, you'll probably want it on the left. If the navigation aspect is less important to you than making sure your viewers see your video in all its full-screen glory, you might want to place it on the right.

Finally, you have the choice of whether to **Play movies in sequence**. This option has an effect not on the menu's appearance, but rather on the behavior of your video content. When this option is checked, whenever the user finishes viewing one of the videos in your menu, the next video in the series queues up and begins to play. This is a handy feature if you have a series of videos that build upon each other, such as step-by-step tutorials. It can be a real convenience for users, who aren't constantly having to click in order to proceed in the series. The menu provides visual feedback using an underline (as well as the defined Item rollover color; more on that in a second) to make clear exactly which video in the sequence the user is currently watching.

Colors

In the **Colors** section, you have the option of defining a custom color scheme for your menu. You can set the color of the following menu components:

- **Movie background.** This is the background color that displays behind your video. You will only see it if the video in question isn't large enough to fill up the entire playback area.

- **Menu background.** This is the background color of the navigational bar that displays the individual menu items.

- **Menu title.** The color of the menu title you entered.

- **Item normal.** This is the color of a menu item in its normal state (i.e., not actively playing or being hovered over).

- **Item rollover.** A menu item becomes this color whenever the user hovers over it with the mouse cursor. In addition, any *active* menu items (where its corresponding video is currently playing) display in this color, plus have an underline, so as to let the user know which video is currently playing.

Menu List

At the bottom of the Menu tab, you'll find the **Menu List**, where you can assemble all the SWF files that go into your project. Right now, the list window is empty. Let's remedy that. We'll navigate to some SWF files and add them to the list. If you don't currently have any SWFs on your machine and you can't wait to get cracking, there are some on the CD-ROM in the folder for this chapter.

There are a few different ways to **add files to the Menu List**:

1. Click the **Add SWF movie** button, which is located to the right of the list. It looks like this: 🔳.

2. A dialog pops up, allowing you to navigate to your desired file. Just double-click the file, or single-click and then click **Open.**

3. Repeat this step for each individual SWF file you want to include (for some odd reason, multiple selections don't work here).

or

1. Click the **Add all SWF movies in folder** button. It is also to the right of your Menu List, and looks like this: [icon] .

2. A Browse for Folder dialog opens, which lets you open the contents of an entire folder. Browse through the file list by clicking the + to open folders or by double-clicking on the folder itself.

3. When you've navigated to the desired folder, click the **Open** button to add *all* SWF content in that folder to your menu list, organized in alphabetical order. However, for SWF files produced in Camtasia Studio, this is often less than ideal, since Camtasia Studio can produce a number of by-product SWF files, such as video preload movies and the playback controller. Both of these become superfluous when creating a Flash menu with Theater, since Theater efficiently creates only *one* set of these files that work with every video in your project. It is therefore not necessary to add these files.

   or

1. Open a file window in Windows Explorer. This can be done by right-clicking on your **Start** button and then choosing **Explore**.

2. Move and resize your Explorer window so that this window and your Camtasia Theater window are side by side.

3. Click and drag a SWF file from your Explorer window to the Menu List window inside Camtasia Theater. With this method, it is possible to select multiple files using **Ctrl-click**, and then drag them all over at once.

As mentioned, when adding your SWF files to the list, you need only worry about the actual video SWF file. It is not necessary (or desirable) to add the SWF files of your controller or preloader. In fact, you should be producing the SWFs using the **Legacy** template exclusively, and playback controller files should therefore not be present in the folder at all.

Now that we have some video files to play around with, let's see how we can manipulate the Menu List window and the files it contains. First off, note that the window is divided into two columns: Menu item name and Menu item file.

Your file's **Menu item name** is the title of the menu item that will
actually appear in the navigation menu. By default, it takes its name
from the file name, but a double-click in this field will select the name
so that you can type a replacement. The **Menu item file** can be similarly replaced with a double-click in its field. This time, the **Add
movie items** dialog appears once again, and all you have to do is
select a new file and click **Open**. But rather than merely adding a new
file, the newly opened file replaces the file you double-clicked. The
Menu item name for the file also changes accordingly, even if you had
previously edited it.

Now let's talk about arranging our items into some kind of order.
While Camtasia Theater lacks the autosort tools of MenuMaker, it is
possible to manually change the sort order of your individual items.
This process can be a tad labor intensive if you're adding a long list of
files, so it's helpful to add these files in the order in which you want
them to appear, so that your sorting tasks are minimal.

To **change your sort order**, simply follow these steps:

1. Click once on the menu item you wish to move (on either
   field).

2. Click the **Move movie up** or **Move movie down** button to
   shift your menu item up/down by one slot. These are
   located to the right of the Menu List, and look like this:

3. Continue until the video is where you want it. If one of the
   arrows is grayed out, that means that the menu item is
   already at the top (or bottom) of the list and cannot be moved
   further in that direction.

4. Repeat for subsequent menu items. Sorry, no multiple selections are possible in the Menu List; all files need to be
   moved one at a time.

If you want to remove any items you've added, just select it and click the **Remove movie** button to the right of the Menu List: ✖.

We have export options down at the bottom of the tab, but before we compile our final presentation, let's first have a look at the Controls tab.

Controls Tab

The **Controls** tab is where all the settings related to your video controls are located. The video controls constitute the scrubber bar and accompanying buttons that control the playback of your video. The Camtasia Theater control bar looks just like the "classic" control bar in Camtasia Studio. It is the only control bar currently available in Theater, and it looks like this:

Camtasia Theater provides your viewers with precise controls to command all the action.

This control bar gives the user the following controls:

- **Play.** The playback head begins to move through your video.
- **Pause.** This stops the playback head at the current point.
- **Stop.** This stops the playback head and returns to the beginning of the current video.
- **Scrubber bar.** This bar gives the user precise control over the location of the playback head. Clicking anywhere on the black portion of the bar makes the playback head jump to that exact location in your video. Your users can also click and hold on the playback head itself, and then drag it to a new location.
- **Rewind** and **Fast Forward.** Clicking these buttons will send the playback head backward or forward by a certain percentage.
- **About/File Info.** Clicking the button marked with the Camtasia Studio logo will bring up a special box with two tabs: **About**, which will display up to eight lines of custom information you enter on the Controls tab of Camtasia Theater, and **File Info**, which will provide the file's URL, size (in KB), and duration (in number of frames). This box can be disabled on the Controls tab.

The Controls tab is where you can adjust both the look and functionality of your control bar as well as determine how (or *if*) a preload movie is displayed. The tab has three sections: General Properties, Duration/ Elapsed Time Properties, and Preload Movie Properties.

The Controls tab on one of my current projects.

General Properties

The **General Properties** section of the Controls tab contains a collection of a few essentially unrelated commands that don't really fit anywhere else. As such, it's easy to forget they're there, even though these commands are actually quite useful. To wit:

- **Paused at start.** Checking this box will start the video in paused mode, so that the user must actually click the Play button in order to begin viewing. Note that this option pauses at the beginning of *every* video in the series, not just the first one.

- **Movie controller color.** You may find the gray control bar a tad on the blah side, so why not give it a little color to go along visually with the color scheme of your videos? A click of this button will allow you to choose from a broad palette of colors. The current color displays in a little square preview box.

- **Show About box.** When describing the control bar, I mentioned the About/File Info box as a way of providing custom information about your video project. I also mentioned you could turn it off —

simply clear this check box, and the About button will no longer display on the viewer's control bar.

- **About text.** Provided the Show About box check box is enabled, this text field will let you enter up to eight lines of text that your audience will see whenever they click the About button on their control bar. You can use this space for anything from copyright information to a web URL to a "last edited on *x* date" info window. When viewers click the About button, they're requesting more information: who made it, when, etc. It's up to you to determine for your specific audience what they'll likely want to know, and then provide that info.

Duration/Elapsed Time Properties

If you take another look at the control bar from a few pages ago, you'll notice that there's a small info window to the right of all the control buttons. This window shows the *elapsed time* (exactly how much time has elapsed since the start of the video) as well as the *duration* (the total length of the video). You can easily change the format of this information or remove it entirely. We'll discuss each of these options in turn.

First, you have to decide if you want to include this information at all. The check boxes **Show elapsed time** and **Show duration** are checked by default. If you want to exclude one or both of these elements from your control bar, simply clear the appropriate check boxes. If neither box is checked, the elapsed time/duration information window will be missing from the control bar. If either box is checked, you have a few additional options that control the format of the information.

In the **Display format** drop-down list, you can choose what time elements you want displayed, and how. Just click in the drop-down and select an option. Here's how these formats break down: The capital letters **HH**, **MM**, and **SS** represent the number of hours, minutes, and seconds, respectively, that are present in the elapsed time or duration. The lowercase letters **h**, **m**, and **s** are the actual acronyms for these time elements. Say, for example, your video has a duration of 3 minutes and 28 seconds. If you selected HH:MM:SS, the display would read 00:03:28. If you selected MMm SSs, it would read 03m 28s. If both **Show elapsed time** and **Show duration** are checked, then your format selection affects them both — there's no way to select a different format for each.

Now that you've chosen a format, you also have a bit of control over how the text itself looks. While you can't choose a font size due to the fixed size of the control bar, you can choose between Times New Roman and Arial for your **Font** as well as select a **Font color** by clicking the appropriate control and selecting from the list of options. Remember, the window's background color is always white, so it's important to select a relatively dark color in order to maintain a legible level of contrast.

Preload Movie Properties

As you continue to work with Camtasia Studio and the complexity of your projects increases, you're likely to end up creating some pretty lengthy videos. Depending on the type of content and the amount of compression, you could end up with rather large file sizes, accompanied by some long load times that your audience is forced to put up with. Your users might start to wonder what exactly is going on after staring at a blank screen for 10, 20, or even 30 seconds after they clicked to begin the video. While the black portion of the scrubber bar will begin to fill as the video loads, this may not be enough of a visual indicator that something is in fact happening, and that the user should hang on just a few more seconds for your presentation to start.

This is where a *preload movie* comes in. This movie is a small SWF file (often called a *stub movie*) that informs the user that your video is in fact *loading already, so just cool your jets and watch the pretty animation*. These movies are generally very small in size — you want it to load instantaneously, after all; otherwise you'd need a preload movie *for* your preload movie! Most have some kind of simple animated sequence, from a standard loading bar to a cute/humorous segment that gives the audience something engaging to watch while they're waiting for the actual video*. Camtasia Studio comes standard with a very serviceable preload movie (located in the Resources folder in your install directory), and Camtasia Theater thoughtfully links to the movie by default so that you don't have to go searching for it.

---

* To give you a sense of the possibilities, I have also taken the liberty of putting a few additional preloaders that I created onto the companion CD-ROM. They're free and freely distributable, so feel free to use them in your own projects at will. Enjoy.

Now, let's talk about exactly how we add a preload movie to the videos in your menu. Here's a breakdown of the controls you have at your disposal:

- **Show loading movie.** A click on this check box gets the process started.

- **Match movie size.** To save on file space, preloaders generally have very small dimensions. Clicking this option automatically scales your preload movie up so that its dimensions match that of your video. If unchecked, the preload movie displays at its original size, possibly revealing the background color of your project.

- **Loading movie URL.** This field is where you enter the location of the preload movie. This location can be a file path, and the file will therefore be included in the exported menu folder. You can click the **Open** button to help you browse for it. The location can also be an externally referenced web URL, either absolute (e.g., http://www.mywebsite.com/preloader.swf) or relative (/videos/ preloader.swf).

- **% of main movie to preload.** This is the percentage of the video that needs to preload before it begins to play. The preload movie plays during this period. The lower you set it, the less time your audience has to wait for the loading video to begin, but the higher the risk of playback being interrupted due to incomplete loading. I tend to ratchet it down (to, say, 10%) if the duration of the video is quite long, as the remaining content would have plenty of time to load in the background during playback. For shorter, sexier (read: big file size) videos, I'll crank it up to around 50%.

- **Minimum preload movie display time.** This is the minimum amount of time for the preload movie to display. Should you have a relatively quick-loading movie, not having a value entered into this field will either skip the preload entirely, or it will appear on the screen for the approximate duration of a subliminal message. So, unless that's your intention, my recommendation is to keep your preload movie going for two to four seconds. That way, a user's fast connection won't spoil the swell branding message you so carefully assembled.

The latter two options (% of main movie to preload and Minimum preload movie display time) go hand in hand. *Both* conditions have to be met before the preload movie quits and the actual video begins. Keep this in mind when setting these values.

Exporting Your Flash Menu

Now that you've visited both tabs in your Camtasia Theater application, you've probably noticed that the same two options appear at the bottom of both tabs, namely a check box called **Launch Menu after export** and, of course, the **Export Flash Menu** button.

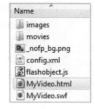

☑ Launch Menu after export

Export Flash Menu

You'll see these options at the bottom of the Camtasia Theater window, regardless of which tab you're currently viewing.

Clicking the former will actually launch the HTML page that contains your menu elements so that you can preview it directly after its production. It's a good idea to keep this item checked. But it's the Export Flash Menu button that gets the whole process rolling. Upon clicking, you're presented with a dialog that prompts you for an output directory. Do keep in mind that the names of the output folder, the SWF video, and the HTML file that displays it are all taken from your menu name, and as such you are not given an option to name the files. Note that you can alter the name of the project folder and the HTML file without any glitches, so if you want accented characters in your menu name (refer to the discussion of this in the "General Properties" subsection in the "Menu Tab" section of this chapter), or if you prefer that the page be named index.html for easy referencing, feel free to change it. However, leave the file names of your SWF files alone unless you're comfortable editing the accompanying XML document (and we'll talk about how to do this in Chapter 16). At any rate, find the directory into which you want your production folder to go, and click **OK**. If a folder with that name already exists in that directory, a warning dialog will appear, asking if you wish to overwrite the pre-existing folder. A click on **Yes** means that the old folder and its contents will be replaced, choosing **No** will give you the opportunity to choose a different directory for your new project folder, and **Cancel** escapes back to the main Camtasia Theater interface in case you need to rethink what your next move should be.

Once you start the production process, a status dialog will update you on Theater's progress. With any luck, you will soon see a congratulatory message telling you that your project was successfully exported. Before moving on, let's talk briefly about the different components of your production folder. Its contents probably look something like this:

Name
📁 images
📁 movies
🖼 _nofp_bg.png
📄 config.xml
📜 flashobject.js
🌐 MyVideo.html
▶ MyVideo.swf

Your **HTML** file (mymenuname.html) is the web page your users will access when they want to open your presentation. This is an automatically created file that already contains all appropriate references to your SWF and XML files needed to view the presentation. When a link is clicked on this page, the user will be presented with the navigation menu, control bar, and the first video of the series.

So what if there are circumstances where you *don't* necessarily want to start with the first video in your menu? For example, you may have a web page that discusses one particular feature of your software, but the video project you created that specifically addresses that feature is the fourth video in a series of 10. You can instruct the HTML file to load the exact video of your choosing with the movie query string parameter. Instead of pointing to www.mysite.com/myvideo/myvideo.html, you can do something like this: www.mysite.com/myvideo/myvideo.html**?movie=4**. This example would instruct the presentation to load per usual, only this time starting with the fourth video in the series.

The folder's **SWF** file (mymenuname.swf) contains the actual menu, video window, and control bar created by Camtasia Theater, but understand that these items are dynamically populated with settings and menu items by the accompanying **XML** file (config.xml). This is a special markup file that puts everything together, containing pretty much all the settings you specified in Camtasia Theater, including the menu tree structure as well as the format of both the controls and the menu. And while not terribly complex, there are two additional folders with project-specific content. The **images** folder contains all the images making up the neat "brushed metal" border effect that appears around your menu, control bar, and video content. The **movies** folder is comprised of your project's SWF videos (including the preload movie if applicable), all assembled in one place. These files are just copies of your original SWFs; the Camtasia Theater export process doesn't alter them in any way.

Now that you know what all these files do, it's time to upload them to your web server. There's no real trick to it; just fire up your favorite FTP client and put the entire folder into a directory of your choosing. As I mentioned, feel free to change the name of the folder as well as rename your HTML file index.html. After all, a link called www.mysite.com/myvideos is significantly cleaner than www.mysite.com/myvideos/mylongandboringfilenamethatiseasily-mistyped.html.

Also, do remember to upload *everything*, the entire contents of your production folder. In addition to not forgetting any files, keep in mind that all those files need to maintain the correct directory structure. For example, your videos *must* be in the movies folder, and if they're not, you'll end up with a beautiful menu that doesn't play anything. And who wants that?

Theater06: A Robust Workaround

As I mentioned at the start of the chapter, the current iteration of Camtasia Theater has some pretty stark limitations in light of Camtasia Studio's current capabilities. It has been in dire need of an update for some time. Fortunately, TechSmith has recognized this and is beginning to work on a solution. While not quite ready for prime time, **Theater06** is a new version of Theater that they've posted to the TechSmith User-to-User Forums, and I've been granted permission to pass it on to you. Since it's not an official release, I will not be going through the application in any degree of detail, but as it represents a number of drastic advancements over the current Theater that are likely to find their way into the very next version of Camtasia Studio, I'll give you the dime tour.

First off, go ahead and open the Theater06 zip file from the CD, and extract its contents to a safe location on your hard drive. There are actually two applications we have to play around with: Theater06.exe and ConfigEditor.exe. Go ahead and open the first one. Via the Open tool or by simply dragging and dropping, you can add SWF and FLV files (or their corresponding config.xml files):

As you can see, this window is relatively bare, without a lot of the formatting choices you saw in Camtasia Theater. Don't worry; we'll come to formatting in a moment. You can click **Advanced options...** to enter a title for the HTML document, to specify a preload movie, or to add basic character formatting to your TOC items. When ready, click **Create!** to produce your web menu.

Now this is where things get interesting. Go ahead and open the second application, ConfigEditor.exe. Using this application, you can edit all kinds of information about your project. To use it, just navigate over to the folder where you exported your Theater06 project, and find the file **config.xml**. Drag that bad boy over to the leftmost pane of the ConfigEditor window, and release. The application window suddenly comes to life with several categories of properties that affect the aesthetics and functionality of your project, and they can all be adjusted:

Don't like the default theme you're given? Just click the drop-down arrow to change it...

So, if you wanted to change the font of your TOC items, make your control bar a new color, pick a different theme, it's rather straightforward to do so. There's a small notes field in the lower left-hand corner that tells you the function of any property you click on. Just below that, you have a **Preset...** button that will let you save a particular set of properties as a preset, so that you can be consistent between projects if desired. We'll talk a lot more about the customization of the config file in Chapter 16.

Summary

For those looking to string multiple SWF files into a cohesive presentation, complete with table of contents, Camtasia Theater is a viable solution. While the application is in need of an update to make it fully compatible with all SWF and FLV content, Theater can still make use of SWF files produced with the Legacy template.

To create a **full web menu using Camtasia Theater**, do the following:

1. Produce all needed SWF files using the Legacy template.
2. Use the **Add SWF movie** command to add your SWF files to the Menu List. Reorder as needed.
3. Give your menu a title, and choose formatting options such as font, font size, alignment, and colors. Choose whether you want the videos to automatically play in sequence.
4. If desired, add an **About** box, format your **Duration/Elapsed Time Properties**, and select a **Preload Movie** to display while the main videos are loading.
5. Choose **Export Flash Menu** to build your menu for upload to your web site.
6. If you have Flash quizzes or FLV files to include in your Theater presentation, or if you just want finer control over the look and feel of the output, the unofficial Theater06 release can provide at least a partial solution.

In the next chapter, we'll be exploring the remainder of our sharing options with tools such as batch processing, Pack and Show, and the Camtasia Player.

Exercises

1. Produce multiple SWFs using the Legacy template to prepare them for use in Camtasia Theater.

2. Add these videos to a new Theater project. Give your project a name.

3. Play with text and background color combinations until you've developed a color scheme you're happy with.

4. Choose a preload movie for your videos. If you find the included ones boring, then keep in mind that the sample movies from Chapter 12 can also be found in this chapter's media folder.

5. Export and preview your menu. Does it look and function as you had expected?

Chapter 15

Other Output Options

At this point we've covered the production options in Camtasia Studio as well as shown how to create an attractive front end for your videos, both for CD-ROM (MenuMaker) and web distribution (Theater). But there are some additional features in Camtasia Studio that can augment your file production, thus assisting you in sharing your videos with the world.

This chapter is divided into three sections. First, we'll discuss the wonders of batch production, helping you take a multitude of files and put them in a desired format. Then we'll talk about using Pack and Show to make EXE files out of videos, helpful in a totally locked-down environment where no additional software may be installed. And finally, we'll go over the Camtasia Player, an elegant little AVI player that is simple without being simplistic.

Assembling Multiple Videos with Batch Production

Say you have created a series of 20 tutorial videos about your company's performance evaluation software, producing them as SWFs to upload them to the corporate intranet. Then you get a call from management. The files are too large, and people are complaining of long download times. So, you begin to pitch the usual list of suspects on how to make the files smaller (try lossy SWF or FLV, more audio compression, reduce frame rate, etc.). You agree on a plan of action. Right before hanging up, your manager says, "Oh, and we need them all by tomorrow." Click.

Time to panic? Nope, not with the magic of **batch production** at your fingertips. Rather than reproduce every single video in the series, you can set up *all* the video files to produce in a specific file format with specific settings. Just start the process and walk out the door at five. Barring a freak power outage, you'll have all 20 videos produced and waiting for upload when you arrive the next morning. So, let's fire up our Batch Production Wizard and go to it. It is launched from Camtasia Studio, and can be run regardless of whether or not a project is currently in memory (the project won't be affected).

You can **launch batch processing** in one of the following two ways:

- From the **File** menu, choose **Batch Production....**

    or

- In Camtasia Studio's Task List, click on **Batch Production** (Produce section).

The Batch Production Wizard appears. This dialog is a multi-step wizard. Our first stop is the **Select Files** screen, so let's do what it says, and add some. Let's click on the **Add Files/Projects** button. A dialog pops up that will let you browse for both video files (including CAMREC files, AVIs, MPEGs, and WMVs) and entire Camtasia Studio project files (*.camproj). Simply browse to the directory where your files are contained, select them (multiple selections are possible by holding down the Ctrl key), and then click **Open**. If your desired files are split across multiple directories, you can repeat the process by clicking **Add Files/Projects** again.

Creating a Production Preset

Choose **Next**, and you'll end up at the **Preset Options** screen. If you created a preset or two back in Chapter 12, "The Production Process," you will see them listed here. If not, the list will be grayed out, and it's up to you to create one. Click the **Preset Manager...** button. The **Manage Production Presets** dialog appears, and if you have any presets created, they'll be listed here. If not, we'll have to create one. To begin a new preset, click **New....**

The **Preset Editor Wizard** comes up, the first screen of which is called **Create a Production Preset**. If you've worked with the Advanced Production Wizard that we discussed in Chapter 12, this new wizard will look rather familiar. The production steps are laid out more or less the same:

1. Choose an output file format.

2. Set your encoding options.

3. Choose a video size.

4. Select additional video options.

But we're getting ahead of ourselves. This first screen differs a little, in that we're provided a couple of text fields that ask for a preset name and a corresponding description of up to four lines. The preset name is the text that you'll see listed when it's time to pick a preset in the future. So, following our example of the 20 videos, I'll enter "Performance Eval Video SWFs" as my name and something like "Lower quality SWF setting in response to manager request 9/30/07" for the description. Resist the temptation to enter setting-specific information in your description, as this info will automatically be listed under Preset information in your Manage Production Presets dialog, anyway. Here's what the dialog will look like once you've completed the preset:

The Manage Production Presets dialog. You've got a bird's-eye view of your preset's name, description, and settings. From looking over this info, you can edit the preset, delete it, or start a new one from scratch.

Back in the Preset Editor Wizard, your next step is to choose a video file format, which in our case will obviously be **SWF**. Click **Next**, and you're presented with the **Encoding Options** screen, which if you'll recall is specific to the chosen output format. To achieve a smaller file size, I'll set Frame Rate to 5 fps, Colors to 16-bit, and Audio Format to MP3 (11.025 kHz, Mono, 16 kBits/sec). Then it's on to the **Video Options** screen. Once you have everything set the way you like, click

Finish to add the preset to your list, where you can select it over and over again on similar projects.

That's the beauty of presets. For every preferred set of output options you have, just set your desired options once, and you don't have to do it again. Ever. Also, you don't have to be in batch production to use your presets. When producing from your current project, you may recall from Chapter 12 that you have the option of choosing one of your established presets to produce your final video rather than using one of Camtasia Studio's two production wizards.

Using Your Presets to Batch Produce

So, once you've managed to create a preset or two, go ahead and close out the Manage Production Presets dialog. This will bring us back to the Preset Options screen in our Batch Production Wizard, where we now have the option of picking a preset from those we just created in the processing of our files. There are two ways to go about it:

- **Use one preset for all files/projects.** Just select a preset right within this screen, and this preset will be used for all files and/or projects you selected. This would be the way to go in the performance evaluation example I gave.

- **Use a different preset for each file/project.** When you click the **Next** button after choosing this option, you get a special bonus screen, allowing you to select a preset from a drop-down list for *each and every* file or project. At the bottom of this screen is an additional **Preset Manager...** button that will let you add, edit, or delete your presets.

So, you've got one option for producing a bunch of file/projects in one format, and you've another option for producing a bunch of file/projects with a different format for each. But what if you have just *one* file or project that you need to convert into a multitude of file formats (such as when you want to give the viewer a choice between different formats or bandwidth requirements)? Well, there's actually a super-secret *third* option to let you do just that. On the Select Files screen, click the **Add Files/Projects** button and select your file. Repeat this step, selecting the same file over and over. You can select multiple instances of the exact same file or project, one for every output preset. Then, on the Preset Options screen, choose **Use a different preset for each file/project**. Click **Next**, and pick a different preset for each instance by clicking a preset name and choosing a preset from the drop-down list, just like this:

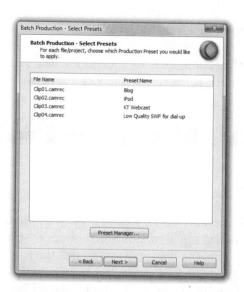

Just keep in mind that if you're using the same file type for more than one preset (multiple AVI presets with different settings, for example), the files will be named by number. That is, the first will be called myfile.avi, the second myfile(2).avi, etc. It may be worthwhile to instead make copies of your file and then rename each appropriately (myfileHQ, myfileLQ, myfileSWF, etc.) prior to doing the batch production.

Finally, a click of the **Next** button will bring you to the dialog's **Finish** screen. Here, you're prompted for an **Output Folder.** Special directories will be created in your chosen output folder to house your new file(s) that bear the name of the original file or project. Either type in the path or simply click the **Open** button to browse for it. Checking the **Show production results** check box gives all sorts of valuable information upon completion of your production, including the start and finish time, the size of each file, and a rundown of all the production settings.

Once you've set your options here, a click on the **Finish** button will set the process in motion. So, feel free to grab a cup of coffee, or if you're working with a whole lot of files, take a little nap under your desk. The **Rendering Batch Production** dialog keeps you abreast of the status of your production, both for the current file/project and overall. From the file list, it's easy to see which files have finished producing and which are still pending. After it finishes, you'll get a handy summary of all production activity, provided you didn't disable the Show production results check box (and I strongly recommend that you don't).

So now you have all those lovely fresh new (smaller) files ready for upload, and you've hit your deadline with flying colors. Management is happy, the viewing audience is happy, and you didn't have to pull an all-nighter to make it happen, which makes you happy too.

Creating Executable Files with Pack and Show

When dealing with the business world, you may find yourself in what is known as a "locked-down" environment, where users are prohibited from installing software, and the kind of file types that the user can actually read is therefore greatly restricted. While a CD-ROM created with Camtasia MenuMaker can alleviate this problem (no install required), there are times when you just want to share a quick file with someone, and the **Pack and Show** feature of Camtasia Studio is ideal for this kind of quick exchange.

Pack and Show takes your video file and packages it in an executable (*.exe) file. While other file types are supported, AVI files receive the greatest benefit from this kind of packaging. As I've mentioned in previous chapters, AVI files recorded with Camtasia Studio are by default encoded with the TechSmith Screen Capture Codec (TSCC). The problem lies in the fact that this codec is *not* included with Windows, so if a user wishes to view your AVI on their machine, they must first install the codec. With Pack and Show, you can:

- Package the codec in with the video for display with the user's default media player. This means that TSCC would automatically be installed, if not already present on the system, prior to starting the video. However, being in a truly locked-down environment (where any sort of installation is *verboten*) would obviously make this option infeasible.

- Or you can opt to package the Camtasia Player along with your video in the EXE. The codec is therefore not necessary, as the TSCC-decompressor is baked into Camtasia Player. Also, since the player does not rely on any external libraries, no installation is necessary. Everything you need to run the video is right there in the EXE.

Pack and Show can package more than just AVIs, however. Below you'll find a list of the different file types that can be stuffed into a Pack and Show EXE file, along with a reason or two as to why you'd want to do it.

- **AVI.** With a Pack and Show AVI, you send a master-quality video to someone without having to make sure they have the TSCC codec installed.

- **SWF.** While designed for the web, the HTML files that contain your SWF video can actually be viewed locally from your hard drive, and this is a good way of sharing small video files that play back virtually anywhere. The same thing can be accomplished by sending the actual SWF video and its accompanying files, but Pack and Show offers the convenience of dealing with a single executable file.

- **MOV, WMV, RM, CAMV.** As you can see, Pack and Show can pack up most of the other file formats produced by Camtasia Studio. However, aside from "proof of concept" uses (i.e., showing a CAMV Pack and Show to your webmaster so that she can see what your video would look like in this particular format without your having to upload it to a server first), these formats are of questionable real-world use when used in conjunction with Pack and Show. Also, keep in mind that EXEs from these formats will open with whatever media player is set as the default on the viewer's machine, so your content may not look exactly the same as you envisioned.

Choosing a File

Let's fire up the Pack and Show Wizard and walk through the process of creating an EXE. From the Camtasia Studio interface, choose **File**, and then **Pack and Show....** Don't worry if you have a project currently open — it won't be affected. The Pack and Show Wizard dialog will appear.

On the initial screen of this wizard, you're prompted for two file paths: one for the file you wish to convert and one for the executable. The former is a pre-existing media file that will act as the source. The latter is the destination, a file that does not yet exist. So, let's choose a source file. You've got three options here:

- Type in a path and file name manually.

- Click the **Open** button, and navigate to your desired file.

- The file path field is actually a drop-down list that contains several of the most recently selected source files. If you have recently created a Pack and Show file from your desired file, you can likely find the file path in this list. Just click the drop-down arrow and select your file.

You probably noticed that after selecting a video file name, a path to the executable file name is filled in automatically, with the same path and the same root file name. For example, if you selected a file called myfile.wmv, the proposed Pack and Show file name is myfile.exe, located in the same directory. You can edit this file path at will with the same three methods mentioned above. Just remember to keep the .exe extension.

Selecting Your Options

Go ahead and click **Next**. The screen that follows will vary based on the file type of the video you've chosen to package. For AVI files, the screen looks like this:

How do you want your EXE-encapsulated AVI file to open?
Including the Camtasia Player is the safest option.

As I mentioned earlier, you have a choice here between opening the file using the viewer's default media player (probably Windows Media Player) and Camtasia Player. While it takes up a few hundred additional K to package the Camtasia Player with your EXE, this file space buys you the assurance that your videos will look terrific, never scaled. You'll read more about Camtasia Player in the section that follows.

If you do choose **Use default player**, note that you also have the option of including an installer for the TechSmith Screen Capture Codec (TSCC). On media players *other* than Camtasia Player, this codec is necessary to decompress and view any TSCC-encoded AVI file (which yours probably is). If you go the route of using the viewer's default player, the only times you would *not* want to check this option are when...

- You know with absolute certainty that every potential audience member already has TSCC installed on their machines (for example, an office environment where all computers share an identical set of software).

- You used a codec other than TSCC to compress your video file during production.

Of course, you could avoid any possible hassle entirely by instead selecting **Use Camtasia Player.** This is a good way of ensuring that every viewer's experience is going to be identical, which will really cut down on your support calls. Also, as you can see in the above screenshot, using Camtasia Player enables you to customize exactly how the video opens and plays by checking off a series of options. These options are based on the command line parameters of Camtasia Player, and are fully described in the section on Camtasia Player later in this chapter.

Choosing a **SWF** file as your video file will give you a screen like this:

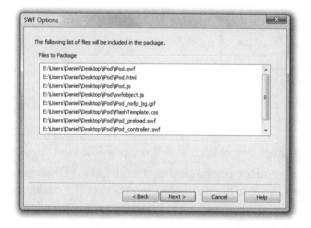

This is just an informational screen; there are no choices to make here. It merely tells you about all the files that will be included along with your SWF video during packaging. On a related note, make sure you keep all the corollary files that were produced when you made your SWF. If any files are missing, you'll receive an error message and will be unable to proceed.

If you select a **CAMV** file as your Pack and Show video, the next screen looks like this:

You'll need to locate the video's SMIL file (created during the production process), and if the video has an audio track, the corresponding RM file as well. Either enter the file path manually or click the **Open** button to browse for the file.

The formats **FLV, MOV, WMV,** and **RM** have no special configuration screens. Packing up one of these file formats will bring you directly to the following step in the wizard, which looks like this:

You have two check boxes here, and three possible courses of action:

- If **Run video after packaging** is checked, then Camtasia Studio will launch the executable upon completion of the packaging process, using whatever media player application is called for to play back the files.

- If the **Package another video** check box is enabled, then the Pack and Show Wizard will reappear following completion of the packaging process, allowing you to package additional files right away.

- If *neither* box is checked, the Pack and Show Wizard will exit back to the main user interface of Camtasia Studio after packaging.

Checking both boxes is not a valid option. If you check one, the other will appear grayed out. Click **Next** to exit the wizard and begin the packaging process. A progress dialog will appear that updates you on the status of packaging. That's really all there is to it.

 A couple of minor caveats, though. Keep the following in mind when using Pack and Show:

- Pack and Show EXEs work best on writable media, such as a hard drive. When packaged on non-writable media like CD-ROM, the executable must first copy the entire video to a temp directory on the hard drive before it can begin playing, which (depending on the size of the video) can lead to unacceptable load times. If you have a full project you wish to put on CD-ROM, please consider using Camtasia MenuMaker instead, which creates aesthetically pleasing presentations that are designed to run directly off a disc.

- When e-mailing your Pack and Show presentations, bear in mind that many e-mail clients block EXE files in an effort to keep viruses and spyware in check. If you need to send someone your presentation via e-mail, try packaging your EXE file in a ZIP file. You won't compress the file any smaller (technically, the contents of your executable are *already* zipped), but at least it will get you past the spam blockers.

Now that you've learned how useful Batch Production and Pack and Show can be, let's move on to the final utility provided by Camtasia Studio to help you share your content with the world, namely the Camtasia Player.

Camtasia Player

When playing back AVI files in a standard media player such as Windows Media Player, if the player window doesn't have adequate space to display the full dimensions of the video file, it will scale the video down so that it fits in the player's window. For cinematic or real-world video, this isn't really an issue (in fact, you probably don't even notice most of the time). For screen video content, such as Camtasia Studio recordings, this convention of scaling content becomes a big fat blurry deal. Icons lose their clarity, text becomes nearly illegible, and the overall result looks, well... crappy.

This is where the Camtasia Player comes in. This media player does not scale content. If the video dimensions are too large for the screen resolution to accommodate, Camtasia Player provides scroll bars to scroll the content. This ensures that your videos will always play full size, and will therefore always look as intended.

The Camtasia Player is a simple AVI player, and it is this simplicity that makes it so useful. In addition to the aforementioned "no scaling" rule, the Camtasia Player offers the following advantages:

- **Convenience.** The TechSmith Screen Capture Codec (TSCC) is built into Camtasia Player. As mentioned in earlier chapters, this codec is highly recommended for compressing your screen videos. However, your viewers usually must have the codec installed on their machines to view your content. Running the video with Camtasia Player removes this restriction. Everything you need is baked right in.

- **Simplicity.** Most other media players bloat their application with adware, skins, unneeded features, and other distractions that divert your viewer's attention from where it should be, namely on your video. Camtasia Player's clean, simple interface is a welcome break from these chaotic and user-unfriendly players.

- **Small size.** When you cut down on the bloat, you cut down on the size. Camtasia Player weighs in at a svelte 476 K, meaning that you can easily include the application with your videos when e-mailing your content to someone else.

- **No install necessary.** The camplay.exe application can be run without any kind of installation. It relies on no external libraries in order to function, which means that you can run Camtasia Player even in a completely locked-down (no installations allowed) environment, which many large corporate and government institutions employ these days. It doesn't make any use of the registry or any configuration files, and doesn't require DirectX.

- **Compatibility.** With such a small footprint, Camtasia Player can easily run on any 32-bit Windows-based operating system (starting with Windows 95). If the user's computer was made any time in the last decade or so, it can run this player.

- **Free!** Camtasia Player is totally free and freely distributable. It's included automatically when you install Camtasia Studio, but anyone can download the player from TechSmith's web site, no strings attached.

In case you can't tell, I'm something of a fan. In fact, I use Camtasia Player as the default media player for all my AVI files.

If you would like to **make Camtasia Player your default player** of AVI files, just follow these easy steps:

1. Right-click on any AVI file.
2. Choose **Open With... > Choose Program....**
3. Locate Camtasia Player on the list of available programs, and select it.

   or

   If Camtasia Player does not appear in this list, click the **Browse** button and navigate to **camplay.exe**. Provided you installed the software into its default directory, camplay.exe is in Program Files\TechSmith\Camtasia Studio 5. Click **Open**.
4. Click the check box **Always use the selected program to open this kind of file**, and then click **OK**.

Now that we've discussed what's so great about this little app, let's get into the nitty-gritty of using it.

The Camtasia Player Interface

The Camtasia Player can be opened in several ways:

- Choose **Start > All Programs > Camtasia Studio 5 > Applications > Camtasia Player.**

- From one of the main Camtasia Studio applications (Studio, Recorder, MenuMaker), click the **Launch other tools** button and select **Camtasia Player.**

- From one of the main Camtasia Studio applications (Studio, Recorder, MenuMaker), choose **Camtasia Player** from the **Tools** menu.

- Depending on your settings, Camtasia Player may also be automatically launched upon conclusion of recording or production.

Camtasia Player's user interface is simple and elegant. It normally includes a title bar, menu bar, toolbar (playback controls), the actual video window, and a status bar at the bottom that shows the playback state, current elapsed time, and total duration. When I say that the interface *usually* includes these elements, I mean that you can turn one or more of these elements off, if desired, by adding some command line parameters (more on that later). But out of the box, your video should look roughly like the following figure.

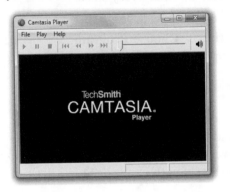

Below are a few simple ways of **opening your AVI video with Camtasia Player**:

■ From the **File** menu in Camtasia Player, choose **Open....**
Then browse to your video and click the **Open** button.

or

■ Click and drag your video icon over the camplay.exe icon, and release. Alternatively, you can also drag your video icon onto the Camtasia Player program window.

or

■ If Camtasia Player is set as your default media player, simply double-click the file.

Obviously, most users will control the playback of your video through Camtasia Player's toolbar. Each of these commands has a corresponding menu option and hotkey. This handy table tackles all our toolbar commands, going in order from left to right:

Button	Menu Command	Hotkey	Description
Play	Play > Play/Pause	Spacebar	Sets the playback head in motion. The menu command and hotkey toggle between play and pause.
Pause	Play > Play/Pause	Spacebar	Pauses the playback head at its current location. The menu command and hotkey toggle between play and pause.

Button	Menu Command	Hotkey	Description
Stop	Play > Stop	Ctrl-S	Stops the playback head, returning it to the beginning of the video.
Beginning	Play > Beginning	Home	Returns playback head to the beginning of the video. Only available when paused or stopped.
Rewind	Play > Rewind	Page Up	Scrolls the playback backward by a small percentage. Only available when paused or stopped.
Forward	Play > Forward	Page Down	Scrolls the playback forward by a small percentage. Only available when paused or stopped.
End	Play > End	End	Sets the playback head at the end of the video. Only available when paused or stopped.
Scrubber bar	---	---	This playback slider can be dragged to any point in the video, and the video will commence from that point. You can also click on any point on the video's Timeline, and the playback head will jump to that point.
Volume up	Play > Volume > Up	Ctrl-Up	Click the Volume button, and then drag the slider up to raise the volume.
Volume down	Play > Volume > Down	Ctrl-Down	Click the Volume button, and then drag the slider down to lower the volume.
Mute	Play > Volume > Mute	Ctrl-M	Click the Volume button, and then check the Mute check box.

Note that there are a few additional commands the viewer has to control their view of the video:

Full Screen	Play > Full Screen	Alt-Enter	Changes the display to full-screen mode, which places the video display in the center of the screen, surrounded by a colored background. All other parts of the window (as well as everything outside the window) are obscured by this background.

Repeat	Play > Repeat	Ctrl-R	Places the playback in repeat mode. When the playback head reaches the end of the video, it will return to the video's beginning and play the video over again. The video will loop for as long as repeat mode is engaged.
Frame by Frame	---	Left arrow, Right arrow	Moves the playback head forward or backward by a single frame. Only available when paused or stopped. You can hold down one of the arrow keys to scrub forward or backward.

Camtasia Player's Command Line Parameters

While the player's basic functionality is pretty easy to grasp, there are also extended functions that will allow you to stipulate how it opens, what components are available to the user, and how the video actually plays. These are controlled by **command line parameters**, little switches in the form of an alphanumeric code that get tacked onto the command to run Camtasia Player.

> Confused yet? Try the following simple example:
> 1. From your **Start** menu, choose **Run...**.
> 2. Type **camplay.exe** and a space.
> 3. Type **/F** and a space.
> 4. Type (or copy and paste) the file path to one of your AVI files. Press **Enter**.

And voilà! Your video opens in full-screen mode. Command line parameters can do much more than that. A full list of these parameters is available in the following table. Remember, the syntax for your command line parameters is as follows:

```
camplay.exe <options> <file path>
```

Note that both the <options> and <file path> arguments are completely optional.

Parameter	Description
/A	Launches with the "Always on top" option. The video window will always remain on top of other windows on your desktop, even if it loses the focus.
/BC RGB(255,0,255)	Sets the background color. This background color is visible only in full-screen or maximized modes. While the background color is black by default, this can be changed by altering the values of the parameter's "RGB" argument. Those three numbers stand for the colors red, green, and blue, respectively. These values can range from 0 to 255. To find out the RGB value of your favorite color, use a graphics utility such as Color Cop, which is included on the companion CD-ROM.
/D	This launches the video as per usual, but prohibits the user from dragging the video window by the video area, which is normally allowed.
/E	This command forces the video to exit after playing through once.
/F	This parameter launches the video in full-screen mode.
/M	Launches the video without the menu bar. In addition to aesthetic reasons, removing the menu bar can help prevent the user from controlling the view of your video (for example, switching to full screen). Of course, the corresponding hotkeys will still function.
/MX	This launches your video with the window maximized. The video window will take up the entire screen, with the video content in the center, enveloped by your chosen background color. Unlike full-screen mode, the title bar, menu bar, toolbar, and status bar all remain visible.
/open	This parameter opens the specified video, but starts the video in paused mode. It will not begin until the user clicks Play.
/play	This immediately plays the specified video. It is the opposite of the /open parameter.
/R	Repeats the video over and over until the viewer stops it by choosing Pause or Stop, or by closing the video window.
/S	This launches the video without a status bar, meaning that the viewer will no longer be able to see the elapsed time or total duration of the video.

Parameter	Description
/ST	Adding this parameter will cause the video to remain on the final frame of the video after playing, rather than returning to the first frame.
/T	Removes the title bar from the video window. This can be used in conjunction with the /D parameter to prevent the viewer from dragging the video window.
/TB	Launches the video without a toolbar. Be warned: This will remove the user's predominant means of navigating your video.

At this point you may be thinking, "Big deal. Opening up files from the command line is a pain. Besides, how does this influence how my viewers will see my videos?" Well, friends, you can easily use these handy command line parameters in batch files, multimedia authoring applications, or scripting languages. Of course, if the thought of working with scripts and batch files makes your eyes glaze over and your palms begin to sweat, keep in mind that you can also attach command line parameters to each and every AVI file in your comparatively user-friendly Camtasia MenuMaker projects. Just start a new MenuMaker project, add some files, choose to open them with Camtasia Studio, and set your parameters. For full details, please see Chapter 13, "CD-based Videos with Camtasia MenuMaker."

Summary

In this chapter, we covered all the remaining options for sharing our video content. These are generally regarded as "niche" options, yet all remain quite useful under the right circumstances. We discussed the following three tools:

- **Batch Production.** This time-saving utility has the power to produce multiple videos based on a given production preset. Additionally, you can produce a single video in more than one format, which is particularly handy when producing multiple-bandwidth versions of a given video for your audience.

■ **Pack and Show.** If you want to package your video into an executable file, you may do so with this tool. It works best for AVI files, where you can package the Camtasia Player and the video content into one file. Just keep in mind that most modern e-mail clients disallow executable (.exe) attachments.

■ **Camtasia Player.** A handy, no-frills AVI player. No installation required, as it doesn't rely on any external libraries in order to function. It's widely compatible and free of cost. Additionally, it won't scale your content, dance with your date, or trump your ace lead. The TSCC codec is built directly into it.

Exercises

1. If you have not already done so, create a Production Preset consisting of your most often-used production settings. Use the Batch Production tool to produce one or more files/projects using this preset.

2. Create a Pack and Show file from one of your AVIs.

3. Set up Windows to use Camtasia Player as your default media player for AVI files.

Chapter 16

Post-Production Customization

If you've read completely through to this point, then you've managed to successfully capture, edit, produce, and hopefully share your content with other people. This brief chapter is a bit of an "advanced topics" course that will teach you how you can change the look and feel of your videos after production has taken place. A lot of what I cover here requires a bit of coding, but don't let that put you off. Customizing your content is actually pretty straightforward, and the programming requirements are thankfully light. While I'm a star at making screen videos, I'm certainly no web developer, and the good news is, you don't need to be. If I can employ these techniques, anyone can, so don't panic.

In this chapter, I'll be walking you through several customization techniques organized into the following sections:

- **Flash Preloader Customization.** This section discusses how to create or modify your Flash preloader movies in order to add your own custom branding and messages.

- **Embedding Your Videos in a Blog or Other Web Page.** Here you learn how to embed your non-ExpressShow Flash content into a blog or other web page as well as place your video behind a video still frame to save bandwidth.

- **Altering the Configuration File.** The final section of this chapter discusses how to use a production's configuration file to alter settings, tweak the aesthetics, and correct errors *without* having to reproduce your Camtasia Studio and Camtasia Theater productions.

Flash Preloader Customization

As mentioned back in Chapter 12, Camtasia Studio comes with a number of stock preloader movies for use in your productions. Some are branded, but most aren't, and they're available free of charge to introduce all your screencasts. But sometimes you want your preloader to have a little extra *something*. It can be your company's logo or some other graphic, or perhaps a bit of text informing your audience that your video will start playing as soon as the percentage bar hits 10%. It can be anything. A Flash preloader file is just a small SWF to introduce the content, and they can run the gamut from humorous animations to corporate slogans to simple "loading…" screens.

In this section, I'll show you how to edit a stock preloader to better fit your needs. Keep in mind that you *will* require a copy of the Adobe Flash authoring tool in order to make any changes. The current version, Flash CS3, costs about $700 when not purchased as part of a bundle.

First things first: Assuming you want to customize a pre-existing preloader and not create one from scratch, you need to locate that preloader's FLA file. A SWF file won't work, as SWF is the preloader's production file, which cannot be edited. You need the original FLA. I have included the FLAs of my preloaders from Chapter 12 in this chapter's exercise folder, which you're welcome to customize to your heart's content. But this time, we're going to be working with one of the stock TechSmith preloaders, mainly because it'll be fun to steal that lovely progress bar that hooks into the video's load status. But we have to find the file first.

Here's how to **prep one of the TechSmith preloaders for editing**:

1. In the drive where you installed Camtasia Studio (usually C:), go to **Program Files\TechSmith\Camtasia Studio 5\Media\Studio\Swf\Preloaders**. This is where all the stock preloader SWFs are located. But there's also a zip file called **preloader_src.zip** that houses the source FLA files. Open it up.

2. Select the FLA file you wish to edit. It's also a possibility that you'll need the **com** folder, as it contains the ActionScript file that controls the more dynamic elements of this movie.

Unzip both the FLA file and the com folder (in its entirety) to an appropriate place on your hard drive.

3. Open the FLA file in the Flash authoring environment. (I'm basing these instructions on Adobe Flash CS3, but earlier versions should work just as well.) It's time to make the preloader our own.

It's not within the scope of this book to give you a complete lesson in Flash development (in other words, I assume that you have some *basic* familiarity with the tool), but I'll give you some brief instructions for executing the most common preloader editing tasks.

First off, if your selected preloader has a branded image, it's very straightforward to replace it. To get rid of the image, just click to select it, and then press **Delete**. But now we need a new image to replace it. It's helpful if the new image has roughly the same dimensions as the one you're replacing.

To **add the new image to your preloader**, do the following:

1. Choose **File > Import > Import to Stage...**, or simply press **Ctrl-R**.

2. Navigate to your new image file and click **Open**.

3. Place the image appropriately on the Stage. For smaller images, you may have to reorder layers and/or create a rectangular mask to serve as a background.

4. If your new background is of a significantly different color from the old TechSmith image, you may need to adjust the font color of any text (if present) so that the text contrasts well with the new background.

For preloaders that have dynamic text and progress bars in them, you can tinker with the ActionScript file TechSmith has also made available. One favorite trick of mine is to adjust the status messaging to let the audience know how much of the video file will need to preload before it begins to play. It's a nice way of tipping them off as to how long a wait they can expect.

To alter the status messages of your preloader, you'll need to **edit the included AS file**, like so:

1. Open the FLA file of your preloader, if it's not already open.

2. Navigate to the AS file by opening **com\techsmith\ preloader\TSPreloader.as**.

3. The AS file will open in Flash. Make sure it's targeted to your desired FLA file by checking the Target field in the upper right-hand corner of the AS window:

    Target: branded_small_preload ▼

    Make sure you're targeting the right preloader! Of course, you can circumvent this risk entirely by only opening one preloader movie at a time.

4. Scroll down to view the **mediaLoadingEvent** function. There's a conditional statement here with two statusMessage strings. It basically says, "If the required percentage has already loaded, display the first text string. Otherwise, show the second." In reality, your audience will rarely see the first string unless the entire video loads before the preloader's miminum display time elapses (the default in Camtasia Studio is three seconds). This typically only occurs when the video is either cached (i.e., they've played the video before and now have a copy on their hard disk) or played back locally rather than viewed online. This is something to keep in mind while testing your menu out.

5. Notice that some parameters are available with which to dynamically build a text string. I'll be making use of the **e.requiredPercent** parameter, which is the percentage required to start displaying the video. It pulls this value from the video's config file. By using a parameter instead of simply typing in, say, 10%, you know that your preloader will be accurate no matter how you set the **Percent of main movie to preload** field in the Flash Options dialog of Camtasia Studio when producing future videos. I can actually stick the parameter in between two text snippets, like so:

```
67    public function mediaLoadingEvent( e:Object ):Void
68    {
69        if ( e.percentLoaded > e.requiredPercent )
70        {
71            statusMessage.text  = "Get Ready!";
72        }
73        else
74        {
75            statusMessage.text = "Video will start after preloading " + Math.round( e.requiredPercent ) + "%";
76        }
77
78        progressMessage.text = Math.round( e.percentLoaded ) + " %";
79        progressBar._xscale  = e.percentLoaded;
80    }
```

6. Feel free to experiment with the other parameters listed in the file's comments. For example, you could build a text string that shows the current number of bytes loaded compared with the total. I have included an example of this in the exercise media for this chapter.

7. Save the AS file.

When the preloader FLA file (and optionally, the accompanying AS file) has been successfully altered, you'll need to produce to SWF. In the **Flash** tab of the **Publish Settings** dialog, you'll need to specify the minimum version of Flash Player that this file can support: Choose Flash Player 7 if you're producing SWF files, or 8 if you only ever produce FLVs. I generally only produce SWFs that will work with versions 7+, as it's just easier.

Each stock TechSmith preloader includes a special layer called **dropShadow** that can produce a neat drop shadow effect around your preloader, but it only works with Flash Player 8 and above. Just turn on the layer's visibility in the Flash timeline if you want to use it.

Now turn your attention to the **Formats** tab, make sure that Flash (.swf) is the only file type checked, and then click the **Select Publish Destination** button to replace the preloader of whatever pre-existing project you wish. If desired, you can also publish your custom works back to where the standard TechSmith SWFs are located, so that you have all available preloaders in one handy location. Just make sure you name it something else so as not to replace your default preloaders.

Now when my audience starts up my video, it looks like this:

Not a bad investment of a few spare minutes, wouldn't you say?

Embedding Your Videos in a Blog or Other Web Page

As we discussed in Chapter 12, every video output includes the option of having Camtasia Studio automatically place your content into a blank web page. It inserts all the code necessary to make it work, and does so pretty flawlessly. But the problem is that you may not necessarily want your video file floating in a blank page, but would rather insert into a pre-existing page where there's already some actual content. Could be a blog entry, an article, a personal page, what have you.

Of course, with all the helper files and such, there's usually a fair amount of code required that you'll need to insert into your content page. With the introduction of version 5, Camtasia Studio has provided a solution in the form of ExpressShow, packing everything you need into one handy SWF file. But what if you're outputting to a format other than SWF, or you want to use a theme other than ExpressShow Onyx? Well, there are actually three different methods of putting your non-ExpressShow content into a pre-existing web page, and I (generous guy that I am) will be showing you all of them. I'm using Flash in these examples because it's almost invariably what you should be using for online distribution, but other file formats can be embedded as well.

Method 1: Screencast.com

If you're uploading to a Screencast.com account, embedding your content into a web page is simpler than you can imagine. After upload is complete, go ahead and visit the video's page, making sure to actually log into your account if you haven't already. As the author of the content, you'll be in what they refer to as Owner View, which gives you access to commands that your users don't have, including a special collapsible pane called **Share this media:**

The second box is the one we're interested in. Simply clicking inside the field will automatically copy its entire contents to your clipboard. Now it's just a matter of pasting it into the appropriate spot in your destination site. You need to open up the page in question so that you can see its source code. Note that the page doesn't have to be locally stored on your hard drive — even blogs, learning management systems, and CRM sites have editing systems that sport a "source view" mode. Check the documentation for your particular system to find out how to gain access to a page's underlying code. Place the mouse cursor in an appropriate spot in the body of your document, and paste.

Another really cool trick for embedding Screencast.com content in a page without actually embedding the video itself is to create a Playlist. If you have a series of videos that relate to a particular blog topic, you can embed a playlist control that will let the user open up each video's page on Screencast.com. This is just a quickie example that I embedded in my blog:

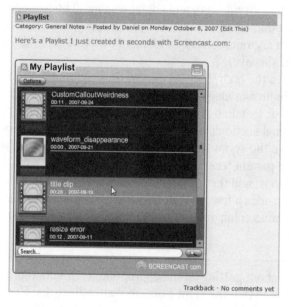

Easy embedding of content is just another of the myriad reasons that Screencast.com rocks for online sharing of your videos. Of course, many folks don't want to invest in a Screencast.com account because they already have a perfectly good file hosting service in place. Or they simply can't because corporate policy dictates that all intellectual property has to reside on company servers. Does this mean you're not able to embed videos? Nope. The following two methods work regardless of your hosting solution.

Method 2: Transfer Code

If you have created a video along with a corresponding HTML page (unavoidable if you're producing a non-ExpressShow Flash video), one possibility is to copy the proper code snippet from that HTML document, and then paste it into the appropriate spot in the target page.

To get at this code, just navigate to the folder where the produced content was placed, and open up the included HTML file. The code we're going to need to see and copy from is located in two sections: the header and the body.

In the header, you have links to two external JavaScript files that you'll need to upload to your web server along with the video. The first one is called **swfobject.js**. It is responsible for detecting the Flash version on the user's machine. If an appropriate version of Flash Player is detected, it also contains the embedding script for dynamically generating the object and embed tags. The second file bears your project name (e.g., *myvideo*.**js**), and contains general housekeeping code such as production-dependent scripting, appropriate routing of movie reference arguments, and handling of SCORM content (including quizzes and surveys).

Moving on to the body, there are a few divs containing the Flash body code, including an elegant error message for those who do not have Flash Player installed or JavaScript enabled (<div> tags represent the individual sections, or *divisions*, of your document). And of course, you have the script that creates a new instance of swfobject, passing on such parameters as the name of the controller SWF, the video's dimensions, and the minumum version of Flash Player required. It then adds a few variables, including the name of the config file, the background color, and the name of the preloader (if you included one).

So, let's talk about getting all the appropriate elements (both file and code snippets) in the right place so that it all works. Here's how to **embed a video in a page by transferring code**:

1. Produce your video and navigate to the folder that contains the production.

2. Using an FTP application (or the FTP feature of Camtasia Studio), navigate to the location of the web page into which you'd like to embed the video.

---

3. Upload the following files to the same directory as the destination web page:

- The controller file (*myvideo*_controller.swf)
- The configuration file (*myvideo*_config.xml)
- The swfobject.js JavaScript file
- The JavaScript file that bears your project name (e.g., *myvideo*.js)
- The actual content (SWF or FLV)
- If applicable, the preloader SWF
- If applicable, the side-by-side camera video FLV

4. Open the destination web page.

5. In the header of this page, you need to reference the swfobject JavaScript file. So, somewhere inside the <head> tag, you need to type the following:

```
<script type="text/javascript" src="swfobject.js"></script>
<script type="text/javascript" src="myvideo.js"></script>
```

In the second line, remember to replace "myvideo" with the name of your actual project!

6. Now, on to the body. Find the location inside the body where you want the video to appear. Enter a few carriage returns to give yourself some space, and then type the following:

```
<div id="flashcontent"></div>
```

This is a placeholder for a piece of content called "flashcontent." Exactly what "flashcontent" is will be defined by the script we're about to insert.

7. Open up the HTML file that was produced by Camtasia Studio. We need to copy some script out of it. Between the <body> and </body> tags, there's the JavaScript SWFObject code we talked about earlier. Copy the entire script, everything between (and including) the <script> and </script> tags.

8. Paste this material into the new document, just underneath the <div> tags you created in step 6. This is what your file should look like at this point:

```
<!DOCTYPE html PUBLIC "-//W3C//DTD XHTML 1.0 Strict//EN" "http://www.w3.org/TR/xhtml1/DTD/xhtml1-strict.dtd">
<html xmlns="http://www.w3.org/1999/xhtml" xml:lang="en" lang="en">

    <head>
        <meta http-equiv="Content-Language" content="en-us">
        <meta http-equiv="Content-Type" content="text/html; charset=windows-1252">
        <title>This is a content page.</title>

        <script type="text/javascript" src="swfobject.js"></script>
        <script type="text/javascript" src="Intro.js"></script>

    </head>
    <body>

        <p>Here's some content.</p>
        <p>Here's the video:</p>

        <div id="flashcontent"></div>

        <script type="text/javascript">
        // <![CDATA[
            var fo = new SWFObject( "Intro_controller.swf", "csSwf", "800", "655", "7", "#FFFFFF" );
            fo.addVariable( "csConfigFile", "Intro_config.xml" );
            fo.addVariable( "csColor"    , "FFFFFF"          );
            fo.addVariable( "csPreloader" , "Intro_preload.swf" );
            if( args.movie )
            {
                fo.addVariable( "csFilesetBookmark", args.movie );
            }
            fo.write("flashcontent");
            // ]]>
        </script>

        <p>Here's even more content.</p>

    </body>
</html>
```

The three script components are 1) the two JavaScript references inside the header, 2) the flashcontent div that represents where the video content actually goes on the page, and 3) the SWFObject code that defines what flashcontent is.

9. Save the HTML file and re-upload to the server.

If you end up with no video (whether with an error message or without), double-check the following:

■ Make sure that you uploaded ALL required files to the same directory as the destination web page.

■ Ensure that your two JavaScript references are inside the <head> tags, and that your second reference is properly named.

■ Check that you didn't forget the flashcontent div. Make sure it also has a closing tag.

■ Make sure you pasted in the entire SWFObject script, and that you actually included the <script> tags.

Of course, if you have a blog, CRM site, or some other sort of online publishing mechanism, you may have already noticed a problem with the above method. Uploading new files to your page's destination directory works well with standard web pages, but many online web publishing systems use a proprietary system for storing web files. As a result, you may not be able to access, or even *find*, the right directory for uploading your files.

Fortunately, the next embedding method, which I vastly prefer, doesn't have this limitation. It allows you to upload your files wherever you wish. As long as your video is publicly accessible, you can embed it into *any* page that'll let you insert a bit of code.

Method 3: Using Inline Frames

An **inline frame** is a special HTML tag that tells the browser to display the contents of another web page *inside* the current page. Its original use was to allow for easy reuse of content, displaying the same article or news segment inside several larger pages. The cool thing is that both pages remain entirely separate entities. They don't have to reside in the same directory, or even on the same server.

This means that you have total freedom in terms of where to upload your content. It also means that you can use the HTML document created by Camtasia Studio during production. No tedious copying of code is required. Just upload the entire contents of your production folder to a web server. The only requirement is that it has to be online *somewhere*.

Then, on your blog or CRM page, you create an inline frame that points to your video's HTML file. It is effectively displayed as "page within a page." The other really cool thing about this method is that it's easy to first point to a dummy page wth a "click here to play" image like this one:

Why would you want to do this instead of instantly jumping right to the video? Well, if you pay for your own web hosting, then it's very likely that you have some sort of limit as to amount of bandwidth your site can consume without having to pay extra. It's possible that not everyone on your page needs to watch your video, and you're wasting considerable bandwidth by letting the video automatically download to their computers if they'll never actually see it. The following procedure assumes that you'll want a bandwidth-saving image to precede your video, but it still works even if you don't. Just skip the step about adding a dummy page and image, and have the inline frame link directly to your content page.

This is how to **embed video** into a content page **using an inline frame**:

1. Produce and upload your video content (including *all* files) to a web server. Make note of the HTML page's URL.

2. Playing back the first few seconds of video, use SnagIt to make a screenshot of the video's title screen, complete with control bar. You can even add a bit of text, such as "Click here to view the video." It's also easy to add a triangular "Play" icon using a character from the Wingdings 3 font (just use the Character Map utility in Windows to select and place this character). Save the file as **still.jpg**.

3. Create a new page and insert still.jpg into it. Place a hyperlink on the image that links to the produced HTML file you uploaded in step 1, and set the target as **_self**. Name this file **still.html**. The code in the page should look something like this:

```
<a href="http://www.mysite.com/myvideo.html" target="_self">
<img border="0" src="still.jpg" width="688" height="575"></a>
```

The actual width and height would obviously conform to the actual dimensions of your image.

4. Upload both still.jpg and still.html to a web server.

5. Inside the code of the content page, create an inline frame that references the still.html file you created in step 3, like so:

```
<iframe width="694" height="582" frameborder="0"
src="http://www.mysite.com/still.html"
marginwidth="1" marginheight="1" scrolling="no">
```

```
Your browser does not support inline frames or is currently
configured not to display them.
</iframe>
```

Notice a few things about the attributes of this tag:

- width and height: I've learned to add seven or eight pixels beyond the actual dimensions of the video or still image, as these are offset by three to four pixels when displayed in their accompanying HTML files.

- frameborder: Make sure there's no border around your frame. It breaks the illusion that the page is a single unified entity.

- scrolling: Set it to "no" to ensure that no scroll bar pops up.

- src: The URL of the web page that contains your still image.

6. Save and re-upload your content page.

That's all there is to it. Inline frames are compatible with all the major web browsers going several versions back. I have yet to hear about any compatibility problems. And the beauty of it is that you really don't have to mess around with a lot of code. But... if you happen to *like* that sort of thing, this next section will really get your blood pumping. Let's turn our attention to the joys of the configuration file and how it can be manipulated to change the look and feel of your video.

Altering the Configuration File

As we've discussed before, Flash production (if you're not using ExpressShow) generates a lot of files. You've got the video itself, the HTML file that contains it, the JavaScript files that generate the needed object and embed tags, and the controller file that contains the control bar, among others. Of course, one of the most important components is a small (usually around 10 K) XML file called the **configuration file (*_config.xml)**. This file is the glue that holds the rest of it together. It is a central repository of information that contains most of the options you set while traversing the Production Wizard. When loading all the files, this config file passes information to the other components. What kind of information, you might ask? Here are a few examples:

- Info about your video components, such as their dimensions, durations, and frame rates.

- The structure and formatting of your table of contents (as well as whether you even *have* a table of contents).

- All the questions, answers, and custom responses of your quizzes.

- The size, location, duration, and actions of all your Flash hotspots, if any.

And a lot more. The cool thing about having all this info in one place is that if you're careful, you can make minor edits to your project after production is complete *without* having to produce again. Particularly if this is a long, involved project that takes considerable time to produce, sometimes it's just easier to go in and edit the XML file if you suddenly caught a typo in one of your quiz questions. Or if you'd like to alter the size of your TOC text. Or if you want to change the URL of one of your hotspots. The possibilities are limitless.

Making Project Changes with XML

In ExpressShow videos, all aspects of the video are contained within the SWF itself. This makes the video very portable and embeddable, but wipes out the ability to make post-production changes. Non-ExpressShow videos have all settings that affect the playback of your video set aside as values inside the config file.

Let's look at how it works (feel free to skip the rest of this section if you already have a handle on XML). XML is an incredibly flexible way of storing text and other data, and it is designed to be accessible (easily read by any database system). All information is contained in *tags*. If you've ever looked at HTML code, you probably know what these look like. You've got an opening tag, whatever content you're wanting to mark, and a closing tag. It looks like this:

```
<tag>The content goes here.</tag>
```

Now, HTML is comprised of a series of predefined tags that web browsers can read and interpret. For example, enclosing a piece of text inside a <b> tag — like this: <b>bold</b> — will produce **bold** text when read by the browser. Unlike HTML, XML tags are completely customizable, meaning that the tag's name can be (within limits) whatever the developer wants it to be (e.g., <mysupercoolwidget>). Obviously, this tag wouldn't mean anything to a standard web browser, so what we need is an interpreter that can correctly parse this information, thereby figuring out what to do with the content contained therein.

In our case, this interpreter is the SWF or FLV video file, which contains the basic bare-bones components of our presentation (menu bar, control bar, video pane). However, these components are generic — your SWF needs the information passed to it by the XML file in order to determine things like the color you want for your control bar or the font size for the table of contents text.

Fortunately for us, this setup is infinitely more flexible than if these settings were "baked" into your SWF. With all the information in your XML file, the content of these tags can be *edited* on the fly, and it's a good way to make quick changes to a project you're generally happy with. In fact, if your project file somehow got lost or corrupted after creating your presentation, it's the *only* way.

Your XML file contains a couple of useful tags that don't correspond to any setting in Camtasia Studio or Camtasia Theater. For example, Camtasia Theater offers no way to turn off the fast forward and rewind buttons on your control bar. But by changing the value of the <ShowFFRW> tag in your XML file, you can make these buttons vanish like magic.

Editing Your XML File

While it may look complicated at first glance, changing the values of your XML tags to change the look and feel of your presentation is actually not that hard, provided you're familiar with the basics. First, let's open up our XML file and see what's there. While there are numerous XML editing applications out there, XML is really just a text format, and as such can be opened with the Notepad application included with every copy of Windows.

Just follow these steps to **open the XML config file**:

1. Choose **Start > All Programs > Accessories > Notepad.**
2. From the **File** menu, choose **Open....**
3. At the bottom of the **Open** dialog, you'll see a drop-down box that lets you specify the file types you wish to view. From this drop-down list, choose **All Files.**
4. Navigate to your project's XML file, and then choose **Open.**

Your project's XML document opens. Now, I mentioned that the value of whatever property we want to change is snugly nestled between that property's opening and closing tags, like this: <tag>value</tag>. The XML file is loaded with these tags. While most control a particular aspect of your production, some tags are there for categorization, with the other tags nested inside them, like this:

```
<category>
<tag>value</tag>
</category>
```

Here are a few handy points to keep in mind when editing your XML file:

- Remember that only the *values* (the data between the opening and closing tags) are to be edited. Do *not* touch the tags themselves! Your SWF will go looking for a tag by its name, and if that tag can't be found, bad things tend to happen (errors, gobbledygook, total refusal to open, etc.). So do be careful. In fact, it's best to make a backup of your XML file before you go messing with it.

- Some tags support only *binary* values, meaning that feature is either enabled or it's not. For these tags, a value of 1 means it's *on*, and 0 means it's *off*.

- Certain other tags will only accept a limited range of values. For example, the <TimeDisplayFormat> tag has only eight acceptable values. For these tags, I will point out what the acceptable values are in the table that follows.

- The values of certain tags are just not meant to be edited, and doing so can lead to problems. Other tags serve no discernable purpose, and are presumably leftovers from previous versions of the software. I'll be skipping these in the following tables, so if you don't see the tag here, then it doesn't behoove you to mess with it.

- For tags that stipulate the color of text and objects, use the desired color's hexadecimal value. You'll need an image utility that will display the hexadecimal value of any color you select. I've always used a small utility called Color Cop. For one thing, it's free, and for another, it rocks. I've taken the liberty of providing you a copy of this handy app on the companion CD-ROM. Each hex value is a string of six letters and numbers. In the XML file, you must precede this string with the characters *0x*. For example, if picking the color white, you would type *0xFFFF*.

Camtasia Studio's Configuration File

The remainder of this section is split into two parts. The first lists all the useful tags for the config files produced by Camtasia Studio. The second part provides the same information about the config file produced by Camtasia Theater, as its configuration is still fundamentally different from that of the main application. Keep in mind that there are some exceedingly useful tags in the config file that *cannot* be controlled from the Production Wizard. These are features that, for one reason or another, have not yet been implemented in the program's interface, and yet you as a savvy, XML-editing Camtasia Studio guru can now use them in your projects.

All tags are listed in the order of their appearance in the document. I also describe what each tag does and, if applicable, what command within Camtasia Studio controls this tag. These commands are found in the Flash Options dialog of the Production Wizard unless otherwise specified.

Keep in mind that many of these settings (such as video size) depend on external factors such as the video file itself or the accompanying HTML file, and as such are not adjustable. If a particular tag isn't mentioned in this table, then messing with it probably does nothing, and might in fact break your project. You have been warned!

Tag	Description	Camtasia Studio Command
CONFIG		
<skinTheme>	Changes the theme of the presentation. Acceptable values: *goog, classic, glass,* and *onyx.*	Flash Templates screen, Theme drop-down list
<autoStart>	A value of 0 indicates that the video will start paused. 1 means that it will automatically begin upon loading.	Controls tab, Pause at start check box
<backgroundColor>	Sets the color of the video's background.	Video tab, Background Color... button

Tag	Description	Camtasia Studio Command
`<showLoadingMov>`	A value of 0 means that no preloader movie will be shown before the main video. 1 means it will.	Controls tab, Show loading movie check box
`<loadingMovPercentToLoad>`	The percentage of the video that needs to load before it begins to play.	Controls tab, Loading Movie... button, Percent of main movie to preload
`<loadingMovMinDuration>`	The minimum duration of the preloader before the video can start to play.	Controls tab, Loading Movie... button, Minimum preload movie display time
`<controllerColor>`	Changes the color of the control bar. Note: The color will actually appear in pastel, much lighter than the hex color you actually chose.	Controls tab, Controller Color... button
`<showAbout>`	A value of 0 removes the About box button from the control bar. A value of 1 displays it.	Controls tab, Show about box check box
`<aboutBoxText>`	Specifies the content of the About box.	Controls tab, About box text
`<timeDisplayFormat>`	This tag changes the format of how the duration and/or elapsed time is displayed in your presentation. The only acceptable values are: SS, MM:SS, HH:MM, HH:MM:SS, SSs, MMm SSs, HHh MMm, and HHh MMm SSs.	Controls tab, Display Format drop-down list
`<ShowDuration>`	Binary tag that determines whether to show the video's total duration.	Controls tab, Show duration check box

Tag	Description	Camtasia Studio Command
\<ShowElapsedTime\>	Binary tag that controls whether to show the video's current elapsed time.	Controls tab, Show elapsed time check box
\<TimeDisplayFont\>	The font of your time display text. While you can enter the name of any font on your system here, keep in mind that it may not display correctly, and that the font in question must also be on the viewer's system in order to display.	---
\<includeScoreInEmail\>	If a scored quiz is to be sent via e-mail, this binary setting determines whether the score is included in the message.	Video Options screen, Quiz and Survy Reporting Options... button, Include score in e-mail check box
\<rememberQuizAnswers\>	Controls whether quiz answers are preserved if the video is closed and then reloaded.	---
\<endAction\>	Determines what happens when the video ends. Acceptable values: *Stop*, *JumpToTime*, and *JumpToURL*.	Controls tab, End action
\<endActionParam\>	If you selected *JumpToURL* for \<endAction\>, this is where you would specify the URL.	Controls tab, End action URL field
\<volume\>	Specifies the initial volume setting as a percentage.	---
\<hasCaptions\>	A binary setting that determines whether captions are available in this video.	Captions pane, Display button

Tag	Description	Camtasia Studio Command
<captionsVisible>	A binary setting that lets you stipulate whether your captions are initially visible, or whether the "CC" button must first be clicked.	Controls tab, Captions initially visible check box
CAPTION > FONT		
<type>	This the font in which captions appear. The same font must be on the user's system as well, so you should choose a common one.	---
<size>	The size of your caption font.	---
<weight>	A binary setting that lets you set the font to bold type.	---
<color>	Choose the color of your captions.	---
CAPTION > PANEL		
<color>	The background color of the closed caption panel.	---
<alpha>	This percentage value sets the background's level of transparency. A value of 1 is nearly transparent, whereas 100 is totally opaque.	---
<speed>	The speed at which the caption panel slides up/down when the closed caption button is clicked. Lower number = faster.	---
TOC		
<backgroundColor>	The background color of the table of contents.	---

Tag	Description	Camtasia Studio Command
<alternatingRowColors>	If you want the background color of TOC items to alternate between two colors, specify their hex values here. These values trump the value of <backgroundColor>.	---
<rowDepthColors>	If you have nested items in your TOC, you can specify different background colors for parent items vs. nested items. These values trump the values of both <alternatingRow-Colors> and <backgroundColor>.	---
<rowRollOverColor>	The color of the row when the TOC item is moused over. The tag <useRollOver> must be set to a value of 1.	---
<rowSelectedColor>	The color of the row when viewing that item's part of the video.	---
<rowIndentation>	The indentation of the TOC rows (in number of pixels).	---
<borderStyle>	The style of the TOC's border. Acceptable values: *none*, *inset*, *outset*, and *solid*.	---
<textColor>	The text color of the TOC items.	---
<fontFamily>	The font style of the TOC items. Use a universally accessible font to ensure consistent viewing.	---
<fontSize>	The size of the TOC item text.	---

Tag	Description	Camtasia Studio Command
<fontWeight>	The weight of the text. You can choose between *none* and *bold*.	---
<textAlign>	The alignment of the TOC text within the TOC pane. Choose between *left*, *right*, and *center*.	---
<textDecoration>	If desired, you can underline each TOC item. Choose between *underline* and *none*.	---
<textIndent>	The indentation of the TOC text (in number of pixels).	---
<textRollOverColor>	The color of the text when the TOC item is moused over. The tag <useRollOver> must be set to a value of 1.	---
<textSelectedColor>	The color of the item text when viewing that item's part of the video.	---
<useRollOver>	This binary tag enables the display of text or row rollovers.	---
<collapsible>	If enabled (set to 1), the TOC submenu items will be collapsible. Only useful with nested TOC menus.	---
QUIZ		
<disableFeedback>	If enabled, this will turn off quiz feedback.	Video Options screen, Quiz and Survey Reporting Options... button, Disable Quiz Feedback check box

Tag	Description	Camtasia Studio Command
<txtQuestionOf>, <txtPrev>, <txtSubmit>, <txtNext>, <txtDone>, <txtPreview>, <txtSend>, <txtMainMessage>, <txtEmailContents>, <txtEmailTo>, <txtAnswersSent>, <txtSummary>, <txtScore>, <txtSummaryTitle>	Specify the actual text string of the various quiz interface elements, both for the quiz/survey itself as well as for the quiz message screen at the end of the video, and for the e-mail message if applicable.	---
PLAYLIST > HOTSPOTINFO		
<start>, <end>	The beginning and end of the hotspot in the video, in seconds.	Timeline
<x0>, <y0>	The coordinates of the upper left-hand corner of the hotspot, in pixels.	Callout Properties pane
<x1>, <y1>	The coordinates of the lower right-hand corner of the hotspot, in pixels.	Callout Properties pane, calculated by adding the width and height to x0 and y0
<pause>	If enabled, the video playback will pause upon reaching the end of the hotspot.	Callout Properties pane, Flash Hotspot Properties... button, Pause at end of callout check box
<url>	Specifies the destination of the hotspot: a particular URL, a time designation, or a marker.	Callout Properties pane, Flash Hotspot Properties... button
<newWindow>	A value of 1 indicates that the hotspot's destination URL will open in a new window.	Callout Properties pane, Flash Hotspot Properties... button, Open URL in new browser window check box
PLAYLIST > CAPTIONINFO		
<Time>	The point in time (in seconds) that the caption is introduced.	Open Captions pane

Tag	Description	Camtasia Studio Command
<Caption>	The actual content of the caption. Use to signify a carriage return.	Open Captions pane
PLAYLIST > TOCINFO		
<node>	Includes the *label*, which is the text of the TOC item as well as the *time* in the video to which the TOC item is linked.	---
PLAYLIST > QUIZINFO		
<time>	The point in time in which the quiz is introduced (in seconds).	Timeline
<title>	The title of the quiz.	Quiz Appearance and Feedback dialog, Quiz name field
<question>	The actual text of a question.	Question pane
<answer>	The text of one potential answer for a question.	Question pane
<response>	Indication of whether a response was correct or incorrect.	Question pane

Camtasia Theater's Configuration File

Because of its different structure, the config.xml file generated by Camtasia Theater is structured a bit differently. In the following table, I summarize all the commands available to you in your XML file (at least, all the ones that actually *do* something). For each tag name, I provide a description of what it does, and also the corresponding command in Camtasia Theater, if applicable. The tags are ordered by appearance in the actual file.

You may notice that between the <config> tags that encompass all the other tags, there are two main categories: movie and menutree. The <movie> tag contains all the tags that influence how the different components are displayed, and it is divided into two subcategories: <controls>, which controls the display of the control bar and preload movie, and **<menuproperties>**, which influences the format of the navigational menu. The **<menutree>** tag stipulates the order and location of your SWF video files.

Tag	Description	Camtasia Theater Command
<AutoStart>	A value of 0 indicates that all videos will start paused. 1 means all videos will automatically begin upon loading.	Controls tab, Paused at start check box
<BackgroundColor>	Enter any valid hexadecimal value to change the background color of your presentation.	Menu tab, Movie Background button
<ShowLoadingMov>	Enter 1 to show a preload movie.	Controls tab, Show loading movie check box
<LoadingMovURL>	The location of your preload movie. This can be either a file path or a web URL (if a file path, make sure you actually add the file to your project). Make sure that <ShowLoadingMov> is enabled.	Controls tab, Loading movie URL field
<ScaleLoadingMov>	A value of 1 indicates that the preload movie will adopt the same dimensions as the video content. 0 will maintain the preloader's original dimensions.	Controls tab, Match movie size check box
<LoadingMovPercentToLoad>	The minimum percentage that your video SWF needs to load before it begins to play.	Controls tab, % of main movie to preload field
<LoadingMovMinDuration>	The minimum amount of time to display the preload movie before it disappears and the main SWF video begins to play.	Controls tab, Minimum preload movie display time field

Tag	Description	Camtasia Theater Command
<ControllerColor>	Determines the color of your control bar. Any hexadecimal value will work.	Controls tab, Movie controller color button
<ShowFFRW>	A binary tag that determines whether or not to show the fast forward and rewind buttons on the control bar.	---
<ShowAbout>	A value of 1 shows the About button on the control bar, whereas 0 turns it off.	Controls tab, Show About box check box
<AboutBoxText>	This is where the content for your About box goes (up to eight lines). Simply press Enter for a new line.	Controls tab, About text (up to eight lines)
<TimeDisplayFormat>	This tag changes the format of how the duration and/or elapsed time is displayed in your presentation. The only acceptable values are: SS, MM:SS, HH:MM, HH:MM:SS, SSs, MMm SSs, HHh MMm, and HHh MMm SSs.	Controls tab, Display format field
<ShowDuration>	Binary tag that determines whether to show the video's total duration.	Controls tab, Show duration check box
<ShowElapsedTime>	Binary tag that controls whether to show the video's current elapsed time.	Controls tab, Show elapsed time check box

Tag	Description	Camtasia Theater Command
<TimeDisplayFont>	The font of your time display text. While Theater will only allow Arial and Times New Roman as values, you can enter the name of any font on your system here. However, keep in mind that it may not display correctly, and that the font in question must also be on the viewer's system in order to display.	Controls tab, Font drop-down list
<TimeDisplayFontColor>	The font color of your time display text (again, only hexadecimal values).	Controls tab, Font color button
<position>	A value of *left* places your navigational menu to the left of your video, while *right* places it on the right.	Menu tab, Menu alignment drop-down list
<background_color>	The background color of your menu, in hexadecimal format.	Menu tab, Menu background button
<title>	The title of your presentation goes here.	Menu tab, Menu title field
<title_color>	The color of said title (hexadecimal values only).	Menu tab, Menu title button
<title_fontsize>	The point size of your title text. You may enter a broader range of values here than is possible within Camtasia Theater.	Menu tab, Menu title font size drop-down list
<item_fontsize>	The point size of your menu item text. You may enter a broader range of values here than is possible within Camtasia Theater.	Menu tab, Menu item font size drop-down list

Tag	Description	Camtasia Theater Command
<maintext_color>	The font color of your menu items (hexadecimal values).	Menu tab, Item normal button
<maintexthilite_color>	The font color of your menu items when moused over or active (hexadecimal values).	Menu tab, Item rollover button
<play_in_sequence>	Binary tag that determines whether the next video in the sequence plays automatically when the current one finishes.	Menu tab, Play movies in sequence check box
<text>	The title of the current menu item.	Menu tab, Menu item name field
<url>	The location of the menu item's SWF file. Unlike in Theater, which will only let you choose a file path, you may enter a web URL here.	Menu tab, Menu item file field (cannot be edited, and no URL may be specified)

As you can see, there's a lot of power packed into those little files. It behooves you to become familiar with your config file so you can make quick changes without having to go back into your Camtasia Studio or Theater project.

Summary

In this chapter, you learned a few handy tricks for tricking out your productions. With a little scripting, you learned how to...

- Create and customize preloader movies by working with FLA files in Adobe Flash.
- Embed Flash videos into your blog, CRM application, or other web page.
- Edit the pants off your configuration file, changing everything from quiz answers to the appearance of your captions pane.

I've opted not to include exercises for this chapter. With such broad possibilities offered by Camtasia Studio's customization options, it's really important just to dig in and experiment.

Thus ends our journey. I hope that by now, you've gotten a real sense of the possibilities offered by this amazing application. If you've read through the entire book and gone through all the exercises, then congratulations — it's likely you're at least 80% as proficient as I am.

Many thanks for your time and attention. If you haven't already, please at least browse the appendices, which include tips and additional resources. If you're in the market for hardware to go with your new software, then the Buyer's Guide is especially worth a look. Have fun!

Tips for Reducing Your File Size

Despite your best efforts to produce high-quality video with a small footprint, there are a number of factors that can bloat the size of your video files. This can be particularly frustrating if your final output destination is the web, where low-bandwidth requirements are the key to success. In this book, I have outlined a number of tips for keeping your file sizes manageable. For your convenience, here they all are in one location.

Keep Your Dimensions Small

It's just common sense. Making a full-screen recording will consume a lot more file space than would recording a small window. In addition, smaller files are easier for the user to play back because you don't have to worry about a user's screen resolution being smaller than the dimensions of your video. Everyone has their own favorite recording dimensions. Mine are 688 x 520, because even users with a maximum screen resolution of 800 x 600 can view your video with space left over for their task bar and the video controls. If the application you're recording absolutely requires a full-screen recording, try reducing your own screen resolution to 800 x 600.

Globally **changing your screen resolution** can be accomplished thusly:

1. Choose **Start > Control Panel**.

2. In Windows XP, double-click the **Display** icon. The Display Properties dialog opens. Click the **Settings** tab.

   or

   In Windows Vista, select **Personalization > Display Settings**.

3. Drag the Screen resolution slider to the left, until it reads **800 x 600**.

4. To save your settings, click **OK**, then **Yes**.

Monitor Your Content

Most problems with file size stem from recording content that is inappropriate for the codec selected. Either choose a more appropriate codec for your content, or edit out the content that your chosen codec doesn't like.

For example, when using the TechSmith Screen Capture Codec (TSCC), you should take care to avoid the following:

- Real-world video
- Animated sequences
- Color gradients
- Lots of fade effects
- Lots of screen transitions (some carry a higher file size penalty than others, so feel free to experiment)
- Superfluous zooming and panning

Several of these tips apply to other codecs as well, particularly in regard to movement. Most codecs have ways of efficiently compressing content that doesn't move around a lot, so keep in mind that dragging large windows around, having lots of scene changes (cuts), and zooming and panning all over the place are likely to show up in your file size no matter what codec you're using. Remember that Camtasia Studio gives you convenient check boxes at production time that let you automatically disable callout fade effects and use instant zooming and panning, so if you have these elements in your production and are unhappy with the file size, reproducing your video with these boxes checked can be an effective quick fix.

Check Your Audio

Have you added voice narration to your video? Many people don't realize this, but your audio track can comprise as much as 90% of your overall file size, depending on your compression settings. While I try to keep my audio very high quality for video on CD-ROM, there are some compromises to be made when bringing your stuff to the web. Try to compress that audio using codecs like MP3 LAME and μ-Law as well as experimenting with different attributes to see what works for you. One thing I can't stress enough: Encode your audio in monaural format! You only have one mouth, right? Choosing stereo is a classic rookie mistake, and *doubles* the file size of your audio with zero increase in quality. So keep it mono.

One final tip regarding audio: If you're adding audio narration, do try to keep your track as succinct as possible, editing out all the internal pauses. Unlike video, where long pauses don't really add much to the file size (provided nothing is changing on the screen), silence in your audio track produces just as much data as the spoken word. Sometimes I look back on some of my earlier work and cringe, thinking, "I could drive a truck through some of the pauses I left in there!" Don't let this happen to you.

Reduce Color Depth

Depending on the codec, you can also save some file space by reducing the number of colors displayed on your screen. I generally like Medium (16-bit); the visual difference between this and 32-bit color depth is nearly imperceptible. Not so with 8-bit color depth (256 colors), so I'd be careful if reducing the color depth this much.

To **change your color depth**, do the following:

1. Choose **Start > Control Panel**.
2. In Windows XP, double-click the **Display** icon. The Display Properties dialog opens. Click the **Settings** tab.

   or

   In Windows Vista, go to **Personalization > Display Settings**.
3. Choose a color depth from the **Color Quality** (or **Colors**) drop-down list.
4. To save your settings, click **OK**, then **Yes**.

Break up Your Video into Smaller Chunks

Fortunately, the pop song adage "breaking up is hard to do" doesn't really apply to Camtasia Studio. Bring your overly large video into Camtasia Studio, add a few markers at the topic transition points, and you can quickly produce a series of videos rather than just one. Yes, technically, the bandwidth savings are an illusion. The users still have to download the same amount; they're just doing it in smaller chunks. True enough. But users will be able to start viewing content much more quickly, as the load time is now split across several videos, thus keeping the frustration level in check.

Try a Different File Format

When producing your videos, if you're not getting the kind of results you expect, it might just be that you're producing into a file format that isn't appropriate for your video's intended purpose. Remember, AVI files work best for CD-ROM, and SWF files work better for the web. WMV files are ideal for real-world video and game captures, while animated GIFs are good for small screen videos that are only a few seconds in length. All file formats have their individual strengths and weaknesses, which are all discussed in detail in Chapter 12, "The Production Process." Matching the content and distribution method with the appropriate file output can have a profound effect on file size, so do your homework before picking an output format.

Try a Different Compression Scheme

And on a related note, even if you're married to a particular file format, there's still a lot you can do to get that file size down by simply playing with the compression settings. Producing to SWF? Try using JPEG compression. Going to AVI? Perhaps the content demands a codec that's more tolerant of high-motion video, such as DivX. If you're doing a lot of transitions and PIP sequences, you'll need to become very acquainted with the various "high-motion" compression options: Flash videos should be FLV, QuickTime should be compressed with H.264, etc. Lossy compression algorithms work much better in these circumstances.

Reduce the Duration of Your Preload Movie

When producing to the web, you have the option of setting how much of the main video you want to preload before it begins. If you have a longer video (hence with more time to load the rest of the video while playing), you can set this to 10% or even less. While this does *not* actually lower the file size, it will feel like it to your audience, who will be spending less time watching the loading screen and more time enjoying your excellent video. However, do keep in mind that this technique does not work with shorter, graphically intense content, because there's a lot to load and not a lot of time to do it. In this case, you'll want to set the preload percentage high, say 50%. Otherwise, the video might pause midway through to finish loading, which as you can imagine is quite aggravating to the user.

Appendices

Recording Alternative Platforms

When crafting your expert tutorials and marketing spots for the various projects related to your work, it's likely you'll be exposed to computing platforms other than Windows. Unfortunately, Camtasia Studio currently supports only Windows XP and later. So what happens if you need to record a Mac or Linux application, or even a mobile program on the Palm OS or Pocket PC? In each of these cases, I can give you a way to record it using Camtasia Studio. While there are some trade-offs, I've found that these solutions do a remarkable job of getting content from other operating systems into Windows, where you can then capture it using our favorite program.

Recording Any Desktop Using VNC

Platforms supported: Windows, Linux, Mac OS, Solaris (SPARC), HP-UX 11

VNC, which stands for Virtual Network Computing, is a software solution that allows you to remotely interact with other computers, effectively viewing (or even controlling) their desktops in a window on your computer. The VNC source code is open-source, and there are therefore about a gazillion variants. Fortunately, that is also what makes it available free for your download. While I've listed the more popular supported operating systems above, you can probably find a version of VNC for just about every operating system out there. It's also available for Java.

VNC has two components: a *server* that offers up the computer as a host, sharing its screen and (possibly) giving up its control to the client computer; and the *client*, which can view the shared content and, if allowed by the server, control the mouse cursor remotely and execute commands on the server machine.

What's important for our purposes is that VNC can take the screen of just about any OS and plaster it all over your Windows desktop. Gee, I wonder if there's some sort of program out there that could capture the contents of that window and save it as a video? Using the Camtasia Recorder, we're going to do just that.

How do we go about this? First, you need a copy of VNC for each operating system you're working with. You'll need to install at least the client portion on your Windows machine (the one running Camtasia Studio). You also need the server portion installed on your source machine.

So where do we download all this wonderful software? As an open-source project, there are multiple developers of VNC, each of whom supports different operating systems. Check out some of these links for different flavors of VNC:

- Real VNC (www.realvnc.com) — The "official" version by the original developers from AT&T labs in Cambridge. Mac and Windows Vista versions are no longer free, though.

- TightVNC (www.tightvnc.com) — An open-source variant. Offers some bug fixes and enhancements, including enhanced compression algorithms.

- UltraVNC (www.uvnc.com) — Brings some security features to the table such as session encryption and Active Directory-based security.

- Vine Server (formerly OSXvnc) (www.redstonesoftware.com/products/vine/server/vineosx) — VNC server software for Mac OS X. They also have a VNC server application for Mac OS 9.

While it's beyond the scope of this book to walk you through the process of capturing every OS out there with VNC, here's a quick getting started guide, using the Macintosh OS X as an example. Please consult the documentation of your individual VNC server application to find out how to get up and running with it, but the client-side setup and the recording process should be the same as in this guide.

Recording Mac OS X Using VNC

To my knowledge, Vine Server is the only free Mac-specific VNC server software out there, although there are several Mac-friendly clients. But it's the server program we need in this case. Before you do anything else, download the software using the link posted above. If you haven't already done so, also install VNC on your client computer (the one that's doing the recording). Downloading from any of the first three links above should get the job done on the client side.

Now that we've gotten that out of the way, here's how we go about getting VNC up and running so that we can **record our Mac application**:

1. On your Macintosh, launch **Vine Server**. Its dialog appears.

2. On the General tab, make note of the **display name** (you'll need this information later when connecting from your Windows PC).

3. In addition, it would behoove you to enter a password into the **Password** field, also noting this information for when you connect.

4. Click the **Start Server** button.

5. On your Windows PC, launch Camtasia Recorder. Choose your capture input: **Screen** if you'll be setting VNC to take over your entire screen, or **Window** if you'll only be displaying VNC in a window.

6. In the Tools Options dialog of Camtasia Recorder, enable both **Minimize before starting capture** and **Pause before starting capture** on the Capture tab.

7. Launch **VNC Viewer.** The following dialog appears:

8. Click the **Options...** button. The dialog that appears will vary based on whatever flavor of VNC you happen to be using. Explore your options. There are two that I usually mess with. The first is **Full-screen mode**. This displays the operating system full screen rather than just in a window. It helps to be able to see the entire server screen without needing to scroll all over the place. Keeping the monitor resolution of the server computer *lower* than that of the client computer helps as well. If you're going to enable full-screen mode, then you'll also want to change a second option, namely to specify a **hotkey** for accessing the VNC menu. Otherwise, you'll have a hard time accessing your own desktop and getting back out of the client when needed. Look around in your Viewer options dialog; it's usually listed under Menu key or something like that.

9. In the server window, type in the display name you noted back in step 2. Click **OK**.

10. If you specified a password on the server side (step 3), you are prompted to enter it. Do so and click **OK**. The remote desktop will appear on your screen.

11. Press your **Record** hotkey (F9 by default) to turn the Recorder on (in paused mode). If you're recording VNC in a window, click the server's desktop window when prompted. Press your hotkey again to get rolling. Record your session per usual. Press your **Stop** hotkey when finished.

VNC Tips

Tip 1: Forget the net. While VNC developers are constantly working to optimize its compression, keep in mind that viewing another computer remotely in real time sucks up a *lot* of bandwidth. If you're going to be making a broadcast-quality recording of this session, you want it to flow as fast as possible so that it doesn't look like your video was made in slow motion. I therefore recommend only recording content sent over a local area network (LAN), rather than over the Internet. If you can, get both machines (server and client) running off the same router.

Tip 2: Juggle computers. If you're fortunate enough to have both machines in the same room, my recommendation is to work from the machine you're recording. While it's tempting to work remotely with the Windows computer while recording, thereby controlling everything from a single console, you want to avoid this. Even on LAN connections, there can be a bit of a lag, and this lag is exacerbated when your commands originate away from the source machine. To your audience, your mouse cursor will appear sluggish, and people will assume that its wielder is either highly uncoordinated or simply drunk.

Tip 3: Keep it simple. While the movement of a mouse cursor and the opening of menus are relatively fluid when viewed remotely, moving windows around or doing other activities with a lot of background changes can eat up a ton of bandwidth, and you're almost certain to see some lag. Keep your actions simple. In addition, just doing things like cleaning up your desktop icons and temporarily removing your desktop wallpaper can also help stream that screen a bit faster (as well as reduce unnecessary clutter).

Recording Any Computer Using an RGB Capture Card

While VNC is a piece of software for broadcasting your desktop onto another machine, there are hardware solutions out there that can do it much more expediently. Using an RGB capture device (often referred to as a "frame grabber"), you can take any VGA input and display it in a window on your Windows PC. What does this mean for you? It means that you can capture the video output from *any* machine that supports VGA output (and virtually all of them do). Using a hardware solution sports the following advantages over software like VNC:

- It tends to be faster. Depending on the specifications of the hardware, you might not notice a lag of any sort. Most cards will post benchmarking results that show how many frames per second you can expect at a particular resolution. Even lower-end cards can handle resolutions of 640 x 480, 800 x 600, and even 1024 x 768 at a minimum of 10 fps, which for our needs is perfectly acceptable.

- There is no configuration needed on the source machine whatsoever. Once you've installed the software and got the system working on the client side, it will continue working, no matter how many different computers you end up connecting to it.

- Because all it requires from the source is a VGA output stream, you can hook up just about any computer imaginable to it. And it doesn't stop with desktop computers, either. Game consoles, medical devices, and scientific equipment with VGA output can be captured just as easily. I have also heard of people using third-party conversion cables to put VGA outputs on their personal digital assistants (PDAs) as well as handheld gaming devices, meaning that these could be captured, too.

But it's not all sunshine and roses in FrameGrabber Land, either. As with anything, there's a flip side. Here are some disadvantages of which you'll want to be aware:

- It's *expensive*, especially when compared to the cost of software like VNC (which is approximately $0). Expect to pay anywhere from $400 to $2,500, depending on specs.

- Most of these devices are PCI cards, which will require you (or someone perhaps a bit more qualified than you) to open your machine and install it. However, I have seen some frame grabbers advertised that convert the VGA signal to USB 2.0, and since all the hardware is external in this case, no such tinkering would be necessary.

- Unlike the DVI output found on most newer video cards, VGA is an analog standard, not digital. As such, the color output can be somewhat inconsistent. For example, when viewed in a window on the destination monitor, what is supposed to be a solid block of color might in fact develop subtle color gradations that will really throw the TSCC codec into a tizzy, thus bloating the file size. While I have seen DVI-based capture cards that might not have this problem, keep in mind that DVI output on computers is still nowhere near as common as VGA, and the range of devices with which you could use the card's digital input are therefore limited.

Performing the capture is relatively simple. Just take a standard monitor cable (usually included with these devices), plug one end into the monitor port on the computer you want to record, and plug the other end into the VGA port of the capture device. Install and launch the included software on your Windows machine, and poof! A window appears on your Windows monitor that shows the desktop of the other machine. This window can be recorded just like a VNC window can, so please consult the VNC getting started guide in the previous section for details in setting up the Camtasia Recorder to capture it.

Recording Palm OS Applications

If you should ever need to record a Palm OS application, it's actually pretty straightforward to do so. All the software you ever need (other than the application you're recording) comes directly from ACCESS (formerly PalmSource). You have a choice between two applications:

- **The Garnet OS Emulator.** This application takes the ROM image from a Palm device and emulates the Palm environment on your Windows desktop. There are even skins to make your desktop "Palm" look like an actual Palm device, rather than just a Palm environment in a window. However, this emulator is only for emulating older versions of the Palm OS (v 4.x and lower). For newer versions of the operating system and the applications that support it, you need…

- **The Garnet OS Simulator.** This is the Palm operating system compiled natively for Intel machines. It doesn't just emulate the Palm OS like the Emulator does — it *is* the Palm OS. Different OS versions are available for download.

Both of these environments include the native PIM (personal information management) applications like Datebook, Address, etc. If you want to record a specific third-party Palm application, you can install it just as you would on a regular Palm.

So how do we get these useful tools? Unfortunately, Palm doesn't just give them away without asking for some information in return. They make you join the ACCESS Developer Network. Don't worry, you don't have to have a computer science degree or work for a software company to join, and it's completely cost-free. Simply go to the web page

http://www.access-company.com/developers/

to read up a bit on the program, and when you're ready, click the **Join ADN Today** link to join. It's nothing too serious, just some basic web form information and a few screens of legalese. Once you're all legal, you can go to the following link to access all Palm-related content, including the download of Garnet OS developer tools:

http://www.developerpavilion.com/palmos

There are some corollary files to use with the Emulator:

- **ROM images.** These are the "guts" of the OS and must be installed. An appropriate ROM file can be imported from any older Palm device you happen to have handy. ACCESS also offers a couple of older basic ones for download.

- **Skins.** These are used to present the image of an actual handheld on the screen, making your recordings a tad more realistic. Unlike a valid ROM image, it is not necessary to install skins in order to run the Emulator.

Here's the process for **recording a Palm application** with Camtasia Recorder:

1. Launch either the Emulator or Simulator. If starting the application for the first time, you may need to specify the ROM image as well as go through the operating system's introductory screens (time zone settings, etc.).

2. If recording an application *other* than the built-in PIM applications, you'll need to install it first. To do so, right-click anywhere on the Palm's window and then choose **Install > Database....** Select any needed PRC (application) and accompanying PDB (data) files, and then click **Open.**

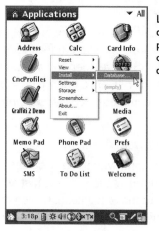

Let's go ahead and install some programs onto our virtual Palm device.

3. Launch your application, and then open Camtasia Recorder.

---

4. If desired, you can change the default mouse cursor to simulate a stylus. In the Camtasia Recorder, open the **Effects** menu and choose **Options....** From the **Cursor** menu, click the **Cursor Setup...** button. Choose **Use cursor from file**, and then click the **Open** button.

Of the many cursors available, there are several that look like PDA styli. Select one and then click **Open**. Click **OK** twice.

5. Select your capture area to include the Emulator/Simulator window.

6. Start recording, and then work as you normally would. End and save the capture per usual.

These applications work extremely well. I've recorded countless Palm applications in the past; they're a snap to make, and they always look great.

Recording Pocket PC Applications

Unlike the Palm OS platform, Microsoft has not created a free, easily accessible emulator for our use. Fortunately, a third-party developer called SOTI, Inc. (www.soti.net) has stepped up to the plate and created a software product that will let you project the contents of your Pocket PC onto the monitor of your Windows PC. You can even overlay a device skin to make it look like just about any kind of Pocket PC device in existence. The product is called **Pocket Controller,** and their professional edition is currently $35.95. It's the best method I know of for getting Pocket PC content onto your desktop, where it can then be recorded.

The one downside is that you need to have access to an actual Pocket PC device (or one of its other supported mobile devices) in order to use it. The program supports a number of ways of connecting the unit to your PC, from LAN (wired or wireless) to USB to Bluetooth to serial. Some connection types are faster than others, but you should be able to find some acceptable way of establishing a connection. Once you have the software installed on both the device and your Windows system, it will beam the contents of your handheld into a window on your desktop. Follow the instructions in the previous (Palm) section to set your capture area, change the mouse cursor to simulate a stylus, and execute the recording.

Putting Camtasia Studio Content on Mobile Devices

Up to this point, we've talked about how to get information from small screens onto your Windows desktop. But what about doing the reverse? This isn't limited only to video iPods — Camtasia Studio can produce videos that look amazing on other mobile devices, too. Now, you'll often require a third-party application to get these videos onto your machine of choice, as these devices and their various media applications generally have a preferred format (some proprietary, some not). The thing you'll need to keep in mind on the recording end is that the dimensions of your videos should be the maximum resolution supported by the device in question, so as to avoid scaling issues. For example, several high-resolution Palms have a screen resolution of 320 x 320. By confining your screen recording to a 320 x 320 area, you can ensure that your content looks great on these devices. No scaling. No scrolling.

Here's a brief list of software that can help get those little videos all ready for display on smaller devices:

- **TealMovie** (http://www.tealpoint.com/softmovi.htm) — Palm devices. Comes with both a Windows-based conversion tool and a media player. The produced file format is proprietary, but file sizes for Camtasia Studio videos are low and the quality is outstanding (practically lossless). Cost: $29.95 for both producer and player.

- **Kinoma Producer and Kinoma Player** (www.kinoma.com) — Palm and PlayStation Portable (PSP) devices. Sports a conversion tool for Windows and a media player on the Palm (the files work with the built-in media player on PSP). Produces videos in MPEG-4 format. Kinoma has an advantage in that their media player is already bundled with several Palm OS devices. Cost: $29.99 for Producer, $24.99 for Player.

- **Pocket DVD Wizard** (www.pocket-dvd-wizard.com) — Pocket PC, Portable Media Center, Palm, PlayStation Portable (PSP), and a host of other portable media devices. In addition to converting DVDs, this handy application will also convert your AVIs, MOVs, or WMVs created in Camtasia Studio. This is a Windows-based conversion application. It is a producer only — you'll still require a player app on the device that can play one of its available output formats (AVI, WMV, MP4). Cost: $28.95 for the producer. Keep in mind that this application's main advantage lies in selecting the proper dimensions, file type, and level of compression for use on particular media devices. With the exception of MP4 output, Camtasia Studio can do all this natively if you know what you're doing.

- **PSP Video 9** (www.pspvideo9.com) — PlayStation Portable (PSP). Donationware app that converts Camtasia Studio AVIs, MOVs, and WMVs for viewing on the PSP's standard media player. Windows-based. Cost: free.

Keep in mind that there are a multitude of player applications out there for the various media devices. Some are commercial (i.e., they cost money), some are open-source (free), and some are bundled with the OS or device. Before dropping a mint on new software, double-check with the free applications to see if they support a file format from which Camtasia Studio can output.

Equipment Buyer's Guide

So you've followed all the suggestions for great-sounding audio laid out in Chapter 10, yet you still end up with sound quality reminiscent of a tin can and string telephone? It may be time for an equipment upgrade. Audio and video equipment can be quite expensive and, as with most things, you really do get what you pay for. But there are ways of getting great quality without breaking the bank, and in this section, I'll show you how. We'll begin by talking about all the links that make up the audio production chain, and for those PIP fanatics, we'll conclude with some general guidelines regarding camera video.

Buying the Right Mic

Let's start with microphones. At its simplest, a microphone is a piece of equipment that converts sound waves into an electrical signal. Sound waves (coming from your voice or a musical instrument) strike a flexible diaphragm at the microphone's head, which vibrates back and forth, modulating an electrical current as it does so. These electrical waves can then be recorded.

There are many different sorts of microphones for equally many purposes, but microphones tend to vary along two individual spectra: type and directionality.

Microphone Type

The microphone type is defined by the exact kind of diaphragm used for capturing sound waves. There are a number of kinds, such as piezo microphones (which use pressure to convert sound to electricity), the antiquated carbon mics, and ribbon microphones (where the diaphragm is a thin metal ribbon). For our purposes, we'll be looking at the three most common types for the recording of narration: dynamic, condenser, and lavaliere.

The diaphragm of a **dynamic** microphone is actually attached to a small metal coil. The coil moves within a magnetic field whenever the diaphragm vibrates, thus producing an electric current in the coil's wire. Sturdy and relatively cheap, dynamic mics are ideal for a simple home studio environment, especially considering that they require no batteries or other external power source (since the magnet moving within that coil of wire produces enough electricity to power it). They are also better equipped to handle high volume levels, though this is more of an issue when miking certain musical instruments as opposed to your own voice. While not as robust as condenser mics, they simplify things by not requiring a power source such as a preamp (more on that in a minute), and the higher-end ones actually produce very acceptable quality.

Condenser mics, on the other hand, require a power source in order to function. In the head of the microphone are two plates, one of which is thinner (often made of gold foil) and acts as the diaphragm. When sound waves hit this thin plate, it moves back and forth, changing the distance between the two plates, and thus modulating the electric current being applied to it. Condenser mics get their power from batteries or from a "phantom power" source such as an external power supply or (most likely in our case) a preamp or sound mixer. Condenser mics aren't anywhere near as rugged as dynamic mics, but they make up for it by being more responsive and accurate than dynamic mics, and thus able to reproduce the subtle nuances of the human voice much more accurately.

Finally, **lavaliere** microphones are small mics that clip to the speaker's lapel. You often see them during televised interviews and talk shows. Technically, lav mics are also dynamic mics (usually), but they're so specialized, I decided to break them off into a third "type." There are essentially two situations in which it makes sense for you as a Camtasia Studio user to employ a lav mic:

- You're giving a live presentation (PowerPoint or otherwise) that you also happen to be recording.

- You're recording camera video in addition to screen video, and you don't want to fidget with a handheld mic or have a studio boom obstructing your face.

Lav mics come in two flavors: wired and wireless. The latter is excellent for presentations. Both have pickup patterns designed to filter out ambient noise and capture the voice of the wearer and nobody else.

Directionality

And speaking of which: Every microphone (not just the lavaliere mic) is engineered to support a particular *pickup pattern*, or *directionality*. A microphone's pickup pattern determines how sensitive the mic is to a particular sound depending on the location of the sound source relative to the mic.

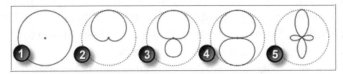

Standard microphone pickup patterns: 1) omnidirectional, 2) cardioid, 3) hypercardioid, 4) bidirectional, 5) shotgun.

An **omnidirectional** microphone is equally sensitive to all sounds, regardless of the direction from which the sound is coming. This is typically a poor choice for recording your narration, since it will pick up all ambient sound: the squeak of your chair, hum of your computer fan, or kids playing on the street outside. I think it goes without saying that none of these will add to the professionalism of your video.

You'll most likely be using a **cardioid** microphone (thus named because the pickup pattern looks like an upside-down heart), which is typically only sensitive in the front. Make sure you're speaking into the correct side! People who want an even tighter pickup pattern should go with a **hypercardioid** mic, which offers even narrower directionality in the front, yet also often has a tiny sliver of sensitivity in the back (never have been able to figure out why).

Bidirectional mics are equally sensitive in the front and back, but not the sides. You'll find this pickup pattern mostly on ribbon mics. Finally, a **shotgun** pattern is like hypercardioid on steroids. With its super-narrow pickup pattern, a shotgun mic can pick one person's voice out of a crowded room. This microphone type is used predominately for television, film, and (as you can imagine) surveillance. Keep in mind that some microphones offer a special switch that will let you actually select from several different pickup patterns — it's something to consider if you have multiple uses in mind, but don't want to buy multiple microphones.

Buying Tips

Okay, so it looks like we've got some choices to make regarding the right microphone. I know that up to now, some of you have been using the microphone that came with your computer. You know which one I'm talking about: It looks like a little beige or black plastic cockroach that's attached to a long thin cable and ends with a stereo mini-plug, perfect for jacking into the mic port of your equally crappy factory-installed sound card. It's not worth the drawer space in which it usually resides — throw it away this instant! Some of you might be using the built-in mic of your webcam or a headset-style microphone/headphone combo. These things have their place, such as for Internet telephony or gaming, just not for recording your dulcet tones for a screen video. Please don't use them with Camtasia Studio (or if you do, don't tell me about it — I'll have nightmares).

If one of the above describes your situation, never fear: There *is* hope for you. We just need to do a little shopping, that's all. For our purposes, we're likely looking for a dynamic or condenser mic with a cardioid or hypercardioid pickup pattern. Some good **dynamic** mic choices include:

- **Shure SM57** or **SM58**. Both of these are good beginner mics that can be had for under $100*. I've heard that the SM57 is better suited to the male voice and the SM58 a more appropriate choice for the ladies, but only testing with your own voice will tell you for sure if that theory holds water.

- A somewhat pricier dynamic mic is the **Sennheiser MD 421 II**. At around $350, if you're looking for a rugged, high-quality alternative to a nice condenser mic, this is the way to go.

- Another dynamic mic choice in the $350 to $400 range is the **Electro-Voice RE20**, which is used mainly in broadcasting. It offers a flat response over a wide frequency range and, as with all dynamic mics, no external power is required.

---

* To help give you a sense of the real-world cost of upgrading your recording system, this and the other listed prices in this appendix reflect "street value," and not the (usually) inflated MSRP. As always, try to shop around for the best price.

So what about the **condenser** side of things? Your choices here are much broader, particularly on the higher end, but here are a few of my faves:

- On the lower end, the **Marshall MXL 2003** can be had for about $150. It features bass roll-off and a –10db switch.

- Similarly, the **NT1-A** by Australian manufacturer **RØDE** is an excellent choice at around $200. I owned its predecessor, the NT-1, and it was a mainstay of my studio for about two years.

- For a little more money, the **Shure KSM27** and **RØDE NT 1000** are both great buys in the $300 range.

- **AKG** and **Audio Technica** are also solid brands that offer great mics at a variety of price ranges.

Though I consider the upper range of condenser mics to be a tad superfluous for most screen video related applications (especially since you'll probably end up compressing the audio, anyway), if you can get your hands on one of these for a reasonable price, go for it:

- The **Neumann TLM 103** is a popular choice for professional voice actors, and can be had for about an even grand.

- Neumann makes even higher-quality mics for studio recording: The **U87** and **U89** are considered by many sound engineers as *the* choice for studio recording, but at a price (usually around a couple thousand, though some vintage versions can fetch an even higher price).

Some online retailers such as ZZSounds (www.zzsounds.com) and Dolphin Music in the UK (www.dolphinmusic.co.uk) let you check out user reviews of their various mics, but there's really no substitute for heading out to a well-stocked music store and auditioning a few microphones using a prepared script. Certain mics are better suited to a particular voice type. Women should be particularly selective, as some mics are just too bright for their voices and can end up making you sound shrill.

One last point about buying a microphone: Be sure to check the store's return policy *very* carefully. As microphones come in close contact with the mouth, many retailers will not accept returns on a mic, once opened, due to health concerns. Make sure you ask before you buy, and don't just take Joe Registerjockey's word for it — ask to speak with a manager.

Microphone Accessories

Now that we've picked out the right microphone, there are a few other items we'll need prior to shopping for a preamp. Specifically, you will need a quality XLR cable to attach the mic to whatever preamp or audio interface you're buying, you'll need some sort of microphone stand, you'll need a pop filter, and finally, you're going to require some quality monitors.

Microphone Cable

First off, we need some cable. Select a high-quality **XLR cable**. Here's a bit of useless trivia for you: XLR stands for Xternal, Live, and Return, which correspond to the three pins at each end of the cable (which in turn are connected to the ground wire, hot wire, and cold wire, respectively). Here are the various factors to consider when buying an XLR cable:

- **Length.** These grounded cables come in a variety of lengths. Pick the shortest available length that will still be sufficient for running from the mic to your preamp. It's not a huge deal, but the longer a signal has to travel, the more it can degrade, so keep the mic cable as short as you can.

- **Balanced vs. Unbalanced.** Make sure that the mic cable you select is *balanced*. Balanced cables have two conductors; half the signal travels on one and half on the other. Balanced cables are quieter because the two conductors tend to cancel out extraneous signals. Even better are *quad* cables, which feature four conductors. The tight winding required when two pairs of conductors are twisted together results in even better rejection of noise interference.

- **Contact materials.** The contacts are those points at the end of each cable that come into actual contact with the mic on one end and the mixer/preamp/audio interface on the other. Typically these are made of tin, silver, or gold, in ascending order of cost and desirability. Buy a cable with gold contacts if you can afford it.

- **Shielding.** Next, you need to concern yourself with the cable's shielding. Shielding covers the actual wires in the cable and has two purposes: It acts as a return conductor for the signal current, and it *shields* your center cable from different kinds of interference, such as that given off by radio waves, power conductors, and those pesky fluorescent lights hanging above you, to name but a few. Shielding also comes in three flavors: foil, spiral, and braided.

Typically, the more copper in the shielding, the better. The foil shields are mostly aluminum, which is not as good a conductor as copper. Braided shielding has the most copper content, and therefore rejects the most interference. It's a bit more fragile than spiral shielding (which can be bent and kinked all over the place with no breakage), but since we're apt to be working in a studio environment rather than out touring with The Stones, I think it's safe to say that braided is best.

■ **Connector quality.** Most cabling companies get their XLR connectors from other manufacturers. As with any industry, there are high-quality manufacturers and there are those who specialize in producing cheap, low-quality knock-offs. You're in good hands if your connectors came from Neutrik or Amphenol.

Bottom line: Cabling is an important link in your chain of audio quality, and it's no place to skimp. Shielding is particularly important due to the potential havoc wreaked by the electromagnetic interference from all your other equipment.

Expect to pay anywhere from $20 to $40 for a high-quality cable of shorter length. Three reputable manufacturers are Pro Co Sound (www.procosound.com), Monster Cable (www.monstercable.com), and C.B.I. (www.cbicables.com). Pro Co Sound's AmeriQuad and Merlin lines are particularly good.

Microphone Stand

One vital aspect of ensuring a high-quality recording is to provide the microphone with a certain amount of stability. *Do not* hold the microphone in your hand while recording! Every tremor, every movement, will show up as noise in your recording. To keep the mic in a stable position, you're going to need two things. The first is a shock mount. This device keeps the mic suspended inside a large ring through the strategic placement of elastic bands.

This is a Neumann TLM 127 inside a shock mount.

Even if the mic stand gets slightly jostled, the shock mount should absorb any impact and allow the microphone to continue doing what it does best. Most high-quality mics will throw in the shock mount for free, or at least have it available as an optional accessory. You might want to make sure that the manufacturer will send you replacement bands upon request, as these do have a tendency to snap occasionally.

The other thing you're going to need, obviously, is a good microphone stand. There are three main types of mic stands, at least for our purposes, and the right one for you will depend on how you have your studio set up.

- **Straight mic stand.** This is the kind of stand you typically saw at your old high school assemblies. A telescoping pole is attached to a weighted circular base. The other end of the pole holds a clip for the mic. These stands come in two sizes: a standard one for delivering a standing performance, and a miniature desktop model for recording while firmly planted in your favorite office chair.

- **Tripod/boom stand.** These stands consist of a tripod that you place to the side or in front of the desk where you're recording, and the tripod attaches to a boom arm that swings over to where you are. The height can be adjusted based on your preference to sit or stand. When giving one a test drive, make sure that the tripod is sturdy, that the screw knobs to adjust the stand are made of metal (not plastic), and most importantly, that the joint connecting the boom arm is both counterweighted and uses some sort of interlocking mechanism in the joint. This helps ensure that the boom doesn't slip, even when you've got it fully extended and attached to a heavier microphone. While marvelously versatile, if you're working in a small space, you might find your average boom stand to be a tad unwieldy.

- **Microphone arms.** These handy devices can be attached to your desk or another piece of furniture (either screwed in or held in place with a C-clamp). The extendable arm can be easily positioned when you need the mic and quickly tucked away when you don't. It uses heavy springs to counterbalance the weight of the microphone, cable, and pop filter. While expensive ($80 to $160), I find them to be the most convenient if you're doing a lot of recording and don't want to have to endure a lot of setup/breakdown time. This is the kind of mic holder I currently use. The only downside is that it doesn't work well with sound booths or other sound enclosures, so if you use one, you're going to have to worry about soundproofing the entire room — more on that later. O.C. White (www.ocwhite.com) makes excellent microphone arms.

Pop Filter

One final microphone accessory you'll need is a **pop filter**. Also called a *windscreen*, this handy tool places a large circle of stretched fabric (usually nylon) between your mouth and the mic. Its job is

A pop filter usually comes attached to a flexible gooseneck for easy positioning.

to dissipate air pressure, and it greatly reduces a phenomenon called *plosives* (those annoying popping "P" noises that can otherwise mar a good recording).

Pop filters also serve a secondary function. Microphones (especially condenser mics) are very sensitive to the elements, and don't like moisture. A nice pop filter is an inexpensive way of keeping you from spitting all over your shiny new mic during a recording session. Expect to pay somewhere in the neighborhood of $20 to $30. Of course, if you don't want to spend the cash, you can quickly and cheaply rig up your own pop filter with a wire clothes hanger and a piece of nylon hosiery. While it doesn't precisely lend a professional look to your studio, it works like a dream.

Monitors

No, I'm not talking about your computer screen. A **monitor** is sound engineering lingo for any speaker device that lets you monitor your output. You can, of course, use the garden-variety speakers you picked up at Best Buy last year, and this may in fact be preferable if you're only creating videos for the web. In that case, you would *want* to hear what the output sounds like on a set of Average Joe computer speakers. But when doing more sensitive work (for example, outputting to DVD), you may need something a bit more heavy duty.

Monitors may look like standard speakers, but they're much more accurate. They can run anywhere from $50 all the way up to $1,200, and come in two flavors: passive or active. *Passive* monitors require a separate amplifier, whereas *active* (or *powered*) monitors have the amplifier built in. A nice pair of these hooked into your audio interface can provide a much better reflection of what you're actually recording.

Headphones are also an absolute necessity, for two reasons. First, they're a great means of hearing what's being recorded during your session in real time. If you're breathing too loudly into the mic, why wait until the end of your recording to find out? Also, headphones are great for picking up on subtle background noise (like traffic outside) that you might have missed when listening through speakers. The ability to hear exactly what the mic is picking up will cut your audio editing time in half, believe me. Just plug 'em into the headphone port of your sound card or audio interface, and you should be good to go. Be sure to opt for a set of closed-ear headphones to filter out external noise (and eliminate possible microphone feedback — ouch!). A decent pair should run you $50 to $200.

Buying the Right Preamp

So, up to this point we've learned that your microphone takes sound waves (your voice) and converts them into an electrical signal. But unfortunately, the signal coming from your mic is too weak to be recorded. We need a device to amplify the signal first. This is where the preamplifier, or **preamp**, comes in. You've got a number of options, from stand-alone mic preamp to mixing board to full-blown audio interface, and we'll talk about each of these.

No matter what kind of preamp you choose, there's one particular feature that's an absolute *must* if you're using a condenser microphone. Since condenser mics require external power in order to function, your preamp is going to need an option called phantom power. Basically, all this means is that the preamp is equipped to deliver power to the microphone so that it can work. If you've got no phantom power, then that $500 condenser mic you just bought will give you $0 of actual use, except maybe as a paperweight.

Analog Preamps

A stand-alone preamp, also known as an **analog preamp,** has but one job: to take an XLR input from your microphone, amplify the signal up to what is known as *line level,* and then pass it on as cleanly as possible. It's called an analog preamp because it doesn't digitize the sound — it leaves that task up to your PC's sound card. Simply attach a cable from the preamp's output port to the microphone jack of your card.

Like anything else, analog preamps come in all price ranges ($50 to $2,000). Here are a few solid choices for your perusal:

- At a mere $50, the **ART Tube MP** preamp is an excellent choice. Rather than using a solid-state amplifier, it makes use of vacuum tubes to amplify the sound, which many professionals claim gives the mic a "warmer" sound. Another good example of a vacuum tube preamp is the **PreSonus BlueTube DP Stereo Tube** preamp, which provides both solid-state and tube amplifiers, letting you set the level of tube amplification (and hence the warmth). It can be had for about $200.

- One of the cleanest preamps you can get for under five hundred bucks is the **AudioBuddy** by **M-Audio**. At just $80, this little workhorse provides excellent low-noise amplification. I used one for a couple of years when first starting out, and it's the starter preamp I typically recommend to my Camtasia Studio training clients.

- On the higher end, the **Focusrite Platinum Voicemaster Pro** ($650) throws in a lot of bells and whistles like no-latency monitoring, vintage harmonics, and voice-optimized EQ. It's an excellent choice, but may be overkill for most users.

If you're working with a lot of other audio inputs (such as musical instruments), then a full-fledged mixing board might suit your needs better. These boards include a boatload of microphone and instrument inputs, and most can provide phantom power to your condenser mic. All those knobs and buttons are also really impressive looking, so if you've got a lot of customers or clients swinging by your office, it can make a nice trophy piece. Be wary, though. I've found that the actual microphone preamps in most mixers can't compare to stand-alone units unless you go really high-end.

Audio Interface Devices

Analog preamps can be had rather inexpensively while still providing clean sound, but there is still a small problem, friends. No matter how nice the signal coming from your preamp may be, once it leaves the preamp, that beautiful signal is now at the mercy of your (probably) factory-installed, OEM, cheaporific sound card. By relying on your sound card to digitize the signal for recording, you're introducing a new link in the chain of your audio quality, and probably the weakest one. Fortunately, there's a wonderful invention created just for computer-based recording, specifically the digital preamp, or **audio interface**.

An audio interface acts like a preamp and sound card in one. It comes in two styles: internal and external. Internal interfaces plug into one of your computer's free PCI slots, and generally come equipped with a series of cables, and sometimes even some sort of external box, for connecting your XLR cables and other inputs. Be sure to read the fine print prior to buying an internal card, though. Many do not include phantom power as part of the package. Additionally, these cards take up one of your precious PCI slots (thus requiring you to open your PC for installation, which is something to think about if you're squeamish about that stuff), and if your main computer goes on the fritz, so does your ability to record.

A much handier way of amplifying and digitizing your sound lies in external audio interfaces. These little miracle boxes have all the XLR and instrument inputs you need to take your content, amplify it, digitize it, and then pass it on via FireWire or USB to your computer, where Camtasia Studio can then record it. No sound card is required for digitization, because technically speaking, the audio interface *is* a sound card, and it's one that typically comes with an infinitely more advanced ADC (that's *analog-to-digital converter* for the acronym-challenged among you). The average sound card can only handle 16-bit, 44.1 kHz, whereas many external audio interfaces can record with 24-bit, 96 kHz fidelity. To take advantage of this, you'll need a more advanced software solution for your audio than the Camtasia Audio Editor (Adobe Audition and Sony Vegas are two such choices).

Now, audio interfaces don't merely consist of a box — there's a software component as well. Each manufacturer has its own proprietary solution, and some are better than others. Before making your purchase, be sure to check reviews of both the hardware *and* software as well as read the company's fine print to determine if all of it is compatible with your PC. No reason to fret, though — most companies do a pretty respectable job of keeping their basic audio drivers updated, and some even throw in some audio recording and mixing software to round things out. For those looking for a heftier software package than Camtasia Studio for recording their audio, this can be a pretty compelling value-add. Or it can be junk. It all depends on the capabilities of the software and your own needs, so do your homework.

Of course, I am prepared to help point you in the right direction. Here are a few recommended audio interface devices you might want to check out:

- **PreSonus FireBox.** I've been using this little $300 audio interface as my main preamp for a while now, and I can't say enough good things about it. It sports a built-in software-based mixer, and is also bundled with Cubase LE recorder/mixer software. Additionally, it includes a headphone jack for low-latency monitoring. The FireBox comes with all needed cables and even a power supply, though technically you don't need it — it can draw power right from your FireWire card.

- **M-Audio FireWire 410.** This is another audio interface in the $300 range. It offers two headphone out jacks with independent level controls, can crank 192 kHz output, and includes the Maximum Audio Tools software package.

- For the USB side of things, the **M-Audio MobilePre USB Interface** offers 16-bit/48 kHz output, two balanced XLR inputs, and is powered by a USB 1.1 connection, all for about $150.

- For about $100 more, the **Edirol UA-25** offers full 24-bit/96 kHz recording. Also completely USB-powered.

All the above units offer phantom power, so owners of condenser mics can relax with the knowledge that their microphones will work with any of these.

USB Microphones

If your head is swimming right now with all the cost and complexity of having to pick up a good mic, preamp, and analog-to-digital converter (not to mention all the cables you'll need to connect them together), there *is* a simpler option I should let you know about. I speak of the USB microphone. Imagine, if you will, a preamp and digitizer *built right into the mic*. All you have to do is jack it right into a standard USB port, and that's about as complicated as it gets on the hardware side. On the software end of things, the same caveats apply here as with the audio interface. Prior to purchase, make sure that the included software is compatible with your operating system, and always make sure you have the latest update to get the best stability and functionality. *Voilà.* You have a complete recording solution in one unit.

These microphones represent the ultimate in portability and convenience, and from the few units I've been able to test, they don't sound too bad, either. Best of all, the cost is pretty palatable, especially considering that everything you need is built in. This is a relatively new product type, and as such, the playing field doesn't yet have many contenders. But there are a few standouts. Here are five units you might want to consider:

- **Samson C01U.** This was one of the first available USB mics, and at $70, probably the least expensive. TechSmith actually sells these from its web site as a Camtasia Studio accessory. Sound quality is decent, but its comparatively high noise floor and lack of ability to monitor input in real time make it a difficult unit to heartily recommend.

- **Samson** also has the newer **GM1U G-Track**, which offers the unique ability to mix tracks directly from the mic. It sports both an instrument jack and (praises be…) a headphone jack for low-latency monitoring of your input. It's available for about $130.

- **Marshall Electronics MXL USB.006.** Also pricing in at the $130 mark, this cardioid-pattern condenser mic sports a three-position attenuator switch to adjust the gain directly from the mic.

Some have claimed that the unit has higher than acceptable self-noise, though.

- **Blue Snowball.** This mic's spherical shape is more reminiscent of a webcam than a microphone. Available for around $100, it features two cardioid (one for voice, one for instrument) and one omnidirectional pickup pattern. A desktop tripod and shock mount are available separately.

- **RØDE Podcaster.** A recent addition to Aussie manufacturer RØDE's already excellent product line famous for low self-noise. This dynamic mic also offers a headphone jack for low-latency monitoring. As a special value-add, RØDE created a special podcast hosting service just for Podcaster owners. This mic can be had for $230.

All of the above mics support various flavors of Windows and Macintosh. Be sure to read the fine print carefully to make sure that your OS is supported.

The Basics of Acoustic Treatment

As you settle in to record your audio narration, you'll obviously need to pay close attention to the acoustics of your recording space. Your two primary concerns are:

- Keeping unwanted sounds and background noise away from your mic, and therefore off your sound track.

- Deadening the acoustics of the room itself so that the sound waves don't go bouncing all over the place, resulting in an echoey, boxy quality to your sound.

To accomplish the first goal, your best bet is to simply find the quietest space in your home or office. You needn't worry about trying to "soundproof" your room — true soundproofing is difficult and outrageously expensive. If you have some cash to burn, you might want to consider double-paned glass on the windows (particularly if you've got a lot of noise from outside, such as traffic, children playing, etc.). If home/office noise is really bad, consider a sound isolation booth. These mini-rooms address both the above concerns wonderfully. They're also cheaper and more portable than truly soundproofing your studio space. You should be prepared, however, to shell out upward of $2,000 for even the smallest, most basic booth. Even so, they can be a bargain if you're losing all sorts of precious time rerecording segments that were ruined due to ambient noise. For those with the inclination, some good manufacturers are listed here:

- WhisperRoom, Inc. (www.whisperroom.com)
- Vocal Booth (www.vocalbooth.com)
- ClearSonic (www.clearsonic.com)

For the rest of us poor souls without an unlimited budget, the following tips will help you achieve maximum noise reduction for minimum dollars:

- Consider recording at different times of the day (or night) if you've got a lot of noise coming from outside. I live near a school, so there are certain times of the day I know to avoid when scheduling my narration.

- Alert your colleagues/roommates/family members whenever you record. You can even invest a modest sum in a wall-mounted "Recording" light to alert any passers-by. I suppose a printed sign taped to the door would work just as well, but what's the fun in that?

- Finally, separate your recording space and your regular workspace if possible. At the very least, either get your computer CPU (with its noisy fan) as far away from your microphone as possible, or simply pick up a quieter machine. If you're serious about creating an ideal recording environment, you need a computer that screams on the inside, yet whispers on the outside. High performance, low noise. Not many PCs out there can rise to that challenge. You can, of course, build one yourself, and a great source of information on constructing a quieter computing environment can be found at www.silentpcreview.com.

Unfortunately, most of us don't have the time, expertise, or even the desire to build a Windows PC from scratch, let alone spend the extra time and dollars on shutting it up. As an additional kick in the pants, it's clear that the major PC makers such as Dell and Hewlett-Packard do not consider noise reduction/elimination a top priority. But there is a PC builder out there who does. **Puget Systems** in Seattle (www.pugetsystems.com) builds custom computers for individuals and companies all over the world. One special service they offer is the construction of quiet, and even totally silent, PCs. My studio machine comes from them, and I can't tell you how happy I am with it. And from the gushing testimonials on their (unmoderated) ratings page, it seems I'm not alone: www.pugetsystems.com/ratings.php.

I recently alerted Puget to the plight of my readers, who must endure amateurish recordings due to the buzz of their noisy PCs. They graciously agreed to help put an end to your suffering: Anyone who mentions this book when soliciting a quote on a new PC will **receive 5% off their total order***. So, if you've been on the fence about getting a computer that doesn't sound like a shuttle launch whenever you press the power button, head on over to Puget Systems' web site, or give them a call at (888) PUGET-PC.

Now, the second challenge lies in making sure that your recording space is "dead" acoustically. Hard surfaces reflect sound waves and give the room an echo. In your recordings, you'll end up hearing the room as much as your own voice — not ideal. For me, this became a real issue when I moved to Spain and suddenly had to contend with marble floors and plaster walls (for some reason, drywall isn't as problematic).

If a voice-over booth is beyond your means, there are some things you can do. Fabrics tend to trap sound waves quite well, so if you really want a dampened recording space on the cheap, try capturing your narration in a walk-in closet that's full of clothes. It's an interior room with no windows, so you won't have outside noise to contend with, and the clothing will keep any errant sound waves from reverberating back into your mic. There are a million of these cheapie techniques, from hanging up heavy curtains and blankets to utilizing strategically placed folding doors or dressing screens that are adorned with acoustic foam. One really simple idea I like is simply mounting your mic in a desktop stand, and then building a little "house" for it made from four squares of acoustic foam (three walls and a roof). Place a towel underneath to keep sound waves from bouncing off the desktop, and you've got yourself a cheap, portable "dead zone" in which to record your narration.

---

* This excludes the purchase of one of Puget's (non-customized) Certified Computer Systems, to which a 10% discount already applies.

Buying the Right Video Camera

Now that we have the audio side of things covered, I'd like to take a brief moment to discuss picking out a video camcorder. With Camtasia Studio's recent support of camera video (and considering the fact that new codecs and file formats have made it more feasible than ever to put real-world video on the web), you may be considering the purchase of a camcorder to round out your content creation arsenal. While a webcam can do the job in a pinch, if you want professional results, you're going to need a more professional solution.

Because the range of devices in this area is so broad (and because my firsthand experience with individual units is admittedly narrow), I'm going to give you some general purchasing guidelines rather than recommend specific brands or models. Individual camcorder models have dozens of distinguishing characteristics, but for the purposes of this guide, I'm going to focus on the few most beneficial to indoor studio recording to complement Camtasia Studio. To wit:

■ **Go digital.** Analog camcorders are quickly going the way of the dinosaur, so if you're buying new, it shouldn't be an issue. With analog cameras, you would need to find some way of digitizing your images so that you can work with them, and it's simply more hassle than you probably need. Among digital camcorders, there are different types, and thus different ways of getting your content into your computer. Some cameras record directly to DVD, letting you then pop the disc into your computer's DVD drive, though these are typically better suited to those who just want to point, shoot, and deliver, with no editing involved. MiniDV camcorders record onto digital tape. To import the content into your computer, you'll need to connect the camera with a FireWire (IEEE 1394) cable. Some cameras are now completely tapeless, relying on a small hard drive to store your video data. Through an attached FireWire cable, these drives can be read and written to just like any other hard drive.

■ **Three heads are better than one.** Digital camcorders are equipped with at least one CCD* (charged-coupled device), which is the sensor the camera uses for recording images. Most sub-$1,000 cameras sport only one of these. The higher-end

---

* CCD sensors are increasingly being replaced by CMOS sensor technology, a less expensive alternative.

camcorders, however, tend to have three — one each specifically engineered to respond to red, green, or blue light. This color separation yields a much higher-quality image. With the increasing popularity of HDV (high-definition) camcorders pouring into the upper cost brackets, many quality low-def units are coming down in price. I've seen 3-CCD cameras as low as $500, and you can expect this trend to continue.

- **Microphone input.** If you've made home videos with garden-variety camcorders in the past, this little tidbit probably won't be news to you. Most cameras' built-in microphones are complete junk. Try to find a camera that has some sort of microphone input (preferably XLR, though most of us mortals can't afford the cameras that offer this amenity). Even a 1/8" microphone jack would be handy, though. And of course, you need a mic to plug into it. If you're doing a "talking head" style video, then a lavaliere mic would probably suit your needs just fine. Another option is a camera-mounted shotgun microphone. These attach to a special shoe on the camera, and many are now custom designed to "zoom in" on a subject in automatic response to the camera's zoom.

- **Get a remote.** Since using a camcorder with Camtasia Studio often means that *you're* the one on-camera, it behooves you to be able to control the unit from a distance. Remote controls are practical for executing new takes as well as zooming in and out. Most of the higher-end models include a remote, and even the lower-budget models have them available as an optional accessory.

- **Video light.** Virtually all lower-end camcorders choke in low-light situations, so make sure your studio is well-lit. While this isn't completely necessary, a nice-to-have feature on your camcorder is an included lamp to brighten up your target when the ambient lighting just isn't enough.

- **Mount it.** Especially if you're taking video of yourself, you should be putting your camcorder on a tripod to keep it steady. Of course, if you want to go cheap, then an old table lamp will work, too. Just pop off the lampshade, and you'll find that the lampshade threads exactly match your camera's tripod mount. (Thanks to *New York Times* technology columnist David Pogue for this one.)

Getting Additional Help

If you've gotten this far, you should have a pretty solid sense of what you're doing. But when working on a project, unforeseen difficulties almost always come up, and it's often hard to know where you can turn. This appendix is a general outline of the various help options you have at your disposal. First, I'll talk about the different choices available from the Help menu, and then I'll follow up with some other possible resources to check out.

Every single application in the Camtasia Studio suite of programs (except Camtasia Player, but that's because it's a stand-alone product, too) has the same set of options in its respective Help menu. I haven't covered them anywhere in this book, and here's as good a place as any. This is what you can find in the Help menu:

- **Camtasia Studio Help....** When all else fails, read the manual. This comprehensive document covers every aspect of the program in great detail.

- **Show Welcome Window.** This option brings up the same dialog that you're usually shown at startup.

- **Support.** Choosing this option brings up the Technical Support dialog, complete with a special field that details all sorts of information about your computer and your settings, including your general system information, the audio and video codecs you have installed, the settings of your various Camtasia Studio applications, and your DirectShow filter info. This information helps TechSmith support personnel better target any specific technical issues you may be experiencing. Choose Copy to clipboard to paste this information into an e-mail, or click Save to File... if you'd rather send it as an attachment.

- **Check for Upgrade.** This option checks online to ensure that you have the most recent version of the application. It's a good idea to check back every few months to make sure you're up to date.

- **Frequently Asked Questions.** This drops you off right at TechSmith's frequently asked questions page for Camtasia Studio. It has a comprehensive catalog of great tutorials and other info for the uninitiated (which, as a graduate of this book, does *not* include *you*, but these documents can be a good refresher nonetheless).

- **Tell a Friend.** This link sends you to a web form where you can send a Camtasia Studio spam-o-gram to any of your friends (or enemies, for that matter). All kidding aside: Yes, this is blatant marketing, but if the program has added meaningfully to your work or your life, why not return the favor? You'll evangelize a terrific product and help out a friend or colleague at the same time.

- **Quick Start Videos.** These are introductory videos made with Camtasia Studio about Camtasia Studio. They're very basic and aimed at total greenhorns. If you've worked through this book, you're way beyond them.

- **TechSmith on the Web.** This isn't really help as much as a few handy links about TechSmith and its products. You've got four links: the TechSmith Home Page, the Camtasia Studio Home Page (handy for when you want to make your purchase), Send Feedback (talk back to TechSmith: feature requests, complaints, etc.), and the TechSmith Products Page (find out about the rest of the product line).

- **Reset Balloon Tips.** In case you forgot what some of those balloons said, you can revive them.

- **About Camtasia Studio.** This has both version and registration information about your copy of Camtasia Studio.

But this is not the end of the resources available to you to get help for your issues. For one, TechSmith offers an online forum where users can go to post questions and help each other out:

http://forums.techsmith.com/

In addition to technical help, the forum is loaded with great information about the logistics of completing your projects: third-party software recommendations, workflow suggestions, and various other tips and tricks. There are several denizens of this forum who are extremely knowledgeable about Camtasia Studio and what it can do, so don't be afraid to ask lots of questions*. You might even find yours truly hanging around.

Finally, if you require any advice about implementing Camtasia Studio for use in your projects, feel free to contact me directly: csbook@dappertext.com. While I'm likely to refer you to TechSmith for any technical support issues, I am more than happy to answer workflow and "best practices" type questions about working with Camtasia Studio. If your needs go beyond the general question or two, I am also available on a professional basis for video creation, training on Camtasia Studio, and one-on-one consulting. For more information, go to www.dappertext.com.

So, if your current project presents you with a real stumper, let me know, and I'll do my best to try to find you a solution. And who knows, perhaps the knowledge gained will find its way into a future revision of this book!

---

* That is, don't be afraid to ask questions *after* following a basic tenet of forum netiquette: Conduct a search of the forum to make sure no one has successfully found the answer to your question before. Sorry, but it's a pet peeve of mine.

About the Author

Daniel Park is a multimedia developer and stand-up technical trainer by trade. He spent three years at TechSmith Corporation (the creator of Camtasia Studio), where he worked in marketing, international development, database administration, and, of course, video creation. He left in 2003 to start dappertext LLC (www.dappertext.com), a consultancy specializing in Camtasia Studio video creation and training, serving clients all over the world.

Daniel splits his time between the United States (mostly Michigan) and Huelva, Spain, where he resides with his wife and son.

Daniel can be contacted via e-mail at csbook@dappertext.com.

Index

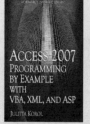

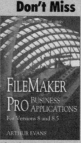

On the CD

The companion CD-ROM contains a trial version of Camtasia Studio 5, free and trial versions of several utilities that can be used with Camtasia Studio, and data files for use in the chapter exercises. These are organized into two folders:

- Software Demos: Contains the trial version of Camtasia Studio 5 and other software; see page 16 for more information.

- Exercise Media: Contains various files to complete the chapter exercises.

 By opening the CD package, you accept the terms and conditions of the CD/Source Code Usage License Agreement. Additionally, opening the CD package makes this book nonreturnable.

CD/Source Code Usage License Agreement

Please read the following CD/Source Code usage license agreement before opening the CD and using the contents therein:

1. By opening the accompanying software package, you are indicating that you have read and agree to be bound by all terms and conditions of this CD/Source Code usage license agreement.

2. The compilation of code and utilities contained on the CD and in the book are copyrighted and protected by both U.S. copyright law and international copyright treaties, and is owned by Wordware Publishing, Inc. Individual source code, example programs, help files, freeware, shareware, utilities, and evaluation packages, including their copyrights, are owned by the respective authors.

3. No part of the enclosed CD or this book, including all source code, help files, shareware, freeware, utilities, example programs, or evaluation programs, may be made available on a public forum (such as a World Wide Web page, FTP site, bulletin board, or Internet news group) without the express written permission of Wordware Publishing, Inc. or the author of the respective source code, help files, shareware, freeware, utilities, example programs, or evaluation programs.

4. You may not decompile, reverse engineer, disassemble, create a derivative work, or otherwise use the enclosed programs, help files, freeware, shareware, utilities, or evaluation programs except as stated in this agreement.

5. The software, contained on the CD and/or as source code in this book, is sold without warranty of any kind. Wordware Publishing, Inc. and the authors specifically disclaim all other warranties, express or implied, including but not limited to implied warranties of merchantability and fitness for a particular purpose with respect to defects in the disk, the program, source code, sample files, help files, freeware, shareware, utilities, and evaluation programs contained therein, and/or the techniques described in the book and implemented in the example programs. In no event shall Wordware Publishing, Inc., its dealers, its distributors, or the authors be liable or held responsible for any loss of profit or any other alleged or actual private or commercial damage, including but not limited to special, incidental, consequential, or other damages.

6. One (1) copy of the CD or any source code therein may be created for backup purposes. The CD and all accompanying source code, sample files, help files, freeware, shareware, utilities, and evaluation programs may be copied to your hard drive. With the exception of freeware and shareware programs, at no time can any part of the contents of this CD reside on more than one computer at one time. The contents of the CD can be copied to another computer, as long as the contents of the CD contained on the original computer are deleted.

7. You may not include any part of the CD contents, including all source code, example programs, shareware, freeware, help files, utilities, or evaluation programs in any compilation of source code, utilities, help files, example programs, freeware, shareware, or evaluation programs on any media, including but not limited to CD, disk, or Internet distribution, without the express written permission of Wordware Publishing, Inc. or the owner of the individual source code, utilities, help files, example programs, freeware, shareware, or evaluation programs.

8. You may use the source code, techniques, and example programs in your own commercial or private applications unless otherwise noted by additional usage agreements as found on the CD.

 By opening the CD package, you accept the terms and conditions of the CD/Source Code Usage License Agreement. Additionally, opening the CD package makes this book nonreturnable.